Remaking Holocaust Memory

Remaking Holocaust Memory

Documentary Cinema by Third-Generation Survivors in Israel

Liat Steir-Livny

Syracuse University Press

First Edition 2019

19 20 21 22 23 24 6 5 4 3 2 1

∞ The paper used in this publication meets the minimum requirements of the American National Standard for Information Sciences—Permanence of Paper for Printed Library Materials, ANSI Z39.48-1992.

For a listing of books published and distributed by Syracuse University Press, visit www.press.syr.edu.

ISBN: 978-0-8156-3632-8 (hardcover)
978-0-8156-3650-2 (paperback)
978-0-8156-5478-0 (e-book)

Library of Congress Cataloging-in-Publication Data
Names: Steir-Livny, Liat, 1973– author.
Title: Remaking Holocaust memory : documentary cinema by third-generation survivors in Israel / Liat Steir-Livny.
Description: Syracuse, NY : Syracuse University Press, [2019] | Includes bibliographical references and index.
Identifiers: LCCN 2018060093 (print) | LCCN 2018061128 (ebook) | ISBN 9780815654780 (E-book) | ISBN 9780815636328 (hardcover : alk. paper) | ISBN 9780815636502 (pbk. : alk. paper)
Subjects: LCSH: Documentary films—Israel—History and criticism. | Grandchildren of Holocaust survivors—Israel. | Collective memory—Israel. | Memory in motion pictures—History and criticism. | Holocaust, Jewish (1939–1945)—Influence. | Motion picture—Israel—History.
Classification: LCC PN1995.9.D6 (ebook) | LCC PN1995.9.D6 S8217 2019 (print) | DDC 791.43/658405318—dc23
LC record available at https://lccn.loc.gov/2018060093

Manufactured in the United States of America

Contents

Preface

The Holocaust was and remains a central trauma in Israel's national consciousness. The memory of the trauma has not faded over the years; on the contrary, Holocaust representations and the public discourse regarding the Holocaust have only grown stronger in recent decades. Surveys indicate that in the Jewish Israeli population in general, the Holocaust is considered a central event, and young Jewish Israelis perceive the Holocaust as the historical event that has had the greatest impact on them and their future, even more so than the founding of the state of Israel.[1] In this historic-cultural environment, *second-generation* and *third-generation* are not only biological but also cultural terms.[2]

The Holocaust has found ample expressions in Israeli documentary cinema from 1945 until the present.[3] An immense change in the number of productions and the nature of the representation of the Holocaust and Holocaust survivors has taken place from the 1980s onward, in great part due to the expanded role of second-generation Holocaust survivors in this process.[4] Third-generation Holocaust survivors were born between the late 1960s and the early 1980s. They grew up in a society in which Israeli media, the fields of education and culture, and public discourse all frame the Holocaust as a current, ongoing local trauma rather than an event that ended decades ago in another place.[5] Since the late 1990s they have related to the Holocaust in a range of cultural fields in art, television, fringe and mainstream theater, alternative ceremonies, literature, and film.[6]

The topic of this book is the under-researched theme of Holocaust memorialization in third-generation Holocaust survivors' documentaries. Although third-generation Holocaust documentaries have been screened in Israel, Europe, and the United States, have appeared at numerous international film festivals, and have won international awards (see appendix), there is little academic research on this subject. There are no book-length works on the Holocaust documentaries of third-generation survivors in Israel, and publications have been limited to several articles and book chapters.[7] Research on Israeli second-generation Holocaust documentaries has primarily been written in Hebrew. Three main books have analyzed representations of the Holocaust and Holocaust survivors in Israeli cinema up to the 2000s in fiction and documentary films.[8] In addition, several articles and book chapters in Hebrew and in English have addressed the depiction of the Holocaust and Holocaust survivors in Israeli second-generation documentaries.[9]

Remaking Holocaust Memory aims to paint the first comprehensive portrait of third-generation Holocaust documentaries phenomenon. It takes a cinematic, cultural, and sociohistorical comparative approach to examine how third-generation filmmakers have responded to second-generation documentary representations. This book analyzes nineteen prominent films that reflect the key tendencies of third-generation Holocaust documentaries. Examples from other documentary films, short documentaries, television documentaries, and episodes from television documentary series that shed light on these features are also discussed. These films are compared to sixteen Holocaust documentaries by second-generation survivors. This broad-based comparison has not appeared in previous research. One of the main goals of this book is to explore how third-generation filmmakers are both affected by and deviate from earlier Holocaust representations. They create a new layer of commemoration that coexists with the former, while constructing new thematic, moral, and aesthetic recollections of the trauma. In so doing they change and extend the nature of Holocaust representation, recollection, and awareness.

Remaking Holocaust Memory is situated at the crossroads of the fields of Holocaust studies, film studies, and memory studies.

Its starting point is critical research on documentaries. It examines the ways in which third-generation Holocaust documentaries represent and narrate reality according to categories defined by documentary theorists—in particular Bill Nichols's six documentary modes of representation of reality (expository, observational, poetic, participatory, reflexive, and performative),[10] and Michel Renov's four modalities of desire (to record, reveal, and preserve; to persuade and promote; to analyze and interrogate; and to express).[11] It highlights the cinematic methods of emplotment, the aesthetic decisions that are made to construct a narrative in terms of the past and the present, and the subjective interpretation of reality.

These documentary modes are analyzed through the prism of transgenerational transfer theories and especially the prime notions of *postmemory*, *after postmemory*, and *prosthetic memory* as defined by Marianne Hirsch, Gerd Bayer, and Alison Landsberg. Hirsch suggested that the Holocaust, as represented in the works of second-generation survivors, is an indirect affinity structured on imagination and memory that is inherited.[12] This is what she termed *postmemory*, which characterizes the experience of those controlled by events that happened before they were born, and who apply their imagination to places they cannot remember.

Gerd Bayer extended Hirsch's definition by coining the concept of *after postmemory* awareness typical of the third generation onward that combines postmemory of the past with a more general perspective on the moral conclusions to be drawn from the Holocaust for future generations.[13] After postmemory implies that the public has historical knowledge about the Holocaust, and engages with it from different perspectives. This concept bridges the gap between the historical trauma of the past, which is receding, and an examination of the impact of the Holocaust in the here and now.

Prosthetic memory was defined by Landsberg to characterize memories of historical events that people adopt as their own even though they did not actually experience them.[14] Prosthetic memory is the outcome of a person's experience with a mass culture technology of memory that re-creates and imparts a history the individual did not live through. Thus, prosthetic memory relates to the works of both second- and third-generation documentary filmmakers who present a trauma they did not experience and was mediated to them through the educational, social, political, and personal spheres.

This book highlights that prosthetic memory changes from one cinematic generation to the other, and shows that postmemory and after postmemory create a dialogue with each other and reflect continuity, while also representing two different sets of themes, aesthetics, and ethical notions. It focuses on this complex relationship in five key areas: (1) gender; (2) Germany; (3) victims' testimonies; (4) the image; and (5) perpetrators, bystanders, and both these groups' descendants.[15]

It approaches gender perspectives by examining the documentation of new feminine subjects that were marginalized in second-generation documentaries. It analyzes the changes in the predominance of Germany and the open debates about Germany as a beloved homeland and a home for Holocaust survivors and their offspring. It shows how third-generation filmmakers dispute previous perceptions of Holocaust survivors' testimonies as facts and reveal the complexity and elusiveness of survivor testimonies. It discusses how visual images are transformed in third-generation documentaries from devices that facilitate the telling of history into the subject of inquiry. It examines how, for the first time, third-generation documentaries also shift the focus away from the victims and their offspring to confront and document the voices, choices, claims, and conceptions of perpetrators, bystanders, and both these groups' descendants.

These issues are examined in-depth in each chapter. The introduction explores the question of truth in documentary cinema, Holocaust documentaries, Holocaust documentaries in Israel, and the working definitions of *second-generation Holocaust survivors* and *third-generation Holocaust survivors.*

Chapter 1, "Depicting Women's Gendered Experiences in the Holocaust," discusses female representations. Second-generation documentaries tend to focus on individual Holocaust survivors and their stories, and devote a great deal of screen time to survivors and their memories, but the unique female experiences during the Holocaust are marginalized. The chapter shows how third-generation documentaries highlight women's specific traumas by addressing unexplored subjects such as pregnancy, abortion, sexual abuse, and their effects on motherhood. It analyzes the third-generation documentaries *Oy Mama* (Noa Maiman, 2010), *The Cemetery Club* (Tali Shemesh, 2006), and *Aida's Secrets* (Alon Schwarz and Shaul Schwarz, 2016), and compares them to the second-generation documentaries *Three Sisters* (Tzipi Reibenbach, 1998), *Girlfriends* (Yoel Kaminski, 1994), and *Love in Auschwitz* (Tor Ben-Mayor, 2003).

Chapter 2, "Back to the *Heimat*: Germany as Home," analyzes representations of Germany. In second-generation documentaries, many films depicted family journeys back to Europe to the families' roots and retraced the familial history before and during the Holocaust (primarily in Eastern Europe). This chapter shows how third-generation documentaries make Germany their main destination. These films also touch on Germany as a home for Holocaust survivors and their offspring—a subject that was marginalized in second-generation films. The films discussed in chapter 2 include *Kleiner Rudi* (Michelle Stein Teer, 2006), *The Flat* (Arnon Goldfinger, 2011),[16] *Farewell Herr Schwarz* (Yael Reuveny, 2013), *Address: Germany* (Ruth Shiloni, 2017) and *My German Children* (Tom Tamar Pauer, 2012), which are compared to the second-generation documentary *One, Two, Three, Four, Adolf Hitler at My Door* (Tami Gross and Yuval Cohen, 2002).

Chapter 3 explores the power of the image. Holocaust representation in art in general, and in films in particular, has elicited debates since the aftermath of World War II. These have dwelled on the ways in which images construct memory, the usage of Nazi footage, and the extent to which the cinematic medium can, and should, attempt to depict suffering. The issue of the image is not addressed directly in most second-generation documentaries. Instead, the image is used as a natural device through which pieces of the past resurface to complete the puzzle of the family's history. This chapter shows how in some third-generation films, images become the central theme.

They are used to reflexively discuss the power of the image, its (mis) representations, as well as the advantages and disadvantages inherent to rebuilding a portrait from historical images. It analyzes the third-generation documentaries *A Film Unfinished* (Yael Hersonski, 2010), *The Green Dumpster Mystery* (Tal Haim Yoffe, 2008), *Numbered* (Dana Doron and Uriel Sinai, 2011), and *A Documentary about the Holocaust* (Itay Ziv, 2012), and compares them to the second-generation documentary *Tango of Slaves* (Ilan Ziv, 1992).

Chapter 4, "The Elusiveness of Memory," deals with the problematic aspects of testimony. In second-generation documentaries, survivors' testimony was presented as historical fact, and was not disputed or critically examined. This chapter shows how the aesthetic, rhetorical, and thematic representations of survivors in third-generation documentaries address this evidence in much more complex ways. It attests to the subjective and partial process of recollection and personal remembrance of the victims. It analyzes the third-generation documentaries *Martin* (Ra'anan Alexandrowicz, 1999), *The Cahana Sisters* (Gilad Melzer, 2006), *Shalom Italia* (Tamar Tal-Anati, 2016), and compares them to the second-generation documentaries *Because of That War* (Orna Ben-Dor, 1988) and *Choice and Destiny* (Tsipi Reibenbach, 1994).

Chapter 5, "Looking beyond the Victims: Nazis, Bystanders, and Their Descendants," discusses the representation of Nazis, bystanders, and both these groups' descendants. Second-generation Israeli documentaries mainly focused on the victims and the ways in which their children were affected by their parents' trauma. This chapter shows how third-generation documentaries represent "the other side" through the personal documents of perpetrators, interviews with second- and third-generation descendants of perpetrators, bystanders, and their offspring. It analyzes how directors have begun to paint a profound portrait of themes not previously explored, such as the private lives of the Schutzstaffel (SS), how the perpetrators' offspring deal with their families' pasts, and the complexity of the term *bystanders* and its many facets. The chapter analyzes the third-generation documentaries *Kleiner Rudi* (Michelle Stein Teer, 2006), *The*

Flat (Arnon Goldfinger, 2011), *Hitler's Children* (Chanoch Ze'evi, 2011), *The Most Beautiful Woman* (Maya Sarfaty, 2016), *The Decent One* (Vanessa Lapa, 2014), and *Out of the Forest* (Yaron Kaftory Ben-Yosef and Limor Pinhasov Ben-Yosef, 2004), and compares them to the second-generation documentary *Healing by Killing* (Nitzan Aviram, 1996).

The comprehensive analyses of the films reflect the zeitgeist of a generation affected by Holocaust commemoration and simultaneously elucidates the trauma in its own way.

Acknowledgments

This book was written at Sapir Academic College and at the Open University, Israel, between 2014 and 2017. I am grateful to Sapir Academic College and the Open University research authorities for providing initial funding for the project. I would like to express my gratitude to Esther Singer, this book's language editor, for her editing, comments, thoughts, and ideas. I would also like to thank Elisheva Lahav for her great help in editing the book's endnotes. I thank the reviewers for their comments, and the cartoonist Yotam Fishbein for allowing me to use his brilliant cartoon for the book's cover. I would like to thank the wonderful people at Syracuse University Press for their professional, diligent attitude and to express my gratitude to Deborah M. Manion, who believed in this project from day one. Finally, my heartfelt gratitude goes to my family.

Early versions of the analysis of *The Flat* and *Oy Mama* appeared in the following publications: "Post-Holocaust Heritage of Trauma: The Identity Crisis of Jewish Immigrants From Germany to Eretz-Israel in the 1930s, and the Transgenerational Transfer of the Trauma in the Israeli Documentary Film 'The Flat,'" in *Post-Holocaust Studies in a Modern Context*, ed. Nitza Davidovitch, Ronen A. Cohen, and Lewin Eyal (Pennsylvania: IGI Global, 2018), 70–84; "Aftereffects: The Representation of the Holocaust, Its Universal Moral Implications and the Transgenerational Transformation of the Trauma, Based on the Israeli Documentary Film 'Oy Mama,'" *Kultura Popularna* 1, no. 51 (2017): 118–35.

Remaking Holocaust Memory

Introduction

Third-Generation Holocaust Survivor Documentaries

Since the end of World War II, there has been an ongoing debate in the Western world on representations of the Holocaust. Can the depths of horror be expressed through art, or should these horrors be discussed solely through the testimonies of Holocaust survivors? Can art represent these atrocities? Should the cultural debate on the Holocaust be limited to realistic representations, or can it be represented fictionally, metaphorically, or even through the fantastic? Is it ethical to use Nazi material in cultural representations?[1] These issues, which were raised as early as the 1940s, are still being debated, since the Holocaust was and continues to be represented—in fact even more so in recent decades—in a range of cultural fields.

The Issue of Truth in Documentary Cinema

John Grierson coined the term *documentary* in 1926 and defined it as the "creative treatment of actuality." In 1935 Paul Rotha called it "the creative dramatization of actuality."[2] The question of "truth" in documentary cinema has been debated ever since. It is sometimes argued that documentary films do not represent reality but rather are a creative treatment of real life that uses components of the "real world" to tell a story. Subjective decisions when directing, filming, and editing compress reality into a narrative. A documentary is not a reflection of reality but a story about reality. Since the

1960s, postmodernist theorists have challenged the notion of objective truth and have blurred what were once clear boundaries between the objective and subjective. Cross-disciplinary approaches to cinema as well as advances in technology and the mimetic capabilities of computer imaging software have also contributed to heightening the problematic nature of documentary truth value.[3] Scholars have noted that no historical text, whether historical writing or documentary cinema, can authentically capture the past. Rather, a specific truth is created through ideologies and emplotment that constitute a narrative. Hence a documentary does not represent objective knowledge, but in fact a partial, subjective history.[4]

In fiction films, viewers are aware that they are watching actors. Nevertheless, fiction films have had a tremendous influence on the way images are created and intensified. Historical fiction films often prompt resentment among historians, who claim that they are inaccurate. They are aware that some viewers relate to them as a reflection of a historic truth and are mindful of the power of the cinema to confer knowledge and strengthen certain beliefs and images.[5] Perceptions of truth are even stronger in the case of documentaries because the "social actors" are filmed in their real surroundings and "act" their lives. A sixty- or ninety-minute documentary is created out of dozens, and sometimes hundreds, of hours of filmed footage. In the editing rooms, most of the cinematic footage stays on the cutting room floor and the final scenes condense real time into cinematic time to fit the story the filmmaker wants to tell. The subjective aspects of filming—the aesthetic choices, the cinematic language, the place of the filmmaker in the film, the selection of the social actors, the soundtrack, the narration and/or voice-over, and the editing decisions as to which parts to include—are all part of the emplotment of truth that goes into producing a documentary.[6] Thus documentaries are not a genuine reflection of reality but rather the end product of an artistic process. They represent an arranged story from a specific perspective that does not mirror the truth but instead reflects the filmmaker's subjective point of view.[7] Amongst the many scholars who have engaged in definitions of documentary and its connections to truth, authenticity, and reality, Michel Renov notes that since the documentary film uses the rhetorical cinematic devices of fiction films, it cannot claim to be objective or be perceived as such. The material is reorganized to correspond to a particular interest. One can analyze the representations, but these do not reflect the truth, since people tend to talk about themselves or others from a subjective point of view, to which one must add the specific perspective of the director. Carl Plantinga noted that "both fiction and nonfiction film are creative in their manipulation of their materials," whereas David LaRocca took the position that there is no difference between fiction film and documentary film and that "all film is fiction film."[8]

Bill Nichols suggested that documentaries are "modes of representation of reality."[9] He reasoned that documentaries cannot be viewed as a "reproduction of reality but as a representation of the world we occupy."[10] The director's point of view shapes situations and events involving real people whose real lives are depicted, and turns them into films that "frame and organize [reality] into a text."[11] Research on documentaries also highlights the components of emplotment, which are often perceived to be a reflection of reality. Brian Winston pointed out that the representation of factual material is mediated by non-neutral features such as the filmmaker and the medium (film, video, new media).[12] For Stella Bruzzi, a documentary is an illusion of an objective film, "a negotiation between reality on one hand, and image, interpretation and bias on the other."[13] She sees documentaries as "a dialectical conjunction of a real space," and the filmmakers that invade it mediate reality.[14]

The title of Elizabeth Cowie's book *Recording Reality, Desiring the Real* summarizes the paradoxical relationship between documentaries and the "true accounts" they purportedly represent.[15] She examines whether the documentary is best defined as filmed reality, a presentation, or a performance of recorded reality. While discussing the problematic relationship between representation and real life, Cowie analyzes documentaries as both an art form and a form of social engagement which informs and educates. Cowie highlights how the "real" is mediated, interpreted, narrated, and represented.

Thus, the documentary becomes prey to a loss of "the real" in its narratives of reality.

Another problematic facet of the perception of the documentary as reality is made clear in Agnieszka Piotrowska's book on psychoanalysis and documentary film, in which she focuses on the encounter between filmmaker and subject in documentaries, and the way these representations are impacted by the bond between the two, which she calls "transference love." In Piotrowska's view, the transretinal love shared by the documentarist and the subject raises profound and disturbing ethical questions concerning the psychological and ethical stakes of documentary productions. She demolishes the notion of documentary "objectivity" and suggests that powerful unconscious mechanisms are generated in the encounter that necessarily run counter to the film's supposedly "neutral" perspective.[16]

In *Representing Reality: Issues and Concepts in Documentary*, Bill Nichols defines documentaries from the points of view of the filmmaker, the text, and the viewer. He classifies these three points of view into six documentary modes of representation of reality, or "basic ways of organizing texts in relation to certain recurrent features or conventions," which he labelled *expository*, *observational*, *poetic*, *participatory*, *reflexive*, and *performative*.[17] The expository mode primarily makes use of verbal commentary and argumentative logic (the "voice of God" commentary). The observational mode is characterized by the nonintervention of the filmmaker. It tries to capture reality, with the filmmaker as a neutral observer who is not a part of the frame ("fly on the wall"). In order to enhance the impression of lived or real time, the camera moves rapidly to keep up with the action, resulting in rough, shaky, often amateur-looking footage aimed at strengthening the realistic effect. In the interactive mode, the filmmaker is more fully part of the film in that he or she looks, listens, speaks, and reacts on-camera (and not only in voice-over) to the social actors. As the filmmaker interacts, questions, and provokes situations, the impact on these situations becomes an integral part of the film. In the reflexive mode the representation itself becomes the topic of cinematic meditation. These films aim to expose the artificial nature of the documentary, as opposed to its perception as truth, and by revealing the process of representation. The audience is made aware of the cinematic language and manipulations. Thus, the reflexive mode of representation primarily involves an encounter between filmmaker and viewer rather than filmmaker and subject. The poetic mode shifts away from reality and deals with the emotional impact of the world documented by the filmmaker. It constitutes a more abstract, lyrical translation of the documented material, and the film revolves around the filmmaker's impressions. In the performative mode, the filmmakers place themselves in the center of the film and the events that are documented are shaped by their actions.[18]

Taking issue with Nichols's perception of the documentary as a "discourse of sobriety," Renov described documentaries as a reflection of the deep desires of the human soul and defines fundamental tendencies or modalities of desire that fuel documentary discourse, which he termed *record*, *reveal and preserve*, *persuade and promote*, *analyze and interrogate*, and *express*.[19] Their friction, overlapping, and mutual determinations "testify to the richness and historical variability of nonfiction forms."[20]

While acknowledging the importance of Nichols's classification, which has become increasingly dominant in documentary research, David LaRocca argued that "Just as the ink dries on such divisions, exceptions arise, questions are asked, and one reaches for an eraser, which is no good against the ink." He proposed including hybrid categories that combine several of the original modes for documentaries that do not fit into Nichols's criteria.[21]

Holocaust Documentaries

The first cinematic records of the Holocaust were filmed by the Nazis. Although filming executions was banned, Reinhard Wiener, a German naval officer, shot 1.39 minutes of footage in 1941 of Nazi-occupied Liepāja, Latvia, showing the Einsatzgruppen shooting Jews into mass graves. The documentary researcher Brad Prager argued that this footage is not a documentary but rather a document, because not all the components of documentary are present since it is not contextualized, it is unframed, and there is no narration, exposition, or intertitles.[22] Seventy-two seconds of a couple of Jews coming out of the Warsaw ghetto ruins were filmed by Nazis during the ghetto's uprising. Other films were shot by Nazis as part of the Nazi propaganda war machine, and are not documentaries but rather deliberate distortions of the real nature of Jewish life under the Nazi regime. For example, the 1944 film *Theresienstadt: Ein Dokumentarfilm aus dem jüdischen Siedlungsgebiet* (*Terezin: A Documentary Film from the Jewish Settlement Area*) was designed to deceive the Red Cross and the world and depict the "decent and tranquil life" of Jews in the ghetto. The film *Das Ghetto* was shot in the Warsaw Ghetto in 1942 but was never completed or released. The Nazis may have wanted to use it as a didactic propaganda film to insinuate that the death and starvation that prevailed in the ghetto were caused by the indifference of the Jewish community's upper class to their brethren. Despite the meticulous twisting of reality that governed the way *Das Ghetto* was directed, scenes from the film have become an integral part of the collective memory of the Holocaust. For years, these staged scenes were depicted as authentic representations of the ghetto. The outtakes, which show Jews being forced into these scenes and highlight their manipulative and unrealistic intent, were only revealed decades later in Yael Hersonski's 2010 documentary *A Film Unfinished*.[23]

Stuart Liebman considers that the first Holocaust documentary was Alexander Ford's *Vernichtungslager Majdanek: Cmentarzysko Europy* (*Majdanek: A European Cemetery*), which was filmed in 1944. The film is a compilation of scenes from the Majdanek extermination camp near Lublin on the day it was liberated.[24] Toby Hagith claims that the film *German Concentration Camps Factual Survey*, which was shot by the British liberating forces in 1945 but was left unfinished, is the first Holocaust documentary.[25] Several other documentaries were compiled of footage filmed by the liberating armies. The films shot in the liberated camps by the American, British, or Soviet liberating forces and turned into documentaries—such as *Memory of the Camp* (Stuart McKalister, 1945) and

Death Mills (Billie Wilder, 1945)—portrayed what the Allied armies found: emaciated prisoners, piles of corpses, and mass graves.[26] Some included scenes in which Germans and Poles who lived nearby were forced by the liberating armies to enter the camps, to see with their own eyes what they had chosen to ignore, and help bury the corpses.[27] These images were distributed worldwide and have become iconic representations of the Holocaust.[28] For example, the American documentary *Nazi Concentration Camps* (George Steves, 1945) and the Soviet documentary *Kinodokumenty o zverstvakh nemetsko-fashistskikh zakhvatchikov* (*Film Documents of the Atrocities of the German-Fascist Invaders*), which represented the Nazi atrocities, were presented to the International Military Tribunal at the Nuremberg trials and entered as evidence.[29] However, these documentaries did not capture the atrocities themselves, only the aftermath. Many Nazi actions were not filmed or photographed, and many documents and visuals were deliberately destroyed by the Nazis, who found ample ways of covering their tracks.[30]

According to film researcher Lawrence Baron, in these initial films, Jews were not depicted as the prime victims of these mass murders. *Death Mills* cites victims "of all the nations of Europe, of all religious faiths, and of all political beliefs, condemned by Hitler because they were anti-Nazi." *Nazi Concentration Camps* alludes briefly to the fact that there were German Jews among the victims.[31] In the immediate postwar years, three documentaries that dealt with Nazi atrocities were awarded Academy Awards: *The True Glory* (Carol Reed and Garson Kanin, 1945), *Hitler Lives* (Don Siegel, 1945), and *Seeds of Destiny* (1946). While they dealt with Nazi atrocities, for the most part these documentaries also downplayed the Jewish identity of many of the dead and the survivors, and discussed Nazi victims without focusing on the Jews and the Holocaust. They tended to subsume the catastrophe that had befallen the Jews under the broader notion of crimes committed against the citizens of Nazi-occupied countries.[32]

From the aftermath of World War II and until the 1980s, only several prominent Holocaust documentaries were produced. Alain

Resnais's 1955 thirty-two-minute documentary *Nuit et Brouillard* (*Night and Fog*) is one of them. To mark the tenth anniversary of the end of World War II, the French Second World War Historical Board approached Resnais and asked him to produce a documentary on the Nazi concentration camps. Resnais wrote the script with the Holocaust survivor Jean Cayrol, a non-Jew who was imprisoned by the Nazis because he was a homosexual. They chose to combine a very poetic narration with black-and-white archival footage, still photographs, documentaries about the camps made by the liberating armies, and color scenes that Resnais himself filmed from what remained of certain camps. The film describes the hunger, disease, inhumane conditions, the brutality of the guards, the daily humiliations, and murders. It reveals the massive death industry, the crematory ovens, and the mass graves found following liberation. The film ends with the question *why*? Resnais, a leftist who was concerned about the universal potential for human brutality, described the Nazi concentration camps as evil perpetrated by humans against other humans. He portrayed it as something that could take place anywhere and at any time. The word *Jews* is only mentioned in *Nuit et Brouillard* twice. This is not a film about the Holocaust of the Jews, but about the Nazi concentration and death camp system. Thus, it is clear why political prisoners and prisoners of war were murdered, but it is unclear why the Nazis murdered millions of Jews and other ethnic minorities. According to the historian Shlomo Sand, a photo of a French policeman from a French transit camp was cut from the film by French censors to conceal the role of the Vichy government in the rounding up and deportation of Jews.[33]

Until the 1980s, documentaries were produced in various countries that reflected on the past from different perspectives. One of the best-known is Marcel Ophuls's 1969 *Le Chagrin et la Pitié* (*The Sorrow and the Pity*), which addresses France's role in the deportation and murder of France's Jews. This film helped change French collective memory (and deliberate omissions) concerning the role of the French authorities during the Holocaust. Marcel Ophuls, the son of the famous Jewish director Max Ophuls, who was forced to stop working in Germany in 1933 when the Nazis came to power, produced this TV film for German and Swiss television. *Le Chagrin et la Pitié* subverted the canonic French narrative that the French had resisted the Nazis. It shows that even though there was a French resistance, there were also many collaborators, and the vast majority of the population was indifferent to what was happening to the Jews as a result of ingrained anti-Semitism and contempt for "the other." Symbolically, the censored photo in Resnais's film was transformed into a documentary of more than four hours by Ophuls. Unlike Resnais's attempt to tell the larger story of the concentration camps, Ophuls undermined the myth of French resistance by telling the story of the city of Clermont-Ferrand. *Le Chagrin et la Pitié* has no narrator and is centered on interviews with thirty-four people representing the voices that many in France had preferred to silence: the collaborators, bystanders, and Nazi sympathizers. French television channels refused to broadcast *Le Chagrin et la Pitié* until 1981.[34]

Other well-known films from that era include the British documentary *Kitty: Back to Auschwitz* (Peter Morley, 1979), in which Kitty Hart-Moxon, a Holocaust survivor, returns to Auschwitz, where she was imprisoned at the age of sixteen for two years, to reenact her life experiences. The 1981 West German Oscar-nominated film *Der Glebe Stern* (*The Yellow Star: The Persecution of the Jews in Europe*), directed by Dieter Hildebrandt, deals with the persecution and murder of European Jews through archival footage from sixteen countries. *Breaking the Silence: The Generation after the Holocaust* (Edward A. Mason, 1984) was produced by Eva Fogelman, a psychologist and the daughter of Holocaust survivors. It was the first portrayal of the characteristics of second-generation survivors and their complex relationships with their parents.

Claude Lanzmann's *Shoah* (1985) is considered to be a milestone in Holocaust documentaries. This nine-hour film took twelve years to produce, during which 350 hours of footage were filmed in fourteen countries. *Shoah* was sponsored by the French Ministry of Culture, and according to the historian Shlomo Zand, covertly by the Israeli Ministry of Foreign Affairs.[35] Whereas *Nuit et Brouillard* was an attempt to summarize the history of the concentration camps, *Shoah* was intended to depict the entirety of the Holocaust (hence its name). The film, however, although ostensibly comprehensive, omits the role of the French. There is no discussion of what happened in France during the Holocaust and no French interviewees are included. Other minorities that were persecuted and exterminated are also overlooked. As opposed to documentaries that were produced before and often used Nazi visual materials, Lanzmann deliberately refrained from doing so. He also did not use the archival footage taken by the Allies that had been the basis for many other Holocaust documentaries. Lanzmann only used interviews with survivors, Nazis, collaborators, and bystanders, who were asked to recall the atrocities. Through them, *Shoah* highlights the deep-seated anti-Semitism of Catholic Poland, where almost all of the extermination camps were located.[36]

Lanzmann argued that he did not want to use scenes filmed from the persecutors' point of view. He claimed that since there are no Nazi film reels documenting what happened in the gas chambers, existing Nazi images can provide no more than a dismal, superficial account of what truly took place during the Holocaust. Lanzmann believed that the solution was to focus on testimonies.[37] By refusing to use materials filmed by the Nazis, Lanzmann established a rule in the ethics of Holocaust documentaries, which he himself broke in his 2013 documentary, *The Last of the Unjust*. In this film, Lanzmann did incorporate several minutes of the 1944 Nazi propaganda film *Theresienstadt: A Documentary Film from the Jewish Settlement Area*. The words *mise en scène Nazi* ("staged by the Nazis") are imprinted in the right corner of the frame throughout all the scenes to remind viewers that this is not the truth but a deceitful representation created by the Nazis.[38]

As one of the most well-known Holocaust documentaries ever made, *Shoah* greatly influenced debates on the subject. In many countries where Holocaust survivors settled, testimonial films began to be produced, mainly by the next generations (although not necessarily by the second generation and third generation in the biological sense). In addition, the aging of the eyewitnesses contributed to the sense of urgency to document. Technological advances that lowered filming costs have also contributed to the wave of Holocaust documentaries since the mid-1980s to the present day.[39] These documentaries deal with the Holocaust and Holocaust survivors, perpetrators, bystanders, and their descendants. Hundreds of documentaries produced have addressed various issues, people, and historic situations during the Holocaust and their long-term aftereffects, posttraumatic stress,[40] the nature of transgenerational transfer, Holocaust commemoration, and its effects on collectives and individuals from all sides (persecutors, bystanders, victims, and their descendants).[41]

Holocaust Documentaries in Israel

Documentaries cannot be separated from the wider context of the cultural setting in which they are produced. Nichols pointed out that "documentary, like other discourses of the real, retains a vestigial responsibility to describe and interpret the world of collective experience . . . it joins these other discourses (of law, family, education, economics, politics, state and nation) in the actual construction of social reality."[42] The analysis of second- and third-generation documentaries in Israel clearly needs to be examined within the broader context of the evolution in awareness of the Holocaust in Israel over the years. Approximately 450,000 Holocaust survivors immigrated to the Jewish Yishuv (Jewish residents living in pre-state Israel; literally, "settlement"), and to Israel after 1948.[43] Their representation in Israeli documentary cinema can be roughly divided into three periods: the 1940s to 1960, 1961 to the late 1970s, and the late 1980s onward.

The 1940s to 1960

The encounter between Holocaust survivors and Israeli society was complex and is still a topic of scholarly debate. Rumors about the murders committed in Europe were cause for solemn mourning within the Jewish community in the Yishuv during and especially after World War II. The shock was mingled with anguish and a desire to help Holocaust survivors. But simultaneously, during and after the war, questions and doubts began to arise as to the response of European Jews to the Nazis during the Holocaust. Alongside the assistance in immigrant absorption that was offered, there were also reservations about the perceived passivity and meekness of the diaspora Jews in the face of the Nazi horrors. In addition, veteran Jewish Israelis often wondered how these new immigrants had survived while six million other Jews had perished. The answers to this question were sometimes problematic.[44]

Some scholars describe these reactions to be a combination of empathy and indifference that involved a desire to help, alongside insensitivity and the careful phrasing of a charged and contradiction-ridden encounter.[45] Others criticize the Jews (and especially the leaders) of the Yishuv and post-1948 Israel for ignoring the survivors' pain, and treating their plight with indifference.[46] Some have noted that the issue of the Holocaust was marginalized within Israeli society and culture until Adolf Eichmann's trial in 1961, thus causing survivors to remain ensconced in their silence.[47] Others feel that Holocaust survivors were not silent, nor were they silenced by other Israelis, but instead played a major role in shaping Israeli awareness of the Holocaust.[48]

Cinema from the late 1940s up to the 1960s was primarily a form of Zionist propaganda aimed at three main target audiences: the intra-Zionist circle (the Zionist movement and its institutions in the land of Israel and abroad), the inter-Jewish circle (the Jewish diaspora worldwide), and the non-Jewish population worldwide. These films were dominated by ideological considerations and espoused Zionist ideals. They served as an artistic ideological platform harnessed by the Zionist establishment to display its political, national, and economic achievements. Zionist institutions such as the Jewish National Fund (Keren Kayemet leIsrael), the Jewish Foundation Fund (Keren Hayesod), and others that were involved in producing films hired directors who were committed to presenting Eretz Israel at its best, and to directing films showing the tremendous progress in the country. These institutions carefully selected themes and intervened in the scriptwriting, shooting, editing, and marketing.[49] The films focused on the Zionist struggle, the establishment of a Jewish state in Eretz Israel, and support for the state after its founding, including the need for donations to the Zionist movement. To this end, many films were produced in English and then translated into numerous other languages for worldwide distribution.

The films emphasized the dichotomy between the Holocaust survivors and the "new Jew"—the prototype of the pioneer spirit leading the Zionist revolution. Although the "new Jew" reflected an ideological vision more than a description of reality, the cultural power of this model was extremely strong. The films represented the cinematic interpretation of the Zionist myth: strong, handsome young men (and beautiful women) working the land, fighting the Arabs, and exhibiting self-sacrifice for loftier national goals. In most cases, they were filmed in the countryside, in open sun-filled frames, and from low angles that elevated these men and women as they dominated and tilled the soil, built new settlements, and inspired the younger generation.[50]

The films necessarily presented a tendentious world view. They were portrayed as reflecting the truth, but in fact represented the ideological worldview of the Zionist establishment's desires and aspirations. The filmmakers created a historical narrative that moved from an abstract national disaster to the national renaissance that was showcased in the films. These documentaries, which fall into the category of Nichols's expository mode, did not contain interviews with survivors. The narrator provided verbal commentary on the visuals, and described a collective transaction from ashes to renewal. Thus, survivors' assimilation in Eretz Israel was always associated with the suppression of their memories. This narrative clearly reflected and corroborated the Zionist account, which regarded the Land of Israel as the only place where survivors could heal and begin a new life. The films presented a process of national initiation that argued for the need to establish and strengthen a Jewish state in the Land of Israel—for example, *The Road to Liberty* (Norman Lurie, 1946), and *Our Way of Life* (Baruch Dinar, 1958).

From 1961 until the Late 1970s

The trial of Adolf Eichmann (1961) prompted a change in perceptions of the Holocaust in Israel. Israelis were exposed to 110 Holocaust survivors' testimonies, which were also heard on the radio and published daily in newspapers. Their stories led to new realizations about the complexity of the Jewish predicament during the Holocaust, such as the difficulties of resistance, the inability to grasp the Nazis' techniques of lies and deception, and confusion about the nature of the camps. After the trial, the Ministry of Education expanded the scope of the school curriculum on the Holocaust. In 1966 and 1967 the first delegations of Jewish teens were taken to Poland on guided school tours to see the remains of the ghettos and the former concentration and death camps. The Holocaust and Jewish diaspora history began appearing in a slightly more complex manner in Israeli culture.[51]

The few documentaries that were produced between 1961 and the late 1970s differed from the earlier documentaries in terms of their greater identification with the Jewish diaspora in Europe before, during, and after the Holocaust. Holocaust survivors were revealed to be a multifaceted group whose members had different opinions, perceptions, and perspectives on the past and the present. Their individual anecdotes shed light on the Holocaust and began to personalize the national trauma. Films started to turn Zionist revival into an in-depth debate on the Holocaust (*Holocaust*, Ben Kurtzer, 1975), and a collective discussion to personal traumas (*Like a Phoenix*, Igal Burstein 1972). Films examined life under the Nazi regime, in the ghettos, and the concentration camps (*Why Not Bomb Auschwitz?*, Hananiah Amotz, 1972), the effects of the trauma on Israelis (*Memories from the Eichmann Trial*, David Perlov, 1979), and the complexities of immigration to Israel (*The 81st Blow*, Jacques Ehrlich, Haim Gouri, and David Bergman, 1974; *The Last Sea*, Jacques Ehrlich, Haim Gouri, and David Bergman, 1979).

The 1980s Onward

During the 1970s, the hold of Zionist ideology gradually began to weaken. The 1973 Yom Kippur War and its severe political and economic consequences were followed by revelations about stagnation and corruption in the left-wing Labor Party, which had been in power since the days of pre-statehood. This led to the rise of the right-wing Likud Party, which came to power in 1977. These political changes coincided with the growing legitimacy of multicultural trends that replaced the prevailing notions of a homogeneous Israeli society. The glorification of the Zionist ethos and the absorption of immigrants was replaced by profound criticism of early Zionism and its treatment of marginal groups.[52]

In the 1980s the Holocaust was made a permanent feature of high school curricula and matriculation exams. High school delegations to former concentration camps in Poland began in 1988, and have become increasingly popular. According to the sociologist Jacky Feldman, since their inception, these trips have become one of the most intensive means of transmitting the Holocaust memory to future generations.[53] In addition, this was the period of time when many Holocaust survivors retired, had more time on their hands, and began to wonder how to communicate their stories to the next generations. More and more Holocaust survivors began to publish their memoirs. Members of the second generation began to discuss the ways in which the trauma had affected their lives, and depict their relationships with their parents in a range of cultural fields.[54]

The international acclaim for Lanzmann's *Shoah*—along with these changes—prompted a burst of Holocaust documentaries in Israel from the 1980s onward. Whereas Lanzmann focused his efforts on interviews with victims, perpetrators, and bystanders, Israeli

Holocaust documentaries focused on stories of survival as filtered through the perspectives of the second generation.[55] The documentaries highlighted individual stories rather than a collective narrative, and addressed the impact of the Holocaust on survivors and their offspring. Michal Friedman refers to this cinematic period as "the age of testimony." These testimonial films turned second-generation directors (not necessarily in a biological sense) into listeners, who were "witnesses through imagination" or "surrogate witnesses," whose gaze and voice defined a new form of empathy toward survivors. Most of these films reflect versions of Nichols's interactive mode.[56] In these films, a compassionate filmmaker interviews and documents the survivor or the survivors and the second generation. Others reflect Nichols's performative mode, in which second-generation directors place themselves in the frame to understand the familial history that affected their lives.

Applying Marianne Hirsch's idea of postmemory, the cinema researcher Yosefa Loshitzky called this category of second-generation documentaries "postmemory cinema." In her view, these films are governed by a diasporic aesthetic. The films represent an imagined collectivity of ghosts and shadows. They express loss and ambivalence toward both their real Israeli homes, and their imagined homes (whether cherished or despised) in the diaspora.[57] The filmmakers did not look for stories of heroism but rather chose to center on the "ordinary person," and dedicated a great deal of screen time to the survivors and their memories—for example, *Because of That War* (Orna Ben-Dor, 1988), *Choice and Destiny* (Tsipi Reibenbach, 1993). Unlike films from previous decades, these documentaries reject the utopian representation of the integration process. They depict the mosaic of identities of Holocaust survivors, who are portrayed in a complex way, living between the past and the present, between the trauma and attempts to build a new life: *Hugo* (Yair Lev, 1989), *Hugo 2* (Yair Lev, 2008), and *Menucha's Film* (Eliezer Shapiro, 2004). Some films describe the journeys taken by Holocaust survivors and their children back to Europe (*Tango of Slaves*,

Ilan Ziv, 1992; *Daddy, Come to the Fair*, Nitza Gonen, 1993; *Pizza in Auschwitz*, Moshe Zimmerman, 2008), or trips taken by the second generation after a parent's death (*Six Million and One*, David Fisher, 2011). Other films criticize the attitudes of the Jewish Yishuv leaders toward European Jews in the Holocaust (*The Drain Dilemma*, Erez Laufer and Nahum Laufer, 2006), the way the memory of the Holocaust has—allegedly—been manipulated in Israel (*The Specialist*, Eyal Sivan, 1999), and the way in which the memory of the Holocaust affects relationships to Arabs in contemporary Israel (*The Servants of Memory*, Eyal Sivan, 1990; *Don't Touch My Holocaust*, Asher Tlalim, 1994).[58]

Over the years, the memory of the Holocaust has become an integral part of Israeli culture. The third generation in Israel was born between the late 1960s and the early 1980s, and grew up as Holocaust awareness was undergoing significant changes. Features of this intense awareness are imprinted on the third generation in different cultural fields, including art, television, fringe theater, alternative ceremonies, literature, and cinema.[59] Their documentaries reveal the extent to which the Holocaust is a living part of their identities. The third generation's profound emotional connection to the Holocaust drives them to create new representations that constitute a new intellectual, ideological, and aesthetic point of view that both corresponds to the former Holocaust narrative, but branches out to encompass other topics.

Second-Generation Holocaust Survivors: Definitions

The definition of *Holocaust survivor* has changed over the years and is still debated. One of the current definitions that was put forward in 2009 states that a Holocaust survivor is "a person who lived in one of the countries that were conquered or were under direct influence of the Nazi regime for any period of time between 1933 and 1945. It also includes the population of survivors, people who had been forced to leave their homes because of the Nazi regime."[60] Therefore, even the descendants of Jews who fled Germany before 1939 are considered to be members of the second and third generations.

The term *second-generation* was coined by Canadian psychoanalysts as a clinical concept, and today is commonly used to denote the children of Holocaust survivors. In the 1960s, when the issue was first studied, it became clear that second-generation survivors shared certain unique mental health problems that unified them as a group. Since then, more than four hundred articles have been written on the question of intergenerational transmission of Holocaust trauma from survivors to their children. In the last few decades, the perception that they are a separate group has been questioned, and in particular whether second-generation individuals are a distinct group in terms of their characteristics, whether this group has unique and/or more substantial psychological disorders than other populations. The interpretations can be divided into three main schools of thought.[61]

The first suggests that the second generation has clear characteristics that are unique and that distinguish them from other groups. These include suspicion, fear, overprotectiveness, interpersonal problems, anger, social detachment, and a constant and haunting preoccupation with the Holocaust. For example, Dina Wardi argued that survivors and their children have common experiences and unique modes of expression, such as profound feelings of grief and guilt, separation difficulties, anxiety, mutual overprotectiveness, identity issues, and emotional overload. In Wardi's opinion, while there are minor differences across families, intergenerational transmission generally takes on very similar forms.[62] Carol Kidron examined second-generation support groups and analyzed their cultural and social identity construction mechanisms. She found that members of the second generation are aware of their legacy, as well as the unique intergenerational transmission they experienced as children. The second generation feels a responsibility and burden on their shoulders, which often results in an inability to construct independent identities.[63] Julia Chaitin noted that even when the second generation deliberately avoids a profound examination of their parents' lives, the Holocaust still has an impact on a deep, subconscious level, which inevitably leads to symptoms and characteristics that distinguish them from the general population.[64]

By contrast, the second school of thought considers that the second generation has no significant psychological disorders, and that the Holocaust had no long-term consequences on their offspring. They dismiss the conclusions drawn by proponents of the first school of thought as stereotypical and plagued by stigma. For example, Yoram Hazan criticized the term *second-generation*, since only one generation survived the Holocaust, whereas the second generation is, in fact, the first generation of freedom. He argued that survivors and their descendants, as a group, are as large and diverse as other groups and populations, and that labeling them is wrong.[65]

Hillel Klein found that post-traumatic stress disorder (PTSD) is not passed down from one generation to the next. Rather, a transmission of certain common motifs, myths, themes, and vulnerabilities takes place within the family and between generations. Thus, the fact that some second-generation survivors undergo therapy for their problems does not justify singling out all of them, since each case must be examined individually.[66] Studies by Abraham Sagi-Schwartz and colleagues showed that there is no empirical proof of intergenerational transmission to second-generation survivors that distinguishes them from the rest of society since their supposedly unique symptoms were found throughout the population. Rather, in their view, intergenerational transference to the second and third generations is a misconception because the findings based on case studies do not represent the vast majority of the population. In their opinion, one of the problems in this type of research is that in many cases, the researchers studied participants undergoing treatment in mental health facilities and associations for Holocaust survivors and second generations do not represent the norm among survivors or among their children.[67]

The third school of thought acknowledges a form of interaction between parents and children that is unique to the relationship between Holocaust survivors and their offspring, but considers that it is expressed in many different ways and varies from family to family.[68] For example, Eva Hoffman takes the view that the term *second-generation* applies homogeneous features to what is a very diverse group. She sees the second generation as an imagined community "based not so much on geography or circumstances as on sets of meanings, symbols . . . that it has in common," which gives its members a sense of mutual belonging.[69] Dan Bar-On interviewed three generations of five families of Holocaust survivors.[70] He described the survivors' vacillations between fear (associated with the past) and hope (associated with the future). He showed how different survivors distribute along this axis from the need to move forward and the feeling of being pulled backward, the need to remember, and the will to live. According to Bar-On, this oscillation is also characteristic of the second and third generations.

Third-Generation Holocaust Survivors: Definitions

The third generation began to be studied in the 1980s, when psychologists in the United States who were treating a seven-year-old boy, the grandson of Holocaust survivors, claimed that the effects of the Holocaust strongly affected him and that the issue deserved comprehensive treatment in the psychiatric community.[71] Since then, psychologists and psychiatrists have debated the term *third-generation* and its characteristics. The many studies dealing with the biological grandchildren of Holocaust survivors fall into three main schools of thought as well.

Some researchers claim that the trauma of the Holocaust is transferred to the second and third generations. Indirect evidence of posttrauma is manifested in the third generation in a number of symptoms that differentiate them from other groups their age. For example, according to Scharf and Mayseless, third-generation survivors in Israel have greater psychological difficulties than the general population, as seen in in adjustment problems and hardships that appear, for example, when they are called up for mandatory military service. The symptoms are similar to the ones also reported by the second generation, including problems in establishing trust, fear that they will be tricked and deceived, suspicion, difficulties in expressing joy and emotion, and yearning for greater intimacy. Studies suggest that third-generation survivors with two second-generation parents present greater symptomatology, including distress and greater social dysfunction. In comparison, children with only one second-generation survivor parent tend to function similarly to other army recruits.[72] The researchers found three patterns of intergenerational transference of trauma that Holocaust survivors passed on to their children and grandchildren via their children. The first was anxiety and concern for survival. The second was lack of emotional support (children of survivors claimed that their parents were unable to develop closeness, affection, and support, and described them as being alienated. Some transferred this pattern to their own children). The third was the tendency to want to please their parents, which was found in both second-generation and third-generation adolescents.[73]

The second school of thought tends to show that the third generation, as a group, does not have distinguishing traits relative to trauma, and that there is no difference between the biological grandchildren of Holocaust survivors and other groups whose grandparents are not Holocaust survivors. For example, Eva Fogelman argued that trauma cannot be transmitted to others. In her opinion, third-generation survivors do not suffer from "silent scars."[74] Sagi-Schwartz, van IJzendoorn, and Bakermans-Kranenburg claim that Holocaust trauma is not transferred to the second generation, and does not skip a generation to the third generation.[75]

The third school of thought notes the wide spectrum of reactions to trauma that do not justify viewing the third generation as one group. For example, Dan Bar-On found two coping patterns, which he linked to universal myths related to relationships with family elders: the Eskimo myth, in which the young send their elders who are no longer needed to die at sea, and the Indian myth, in which venerable elders are perceived as having knowledge and wisdom. In Bar-On's opinion, when the second generation took on the role of creating positive transference from the first generation to the third generation and filtering the trauma for their children, they contributed considerably to the warm relationship that developed between survivors and their grandchildren (the Indian myth). In cases where the second generation did not take on the role of creating positive transference, this was expressed by a lack of closeness and even aversion between the grandchildren and the survivors (the Eskimo myth).[76] Later research carried out by Bar-On and colleagues described the third generation as a heterogeneous group that was freer and more liberated than the second generation, but was capable of hearing the stories of the past, and identifying and containing the pain through their growth and security. Third-generation interviewees were described as having different perspectives on the way the trauma affected them, the way it shaped their identities, and how they viewed their roles in Holocaust remembrance.[77]

Several books published recently draw on third-generation narratives from several continents and highlight the diversity of inherited memory and the transgenerational transfer of trauma, as well as the elements shared by members of this group. The writers show how a range of cultural and historical factors have shaped the third generation. These researchers describe how grandparents' widely different survival experiences and their eventual integration into their new homes after the war influenced the diversity of the third generation. Cultural and political factors, as well as how the Holocaust is remembered, misremembered, and debated in various contexts, influence that diversity as well.[78]

Second-Generation and Third-Generation: Cultural Definitions

Alongside the many studies dealing with issues of intergenerational transfer of trauma to the children and grandchildren of Holocaust survivors, other studies have been carried out that expand the definitions of *second-generation* and *third-generation* beyond biological terms. Some claim that in a broad sense, these terms include all those who were born after the Holocaust. Others include individuals who are not biological offspring of Holocaust survivors but rather express cognitive and emotional identification with the descendants of Holocaust survivors out of a sense of a shared destiny and Jewish identity. Yet others posit that *second-generation* and *third-generation* are cultural terms, especially in Israel, where Holocaust awareness is more intensive and comprehensive than in other places in the world.[79]

In his study on the ways in which groups confront their collective traumas, the sociologist Ron Eyerman claimed that "a cultural trauma" is a historic event in the consciousness of every member of the collective and that this memory undergoes constant reinterpretation. Different generations have different perspectives on the event as a function of emotional and temporal distance, and also because of altered circumstances and needs, but all generations interpret the event as a primal part of their identity.[80] The sociologist Jeffery Alexander argued that any event—as horrific as it may be—will only turn into a trauma for the collective if members of the elite define and construct it as such. He argued that collective trauma is constructed by "memory agents"; namely, members of the hegemony who feel this event will affect collective memory and identity in the present and the future. These "memory agents" construct the trauma as "collective" through a lengthy cultural process of narration and signification.[81] The historian Dominick LaCapra claims that the danger inherent to the disintegration of distinctions between different time periods and the merging of the traumatic past with the present is relevant not only for those who experienced the trauma themselves but also for groups and societies that are linked to those traumas. Both groups and societies can act out a trauma, become trapped in a situation that commingles past and present, and reconstruct the trauma, or certain aspects of it, in different ways.[82] Another term that can be used to describe Holocaust memory in Israel is *secondary traumatic stress*, in which those who were not directly involved in the traumatic events are exposed to its stress. Secondary traumatic stress can be found in friends and relatives of traumatized individuals as well as in wider circles. Research has found that indirect exposure to trauma through intense cultural and media debates (television, radio, journalism, the internet, etc.) can affect people who were not involved, causing PTSD symptoms such as stress and anxiety, albeit less intensely.[83]

As noted, Holocaust awareness in Israel has only grown stronger in recent decades.[84] The historian Amos Goldberg argued that the way Holocaust memory has been shaped in Israel suggests that Israeli society is posttraumatic and acts out the Holocaust.[85] Studies have shown that the second and third generation's knowledge of the Holocaust, and the ways in which the Holocaust has forged their identities, is similar to that of Israelis of the same age who are not the biological offspring of Holocaust survivors. Elsewhere, however, there is a huge gap in knowledge and perception of the Holocaust between the biological offspring of Holocaust survivors and other Jewish people of the same age.[86] Therefore, in Israel, where Holocaust awareness is so intense, the terms *second-generation* and *third-generation* can refer not only to the biological offspring of Holocaust survivors but can also, as a cultural term, define Jewish Israelis who grew up in an environment saturated with Holocaust awareness, anxiety, and stress.

This book analyzes documentaries directed by members of the third generation, including the grandchildren of German Jews who fled to Eretz-Israel after the rise of Nazism but before World War II, the grandchildren of Holocaust survivors who lived in Nazi-occupied Europe during World War II, and Jewish Israelis who were born between the late 1960s and the early 1980s. They are compared to films directed by sons and daughters of Holocaust survivors and directors who are not children of Holocaust survivors, but belong chronologically and culturally to second-generation Holocaust survivors. *Remaking Holocaust Memory* concentrates on documentaries made by third-generation European survivors. The few documentaries by second- and third-generation North African descendants, which deal with the persecutions in North Africa, have been analyzed elsewhere in contemporary research.[87]

1

Depicting Women's Gendered Experiences in the Holocaust

In the first decades after World War II, there was scant research on the role of gender, or the differing experiences of men and women in the Holocaust. Women's lives were perceived to be an integral part of men's experiences and were researched as such. The few attempts by female scholars to research women's experiences as a separate theme were met with strong opposition from other academics who argued that women were murdered because they were Jews, not because they were women per se, and that the Final Solution did not differentiate between genders. Gender-based studies were viewed as a "shameful" product of feminism, and some academics even claimed it could lead to Holocaust denial.[1]

From the late 1970s onward however, gender-based studies dealing with women in the Holocaust began appearing more frequently. This line of research intensified in the 1980s and 1990s, but still elicited opposition.[2] Today, however, studies on women in the Holocaust have increased, and international conferences on the subject and art exhibitions have been held.[3] In addition, since the 1980s, more women have written autobiographical texts.[4]

Current research addressing gender perspectives on the Holocaust tends to take the position that women's and men's trajectories in death or survival were both similar and different, given female physical features and sociocultural norms. Myrna Goldberg argued succinctly that they had "different horrors, same hell."[5] Jewish women suffered as Jews, but also as women. Thus, although the Final Solution did not differentiate between men and women, gender provides yet another lens through which life and death in the Holocaust can be examined. Pregnancies, abortions, childbirth, attempts to maintain femininity, physical and body changes, make the female experience different from that of men. Social and psychological distinctions between men and women also affected the ways in which they lived and died in the patriarchal world under Nazism.[6]

This change is also reflected in Israeli documentary cinema. This chapter discusses the representation of women's specific experiences during and after the Holocaust. It analyzes *Oy Mama* (Noa Maiman, 2010), *The Cemetery Club* (Tali Shemesh, 2006), and *Aida's Secrets* (Alon Schwarz and Shaul Schwarz, 2016), which are compared to the second-generation documentaries *Three Sisters* (Tzipi Reibenbach, 1998), *Girlfriends* (Yoel Kaminski, 1994), and *Love in Auschwitz* (Tor Ben-Mayor, 2003).

Marginalization of Female Experiences in Second-Generation Documentaries

Second-generation documentaries tended to present individual narratives rather than the collective story that appeared in films of previous decades. The protagonists were often Holocaust survivors, and the films dealt at length with their experiences under the Nazis, while marginalizing the story of national redemption. These films innovated the cinematic documentation of Holocaust survivors by placing them in the forefront.[7] When viewing this change through the perspective of gender, however, it becomes apparent that most of the narratives in second-generation films have to do with men or overlook women's specific experiences in the Holocaust that relate to gender. Documentaries made by second-generation survivors prompted a revolution in Holocaust documentation in Israel by placing the "everyman" in the center (with the emphasis on *man*), as, for example, in the following films: *Daddy, Come to the Fair* (Nitza Gonen, 1993), *Hugo* (Yair Lev, 1989), *Hugo 2* (Yair Lev, 2008), *Pizza in Auschwitz* (Moshe Zimmerman, 2008), *Six Million and*

One (David Fisher and Irit Shimrat, 2011), *Tango of Slaves* (Ilan Ziv, 1992), and *The Kozalchik Affair* (Roni Ninio, 2015). When a female Holocaust survivor does appear, she is usually the partner of the male protagonist—for example, *Because of That War* (Orna Ben-Dor, 1988), *Choice and Destiny* (Zipi Reibenbach, 1993), or part of a group of men and women—such as in *Kapo* (Tor Ben-Mayor and Dan Setton, 1999). Only a few second-generation women made Holocaust documentaries—for example, Orna Ben-Dor, Zipi Reibenbach, Nitza Gonen, Ronit Weiss Berkowitz, Nurit Kadar—and in their films, they documented men (Gonen), or men and women (Ben-Dor Niv, Ronit Weiss Berkowitz, Reibenbach's *Choice and Destiny*). Some films focused solely on women Holocaust survivors—for example, *Girlfriends* (Yoel Kaminski, 1994), *Three Sisters* (Tzipi Reibenbach, 1998), *My 100 Children* (Amalia Margolin and Oshra Swartz, 2003), and *Hanuszka* (Nurit Kedar, 2006).[8] Although they were groundbreaking in that sense, they for most part did not highlight gender-related subjects or examine the elements specific to women's experiences during the Holocaust.

Girlfriends, directed by Yoel Kaminski and released in 1994, tells the story of a group of women from the town of Liepāja, Latvia, who eventually survived the war. The film alternates between two time lines: in the first Kaminski covers prewar Liepāja up to liberation. In the second, which is set in the present, Kaminski films his mother and her friends as they play cards, dine, and laugh, while at the same time recollecting the atrocities. Kaminski surrounds the story with maps, historical photos, and scenes in which he interviews his mother and her friends. The women are the focal point, and the story of Liepāja is told from their perspective.

The interviews provide fleeting glances into each woman's personal experiences during the Holocaust rather than painting a complex portrait. The individual voices and stories are interwoven with the maps, footage, and photos to drive the narrative of the town's destruction. In addition, the director deliberately does not identify the women until the last sequences of the film. Instead, viewers see the women, hear parts of their stories, but do not know their names, thus depriving them of their identity and preventing viewers from relating to these women as separate individuals. In the final minutes of *Girlfriends*, Kaminski's camera pans across the women's faces and their names appear for the first time: Berta, Zila, Roza, Zenia, Luba, Dora, and Micky. But this is too little, too late. The film starts with group shots showing them interacting socially, and ends in a group, as the camera pans between them. Even though Kaminski's mother and her best friend, Zila, are more conspicuous than the others and receive more screen time, their stories are also incomplete, and do not enable viewers to understand their fate during the Holocaust. The historical narrative revealed through their testimonies is not unique to women during the Holocaust. They talk about the hunger, murder, and deaths that still haunt them, but do not discuss specifically female issues. Thus *Girlfriends* is more about friendship and less a film about womanhood in the Holocaust.

In her book *Israel and the Daughters of the Shoah: Reoccupying the Territories of Silence* Ronit Lentin writes about second-generation female writers and directors who engage with the Holocaust and the transgenerational transfer of the trauma. She claims that directors such as Orna Ben-Dor and Tsipi Reibenbach "reoccupy the territories of silence" of their parents and themselves as second-generation women.[9] *Because of That War* (1988) was the first documentary to highlight the stories of survivors (Jacko Poliker and Halina Birenbaum), and their relationship with their children (the musicians Yehuda Poliker and Yaacov Gilaad).[10] In *Choice and Destiny* (1994), Reibenbach interviews her father and highlights the trauma of her mother, who sits in silence throughout most of the film, although her body language expresses anxiety.[11] As in any other text, the authorial subjectivity—in this case, of the women directors—is figured in the films,[12] but in these documentaries the women do not discuss specific gender-related issues when describing their lives during the Holocaust.[13]

Three Sisters, directed by Tsipi Reibenbach and released in 1998, depicts her mother and her two aunts, making this a pioneering documentary since both the protagonists and the director are women. Beyond dealing with the Holocaust, it is also a story of old age. Esther is the youngest sister, Karola the eldest, and Fruma (the director's mother) is in the middle. Although they are in their seventies, the sisters still cannot bring themselves to discuss the Holocaust, even among themselves. Karola stays silent. Fruma tries to write what she remembers in her notebook. Occasionally they talk on the phone. Reibenbach defines the documentary as "a film about trauma," about the inability to work through memories, and about the tacit code of silence between the sisters.[14] Lentin points out how their silence affected the director's aesthetic choices. For example, the first scene of the film is almost completely silent as the camera moves from an old picture of the three sisters as young women to Fruma sitting in the kitchen writing in her notebook. The only sound is her low voice-over as she mumbles broken sentences how she wanted to find her sister in the camp. A telephone ringing breaks the extended silence.[15] Instead of talking about the trauma that has shaped their lives, the sisters spend their days taking care of their ill husbands. In her film, Reibenbach not only breaks with the dominance of male representation but also the long-held practice of glorifying young people and ignoring the elderly in Israeli cinema. The scenes in *Three Sisters* follow the sisters as they go through medical exams and illnesses in a very personal way, thus upending the taboo of exposing the elderly naked body. The film reveals the hardships and strengths of older women who need to deal with their posttrauma and aging while caring for their husbands.[16]

The first attempt to deal with specifically female experiences was the TV documentary *Love in Auschwitz*, directed by Tor Ben-Mayor and released in 2003. The documentary presents two stories. The first, entitled "A Different Love," is about Helena Citronova (Zippora Tahori), a Jewish woman, and her relationship with the SS officer Franz Wunsch. The second is the love story between Zila Sivolska, a Jewish prisoner, and York Bialski, a Polish prisoner. Although love stories between Jews during the Holocaust had been presented in other TV documentaries, they tended to be part of a narrative on Jewish ways to maintain the human spirit under Nazism.[17] Relationships between

Jews and Gentiles and Jews and Germans were not discussed. Tahori's story touches on a taboo and reveals that she survived thanks to the fact that Wunsch was in love with her, and aided her and her sister. This is shown through a combination of interviews with Tahori (which constitute the main part of this sequence), old pictures of her, and evocations of the Holocaust (a barbed-wire fence, sounds of dogs barking, trains, railways, and people screaming in German).

Love in Auschwitz reveals that in 1942, when Tahori was twenty years old and an inmate at Auschwitz, she was told to sing at a birthday party for the Austrian SS officer Wunsch, and he fell in love with her. In the film, which is accompanied by some photographs of beautiful Tahori in her youth and one picture of young Wunsch, she talks about how he left her love letters, and saved her sister, Rosa, from the gas chambers. Although Tahori talks about Wunsch's striking attitude, she marginalizes her part in the relationship and several times claims "he was madly in love with me." In one scene Tahori says that she thought Wunsch was handsome, but she immediately rejects her own statement: "Who thought about them as men? They were the SS, murderess of the Nazi machine." Eventually, though, Tahori admits that toward the end of the war she had feelings for Wunsch.

Tahori tells the story didactically, but sometimes bursts into tears.[18] *Love in Auschwitz*'s director, Tor Ben-Mayor, does not pry too much into her story. He lets Tahori tell it without asking too many questions about the profound nature of Tahori and Wunsch's relationship and how it unfolded in the camp, and does not add hidden details in the narration. Ben-Mayor also does not judge Tahori, nor does he confront her choices. The complexity intensifies when it is revealed that Wunsch looked for Tahori after World War II. He gave up after searching for two years, settled in Vienna, and started a new chapter in his life. In 1972 Wunsch was charged with war crimes. His wife wrote to Tahori, asking her to testify in his favor. Tahori agreed, and stated at the trial that she knew he was cruel to other inmates, but that he had saved her and her sister. Wunsch was acquitted, and Tahori never saw him again. The sequence ends with a close-up of the photo of Tahori as a young woman, accompanied by her voice-over stating, "I lived in a different world, I didn't believe there was a human world, I lost all sense of proportion, everything, I didn't care." Tahori's statement provides an apologetic overtone to the hesitant way she describes their relationship.

Third-Generation Documentaries: The Gender Perspective

The third generation grew up in an era in which the position of women in Israeli society and in the Israeli film industry was undergoing a change. Within the last ten years the number of films, both fiction and documentaries directed by women, has grown tremendously, and deal to a greater extent with more female-related themes.[19] The number of female documentary directors has doubled to reach approximately fifty, and the number of female documentarists who deal with the Holocaust is rising.[20] These women grapple with a range of Holocaust-related subjects from their own perspective, tell the stories of female Holocaust survivors, the offspring of Holocaust survivors, and themselves, the granddaughters, in feminine narratives that include many gender-related issues. A similar emphasis on women and their experiences also appears in documentaries directed by third-generation male directors—for example, *Aida's Secrets*, *Watermarks*, and *The Cahana Sisters*. The filmmakers build upon the important framework found in second-generation documentaries featuring personal stories to construct a much stronger female presence by highlighting the women's specific experiences in the Holocaust and its aftermath.

A good example of these differences in the cinematic perspective of third-generation documentarists emerges when comparing *Love in Auschwitz* and the way the third-generation director Maya Sarfaty addressed Tahori's story in her 2016 film, *The Most Beautiful Woman*, which won the American students' Academy Award for best foreign documentary in 2016. Making Tahori's testimony the center of the sequence in *Love in Auschwitz* was very typical of second-generation documentaries. By contrast, *The Most Beautiful*

Woman is Rashomon-like in that Tahori's testimony is just one of an ensemble of voices that also include her children, her sister, her sister's daughter, and Wunsch's and Wunsch's daughter's perspectives (see chapter 5).[21] The fact that Tahori is not the only one explaining or defending her actions makes it stronger: "What can you expect of a sixteen-year-old who was taken to an extermination camp?" asks her son Israel. "Is it your decision to make? I don't know, maybe he was her ray of light in the darkness." Tahori's niece Micky says that she hopes Tahori loved Wunsch, that she was given a little warmth and support, "and a reason to get up in the morning in Auschwitz." In addition, unlike the apologetic undertones and the way Tahori was described as a passive victim in *The Most Beautiful Woman* her testimony is hurtful but much less emotional, and Tahori admits in more detail that when Wunsch approached her, she saw his human side.

Feminine Justice in Oy Mama

In *Oy Mama*, directed by Noa Maiman and released in 2010, Maiman presents the specifically female events of her grandmother Fira's life. She tells the story of how she was saved by a Polish woman, Stacha, during the Holocaust, and how, in present-day Israel, she tries to save her Peruvian caregiver, Magna, and five-year-old daughter, Firita, from deportation. *Oy Mama* is a female-directed film that deals with women's issues and highlights female solidarity in the past and the present. The film touches on women's Holocaust experiences ignored in earlier documentaries, such as pregnancies and abortions in the ghettos, and women's solidarity that crosses time lines, geographical borders, nationalities, and generations.

At the same time, the male perspective is marginalized in *Oy Mama*. Noa's grandfather died before the film was produced, and although he is mentioned, the focus is on Noa's grandmother. Throughout *Oy Mama* Noa speaks with family members, but the role of men is kept to a minimum. Her father is the only one who is given several minutes of screen time, when Noa interviews him and asks how the Holocaust shaped his life. Her brother is in New York, so she is the one who talks about him in her voice-over, and his presence in the film is reduced to a short Skype conversation. Most of the screen time is devoted to Noa herself, and to Fira, Stacha, Magna, and Firita, who champion female justice.

The Female Perspective

In many third-generation-directed documentaries, the directors make themselves and their attempts to cope with the Holocaust the main topics. These films fall into Nichols's performative mode category, in which the documented events are shaped by the filmmaker's actions, who takes an active part in the scenes.[22] A subgenre of the performative mode is "I movies," where the directors focus on themselves, their families or friends, their encounters with their surroundings, and the conflicts that consume them. Beyond documenting an individual story,[23] these films also tend to reflect wider cultural, social, political, historical, and/or economic issues.[24] Renov's "domestic ethnographies" stake out a mode of autobiographical practice that couples self-interrogation and the documentation of a family member with ethnographical concerns, since "in an era of great genealogical curiosity such as our own, shared DNA becomes a powerful incitation to documentary practice."[25] Renov argues that the films that emerged in the 1970s and gained prominence by the 1990s are linked to the identity politics that developed in the 1970s, and have turned the spotlight on self-observation related to the family, the community, and ethnic/national/gender backgrounds. In these documentaries, subjectivity is not shameful but rather is the basic assumption—it is the filter through which the world is documented.[26]

Oy Mama is a case in point. Many scenes deal with the ways the Holocaust has affected Noa and her family's life and identity, but also tells a wider story of womanhood, trauma, and transgenerational transfer of trauma. Noa appears in many scenes, reveals her feelings, narrates the film through voice-over, and describes her thought processes. Her journey to the past is a self-reflecting exploration no less that it is a story about her grandmother. In *Oy Mama* Noa tries to understand why she wants to preserve and perpetuate, and why she is living her grandparents' past. Noa confesses in her voice-over how the process of becoming the family historian and the many interviews she conducted with her grandmother were difficult for her emotionally. The interviews drew her even further into her grandmother's world, until "everything was blurred for me—the past, the present, her memories and my imagination," she states in her voice-over while presenting a photomontage of two photographs of herself and her grandmother. Noa admits she felt overwhelmed by memories until "I felt I was losing my grip. At the end of the visit to Poland, I had to take a break from everything. Even from my grandmother. Once I had recovered enough strength, I could go back to my grandmother." In *Oy Mama* Noa expresses her hope that this cinematic journey can help her take the burden off her grandmother's shoulders and, no less, "from myself."

As noted, Hirsch, who analyzed cultural works by the second generation, coined the term *postmemory*, which is defined as an indirect affinity, structured by the imagination and memories that characterizes the experience of those controlled by events that happened before they were born.[27] The scholar Hilene Flanzbaum suggested that postmemory can also be applied to third-generation survivors who engage with places where they have never set foot, and traumas they have not personally experienced.[28] Landsberg made the case that memories do not have rightful owners, and can be espoused by people who did not experience them. According to Landsberg, "Prosthetic memories are adopted as the result of a person's experience with a mass cultural technology of memory that dramatizes or recreates a history he or she did not live."[29] This inauthentic experience is constructed through deep identification with others' memories, which dissolves the dichotomy between the natural and the artificial. People experience history that is not their own in a personal and even physical way. While these experiences are not authentic in that they are not an actual experience of the remembered event, they are nevertheless acutely felt. Landsberg talks about the important role of the media in conveying these memories, but in some cases, these are grafted onto close and intimate encounters with the people who had the actual experiences.[30] These theories are applicable to men and women alike, but *Oy Mama* emphasizes female postmemory and prosthetic memory by documenting the close, almost symbiotic, relationship between a grandmother and a granddaughter, which deals in particular with female issues.

The strong emotional bond between the grandmother and the granddaughter is reflected in the aesthetics of the film. Noa films herself surrounded by piles of documents, photographs, and old items belonging to her grandmother, while relating in voice-over: "In recent years, I have been sinking into recollections that are not mine." As she arranges her grandmother's pictures, Noa says, via voice-over, that Fira would not have believed how deeply involved she (Noa) has become in Fira's past. The strong ties between them affect the way the scenes are photographed. Most consist of a two-shot of Fira and Noa, who sit together and talk. Many times, Noa touches or strokes her grandmother's hand. This physical intimacy strengthens Noa's dominance in *Oy Mama*, just as Fira's stories govern her.

Landsberg suggested that the past people claim and "use" in their prosthetic memory is part of an identity-forming process.[31] The blurring of the grandmother's past and the granddaughter's present is also reflected in the way *Oy Mama* is edited. Fira's testimonies do not emerge as a linear narrative but rather are spread over the film, and are integrated into scenes that describe Noa's feelings, her research, and her descent into these memories. In the interviews themselves, Fira often starts telling her stories, but finds it hard to finish them because of the emotional burden. She stops, and Noa completes the missing part via voice-over. For example, when Noa asks Fira to talk about her separation from her husband, Roman, the scene becomes so difficult for Fira that she becomes confused, needs a glass of water, and cannot continue. Only through the distance created by the editing room is Noa able to add the end of the story, in her voice-over, that Roman was murdered at Treblinka. Thus, the historical narrative is presented by both by Fira and by Noa. This cinematic choice breaks down the barrier between the direct witness and the granddaughter, who is submerged in memories that are not hers.

Toward the end of *Oy Mama*, Noa films herself packing the family photo albums and documents into boxes while she explains the meaning of the end of the process for her:

> In these boxes are stored large and small items—my grandmother's past, the memories, the nightmares, the dreams; everything. I am closing them in "Pandora's boxes" to make room for life and to leave the dead behind, to lift this journey off her burdened shoulders and perhaps, to get away from it myself.

The focus on the *I*, both in this scene and throughout *Oy Mama*, reveals that the film is not just Noa's grandmother's journey into the past but, to a great extent, also a journey of a granddaughter into the history that does not let go. Noa closes the box and pushes it aside, and in this way, concludes the film. But Noa's inability to let go of the past is expressed symbolically after the fade-out to black at the end of the film. Even though the film was aesthetically "supposed" to end, Noa adds scenes from an interview with her grandmother, in which she asks Fira to continue telling her stories ("a few more minutes"). "Maybe I am talking too much," Fira protests. Noa answers, "No, you are not talking too much, you are not talking enough." Afterward, Noa continues to extend the end of the film, and before the final credits, adds a written acknowledgment to her grandmother and grandfather, and mentions that her grandfather's first wife and children were murdered by the Nazis. "I am also living for them," Noa adds in the subtitles, thus making it clear that the box that she tried to close and set aside in the final scene has indeed not closed the door on the past.

Unique Female Experiences

The dominantly female perspective is apparent in the themes Noa chooses to relate to while discussing her grandmother's experiences.

Noa emphasizes the suffering of women, sisterhood, and romance. Fira talks about how she married Roman a few weeks after the war started. They moved together with her parents to the Warsaw Ghetto, where they shared a one-bedroom apartment. Even the anecdotes emphasize strong female bonds. For example, Fira mentions that if she had a fight with Roman, she would go to her mother's bed in the shared room until her father would send her back to her own bed.

As noted earlier, studies on gender and the Holocaust have dealt with the elements that women alone experienced, such as pregnancies and abortions. In some ghettos, pregnancy was forbidden, and Jewish doctors performed abortions to save women's lives; in other places, Gentile doctors saved Jewish women by performing abortions.[32] Noa's interest in women's topics prompts her to steer the conversations in that direction. "You told me once that in the ghetto you were pregnant," Noa says. "Should I talk about it?" Fira asks quietly, as though the camera cannot hear her question. "Yes," Noa replies. Fira hesitates, wiping away a tear. She says that when she was five months pregnant, she and Roman went to a doctor, who advised her to have an abortion—otherwise she would die.[33] Even though the doctor warned Fira that she might not be able to get pregnant again since this was her first pregnancy, she made the decision to go through with it. Fira describes, in a detached manner, how she and Roman had to sneak outside the ghetto to a clinic run by nuns; she and Roman took off their armbands before they entered; she laid down on a bed next to an elegant lady; an SS officer entered and gave the lady flowers and candy. She tells the story, holding on to the smallest details ("I started bleeding at two o'clock"), and repeating the nuns' words. These details are probably Fira's way of working through the trauma by creating emotional distance. The aesthetic cinematic choices echo this, as Noa does not add a melodramatic soundtrack, old pictures, paintings, or illustrations, but leaves it as is: a conversation between two women, which lays bare the harsh personal choices that women had to make during the Holocaust. Fira tells Noa that while she was bleeding and dizzy, she told the doctor, "I don't want another Jew to be born. I don't want this baby." The doctor also told Fira that when non-Jewish women come to the clinic for an abortion they shout, "Oh, Jesus," in their pain, while Fira shouts, "Oy, mama," which could have exposed her Jewishness.

Fira's other recollections also reflect the intimacy and love between herself and Roman. Other stories describe the way in which circumstances dictated that young women needed to become the dominant figures in their households as the situation deteriorated and the men were deported or killed.[34] For example, in one scene, Fira tells Noa that she understood that the Germans were sending the Jews to their death, and not to work, whereas her father refused to believe it. He died of a heart attack in the ghetto (a tragedy regarded by Fira as "the best gift I ever received," since he died of natural causes). Fira's brother disappeared, and she was left with her mother. Fira decided that she would not let the Nazis kill her or her mother, and that it would be better to commit suicide when the time came. She asked a friend who worked in a laboratory for cyanide, gave it to her mother, and told her to take it when the Germans came to the door. Unlike Fira's father, Roman understood what was happening, and arranged a hiding place for Fira and her mother in the house of a Polish woman named Stacha. Hiding Jews was not a uniquely female experience, as many stories involved men and families who helped Jews and hid them, but *Oy Mama* emphasizes the different needs of women and their specific mechanisms to feel alive in an environment permeated by death.

The 2008 Yad Vashem exhibition *Shades of Light: To Be a Woman in the Holocaust* displayed women's pictures, items, and documents in an attempt to capture the experiences of women in the Holocaust. Yehudith Inbar, the exhibit's curator, stated:

> I had the feeling that women's stories should be told separately, by highlighting them in a different light. . . . Now, in retrospect, by the reactions of women Holocaust survivors and their daughters, I can safely say that we were right in assuming that there are unique elements in women's experiences in the Holocaust that have not been discussed before.[35]

The exhibition showed that attempting to remain "human" during the atrocities took on special gender characteristics. For example, a concentration camp inmate was able to make a bra. She had lost her family and her child, and that seemingly insignificant undergarment was an act of survival for her. It was also a social process, which involved the assistance of many other female inmates in getting the basic materials: a piece of fabric, thread, a shard of broken glass to cut the fabric. Afterward there was pride, because the women had created something which was almost impossible to make. It was a way of breathing, of living. The same was true for discussions of recipes. This was a world of women's fantasies, dishes, and memories that were connected to their previous lives. It was an attempt to maintain a woman's tradition, even in the face of death and functioned as a survival mechanism.[36]

In describing Stacha's act of rescue, and her relationship with Fira, Noa's voice-over states she is emphasizing "little Holocaust stories" about the everyday, which "created a different kind of heroism for me—women's heroism." She talks about sisterhood ("from the first instant we were like sisters," Fira says) and women's ways of trying to feel feminine. Fira recalls, with shining eyes, how Roman, who hid for some time on the Aryan side and pretended that he was not Jewish, would come to Stacha's house every week and gave them identical presents, such as bracelets. Fira could not leave the house for two and a half years, and could not shower because the shower was outside. One night, in order to cheer up Fira, Stacha brought dresses and a bottle of wine to the living room. She, Fira, and two other hidden women got dressed, put on makeup, and held a small party during which they sat together, cried, and laughed to feel alive. "It felt like freedom," Fira recalls.

A Chain of Female Justice

Studies have shown that the pride the third generation manifests in their grandparents is often channeled into sensitivity to other victimized groups and political activism.[37] The Holocaust commemoration scholars Alan Berger and Victoria Aarons argued that third-generation artists contemporize the Holocaust by negotiating it as a parallel event to other more contemporary tragedies. These parallel stories are not presented for comparison, but enable ethical responses to emerge because these more recent events provide an available, attainable language of pain.[38] Hirsch suggested that postmemory can lead to an ethical relationship with the oppressed or persecuted other.[39] Michael Renov discussed the historical context for the explosion of personal nonfiction filmmaking in the 1980s and 1990s, and analyzed films in which the subjectivity of the filmmaker, the autobiographical practice, is expressly defined in relation to political struggles.[40] In their book, *The Act of Documenting*, the documentary researchers Brian Winston, Gail Vanstone, and Wang Chi discuss documentaries' power to change the world.[41] In *Oy Mama* the perception of female bravery does not end with Holocaust recollections. Rather, beyond the personal family story of the Holocaust and its transgenerational transfer, Noa uses this narrative to address the issues faced by foreign workers in Israel and specifically Fira's relationship with Magna, her foreign caregiver, and Magna's little daughter, Firita, who are facing deportation to Peru.

The issue of foreign workers in Israel has been part of the Israeli public agenda in recent years. In the late 1980s, foreign workers came to Israel from many countries, and were employed mainly as household workers, caregivers, and agricultural and construction laborers. Those who stayed legally, and others who stayed illegally, put down roots in Israel, raised families, and had children. Since the 1990s, attempts have been made to reduce the number of foreign workers in Israel by deporting illegal workers. The current struggle has revolved not only around the workers themselves but also their Israel-born children.[42] In August 2010 the Israeli government adopted an interministerial committee's recommendations to examine the status of children of foreign workers (Cabinet Resolution 2183), and decided to grant residency to hundreds of children who met specific criteria, and to deport children who did not meet them. Activists, such as members of the Israeli Children's Association and others working for this cause, protested the deportations, sometimes capitalizing on the Holocaust to make their point. Websites dealing with foreign workers and their rights also fight for the rights of Holocaust survivors to pensions and compensation payments,[43] and the responses from Holocaust survivors to this issue have been reported widely in the media.[44] Public figures and academics have turned the spotlight on the universal lessons of the Holocaust that they believe should be implemented in Israeli policies towards foreign workers.[45]

Noa became active in the fight against the deportation of the children of foreign workers in 2009, and volunteered in the Israeli Children's Association. She even announced that if the children were deported, she and other activists would hide them. "The connection to the issue was prompted at the most personal level when my grandmother, a ninety-five-year-old Holocaust survivor, asked us to take care of her 'granddaughter' Firita," Noa adds in an interview:

> My grandmother was terrified of the whole idea, and we were all concerned about the fate of our friends when the Oz unit [the unit that tracks illegal workers to deport them] started to operate. . . . My grandmother, a Polish Holocaust survivor, was hidden for two and a half years. I'm not comparing things, but there is a kind of female kindness prevailing and perhaps an attempt by my grandmother to bring good to the world.[46]

According to the historian Gulie Neeman-Arad, in recent decades cultural commemorations of the Holocaust in Israel have attempted to modify the canonic narrative from specifically Zionist to universal humanistic lessons.[47] In *Oy Mama* Noa blurs the boundaries between the Holocaust and the struggle of the foreign workers,[48] since the film alternates between two time lines: the past, when Fira was hidden by Stacha, and the present, when Fira tries to help Magna.[49] The idea that unites these two time lines is the notion of female kindness, and its wider effects. Noa asks Fira if she thinks this contemporary story resembles her own. Fira notes that there is some resemblance but that fundamentally these stories are quite different because Stacha risked her life and could have been murdered by the Nazis because of her actions. Thus, Noa's use of the Holocaust to describe the distress of foreign workers is not a comparison between situations, but points to a more universal lesson of the Holocaust that should be firmly entrenched in Israel.

Oy Mama does not only represent the foreign workers' issues in general but also focuses on the challenges faced by female foreign workers. It emphasizes Magna's troubles, and documents Fira's efforts on her behalf when she became pregnant. Magna, sitting next to Fira, tells Noa that she was sure she would be fired, until Fira, who at that time was already living in a retirement home, fought for her. Since the retirement home clientele resented having a noisy baby living there, Fira hired a lawyer, who examined her contract with the home. "Nowhere was it written that I cannot have children," Fira remarks. She was finally able to convince the home to allow Magna and baby Firita to stay with her. Eventually, all the elderly residents became enamored with the baby.

The importance of a female chain of justice is clear from the first scene of the film. In this fifty-minute Holocaust documentary, Noa devotes the first seven minutes to the story of Magna and Firita, and Fira's role in fighting for them. They also appear in many other scenes, which turns their story into a dominant element in *Oy Mama*. The film opens with little Firita running around the retirement home shouting, "You can't catch me, you can't catch me." The symbolism of her game is quickly revealed as the film begins to introduce the story of her immigration problems in Israel. In later scenes, as Noa's voice-over tells the story of Firita and Magna, "You can't catch me" becomes more than a child's game—it is a challenge to the authorities.

Oy Mama reveals how individuals receiving care transfer their emotions from someone in the past to someone in the present. Fira transfers her feelings for Stacha to Magna and Firita. While Magna physically cares for Fira, it is in fact Fira who is portrayed in the film as being a strong, dominant woman, who takes Magna and Firita under her wings and protects them. Fira tries to give Magna a home and shelter, just as Stacha had given her one. The parallel between the past and present is clearly echoed in a scene in which Fira says that with all her heart, she was giving back to Magna that which Stacha gave her.[50] Noa's brother also states that "there is something symbolic when someone helps another person at some point, and years later, life comes back in the same way. Basically, Magna and Firita also owe a favor to that Polish woman."

The question of who is saving whom arises again in the story of Romek, Stacha's nephew. The film shows how Fira and her family worked for years for Stacha to be given the title of Righteous Among the Nations, but Yad Vashem only acknowledged Stacha after her death. *Oy Mama* shows how the Maiman family located Romek, and brought him to Israel to accept the award in Stacha's name. Against a backdrop of scenes of Romek's visit to Yad Vashem, Noa wonders in her voice-over whether Romek's visit to Israel to accept the title after battling cancer had perhaps given him a few more years to live. If so, her grandmother may be "the one who saved a Polish person."

In one of *Oy Mama*'s first scenes, Fira teaches little Firita a Polish lullaby, and they sing it together. Noa uses this duet as a soundtrack for other scenes showing Fira, Magna, and Firita's daily life. The contrast between these scenes that illustrate everyday life in Israel, and the song that is associated with Fira's European past captures the similarities between times and places. Noa's attempt to blur the dichotomy between native Israelis and foreign workers is also reflected in the scenes that document two major myths in Israeli culture: Holocaust Martyrs' and Heroes' Remembrance Day, and Independence Day. In one scene, Firita tells Fira enthusiastically that she learned about the Holocaust in kindergarten, and "the soldiers fought the Nazis." In another scene, Noa films the celebrations in the kindergarten in Herzliya where Firita plays the part of an Israeli soldier in a class pageant. She wears a T-shirt with the Star of David, an army cap, and she salutes like a soldier. The film thus implies that Firita has already absorbed all the Israeli myths, but that the Israeli government refuses to acknowledge it.

Toward the end of *Oy Mama*, against background images of Magna and Firita, Noa's voice-over states that Magna and Firita have been temporarily allowed to stay in Israel. Firita's aunt had been deported a few years earlier, and Firita's father is pending deportation. Noa concludes by transitioning to discussions with her grandmother about how the Holocaust affected her. ("Is the woman you were before the war and the woman you were after the war one and the same?") This thematic shift reflects the need to examine the effects of the Holocaust in the years that followed, both on a personal level (her grandmother's life, and the way the trauma was transferred to her family), and in a collective manner; in other words, how Jewish Israelis, remembering what they have been through, should treat foreigners and others.

Motherhood in the Aftermath of the Holocaust in The Cemetery Club

The ways in which motherhood was affected by the Holocaust have seldom been documented. The second-generation documentary *Because of That War* touched on this theme in scenes in which the survivor Halina Birenbaum and her son Ya'acov Gila'ad talk to the camera about the ways in which her traumatic experiences became part of her motherhood: she sang songs from the ghetto; made him a rag doll like the one she had; when he got bad grades she yelled at him, "Is this why I survived Auschwitz? To see you come home with such grades?" Gila'ad says that in their home the dead were no less alive than the living, and Halina confesses that the fear that her son would grow up to be "like them" (the Nazis) shaped her motherhood.

The Cemetery Club, directed by Tali Shemesh and released in 2006, is an intimate family story in which the female director Shemesh documents her eighty-five-year-old grandmother Minia Rubin, and Minia's childhood friend from Łódź and future sister-in-law Lena (Shemesh's eighty-year-old great-aunt). The film's aesthetics reflect what Nichols refers to as the *interactive mode*. The filmmaker is part of the film, as he or she appears on-camera, and not only in voice-over, by listening, speaking, reacting, and provoking situations.[51] Shemesh photographs herself in some of the scenes.

She documents the discussions and arguments that she has with Lena and Minia, along with scenes of reconciliation and strong emotional bonding.

Rather than focusing on past atrocities, *The Cemetery Club* centers on the subjects' contemporary lives, a cinematic choice that enables Shemesh to broaden the portrait of female Holocaust survivors. A more complex picture is thus presented which encompasses many other facets of these women's lives. It reflects the trauma of the Holocaust, without neglecting other traumas that affected their lives. They are not only "female Holocaust survivors" but rather women whose personalities are defined by much more than their identities as Holocaust survivors.

Celebrating Old Age

Unlike *Three Sisters*, *The Cemetery Club*'s focus is not on decline in an elderly age, but on exuberance, on an attempt to live life to the fullest, even when the body starts to decline. Lena and Minia are members of what Shemesh calls "the cemetery club," a group of about twenty elderly Holocaust survivors who live in Jerusalem and who, for the past twenty years, have met every Saturday morning on Mount Herzl. Sitting among the graves of the nation's dignitaries, they discuss matters both sublime and elevated, such as philosophy, poetry, and history.[52] They refer to themselves as the "Mount Herzl Academy," and act in accordance with the strict rules that they themselves formulated—the meetings take place only on Saturdays, each member must bring their own chair, they eat lunch together, and the chairperson prepares topics for discussion in advance. Shemesh documented these meetings over a period of several years, and in doing so, revealed the wonderful way these elderly people have chosen to maintain their spirit and energy. As they themselves expressed it in the set of regulations they created, their goal is: "To lessen loneliness in the golden age, to foster friendship, and to help each other." The film portrays a powerful, strong-minded active group of educated people, who even in old age do not relinquish their right to state their opinion.

The Cemetery Club depicts them as a group of people who constantly live in the shadow of death: the Holocaust in the past, and now their mortality. The gatherings are conducted in a cemetery, which for them is a very natural place to meet, talk, and dine. During the meetings, the group reads and analyzes poems that deal with death, and eulogizes deceased group members. In between the cemetery scenes, Shemesh shows the group attending their friends' funerals and documents the group becoming smaller from year to year. However, these scenes are not presented as sad or depressing. On the contrary, Shemesh films them in the same natural way that they experience it, and since they accept the inevitable, there is nothing depressing about it. Rather, its very naturalness results in gently amusing scenes. The survivors are presented as people who are not only acquainted with death, but live peacefully in its shadow.

In her book *Psychoanalysis and Ethics in Documentary Film*, Agnieszka Piotrowska discusses the deep bond between filmmaker and subject, which she calls "transference love," which influences the representation.[53] According to Renov, for the domestic ethnographer, there is no fully external position possible, and the filmmaker's subjectivity is explicitly aligned with familial or close social affiliations.[54] Shemesh's intimate acquaintance with Lena and Minia, and her loving perspective, enable her to represent the lives of the elderly in tragicomic scenes in which the humorous does not denigrate the survivors but rather deepens the empathy toward them. For example, in one scene, Shemesh's camera moves from an elderly man who lectures enthusiastically about Kant, and his wife, whose attempts to light a cigarette are repeatedly foiled by her shaking hands. As he talks, she is completely focused on her physical disabilities. The parallel editing of the film shifts between these encounters, individual meetings with Shemesh, Lena, and Minia in their homes, and extreme long shots of the elderly marching through the cemetery carrying their folding chairs on their way to the meeting point on Mount Herzl. The cinematic repetition of these surrealistic scenes gives the film a comic angle, which highlights their efforts to maintain their vitality.

The Cemetery Club portrays Lena as a symbol of feminism—a strong, successful, opinionated career woman. It opens with Lena expressing her disapproval of the film's title. The title appears onscreen anyway, but Lena contends that *The Cemetery Club* is not appropriate. "It is not a 'cemetery club' . . . It has a completely different meaning. It is the 'Academy of Mount Herzl,'" she insists. Lena's refusal to accept the director's decision is both humorous and also highlights her strong will. This stubbornness is apparent throughout the film in other scenes, and is presented through a combination of drama and humor. Lena argues with Shemesh about the shooting of the film ("What else do you want to do with me? I want to know. I'm allowed to know"), voices her indignation regarding the way the film is structured ("I didn't know that we were going to be the lead actresses. I cannot appear as 'Mrs. Know-it-all'"), objects to the film's synopsis, written by Shemesh, as being exaggerated (since in describing Lena, it says, "There is no book she hasn't read and there isn't a topic she doesn't have a solid opinion about"), and demands that it be changed. Minia, on the other hand, allows Shemesh to document her as she wishes, and answers all her questions without argument.

The Cemetery Club focuses on Lena and Minia's present-day lives. It presents a complex portrait of two contrasting feminine personalities, and is composed of scenes that show various aspects of their daily lives, the ways in which they cope with their memories, and their relationships. They are both retired; Minia is a mother of two, and is now a widow. Lena was a legislator. She is also a widow and a mother of two. Lena is dominant and charismatic; Minia is quiet and introverted. Unlike Lena, who states that she never experienced great love, choosing instead a man she trusted for a husband, Minia is described as a woman who was in love with her husband until the day he died. Lena is down-to-earth and practical, and is photographed in her house with her vast library in the background, whereas Minia is documented as she roams the fields near her home and gazes at the clouds. She tells Shemesh that she sees her husband in the clouds, and dreams about him every night. "Your grandma is more feminine," Lena states. "She has something very unique and she is special. You need a very special character to stay in love until the end like that. Not everyone is capable of that."

Motherhood, Career, and Life Choices

Minia is characterized as a woman who has dedicated her life to her family, while Lena has chosen career over family. She needs to be center stage, and during the Mount Herzl gatherings she speaks up loudly and with confidence. When anyone tries to argue or hush her, she rebels ("Now *I'm* talking!"), while Minia sits in the corner, observing.

Combining both tragedy and comedy, *The Cemetery Club* documents the complex bond between the two women, which goes beyond their shared Holocaust past. Shemesh shows their petty fights, in which they tease and bicker in a way that highlights the differences between them. For example, on many occasions, Lena stresses their intellectual gap. "We have other areas of interest," she says condescendingly to Minia, who dares to interrupt one of her stories. "You know about chickens, dogs, cows, horses, flowers, and the art of cooking. I don't know anything about these topics, but there are things that you didn't learn—literature, history, and law." Even their approaches to everyday life are different: Lena often attacks Minia's ignorance, and elaborates time and again on the number of years she went to school, whereas Minia responds somewhat ironically, "What can I do [about the fact] that I'm so ignorant? . . . I didn't know that my sister-in-law was so well-educated that I could not open my mouth in her presence." These comic scenes help negate the homogenous image of 'the female Holocaust survivor' by adding multifaceted dimensions as the intricacy of their relationship emerges. Lena indeed tyrannizes Minia, but also loves and appreciates her deeply. When one of the other women in the Mount Herzl Academy takes a seat next to Lena in what is Minia's place, Lena rudely makes her stand up, whispering to Minia, "She wants to control everything and separate us."

The Cemetery Club provides a glimpse into the choices and life experiences of female survivors in the aftermath of the Holocaust. It hints at a patriarchal world in which being a mother while trying to break the glass ceiling and develop a serious career was not taken for granted. It exposes viewers to the complexity and tragedy that accompanied these choices. In that sense, the film broadens the topics represented in Holocaust documentaries, as Shemesh not only changes the perspective and themes but also confronts the basic premise of second-generation documentaries, which are mainly seen through the lens of the Holocaust. *The Cemetery Club*, like other third-generation documentaries—*Aida's Secrets*, *The Cahana Sisters*, *Numbered*, and *Farewell Herr Schwarz*—includes the additional traumas endured by female survivors. For Minia, it is the death of her husband. In second-generation films, the men (and the few women) that were documented were sometimes represented in temporary states of acting out, as the past and present blurred into one. When Shemesh follows Minia as she imagines seeing her dead husband in the clouds, the filmmaker presents her in the same post-traumatic situation—only now, it is not the Holocaust that acts out, but another trauma. When discussing the Holocaust, Minia appears calm and relaxed, seems to distance herself from the past, and to work through the trauma. The mention of her deceased husband, however, staggers her emotionally, and she finds herself unable to work through his death.

Lena is haunted by the choices she was forced to make as a mother. In her daily life, Lena appears to be very tough; somebody who handles her affairs with an iron fist. But when Shemesh pushes her to talk about the Holocaust, this image crumbles, and the softer person behind her mask is revealed. The interviews expose Lena's near-inability to discuss her Holocaust experiences. On a trip to the Dead Sea, which is captured in scenes that intensify the theme of death overshadowing the film, Lena is filmed lying on a bed with her back to the camera. It is only in this position that she can begin to explain that she is haunted by a past that constantly appears in nightmares. Lena describes herself as "traumatized." Being aware of the power of a camera, she admits it only when she can control the scene—she talks, but only on her terms by not allowing the camera to capture her facial expressions.

Since Lena is so cognizant of the situation, Shemesh can only document the fragile woman behind the tough image in voyeur shots. In one scene, Shemesh asks Lena, who is sitting in her study, to talk about the Holocaust. It begins like a regular interview in medium shot, which is commonly seen in second-generation films. "One cannot forget events which are landmarks of my life," Lena begins with her featured poise. She describes how her father died of hunger, how her brother was sick and believed the Nazis when they said the Jews would be transported to the East to work, and how her sister caught typhus. She remembers the instant they got to Auschwitz: "When they opened the train cars I saw many girls with shaved heads who ran around and screamed, 'Bread! Bread!' We thought we had come to an asylum. These are things no one can forget." When Lena starts to talk about the hunger, though, the flood of words stops. She tells Shemesh, "In the ghetto I was always hungry. Half a year after the war broke out we didn't have money to buy food, even when there still were products in the market." Then Lena stops. The emotional burden is too great. Instead of admitting that she is unable to continue with the interview, she says that her stomach hurts, and therefore must stop the conversation. The camera follows Shemesh and Lena in voyeurs shot as they enter the kitchen. Through the half-closed door, the camera documents how the mask of rigidity crumbles and the vulnerable woman behind the tough lawyer appears—"You are not mad at me, right?" She leans on Shemesh and hugs her: "You don't know how much I need a family, something to lean on." This soft, broken Lena is the opposite of the image she presents when she knows the camera is filming her. She tries to pull herself together and goes back to her original excuse: "I must eat. I'm very hungry." But while she nibbles on crackers, Lena continues to talk to Shemesh about her need for emotional support. Her inability to continue her personal story, and the marked change in her personality, attest to her complex personality.

The same pattern is apparent when Lena tries to talk about another trauma in her life: the relationship with her son Yoram. Lena is filmed in a similar position to the Holocaust interview. She sits in her study near her desk (medium shot) and addresses Shemesh, who sits in the margins of the frame. Lena discloses that when she and her husband came to Israel, she sent her two sons to an orphanage while she went to study, and during that time her husband lived in an immigrant shelter. Lena, who throughout the film is self-critical, describes what she did as "not reasonable." She continues, "A reasonable person wouldn't have done it." But she also explains that, at the time, she thought it was the right thing to do and that it was a great thing that she could study. "Do you regret it?" Shemesh asks. "I cannot regret it because I don't know what I would have done if I hadn't done it," Lena answers. She presents pictures of her son Yoram to the camera and remarks that Yoram has still not found his place in life. When he lived in Israel, he "replaced jobs like socks," never married, and in 1992 left Israel and disappeared. "You didn't think to look for him?" Shemesh asks. As in the previous scene, Lena once again stops talking and leaves the room. Up until that moment, Lena has talked about her son with detachment, as if working through the issue. Now she bursts out, "Perhaps you should stop questioning me?" Lena becomes angry, exclaiming, "I won't answer any of your questions," and runs again to the kitchen and from there to the porch. The cameraman secretly follows Shemesh as she runs after Lena, and again, only via a voyeur shot that glimpses them on the porch reveals the vulnerable, injured side of her personality she wants to hide. Standing close to Shemesh, Lena whispers that Yoram does not want to be found. Even when he was told, twelve years ago, that his father was on his deathbed, he did not call or come to visit before his father passed away. Here, too, Lena's emotional suffering is expressed physically: she complains of a headache, and the interview ends.

Thus, unlike most second-generation documentaries,[55] *The Cemetery Club* reminds viewers that Holocaust survivors experienced a great deal in their post-Holocaust lives, and that the posttraumatic effects of the Holocaust cannot account for all their behavior.[56] Consistent with this view, *The Cemetery Club* and many other third-generation documentaries that will be analyzed in the next chapters, permit a more profound look at the life of Holocaust survivors. Echoing the vast research on documentary and truth, the film also attests to the problematic nature of documentary films as reflections of reality, by showing how the two most honest scenes about Lena were documented without her knowledge or consent.[57]

Sexual Abuse and Women's Choices in Aida's Secrets

Throughout history, during conflicts, women's bodies have been considered spoils of war. The conqueror invades a woman's body just as he invades her country. Even when soldiers or members of the conquering population are forbidden to have sex with the occupied population, these prohibitions are often disregarded. The law and gender researcher Nomi Levenkron has pointed out that the message conveyed to women who were raped during wartime was clear: commit suicide or live in shame. Women who took their own lives rather than be raped were regarded as martyrs and almost sanctified, and women who were raped but lived were often denounced in their communities. Women who traded sex for food were looked upon as prostitutes and not as human beings fighting to survive. In addition, their suffering did not end after World War II, because they were marked as prostitutes and as promiscuous, and also because they had to deal with posttrauma, unwanted pregnancies, and sexually transmitted diseases.[58]

The exact number of women, both Jewish and non-Jewish, who were raped and abused during the Holocaust is unknown. According to the Nuremberg Laws, sexual contact between Nazis and Jewish women was forbidden. However, testimonies and victims' memoirs reveal sexual exploitation during the Holocaust by the Nazis, Jews, and local Nazi collaborators in different countries.[59] The Yiddish literature researcher Hannah Pollin-Galay noted that Jewish women's testimonies about Lithuanian aggressors who raped women can be found in early postwar sources (1945–48).[60] The film researcher Yvonne Kozlovsky Golan reported that there are several oral testimonies by North African women regarding sexual abuse.[61] The historians Na'ama Shik and Judy Tydor-Baumel Schwartz claim that shame was not characteristic of the first decades after the war and only developed from the 1970s onward. They argue that the autobiographical memoirs of female Holocaust survivors published since the mid-1970s in fact marginalized sexual experiences. In that sense, they differed from the memoirs of women published in the 1950s and 1960s, which dealt more overtly with sexuality during the Holocaust, probably because the feelings of shame grew stronger over the years.[62] However sexual abuse was marginalized in mainstream Holocaust research before the turn of the century. The first comprehensive book on sexual abuse was only published in 2010, and it is rarely mentioned in museums and educational settings.[63]

In the 1940s and 1950s, Holocaust survivors in Eretz Israel and Israel were met with empathy and honest attempts to help them, but also with suspicion.[64] Israelis wondered how and why they had survived, while six million other Jews had perished. Sometimes the claim was even made that "the best had been killed." The thought was that those who had survived had probably been able to get by, and not always with integrity.[65] Attitudes toward women in the Holocaust were very wide-ranging. Mothers and female combatants were sometimes depicted as heroes.[66] At the same time, however, female Holocaust survivors were also depicted in Israeli public debates and popular culture as women who had committed sexual acts in order to survive.[67] This combination of the Holocaust, sex, and sadism appeared in Israeli poetry, cinema, and literature, as well as in public discourse and interpersonal relationships, and often took the form of thinly veiled accusations.[68]

Third-generation documentaries also break the wall of silence surrounding the topic of sexual abuse and explore this topic. The sexual stereotypes that appeared in the first decades of Israel are discussed in the Israeli documentary *Stalags* (Ari Libsker, 2007), which deals with the way sex, Nazism, and the Holocaust have appeared in the public sphere and Israeli literature since the 1950s. "The sexual images in these books infiltrated Israeli Holocaust commemoration and are used as well in contemporary Israel," Libsker says in his voice-over as he films Israelis in schools and streets standing at attention as the two-minute siren blares on Holocaust Martyrs' and Heroes' Remembrance Day. The shots are still—the people stand frozen, as if to symbolize that the pornographic aspects of the Holocaust had become fixed in Israeli Holocaust commemoration from the 1940s until the present.

In the TV documentary series *Vacuum*, which aired on channel 23 in 2010, the media journalist and activist Gal Gabai shed light on tendentious subjects in Israeli society. In the episode titled "Secrets," she discussed the silence concerning sexual exploitation during the Holocaust. Gabai implements Nichols's performative mode as she interviews people on-camera, inquires, urges actions, verifies archival documents, and states her opinions as one of the interviewees. In this episode she turns against Israeli society, which has morally judged women who were forced to prostitute themselves during World War II, tries to determine whether there were Jewish prostitutes, and criticizes the Israeli myth that glorifies women who chose to commit suicide to preserve their purity. The interviews expose the disagreements between scholars on the topic of Jewish prostitutes under Nazism. They raise the question of the authenticity of Paul Goldman's famous photo of a woman's chest with a tattoo marking her as prostitute. They also emphasize that the story about the ninety-three girls from Kraków who chose to commit suicide rather than be raped by the approaching Nazi army has never been verified historically. Nonetheless, it has become an Israeli myth, part of the education system, and is commemorated in streets names. In interviews with Shosh Navon, whose survivor friend confided in her that she was forced into prostitution, she persuades the survivor to write an anonymous letter as testimony. In the letter, which appears on screen at the end of the episode, the survivor states that she was forced into prostitution at the age of fourteen and has had to live with this secret her entire life. As the end titles appear, Gabai's voice is heard as a call to action—that if women stop being ashamed of the horrible position that was forced upon them and will stand up and testify, it will allow others who were sexually abused to understand that they are not to blame—"they are pure."

The television documentary *Screaming Silence*, directed by Ronnie Sarnat and Gil Lesnik and released in 2015, is a fulfillment of Gabai's wish. It consists of a frightening collection of rape testimonies by Holocaust survivors. One after another, men and women who were young children and teenagers during the Holocaust tell the directors how they were raped by Germans, Poles, and even Jews. This is the first film entirely devoted to this topic that presents the testimonies which for many years the survivors preferred to hide. It is a collection of straightforward interviews with survivors, who tell the camera about their rape during the Holocaust. Some describe it in graphic detail—others blur the specific details, but the event is clear. Some cry during their testimony—others tell their stories from an emotional distance. The range of testimonies from different localities, the different perpetrators, and the nature of the instances are visualized in minimalistic cinematic language. There are no illustrations, archival footage, or sound dramatization. There are only a few still photos that show how young they were. Sarnat says that at first, she was afraid of making a pornographic narrative because the film focuses on the victims' descriptions of the rapes, but later decided that the events would be situated once the survivors were shown to be full characters, before and after the Holocaust. "I don't think that after you have seen the whole film you think it is pornography. I think it only raises the question of why this topic has been ignored for so long."[69]

Aida's Secrets, directed by Alon Schwarz and released in 2016, addresses a personal story of sexual abuse, its consequences, and its effects on life and motherhood. The film not only relates to this silenced theme and dismantles accusations, but also very gently portrays the horrific choices made by women who had to live with the consequences of this abuse. The film traces the incredible story of Aida (originally Jadwiga), a mystery woman who gave birth to two boys, Izhak and Shepsel, in the Bergen-Belsen displaced persons (DP) camp after World War II. The brothers were separated as babies, and Izhak was sent to Eretz Israel, while Shepsel was sent to Canada. Neither was told that the other existed. The film catches up with the two brothers more than six decades later as they reunite and investigate their mysterious family history. Together with the director, the two brothers try to understand their mother's life, during and after World War II. They have many questions: When did she get pregnant? Who was the father? Do they both have the same father? Why did she send Izhak to Eretz Israel, but did not immigrate there herself? Why didn't she contact her second son, Shepsel, and what happened to her great love affair with her husband, Grisha? The film's main theme, therefore, is a profound look into the complexities of women's choices during and after World War II that highlights the specificity of female experiences during the war, and their effect on their lives afterward.

Aida's identity is revealed slowly throughout the film, as the director and his crew collect one piece of the puzzle after the other from relatives, friends, and archives around the world. A story of female suffering, sexual abuse, and recovery is revealed. The number of secrets, lies, and melodramatic turmoil in the film made the reporter Zion Nanus claim, correctly, that if the plot of *Aida's Secrets* had been handed to a Hollywood studio as a fictional script, it would have been rejected as being too unbelievable.[70]

Even though the central part of the film is constructed as a detective story in which leads are discovered one after the other, the film begins and ends with funeral scenes, with the voices of Aida's friends describing her as a person. Before viewers see Aida's old photos, home videos, or meet her in her retirement home, they already know that "she never hurt anyone," "she was always nice," "you could have trusted her with everything." "You'd never know what really happened," another relative says. "Something has to come out. You cannot bury everything in the ground," reflects another. These short shots that compose the film's teaser use the funeral as a symbol of Aida's attempts to bury her past. The mystery lady that these friends and relatives talk about, will, at the end of the film, take parts of her past with her into the grave.

Aida's Secrets opens with Izhak, who, at the age of sixty-seven, lives on an Israeli moshav. Izhak is full of life, and takes great pride in his family. He is a gardener, and is filmed in open green fields, roaming the areas of the moshav.[71] He discusses the fact that he is adopted and has a mother in Canada. When Izhak tells the director, Alon Schwartz, about his childhood revelations, he seems to go back in time: when describing his biological mother, he is as enthusiastic as a wide-eyed child seeing his mother for the first time. "One day—I was seven or eight—the children came and told me that my parents were not my real parents." When he confronted his Israeli parents, they first tried to lie, and then confessed that he had a biological mother living in Canada. This scene is the first time that Aida's picture as a young woman appears on-screen. From then on, the pursuit of Aida and her secrets begins. Even before she appears in the film, her character is developed out of anecdotes, memories, documents, pictures, and home videos contributed by her friends and relatives, thus increasing the mystery.

Izhak says that Aida looked for him, found him, and decided that she would come to Israel for his bar mitzvah. While Schwartz screens home videos of a beautiful, elegantly dressed young woman who smiles and waves at the camera, Izhak's voice-over highlights how impressed he was by her beauty, but how awkward the first conversations with her were. From then on, *Aida's Secrets* is composed of sequences that reveal one secret after the other. This aesthetic decision helps create a detective-like structure. In that sense, *Aida's Secrets* resembles other third-generation Holocaust documentaries in which the directors unfold an investigation that reflects their journey to discover family secrets and marginalized family histories—for example, *The Flat*, *Farewell Herr Schwarz*, and *The Green Dumpster Mystery*. This attempt to maintain step-by-step discovery affects the cinematic structure: when an interviewee reveals too much, the interview scenes are separated and appear in different places in the film, sometimes many scenes apart from each other, to reveal the mystery layer by layer. Slowly, Schwartz leads the viewer from one turning point to the next, without stopping, continually creating the feeling that the final secret is being revealed, until the next sequence appears, which upsets everything again. This creates a deep and complex portrait of female suffering, survival, and choices.

Izhak relates that when he asked Aida about his father's identity, she answered, "His name is Grisha. He died in the war. He was a good man. I don't want to talk about him." Schwartz focuses on two photos from the displaced persons camp that Aida showed Izhak. One is a photo taken during a picnic, in which the young Aida is seated holding baby Izhak. Next to her is a man holding another baby. The second picture features a handsome man in the displaced person's camp. He has a tattoo above his left nipple. These two pictures reappear again and again throughout *Aida's Secrets*, like memories that cannot be buried, but keep on surfacing, leading the search and the surprising revelations.

Alon Schwartz, the director, is Izhak's nephew. He grew up in the same moshav and has known Izhak all of his life. The film adheres to what Nichols calls the *interactive mode*: Schwartz is involved, but this is not his personal journey. His intimate acquaintance with the social actors enables him to document very personal scenes. His discoveries propel the film, and his voice-over is featured in many scenes, as he tries to make sense of all the mysterious revelations. Schwartz relates that, inexplicably, Aida chose to show the picnic picture to Izhak's adoptive family when she went to his bar mitzvah. She pointed to a little boy in the photo and said, "This is Izhak's brother. He is blind. Don't tell anyone about this." True to their word, they did not mention it to anyone, and lived with this secret for years. Schwartz tells viewers in his voice-over, "I was six or seven when I discovered that my uncle Izhak has a blind brother and I shouldn't tell him."

According to Schwartz, Izhak began digging into his past upon returning from a trip to the former concentration camps in Poland with his granddaughter's high school class. He did some research at

Yad Vashem and found the DP record cards with emigration stamps for four people.[72] According to the records, Izhak had been sent to Israel, while Aida, Grisha, and Shepsel were sent to Canada. The research led to Izhak's discovery that he had a brother he had never met. Schwartz documents the moment when he confesses to his uncle that he had known all along about the brother. Izhak is astonished and angry. He is upset because he knows that Aida is currently in a retirement home, her memory betrays her, and probably she will not be able to tell the story and help him find his brother. Schwartz turns the search for his long-lost uncle into a mission. He begins to investigate it on a genealogy website, starts looking for information, and combs through archives, libraries, and research institutions in various countries.[73] Against a backdrop of certificates and pictures from the Bergen-Belsen DP camp, Schwartz announces in his voice-over that he has found documents that contain evidence of Aida and Grisha. According to the documents, Izhak was born seven months after the end of the war. Even though Schwartz hints to viewers that Aida was already pregnant when she got to the DP camp, he does not pursue this information, and announces that Lawrence, the investigator from the genealogy website, has found Izhak's brother. He is alive and lives in Winnipeg, Canada. On-camera, Schwartz captures the moment when he tells Izhak the news. He then travels with him to Canada and documents the emotional and tearful reunion.

Unlike many second-generation films that represent the past and present in a gloomy atmosphere, many third-generation films—such as *The Cemetery Club*, *Shalom Italia*, and *Numbered*—are much lighter in tone, even when documenting devastating stories. *Aida's Secrets* is representative of that approach. Even though the film has many dramatic (and even melodramatic) moments, and deals with the impossible choices of a woman trying to survive, it is not gloomy. Izhak is a naïve and charming man, and Shepsel uses a great deal of humor and irony—"You have a bigger nose than mine," he says to Izhak at their first meeting; "It would be hilarious if I got killed now," he says to the crew as he steps out of the car to meet his mother for the first time. Additionally, Schwartz chose a light, jazzy, Woody Allen–style soundtrack to accompany many scenes, which eases the atmosphere and moves viewers from tears to laughter, as the layers of Aida's secrets are revealed.

Second-generation Holocaust documentaries on Holocaust survivors and their stories have always documented them with much respect, even when describing multifaceted and problematic relationships from their children's perspectives. Through Shepsel, Schwartz fractures this deference. In contrast to Izhak, who accepts things as they are, Shepsel is more critical when it comes to their father, and feels much more hurt. He tells Izhak that Grisha was not a warm person. As he puts it, "The camps took it away from him." In later conversations, he claims that Grisha treated him "like shit," and left nothing for him in his will. The development of Grisha's character throughout the film reveals another theme that was left untouched in previous Israeli documentaries which focused on the atrocities and suffering of the survivors. *Aida's Secrets* addresses a different side of survivor narratives, since it describes Grisha as a "Jewish mobster," who used his status in the DP camp to deal food and favors (to "arrange" goods in camp lingo).

Through the documented conversations between the brothers, viewers discover that Shepsel only found out at age sixteen that the woman who raised him, Grisha's wife, was not his real mother. Now, in his late sixties, Shepsel discovers that his biological mother had been living only a two-hour flight away from him for all these years. The brothers make arrangements to meet her. "I am entitled to have questions," Shepsel says angrily, wondering how she completely abandoned him. The portrait of a deserting mother is balanced by Izhak and his family. "Don't blame her," Izhak says, "She is a good woman." Izhak's wife takes this same viewpoint when describing how well Aida treated their children when she came to visit in Israel. The camera backs up her stories while showing home videos of Aida with Izhak's family, including scenes in which she hugs and kisses his children and seems very happy with them. The mother who searched for and eventually found Izhak, who traveled to Israel many times to meet him, and kept in touch with him all these years trying to compensate for the fact that she sent him away contrasts with her complete denial of Shepsel. Even before the audience sees Aida in the present, this creates the image of a complex woman.

As they get ready for the meeting, the brothers and Schwartz compare the pictures that each has of Grisha. Schwartz notices an inconsistency: Grisha has a tattoo near his left nipple, while the man in the picnic photograph from 1947, who Aida claimed was their father, does not. Shepsel's daughter tells them that they must consider that perhaps Grisha did not father both of them. As in the other scene, which revealed that Aida was pregnant when she arrived at the DP camp, Schwartz leaves this item hanging and overshadows it with the excitement of the meeting between Aida and Shepsel. But, just as in the discovery regarding the pregnancy, in later scenes it emerges as one of the main themes. Toward the end of *Aida's Secrets*, it becomes clear that although Aida is indeed their mother, Grisha is not Izhak's father.

In order to prolong the moment before the meeting with Aida, Schwartz uses parallel editing between scenes of Aida getting ready, and the two brothers en route. This is the first time that Aida is shown in the present. She is shot in a close-up, looking straight at the camera, and it is difficult to tell whether she is cognizant of what is taking place or not. Another aesthetic choice Schwartz made was to film using two cameras. For example, in the meeting scene, the camera is located next to Aida in her room, and films Izhak and Shepsel from her perspective as they enter, while Schwartz, who holds the second camera, enters with them. "Shepsele," she says as they enter, "my little Shepsele." They hug, the brothers cry, and Schwartz, holding the camera, is crying as well. Although the emotion is real, the documentation of the surprise is questionable. In an interview, Schwartz remarks that they could not make the visit a complete surprise due to health concerns voiced by the nursing home staff, so Aida was notified in advance that Shepsel would be coming to see her.[74]

Motherhood: Choosing to Forget

The discovery that Izhak has a brother, their reunion, and Shepsel's meeting with Aida all take place in the first half hour of the ninety-minute documentary. Thus, most of *Aida's Secrets* is not devoted to these themes but rather to an attempt to understand Aida's world: her story, her experiences, her choices, her lies and deceptions, and the reasoning behind them. In this sense, meeting Aida in person, which should have been the film's climax, is not the end of a journey, but its beginning. The film's title therefore encompasses much more than Aida's choice not to tell Izhak that he has a brother. The snippets from Aida's life that are revealed in the hour of the film following their reunion make it very clear that women's experiences under Nazism is a topic that requires special and separate acknowledgement.

During the next hour of *Aida's Secrets*, Shepsel and Schwartz, who are increasingly suspicious, and have not received definite answers to their questions, try to put the pieces of the puzzle of Aida's life together. Schwartz films Shepsel and himself as they travel from place to place, meet with relatives, scan documents from archives around the world, and try to find answers since Aida will not cooperate.

Aida appears to be an elderly woman who has difficulties remembering. Throughout her meetings with Shepsel, she has the same impassive expression—she also appears to be frozen, and does not look her sons in the eye. She never expresses excitement or a change of mood. But when Shepsel meets with her several more times, Aida understands what is going on around her, chooses when to take part in the conversations, and when to stop them. Thus her "inability to remember" may also be an escape route, a way to avoid issues she does not want to deal with, and a way to resist Shepsel's and Schwartz's attempts to find out the truth about her life.

Aida's response or lack of response raises difficult ethical questions. The contemporary literature on ethics and documentary cinema has defined several issues related to the director's personal commitment to himself/herself, the people documented, and the audience, such as the public's right to know, the right to an artistic expression, the participants' consent, and their rights to privacy, information, and reputation.[75] Researchers have argued that even though the documentarist has the right to artistic expression, the rights of the people who are filmed must be respected as well. This participants' agreement, or the harm principle, can be evaluated by the way the filmmaker indicates their intentions to the participants and allows them to take part in the film as they see fit, or refuse to be filmed.[76] Sometimes the influence of the director or others involved in the documentary can overcome the better judgment of those filmed. Ethically, the filmed cannot consent to their own injury.[77] But what happens when ethical notions clash? What if the public's right to know, or the right to artistic expression, undermines the participants' rights? What if respecting the rights of the participants means not presenting the truth?

Aida knows that she is being filmed. She does not talk much, but when she does, her reluctance to expose the truth about her life is very apparent. "Sometimes it's better we don't know," Aida says to Shepsel when they meet. In another exchange, Shepsel confronts Aida with the picnic photo and demands to know who the people are. "Aida, Izhak, Shepsel," Aida says slowly, and then stops. "What is it?" she asks, as if understanding that she has been trapped. "Do you remember who this guy is?" Shepsel asks her. "I remember," Aida says, smiling slightly, and then is silent. "I think she understands what is going on," Shepsel says to Schwartz after they leave her room. Aida's choice to keep her secrets is clear. These scenes represent the complex ethical problems within a documentary and the unresolved clash between the search for the truth and the rights of the filmed protagonists. Aida's children's wish to discover the truth about their life is clear, but there is a difference between an intimate familial search and a documentary. Had Aida been in better shape mentally would she have agreed to take a part in this documentary? Wasn't the harm principle violated in this film? If Aida could really understand what the film is about, would she have agreed to be documented? These troubling questions remain open. These ethical questions also arise in other third-generation Holocaust documentaries—such as *The Flat* and *Farewell Herr Schwarz*—in which the directors dig into Holocaust survivors' lives after they have passed away.

Women in the DP Camps

The global search to reveal Aida's secrets also turns this film into the first Israeli cinematic attempt to explore the way women returned to "normal" life in the DP camps, a theme well-known to researchers but neglected in Israeli culture and cinema.[78] DP camps were filmed and represented in documentaries produced by Jewish American organizations such as Hadassah and the American Jewish Joint Distribution Committee (JDC) during the late 1940s.[79] The film *Lang ist der Weg* was filmed in the Landsberg DP camp in 1947 by Israel Becker, a Polish Jewish actor who survived the war by fleeing to Tashkent, Uzbekistan. The film is a docudrama that depicts the life of two Jews (portrayed by actors) against the backdrop of real DP camp's lives. Years later, the American film *The Long Way Home* (1997), which described the life of survivors after liberation and devoted many scenes to life in the DP camps, won an Academy Award for best documentary feature in 1998.

This important historical era, however, was marginalized in Israeli cinema, either in fiction or in documentary films. The Zionist cinema did not address this issue because its goal was to show that survivors could only heal and begin a new life in Eretz Israel. The time that survivors spent in DP camps thus interfered with this political statement and its depictions were marginalized in films.[80] Later documentaries, from the 1980s onward, dealt with individual survivors' stories about the Holocaust and did not deal with life in the aftermath of the war in Europe before immigrating to Israel. A unique exception is Yael Katzir's 2015 *Shores of Light.* The film discusses the warm relations between Holocaust survivors in DP camps in southern Italy and the local Catholic population. The film represents the coming back to life, which included multiple marriages and a baby boom. *Aida's Secrets* recollects the vibrant and sometimes wild social life that flourished among young survivors in the DP camps in Germany, and the ways in which it affected women in particular.

The DP camps are portrayed in *Aida's Secrets* through films Schwartz found in the JDC's archive, the testimony of Marisha, one of Aida's friends, the photo album of Zipi, a female volunteer from South Africa who was a kindergarten teacher in the DP camp and had an affair with Grisha, and through the testimony of Sid, one of Grisha's relatives. Whereas Sid focuses on Grisha as a heartbreaker and "freelance" mobster, the other photos and testimonies depict a world in which women wanted to start life anew by celebrating, dancing, falling in love, and having babies. In a reality of poverty and uncertainty, starting a relationship was a given. Marisha relates that one night, she returned late from a party to find that her roommates had locked their door and she had nowhere to sleep. She spent the night in Aida's apartment, and from then on, they partied together. Marisha knew her secrets, kept them to herself, and only reveals them in the film when commenting on Aida's attempts to conceal her secrets.

The editing of the scenes helps Schwartz create a chronology of the events, but simultaneously make the viewer forget about Aida's pregnancy. In a film so full of details, this information is drowned out in the flood of the reunion. In fact, though, it is a cinematic manipulation that will help Schwartz wait until the end to expose one of the film's most prominent secrets—that Aida became pregnant during the war, and not after she met Grisha in the DP camp. It is only much later in *Aida's Secrets*, while talking to Marisha, Aida's friend from the DP camp, does Schwartz indicate that Aida was actually a Catholic fourteen-year-old from Łódź, Poland, when the war broke out. Together with other Poles, Aida was sent to Germany to work. She worked in German households and was sexually abused. When the war ended, she was pregnant and alone, with nowhere to go. She ended up in the Bergen-Belsen DP camp, and met Grisha, who was Jewish. They got married, she gave birth to Izhak, and had another child—Shepsel. She saw herself as Jewish, insisted that her children be raised as Jews, and sent Izhak to Israel. When she wanted to reunite with him, the state of Israel would not approve her immigration request because she was not Jewish, and she immigrated to Canada.

Similar to the way *Oy Mama* extended Holocaust commemoration by pointing to universal lessons, *Aida's Secrets* extends Holocaust commemoration by inserting universal aspects of women's victimhood and turning the spotlight on the suffering of other groups during World War II. Schwartz edited the film so that the secret that Aida is not Jewish would be discovered only toward the end of the film. Up to that point, it appears "obvious" that the film is about a Jewish Holocaust survivor. The late revelation forces the audience to consider broader aspects of women's suffering during World War II.

Even though Schwartz's detective work is very impressive, there are still many unanswered questions by the end of *Aida's Secrets*. Who was Izhak's father? Why did Aida choose to abandon Shepsel and only contact Izhak? Why did her relationship with Grisha end and when? In addition, there is one last secret that is revealed as the film ends: Aida had a third child in Canada, and she gave him up. As this last secret is revealed after her death, it is clear that Aida's world will always remain a mystery. In the end, as Schwartz again returns to scenes of Aida's funeral, it is obvious that some secrets will never be resolved. It marks the small victory of a woman who had to fight the men in her life even in her old age to keep some of her secrets to herself.

2

Back to the *Heimat*

Germany as Home

In early Holocaust documentary films, Germany was absent. Poland was represented briefly through documentation of the liberated concentration and extermination camps, and as a general space of death and destruction. The films concentrated on the successful transition from death to revival in Israel. In the 1970s, several Holocaust documentaries began to discuss also prewar life in Europe and briefly illustrated Jewish life under Nazism from 1933 through World War II—such as *The Last Sea* and *The 81st Blow*. From the 1980s, in second-generation documentaries, many films have represented survivors' or second-generation journeys back to Europe to retrace the trajectories that led families to destruction during the Holocaust, primarily in Eastern Europe—for example, *Tango of Slaves* (Ilan Ziv, 1992), *Daddy, Come to the Fair* (Nitza Gonen, 1994), *Pizza in Auschwitz* (Moshe Zimmerman, 2010), *The House that Wasn't There* (Nitzan Carmeli, 2010), *If You Stay Alive* (Zvika Nevo, 2012), *Six Million and One* (David Fisher, 2012), and *Tunnel of Hope* (Dror Swartz, 2015). In most of these films, the trauma-inducing setting serves as the backdrop for the victims' testimonies and/or their children's mental and geographic journey into the past. Attempts to interact with the local population are minimal.[1]

By contrast, as shown in this chapter, third-generation documentaries make Germany their main destination. These films touch on subjects that were marginalized in second-generation films; namely, Germany as a beloved homeland and a home (physically and mentally) for Holocaust survivors and their descendants. The films discussed in this chapter include *Kleiner Rudi* (Michelle Stein Teer, 2006), *The Flat* (Arnon Goldfinger, 2011), *Farewell Herr Schwarz* (Yael Reuveni, 2013), and *My German Children* (Tom Tamar Pauer, 2012), which are compared to the second-generation documentary *One, Two, Three, Four, Adolf Hitler at My Door* (Tammy Gross and Yuval Cohen, 2002).

Second-Generation Documentaries: Germany as Scenery for an Inner Jewish Dialogue

One, Two, Three, Four, Adolf Hitler at My Door, directed by Tammy Gross and Yuval Cohen and released in 2002, is exceptional compared to other second-generation documentaries because director Tammy Gross visits Germany. Gross is the main protagonist in the film. She appears in most of the scenes; she narrates other scenes by voice-over. Throughout her journey Gross explores how Jewish Israelis currently living in Germany try to ignore/repress/dismiss Germany's past and build their lives in the country that was responsible for the annihilation of European Jewry. Gross's mother left Germany before World War II, lost her entire family in the Holocaust, and swore she would never set foot on German soil again. "Now I'm here. I'm a journalist. I suggested to my editor that I would do a report on Israelis who currently live in Germany. How can they?"

Germany forms the scenery, and the interviewees are mainly former Jewish Israelis who talk about their ability to live in Germany despite the past, thus generating an inner dialogue from the perspective of the victims' offspring. The interviews, which often include close-ups to show the interviewees' emotions, reveal the complexity of the Israeli German identity through linguistic, visual, cultural, and historical subtexts. Gross illustrates her amazement that Israelis can live in Germany through her aesthetic choices, the way her encounters are edited, and the people she talks to: a judge whose world is dependent on words and accurate formulations but gets stuck in the middle of a sentence between German and Hebrew, a plastic surgeon who hides his Israeli identity behind a German mask, the successful artist who hides her fears behind her art, and the history professor who cannot muster the tools of his academic trade to confront Holocaust representations. Gross does not challenge any of them, but the way these encounters are represented cinematically conveys her negative attitude toward their choices.

Dr. Ruth Hertz, a judge who lives in Cologne (Köln), sees herself as an integral part of Germany. She loves her job, her friends. She claims she also loves Israel and that Hebrew is her mother tongue, but in the middle of the interview, which is conducted in Hebrew, Ruth gets stuck—"I think I should say it in German," she says—and switches to this language. Thus, even though in her monologue Dr. Hertz represents a harmonious combination of the two identities, linguistics underscores the fact that the connection between the two worlds is not seamless.

Dr. Yoram Levi, a plastic surgeon, talks about the German culture in which he grew up in Israel. This attraction to German culture and aesthetics has influenced his life. "I wanted my children to get to know art and culture." He feels very detached from the Levant ("I do not like the Arab or oriental culture"), but at the same time declares, "I'm not a German, I'm absolutely an Israeli." In this interview, Gross discusses possibilities for plastic surgery of her face, and during their dialogue, she is not shot sitting across from him but rather through the many mirrors in his clinic. This focus on facial alternation subtextually symbolizes Dr. Levi's life as a masquerade, a German "facelift" on a Jewish Israeli identity, which creates a German on the outside but leaves the Jewish Israeli on the inside.

Naomi Tereza Salmon moved to Germany from Jerusalem. She is a well-known photographer whose works are exhibited internationally, and the wife of the current director of the former Buchenwald concentration camp. Naomi refers to life in Germany as a "willing exile." She lives in Germany but feels secure because of Israel ("I have a place I can escape to"). She engages in German life but says that she still has to "deconstruct the fear," and does not board a train without making sure she has something to eat. Naomi's interview reveals that the successful artist who is plunged in the German art scene harbors a frightened Jew, traumatized by the echoes of the past.

Professor Michael Wolfson was born in Tel Aviv but emigrated to Germany with his German-born parents when he was seven years old. At the age of eighteen he returned to Israel and was drafted into the Israeli military, but returned to Germany when he was twenty-one. Michael is a history professor who teaches in an officers' academy of the German army. He educates German cadets about their nation's past so that they can construct its future. The scenes illustrate his difficulties investigating the past and facing atrocities. For example, Wolfson had never visited Dachau. He goes there with Gross for the first time, when she asks him to accompany her, but refuses to look at the pictures in the exhibit, saying that looking at these pictures comes down to humiliating the victims once again. But he does not have an alternative. Wolfson does not know the "right way" to commemorate. Thus, he cannot use his professional academic arsenal to face the traumatic story of his people and his family.

In a class scene, Gross begins to touch on a subject that third-generation documentaries explore extensively; namely, the way the younger generation in Germany deals with the past. The cadets' answers to Gross's questions about how they deal with the Holocaust reveal their ambivalence and the hurdles a generation confronted with historical evidence must overcome. They talk about the need to "remember and not forget," but claim that "not all their grandparents took an active part 'in it.'" The Nazis were just "a group of criminals," or that "it does not matter what they [their grandparents] did, the feeling of love toward them overcomes historical admonition." Others claim that "It is hard to decide today who is to blame . . . it did not only happen in Germany," and "we cannot prove what actually happened there."

To help explain her inability to accept her interviewees' choices, Gross depicts the way the Holocaust affected her identity. She says in her voice-over that as a child a relative came to the house and asked to talk to her mother. Behind closed doors, she could hear her sobbing. Even though her mother never discussed what was said, the Holocaust was always a part of her Israeli identity and still is. Gross emphasizes the shadows of the trauma that act out in her present in two cinematic ways. In between her documented encounters in Germany, she intersperses illustrative scenes of a little girl while she describes parts of her childhood. As the little girl stands in front of a mirror, Gross says in her voice-over that as a child she used to stare in the mirror for hours, imagining that an SS officer was standing behind her, deciding whether she was pretty enough. This connection between the Holocaust and sexuality also appears in another scene. She films a forest and adds a scene of the little girl, this time reading *Little Red Riding Hood*: "In this book in our home, Little Red Riding Hood had a yellow badge, and the wolf had a small moustache like Hitler's."[2] To highlight the Holocaust's effect on her life, Gross returns to the scenes of the little girl in other sequences. In one, she jumps rope and paraphrases a well-known children's song, by changing the words to the title of the film: "One, Two, Three, Four, Adolf Hitler at My Door."

The Holocaust's effect on Gross's childhood is also accompanied by scenes that aesthetically meld the traumatic past with contemporary life in Germany. For example, Gross is filmed entering Dachau. The camera pans as she walks behind the barbed wire, and in the soundtrack, an actress reads letters Gross's mother received from her family in 1941 before they were murdered. In other scenes, Gross is filmed roaming the streets of Berlin, and in parallel editing, the camera moves between these scenes and the same scenes that are shot in grainy black and white to resemble old footage.

At the end of *One, Two, Three, Four, Adolf Hitler at My Door*, Gross returns to her Israeli apartment. She is filmed through an open door in a voyeuristic scene putting pictures inside a box and closing it. In her voice-over, she says that for the first time in her life she decided to verify her mother's family's story. This combination of the open (door) and the closed (box, closure of a family story) implies that the journey's end will not be the end of her involvement in the family's past. In the final scene, Gross screens a picture of herself as a child, while on the soundtrack she reads part of a letter her aunt wrote from Germany to her mother at the beginning of the 1940s: "I dreamed

I went to buy a necklace of black diamonds. I woke up, and I was agitated." As the scene fades to black, the last sentence of the letter is heard—"I thought to myself I hope everything will work out." The black visual symbolizes the shattered dream. The cinematic choice to end the film with this frame emphasizes that there cannot be a closure to this tragedy. The deceased family from Germany will continue to haunt the little Israeli girl who grew up in the shadow of the trauma and will not enable her, as did her interviewees, to live in Germany.

These fascinating encounters with former Israelis reveal a theme that was completely marginalized and silenced in Israel up to the 2000s. But *One, Two, Three, Four, Adolf Hitler at My Door* does not depict encounters with Germans in-depth. The scene in the history class is the only one in which the film detours from the inner Jewish Israeli dialogue. By contrast, third-generation documentaries break out of the victim perspective, address different generations of Germans and the way they cope with the past, highlight the hybrid identity of Jewish immigrants from Germany who miss the country they had to flee, and discuss Germany as a home for Holocaust survivors and for their descendants after World War II.[3]

Third-Generation Documentaries: The Complex Relationship with Germany

Third-generation documentaries follow the trend of representing journeys to Europe. Grandchildren travel to Europe with their grandparents, or after their grandparents' death. But unlike second-generation documentaries, this time Germany becomes the dominant space. Central themes that appeared in second-generation documentaries such as historical events during the Holocaust, stories of life in the ghettoes, and concentration camps are marginalized. Instead, the films concentrate on other topics that tended not to be discussed previously, such as Jewish Germans' attachment to the homeland that betrayed them, their emotional connection to German places and people after the Holocaust, the way they interact with Germans, and how three generations of Germans are dealing with the past.[4]

The German Past in the Israeli Present in The Flat

In *The Flat* (2011) director Arnon Goldfinger reveals a family secret: his grandparents, Kurt and Gerda Tuchler, maintained close contact with a Nazi couple, the von Mildensteins, before and after the Holocaust. The Tuchlers immigrated to Palestine in 1936 and moved into an apartment on Gordon Street in Tel Aviv, where they lived for the rest of their lives. *The Flat* begins after the couple has passed away, and the family needs to empty their apartment. *The Flat*'s plot is like a detective story in which the items found in the apartment slowly reveal the hidden truth. Goldfinger finally goes to Germany to better understand the taboos surrounding this relationship. His exploration of the events sheds new light on the complex identity of Jews who fled Germany after the Nazis came to power but could not detach themselves from their homeland and its representatives.

The Flat came about unexpectedly. As a boy, the vanished German world of his grandparents fascinated Arnon Goldfinger. When he grew up, he wanted to make a film about the European codes of the Jewish immigrants from Germany: "The very cultured and very narrow world in which I had been living all my life in a game of longing and revulsion." After his grandparents passed away, Goldfinger and the photographers Talia (Tulic) Galon and Philip Belish shot the clearing out of the apartment, but did not know what direction the film would take. "One day, Tulic said to me: 'Listen, this is a film about nothing. This is *Seinfeld*; that is what's happening here.' We did not understand where we were going. I remember telling her that I felt like a fisherman, waiting and waiting with my fishing rod for a nibble. We waited." Like any good detective film, the discovery arrived. Among the artifacts found in the apartment were stacks of the old German newspaper *Der Angriff.* Goldfinger's mother began to translate for him. They discovered a series of articles describing the von Mildenstein's visit to Palestine and the couple that accompanied them—Goldfinger's grandparents. "It took me a while to realize that this was the turning point in the film," Goldfinger says. "Only then, I started to ask, read, explore, and get involved, and suddenly everything became very interesting."[5]

The Flat repeatedly returns to the high stairwell with its hollow core outside the Tuchlers's apartment, which is suggestive of the vortex into which the past has vanished.[6] The first scene of the film ends with a close-up on a shutter that opens and closes. This motif appears several times in *The Flat* and symbolizes the silenced memory that is locked inside the apartment and the reopening of past secrets.

Yekkes in Eretz Israel

Jews began to leave Germany in the 1920s, primarily because of the economic crisis that followed World War I. Another factor was the rising anti-Semitism. In the 1920s most Jewish Germans immigrated to the United States, and only a few thousand settled in Eretz Israel. After Hitler's rise to power in 1933, emigration rose dramatically. This time most Jews headed toward Eretz Israel because immigration to the United States was restricted as of 1924. In contrast, Eretz Israel under the British mandate prospered in the first half of the 1930s and became a desirable destination for Jewish immigrants. Eretz Israel also benefited from the "transfer agreement" between the Jewish Agency and the Nazi government, which enabled immigrants to transfer their capital from Germany.[7] From 1933 to 1939 roughly fifty to sixty thousand immigrants immigrated to Eretz Israel from Germany, Austria, and Czechoslovakia. Even though they accounted for about a quarter of the immigrants of the Fifth Aliyah—the fifth period of mass immigration to Eretz Israel—it is traditionally called the German Aliyah because of the mark these immigrants left on the Yishuv's economy, trade, industry, higher education, architecture, law, banking, culture, and cultural activities.

These immigrants settled mostly in urban areas such as Tel Aviv and Haifa, but also founded towns and cities—including Nahariya, Shavei Zion, Kfar Shmaryahu, and Kiryat Bialik. Some five thousand immigrated within the framework of Youth Aliyah that took place from the Nazi rise to power up to the outbreak of World War II. They were absorbed primarily in kibbutzim and moshavim, and some took part in founding new settlements.[8] Many adults came with their own capital and set up factories such as Teva, Osem, Ata, Prigat, Strauss, among others. They introduced comfort and aesthetics as ideals to strive for, laid the foundations for professional advertising agencies championing Western European lifestyles, and modified the urban landscape in the sense that they developed the hotel industry and introduced café culture to Israel.[9]

The Jewish German encounter with the Jewish Yishuv was not easy—differences in mentality between Eretz Israelis and the more restrained German Jews often ended in discord; the Nazis' intensifying brutality led many Jews in the Yishuv to challenge the immigrants' wish to preserve German culture in Eretz Israel. There were protests against the continued use of the German language—for example, in German-language newspapers—and there were even cases of harassment. The overt expressions by German immigrants of the superiority of their culture did nothing to facilitate their relationships with the Jewish community in the Land of Israel. The derogatory term *Yekke* to describe the habits and mentality of German Jews dates back to the 1930s. It was a code name for a polite, tie-wearing, punctual, intelligent, stiff, nerdy, and humorless individual, the antithesis of the "new Jew," the model of Zionism in Eretz Israel, who was described as blunt, free-spirited, and even a bit rude. According to the *Yekkes Dictionary*, "some argue that the origin of the nickname is the jacket (*Jacke*) that Jews of Central European origin used to wear. Others claim that the name is an acronym for the words 'difficult for a Jew to understand.' Still others associated the term with 'Yek' or 'Jacke,' the village fool."[10]

The Attraction to Germany: A Combination of Nonhuman and Human Objects

The Actor-network theory (ANT) was developed in the 1980s primarily by the sociologists Michel Callon, Bruno Latour, and John Law. Unlike other approaches that focus on the analysis of the relationship between people, ANT analyzes connections between people and objects. ANT theorizes that the world is an "assemblage" of human and nonhuman factors that affect each other. Nonhuman objects play a central role in shaping social processes and situations and are just as important in creating social situations as humans and should be related to while dealing with social phenomena. ANT describes human and nonhuman as "actants." Hence, only a combination and the interaction of material and human elements can explain social situations.[11] Goldfinger's portrait of his grandparents' world can be analyzed through these human and human-object relations. It operates on both levels to better understand the "network" of Jewish Germans in Eretz Israel. His grandparents' relationship choices may have been radical, but their attraction to their former homeland reflects the mainstream feelings of most German Jews who had to immigrate to Eretz Israel in the 1930s.

The Jewish and Hebrew literature researcher Barbara Mann claims that "space" denotes an area in which a group performs rituals, develops habits, and maintains social institutions. When these actions become inseparable from the space in which the group exists, that space becomes a "place." The connection between actions and place defines the authenticity of both, enabling the group to realize its existence more fully. As a result, space becomes moveable while place remains anchored. If the group shifts its geographic location, the new location becomes the "space" where the displaced group attempts to recreate or commemorate its original "place," although full authentication might remain impossible.[12]

The historian Guy Miron discusses individuals' tactical struggle for space when combatting the strategies of hegemonic power.[13] It can be claimed that the construction of an inner space as a German haven was these immigrants' tactic in their struggle to preserve their culture in the Levant. According to Miron and Dorit Yosef, German Jewish middle-class life in Eretz Israel and Israel was based on an adaptation of the domestic practices of the German bourgeoisie.[14] Many of them turned their homes into a replica of their previous homes in Germany. In their private spaces, the interior design tried to duplicate what they had left behind: grand pianos, dark heavy armchairs, dressers proudly bearing porcelain, bookshelves filled with the works of Schiller, Goethe, Heine, and others. German food was cooked in many of these homes, and the afternoon nap between 2:00 and 4:00 (*shlaftshtunder*) was a fixture.

Arnon explains in the film's synopsis:

> The flat, on the third floor of a Bauhaus building on Gordon Street, in Tel Aviv, is where my grandparents, Kurt and Gerda Tuchler, lived since they immigrated to Palestine. Apart from the view of Tel Aviv from the windows, you might have thought that this apartment was located in the heart of Berlin. The apartment just stood there, furnished in heavy European style, loaded with German literature, and drenched in layers of dust and history.

Early on in *The Flat*, Goldfinger discusses his childhood memories:

> When I was a child, I loved to come here. Once a week. I would cross the center of Tel Aviv, go up three flights of stairs and arrive in Berlin. My grandmother, Gerda, lived there for seventy years, as though she had never left Germany. Despite living in Israel for so many years, she did not speak Hebrew well, and I did not want to learn German, so we sat and chatted in English as if we were in a café in Europe, with apple strudel and Swiss chocolate.

The Tuchlers's preservation of German culture is revealed in the objects that the family finds in the closets in the apartment that are unrelated to the Middle East and represent an attempt to perpetuate the world they were forced to leave behind: fancy dresses, elegant gloves, fur coats, and a huge collection of wallets and handbags. Through his grandmother's fashion items, Goldfinger manages to portray the hybrid world of a generation. The books on his grandparents' shelves also testify to the importation of German culture to Tel Aviv. While emptying the apartment, the family asks Micha, an expert collector of German books, to assess their collection. He also confirms the hybrid identity of this generation: "They lived here for at least fifty years, but their hearts remained in their first twenty years of life in Germany . . . I'm sure they suffered greatly."

The architecture scholar Clare Cooper Marcus, who researches peoples' emotional ties to their homes, notes that one's home is a symbolic mirror of one's self. Similar to the actor-network theory, she emphasizes the combination of material and human and argues that people express who they are through their décor and furnishing choices. Personal crises and changes affect interior design and the choice of objects. They invest objects and places with emotions "as it serves the deeper, largely unconscious process of individualization, or becoming who we truly are." Marcus's interviews suggest that it is the movable objects in the home that are symbolic of the self, and who we are, and perhaps who we were and who would like to be.[15] These elements can be projected onto *The Flat*. The documentary researcher Carmel Gotliv Kimhi argues that Goldfinger applies a topoanalysis of the grandparents' flat in *The Flat*; in other words, an examination of an intimate space that reflects its owners' inner worlds.[16] The objects documented tell a story of people who emigrated from Germany, lived in Israel, but kept on dreaming about their former homeland. Simultaneously, it also subverts the Zionist national story in two ways. Documentaries in the first decades of the state of Israel focused on the outside as a space that should be built-up and cultivated. The private home was not mentioned or viewed. A film that concentrates on the inner space of one Tel Aviv apartment thus deconstructs this national story and highlights the private over the collective. The historian Ofer Ashkenazi suggested that the film uses place and transitional areas to undermine familiar Zionist clichés and the ideological premises they propagate. By showing that his family's secrets cannot be integrated into the national ethos of identity formation, Goldfinger thus hints that the ways identities were constructed in Israel are much more complicated and deviate from the national narrative.[17] No less important is the representation of the apartment, its accoutrements, and its Berlin identity since the legitimacy ascribed to this identity conflicts with the national narrative in Israeli culture and cinema on integration and the abandonment of one's previous "exilic" life.

The media historian Na'ama Sheffi writes that the essential problem of these immigrants was their sense of resounding failure when attempting to assimilate into German culture and the German space. In their lives in Israel, German-speaking Jews not only mourned their foreignness in the country but also their forcible removal from their ideal cultural environment. In fact, they mourned a country that had ceased to exist for them.[18] "My feeling is that although most of the immigrants had actually arrived, the ships are still on their way," writes the cultural scientist Joachim Schlor, thus suggesting metaphorically that many of them never detached themselves from their German homeland, despite the Holocaust, and never fully integrated into Israeli culture.[19] This crisis is reflected not only in the artifacts but also in the Tuchlers's choices of friends and acquaintances.

The objects in the apartment do not only testify to the need to preserve German culture but also help reveal hidden human relationships. From the *Der Angriff* newspapers found among the artifacts, Goldfinger discovered that in the 1930s, a Nazi officer named Leopold von Mildenstein, who supported the emigration of Jews to Palestine as a solution to the "Jewish problem," toured Palestine for about six months. Von Mildenstein wife's and the Tuchlers joined him on this visit. The photographs that Goldfinger finds reinforce the discovery that a close relationship existed between the two couples. However, this is only the beginning of the revelations. Goldfinger, who digs deeper, discovers that the relationship between his grandparents and the Nazi couple did not end there. Details collected about von Mildenstein from archives and conversations with people who have researched von Mildenstein's history slowly reveal that the friendship between the two couples resumed in secret after World War II. This included visits by the Tuchlers to Germany, and the exchange of family photos and gifts. Goldfinger's astonishment intensifies when he discovers that von Mildenstein was a top-ranking officer in the Nazi regime—he was head of the department of Jewish Affairs in the SD (1935–36) and recruited Eichmann for the department. Later he became head of the department in Goebbels's ministry of propaganda (1938–45). As opposed to Edda's notions, her father was abroad only for one year in

1937. Eichmann referred to von Mildenstein as "my mentor," claiming von Mildenstein knew "more than anyone" about the Jews because of his visit to Eretz Israel, accompanied by Goldfinger's grandparents.

In one of his many attempts to understand the relationship between the two couples, Goldfinger turns to a German expert on denial. The expert stresses the complex relationship of Jewish immigrants from Germany to their former culture and claims that through their actions, the Tuchlers sought recognition of their legitimacy as Germans: "Even a persecuted Jew who grew up in Germany and saw in it his homeland wants to believe that there must be at least one good German who accepts you as a human being."

Goldfinger and his mother's lack of ability to come to terms with this relationship is symbolically reflected in their attitude to the objects found in the apartment. Many scenes show family members putting objects in huge plastic bags and throwing them away. Goldfinger shoots the way the family packs up the remains of their heritage and disposes of them. These scenes are repeated several times. This detachment from the objects explains why they cannot understand the Tuchlers's choices. Hence the combination of human and nonhuman objects helps analyze not only the grandparents' world but also the different world of their offspring.

Second-Generation Survivors: The Double Wall of Silence

As noted, from the 1980s onward, second-generation Holocaust survivor directors started to film families of Holocaust survivors—for example, *Because of That War* and *Pizza in Auschwitz*.[20] Other directors filmed their families—for example: *Hugo*, *Hugo 2*, *Tango of Slaves*, and *Six Million and One*. They filmed the survivors' stories and testimonies and talked about the way in which the Holocaust affected the second generation's lives. Despite the debates in the psychological literature on whether the second generation constitutes a separate group with its own psychopathological characteristics, the documentaries refer to second-generation survivors as a separate group that suffers from secondary traumatic stress.[21] Third-generation documentaries discuss the influence of the Holocaust on survivors' offspring but marginalize aspects of victimization and represent different reactions to the past among various family members.[22]

Research shows that there are Holocaust survivors who rarely talked about the trauma they or their families experienced. For some survivors, the need to repress the past was generated by a constant feeling of helplessness. For some, repression was necessary to their mental health after World War II.[23] Some survivors did not talk with their children about the past to protect them and spare them from feeling afraid. Avoiding the past was meant to distance their children from the trauma.[24] The children who felt a "wall of silence" tended to construct a wall in response, to protect themselves from their parents' wall, thus creating a "double wall" of silence.[25] *The Flat* reveals that Hannah, Goldfinger's mother, was born in Berlin and raised in Israel. Her parents never talked about the past. They never told her basic parts of the family's history, such as the fact that her grandmother Susanna was murdered in the Holocaust, and Hannah never asked.

The emptying of the apartment, the sorting of the pictures, documents, books, and clothes opens the door to the past, and Hannah tells Arnon about the way she was brought up. She says that in her youth there were clear dividing lines between what she could ask, and what she could not: "They did not tell us anything, and I did not ask." This unspoken agreement did not disappear at her parents' death. When Hannah clears her parents' apartment, she feels no need to rummage, look at family pictures, or try to discover hidden clues. When Hannah and Goldfinger find an old photo album, Hannah admits that she had seen it before but did not bother to ask her mother about the content. "I was not interested in it," she confesses.

Unlike second-generation documentaries, Hannah is not represented as a victim of her parents' trauma or the circumstances. She is shown as indifferent to the past, their controversial relationship with the Nazi couple, and the fact that they had hidden it from her. The film's English title, *The Flat*, takes on double meaning: it refers to the grandparents' apartment, but it also resonates with Hannah's attitude toward the past and the family secrets. As far as Hannah is concerned, once the apartment is empty, the past is gone. Her imposed discoveries in the apartment completely contradict her attitude toward her parents' past throughout her entire life.

The cinema researcher Odeya Kohen-Raz notes that one of Goldfinger's attempts to persuade his mother to reconnect with the past occurs when he makes her read the end of her grandmother's letter. The letter contains her last words before she was murdered and her request: "do not forget me." Goldfinger begins to read the letter in his voice (the film's voice-over), and then the sound changes to his mother's voice-over in German. He makes her reconnect not only with the family's past she did not want to know about but also to her mother tongue, a symbol of the culture she has alienated herself from.[26] Goldfinger confronts his mother who, unlike him, does not have a deep interest in the family's past, but he is unable to change her mind.[27]

Opening the Doors to the Past

Goldfinger's cinematic decision to dismiss the perception of the second generation as victims of their parents' trauma appears in other third-generation documentaries in which the directors discuss transgenerational attitudes toward the trauma but marginalize the concept of victimization. This may be due to the fact that third-generation documentarists are the first generation to have consistently studied the Holocaust in school, and grew up in a period in which the Zionist myths of the "diaspora Jew" versus the "new Jew" collapsed, the Holocaust became an integral part of Israeli culture and everyday life, and judgmental notions about the Jews under Nazism and the survivors (which elicited a sense of shame for many children) have faded.[28] The intergenerational dialogue they have with survivors is different and is mostly based on curiosity, empathy, and pride.[29] That attitude is apparent in the representation of all three generations and in the general atmosphere of their films. Even if the directors do not understand the life choices of the survivors, they do not criticize or judge but rather contemplate these subjects.

The conflict between the Yekkes and Israeli society often caused their children to be ashamed of their parents' inclination to preserve that tradition. Many tried to detach themselves from it.[30] However, this attitude began to change in the 1980s as the image of the "new Jew" was challenged in turn. The rise of postmodern and post-Zionism refuted attempts to forge one history and one homogeneous mindset. The melting pot turned into perceptions of multiculturalism, and was gradually replaced by the popularization of ethnic roots.[31] Mosaics of memories and identities slowly became the norm, and the stories of communities in Europe, Asia, and North Africa became a source of longing, a basis for identity, and an integral part of the Israeli identity. In this cultural environment, many second-generation immigrants from Central Europe sought to restore the role of their lost past, which was no longer a source of embarrassment. The third generation grew up in a world in which the connection to the past was practically a given.[32]

In the last few decades, second- and third-generation immigrants from Germany in particular and Central Europe in general have been highly involved in the preservation, documentation, and commemoration that define them as a separate group. They run organizations—such as the Association of Israelis of Central European Origin—websites, and initiate and organize conferences and seminars.[33] The Leo Baeck Institute for the study of Jewish heritage in German-speaking countries is preserving and perpetuating new contributions of German immigrants to building the country. Third-generation German immigrants started a Facebook group to work toward preserving and documenting Jewish German heritage. The group's page header reads, "If your memories of your grandmother include nursery rhymes in German or radio silence between two and four—you are in the right place." The group page includes links to the culture of Central European Jews, personal stories, events, and sites associated with the grandparents' histories, etc.[34]

Yekke, which was once a derogatory nickname, has been reclaimed as a symbol of renewed interest in the past. A magazine commemorating the stories of German immigrants is entitled *Yekkington*;

there is a website called Yekke devoted to the history of German Jews whose aim is to preserve their identity for future generations; there is a dictionary that attempts to reconstruct the language of first-generation immigrants called *The Dictionary of Spoken Yekkit*; the concept appears proudly in cookbooks such as *Recipes from the Yekke Kitchen*; there is a museum of German-speaking Jewry called the Yekke Heritage Center; and a book documenting families who came from Central Europe is called *The Book of Yekkes.*[35]

This environment did not change Hannah's detachment from the past. It enabled third-generation Goldfinger, unlike his mother, to reach out to the past his mother refuses to acknowledge. He talks openly and proudly about the stereotypical cultural codes that have been passed down to him. He feels tied to his grandparents not only by blood but also through culture. His behavior reflects the stereotypes that were connected with the Yekim. Goldfinger claims that he is a "Yekke *potz*," and that natural sympathy toward Germany has been handed down to him since childhood:

> The best example of taking Germany for granted happened in 1974 while everyone was cheering for Holland in the soccer World Cup final; I was the only one in the neighborhood who was cheering for Germany, and this was after the Munich massacre. My friends at the time wanted to kill me, but, for me, sympathy for Germany was something uncontrollable that had been passed down genetically, and I did not even think twice about it.[36]

Dan Bar-On suggested that in some families, the third generation have had the chance to fissure the double wall of silence.[37] They do not feel obligated to maintain the silence or the repression, and therefore can bring up previously taboo topics. In *The Flat* Goldfinger voices the family silence and in this process not only reveals secrets but also redefines his identity and forces his mother to disclose things she would prefer to avoid.

Similar to *Oy Mama* and many other third-generation documentaries, *The Flat* is an *I* movie, which reflects Renov's "domestic ethnographies," where the filmmakers place themselves and their relatives in the center of the film.[38] Goldfinger is the protagonist. He appears in the vast majority of the scenes, converses with family members (who are not interested in exploring the topic), motivates the search, and travels to Germany. Goldfinger accompanies the film with his voice-over, sharing every stage of his journey, his dilemmas, and difficulties with the audience. The central topic in the narrative is not only the discovery itself but rather the way he, as a member of the third generation, handles the discovery. Many scenes are devoted to his soul-searching on the subject, his inability to understand, and his great consternation.

Goldfinger is the one who starts reading, checking, and digging through papers.[39] He is the one who decides to stop living with the feeling that "we are a family without a past," and to bring the stories that had never been told to the surface.[40] *The Flat* shows that it is much easier for the third generation to dare, ask, and explore than their parents, the second generation, who have chosen silence.[41] Like other third-generation documentaries, *The Flat* examines the German side and as part of Goldfinger's journey into his grandparents' relationship, he meets several times with Edda, von Mildenstein's daughter, who knew about the friendship, and refuses to acknowledge her father's deeds (see chapter 5).

Blurred Boundaries and Ethics

Similar to *Aida's Secrets*, in which the director and Aida's sons dig into her past without her consent, *The Flat* also raises ethical questions. An issue that continues to resonate at the end of the film is whether Gerda, Goldfinger's grandmother, wanted their secret to be discovered. At the end of *The Flat*, before Goldfinger and Hannah leave Berlin, they try to find Hannah's great-grandfather's grave. In heavy rain, they walk through the cemetery but are not able to locate it. Goldfinger confronts Hannah: "What would your mother have said if she could see you now?" "She would have said that I was rude . . . It was none of my business . . ." This statement is left unanswered and leaves viewers with ethical question marks. Does this search invade the survivors' privacy? "This is a question I'm constantly wrestling with," Goldfinger says:

> On the one hand, I say to myself—if she did not want us to discover what happened, why didn't she throw the newspapers out? She had plenty of time to get rid of them. Possibly in her subconscious, she wanted us to discover them one day. On the other hand, I guess that if she had wanted us to discover it, she would have just told me, so she may have kept all these papers simply out of weariness, forgetfulness and habit, and not because of any conscious or unconscious decision. We will never know. Maybe she could not cope with it; maybe she did not think it is right to involve us. Anything is possible.[42]

There is in fact a dual ethical problem because Goldfinger not only revealed a family secret—and told his family—but documented it on-camera and allowed it to be distributed it all over the world. The combination of the family's inability to understand the Tuchlers's relational choices and the ethical questions left unanswered does not provide, at the end of the film, the long-awaited catharsis.

Goldfinger states that he was concerned about a negative reaction from Yad Vashem since *The Flat* does not show any survivors, but after showing it in Jerusalem he was told by a Yad Vashem representative, "This is the new direction. These are the films we are looking for, because you present a new phase in the connection between the current generation and the Holocaust."[43]

The Attraction to the Past in Kleiner Rudi

On the 750th anniversary of Norden, Germany, the town's residents invited a group of Jews who lived in Norden before World War II to inaugurate a monument memorializing Norden's Jews who were murdered during the Holocaust. In *Kleiner Rudi*, director Michelle Stein Teer travels with her eighty-five-year-old grandfather, Rudi Wolf, back to his hometown. Rudi immigrated to Israel in 1936 within the framework of Youth Aliyah. His family and many of his friends who had stayed behind in Norden were murdered in the Holocaust.

Rudi's memories of Germany, like that of other Jewish Germans who emigrated from Germany before World War II broke out, are not replete with persecution and atrocities, but are primarily good, despite the events that occurred after they left. Similar to *The Flat*, Rudi's character reflects the complex relationship of German Jews with their homeland. Rudi's attraction to German culture and space and his simultaneous repulsion are depicted throughout the journey. At the beginning of *Kleiner Rudi*, on the train to Norden, Rudi drinks beer like the locals do, and expresses German patriotism when telling Stein Teer that the local football (soccer) team won the German championship. When they get to Norden, and Rudi meets his old friends, he seems rejuvenated, more alive, and full of energy. Stein Teer follows Rudi's rituals with love and affection. "The Yekkes are discussing their plans for the week," she giggles in the voice-over, while showing Rudi and his friends reading the itinerary over and over again. She lets herself get sucked into their world, and films for posterity the tea-drinking ritual the hotel proprietor teaches her, which involves steeping the tea leaves for precisely four minutes.

Rudi's lecture to the high school students shows that he still cannot grasp what his beloved homeland did to the Jewish people. His family members were German patriots. His grandfather fought in the German army in World War I, and was even awarded the Iron Cross for bravery. Rudi says that he sees the German culture as sublime, which is why he wants the students to understand the dissonance that has affected him all these years: "I do not blame the generation that was born after the war. I'm sure you have a hard time dealing with the past. You too cannot forget. It is a part of your culture. It is uncanny that these things happened in such a civilized state as Germany, but they did, and this is the awful truth." Rudi confesses that if things had been different, and the Nazis had not been anti-Semitic, he probably would have stayed in Germany, got drafted, and maybe even "got killed in Stalingrad while defending the fatherland." This stance would have been seen as outrageous in the Zionist narrative characterizing the first decades of Israel, which represented Europe as a cursed environment of death and Eretz Israel as a place of life and rejuvenation. It illustrates the long way documentary cinema and Holocaust awareness in Israeli culture have come over the years. Sentences that would have been considered blasphemy in the first decades after World War II and were not discussed in the 1980s and 1990s are now regarded as an integral part of a complex narrative in post-millennial documentaries.

The film's title also implies Rudi's strong connection to German culture. Even though in the film he is an Israeli grandfather, part of his personality will always remain "Kleiner Rudi," the little boy from Norden. However, at the same time Rudi confesses to Stein Teer that he has mixed feelings about German culture, since in his opinion German education caused his father's death—after Rudi's parents sent him to Eretz Israel his father came to visit him but decided he could not stay because it was illegal. "The good German education" caused Rudi's father to return to Germany because he would not do anything illegal. His father was later deported to Auschwitz, where he was murdered. Rudi tells this story to the high school students, who sit quietly and listen. "Are you always so disciplined?" Rudi asks with a smile at the end of the lecture, thus underscoring the stereotype of German neatness and order in the past and the present with its negative and positive sides. When Rudi takes Stein Teer on a tour of Norden, he talks about how it looked in the past, though he tries to be restrained and avoid being nostalgic: "I have mixed feelings," he says. Throughout the visit, it becomes clear that Rudi cannot deal with the Holocaust. In his stories, he focuses on the prewar years. When his friend Lina wants to show him a book containing the names of Jews from Norden that were murdered in the Holocaust, Rudi says that they do not have a time for it—they need to go back to the hotel. But even he cannot keep on repressing the trauma. When Rudi and Stein Teer travel to Norderney, which was one of the Nazis' favorite resorts to attend a formal reception, Rudi gets upset because "It is a German resort." Half of the four hundred Jews who lived in Norden before World War II were murdered in the Holocaust. The unveiling of the monument in their memory forces Rudi to confront what he has been trying to escape. When the names are read out loud, and thirty of them are his family members, it is the first and last time in the film in which Rudi breaks down and cries. As is the case for *The Flat*, *Kleiner Rudi* does not concentrate solely on the victims' side but rather dedicates a great deal of screen time to examination of "the other side"—in this case four generations of Norden Germans and the way they cope with their past (see chapter 5).

Switching Sides in Farewell Herr Schwarz

Farewell Herr Schwarz, directed by Yael Reuveni and released in 2013, depicts another complicated relationship with Germany. Director Yael Reuveni traces the story of her grandmother Michla, and Michla's brother Feiv'ke (later, Peter) Feibush. They were separated when World War II broke out, and Feiv'ke was drafted into the Polish army. During the war, Michla was told that Feiv'ke had been murdered in Treblinka, but after the war, when she traveled to Łódź, an acquaintance told Michla that Feiv'ke had survived and if she would wait at the train station, he would bring Feiv'ke to her the next day. Michla waited, but Feiv'ke never came. Afterward, Michla was told that Feiv'ke burned to death in his sleep in a shelter for Jewish refugees in an attack by Polish nationalists. Years later, the truth was uncovered. In fact, Feiv'ke did not die. He decided to stay in East Germany, changed his name to Peter, married a Gentile woman, started a new life, and never tried to contact his sister. He buried his Jewish identity and took on a new German identity as Peter. Feiv'ke's son Uwe discovered the truth after his father's death in 1987. He went through his father's documents and put the puzzle pieces together. In 1995 he contacted Michla's daughter (Reuveni's mother) and told her the story. Thus, Michla lost her brother three times: first, when she thought he had perished in the Holocaust, then when she thought he had died in the shelter fire, and finally when she found out he had chosen to live his life without contacting her. Reuveni, who grew up in the shadow of her grandmother's trauma, explores her own complex relations with Peter's decisions, against the backdrop of her personal identity crisis and life choices.

The Return to the Past as Soul-Searching

As in *The Flat* and *Aida's Secrets*, *Farewell Herr Schwarz* reveals that when survivors pass away, it is not the end of their story. Rather, their death can be the impetus for in-depth airing of painful stories that were suppressed or marginalized. It is what Victoria Aarons and Alan Berger refer to as "narrative journeys back to the point of traumatic origin."[44] Some historians have argued that it is impossible to describe the events of the Holocaust as a coherent story with an orderly beginning, middle, and end since there will always remain parts that are unclear and elusive. Thus, they challenge narrative attempts to fully understand these historical events or give them meaning. Such stories bypass what cannot be represented, since the traumatic experience leaves lacunae that cannot be expressed.[45] Unlike many second-generation documentaries that represent the hunt for stories and facts that will produce a coherent life story, third-generation documentarists are more interested in specific life choices. Filmmakers return to the past to complete a task that their second-generation parents did not do. Their purpose in trying to unravel untold stories or solve a mystery is to try to understand the survivors' life choices more than tracing their specific history.

In third-generation documentaries such as *The Flat*, *Aida's Secrets*, or *The Green Dumpster Mystery*, the directors represent the discovery little by little. By contrast, Reuveni edited *Farewell Herr Schwarz* differently since it begins after the mystery of Peter's so-called death has been solved. Thus, the detective side of *Farewell Herr Schwarz* is not about solving a mystery, but about the *why*. It constitutes a cinematic attempt to soul-search Peter's inner world in order to understand his decisions.

Reuveni's trips to Schlieben and her interviews with the villagers and Peter's family are aimed at a better grasp of Peter's mental processes. The film focuses on Reuveni's emotions during the trip and, like *The Flat*, her inability to grasp the survivors' life choices. These govern the questions Reuveni asks the three generations of German she encounters, and presents in her voice-overs, which accompany many scenes.

"He had his reasons," a family relative concludes, but this is not enough for Reuveni. "This could have been the end of my journey," she says in the middle of *Farewell Herr Schwarz*, when she discovers details about Fie'vke's life. But it is not the end of Reuveni's journey and not the end of the film, as *Farewell Herr Schwarz* not only deals with uncovering his reasons but also with the third generation's inability to reconcile themselves with the first generation's choices. Reuveni feels compelled to dig deeper. During this process, she discovers that she is also drawn to Germany as a home. Thus, the soul-searching represented in *Farewell Herr Schwarz* is double and is comprised of an attempt to understand Fie'vke's choices and an attempt to come to terms with Reuveni's own emotions toward postwar Germany and Germans.

Germany as a Home for Holocaust Survivors

Farewell Herr Schwarz is composed of three separate parts, offset by black screens and the titles "First Generation," "Second Generation," and "Third Generation" in Hebrew and in German. These titles do not refer solely to Jewish Israelis. In the titles that appear at the beginning of each part, Reuveni visually combines the phrase *first-generation*, *second-generation*, and *third-generation* with the same phrase in German. The "First Generation" sequence represents Michla's and Peter's story but also that of the people of Schlieben. "Second Generation" discusses her mother and Peter's children, and the "Third Generation" sequence discusses herself, her brother, and Peter's grandson, who is Reuveni's age. The sequence dealing with the survivors reveals the enormous disparity between the two siblings. Peter and Michla appear to have chosen utterly different ways to deal with their past. Michla immigrated to Israel and refused to travel to Germany, while Peter made Germany his home. Michla tried to work out the trauma by telling her granddaughter about the atrocities, while Peter's silence points to his inability to do so.

Although Reuveni meets with people Peter knew, his family members, travels to the places where he chose to spend his life, she cannot grasp why a former Jewish prisoner would want to return to the place where he was imprisoned to start a new life amongst Germans by denying his identity. Reuveni discovers pictures from various periods in Peter's life, learns that the villagers loved him; that he never talked about the past, and was never asked about his. All of Peter's friends and relatives knew that questions about the past were taboo. Even those closest to Peter knew little, if anything. "There is something troubling in trying to imagine him here," Reuveni says. "Here is his house, the little shop he managed, the people who knew him." In her attempt to picture Peter's life in Schlieben, Reuveni shows that prosthetic memory can relate to the aftermath of the Holocaust, and not only the Holocaust per se. For her, as Michla's granddaughter, trying to imagine Peter's life in Schlieben is traumatic.

Reuveni's amazement grows as she interviews the people of Schlieben and find out they knew about the Schlieben-Berga concentration camp (the third largest of over 136 satellite labor camps associated with Buchenwald), and that some of the locals even served there as guards. One of Peter's relatives tells Reuveni that after the war, they did not talk about it. Peter, who apparently was aware of this, settled among them and did not talk about his past. The image that shocks Reuveni the most is related to Peter's new family. While visiting Helena Kruger (Peter was married to her husband's sister), and browsing through a family album, Reuveni discovers a photo of Otto, Helena's husband, who later became Peter's relative and close friend, wearing a Wehrmacht uniform. Kruger tells Reuveni that Peter knew this and accepted it. Reuveni is unable to cope with his indifference. Throughout *Farewell Herr Schwarz*, Reuveni struggles to understand Peter's choices, but this does not imply that she judges him. In an interview, Reuveni notes that when she began to dig into Peter's story she was judgmental, but "the film made me look again at my grandmother and realize that in a way her choices were just as strange as his." She comments that:

> Peter lived like the last Jew on Earth and remained in the landscape of his disaster. She left that landscape and never came back but was always surrounded by people who had been through similar things and reflected her pain. Maybe for him there was a certain kind of release or freedom in not meeting people who had gone through similar things. Maybe he made the healthier choices.[46]

The TV documentary *Address: Germany*, directed by Ruth Shiloni and released in 2017, also deals with Holocaust survivors who have chosen to live in Germany. Unlike *Farewell Herr Schwarz*, Shiloni presents her discussions with living Holocaust survivors, listens to their stories, and tries to understand why they chose to start their lives over in Germany. While scenes of contemporary Germany are being screened, Shiloni discusses the forty thousand Holocaust survivors who decided to live in Germany after the war, "not in the shadow of the past, but within the past." This is not an *I* movie but rather a moderate version of Nichols's interactive mode. Shiloni accompanies the film with her voice-over, but acts more as a narrator and translator of the scenes than an active participant in the frame. Throughout *Address: Germany* Shiloni presents different perceptions of Germany, but her cinematic choices are used to reinforce her initial observation that Germany is a cursed soil.

The question *why* is not fully answered. Schwartzbaum and the other survivors who are filmed do not—and perhaps cannot—fully explain why they chose to stay in Germany. As noted, Leon Schwartzbaum married a Gentile; Erna De-Friz returned with her Holocaust-survivor husband to Lathen, his hometown, had a baby, and was too poor to leave; Bella Shopak had a business in Germany, so she returned ("I could afford to send my children to study in England because it was easier here"); Liezel Binzer survived the war but could not leave her traumatized parents behind to immigrate to Israel.

Shiloni's inability to accept that there may be differences between Nazi Germany and contemporary Germany may help explain why *Address: Germany* begins and ends with Schwartzbaum, who has lived in Germany since World War II ended, but loathes Germans and believes they can start "another Holocaust." Toward the end of the film, Shiloni and Schwartzbaum drive to the woods where he walked in a death march. As Schwarzbaum looks out the car window he talks about the Germans who saw him and his fellow inmates suffer, but "looked the other way," and today are indifferent to the issue of Germany's past. Shiloni supports this combination of past and present by superimposing the scenery of the contemporary forest with wartime photographs of inmates in striped uniforms. "The years that have passed since the death march through these woods have not changed his perspective on human nature," she says while this superimposition is presented. "The Germans have destroyed my life," Schwartzman says later, as they return to his home. "People are always asking me, 'why did you stay here?' . . . Sometimes I think that it was a mistake to stay here," he adds, and says that he has not really felt at home all these years in Germany. While Schwartzman is being filmed in his home, Shiloni says that his will leaves everything to the state of Israel. In her view, this decision is a small victory: "After his death, he will not leave a thing on that cursed soil." *Address: Germany* ends with the two of them dancing. Thus, like Reuveni, Shiloni also embarks on a journey to understand how a survivor can decide to live in Germany after World War II, but unlike Reuveni, the survivors she interviewed have not renounced their relatives or their identity to build their lives in Germany. Even though their choices are less complicated than Peter's, Shiloni has a hard time understanding or accepting them, whereas Reuveni makes peace with Germany as home.

The Different Attitudes of Two Generations toward Germany

The part of *Farewell Herr Schwarz* titled "Second Generation" depicts the similarities and differences between second-generation Holocaust survivors in Israel and second-generation Holocaust survivors in Germany. Unlike second-generation documentaries, which often focus on the second generation's complex and difficult relationship with their parents, in *Farewell Herr Schwarz*, like other third-generation documentaries, the attitude toward the survivors is much more restrained. Third-generation directors address the way the Holocaust affected their parents but do not highlight their parents' victimization. Etti, Michla's daughter, says that Michla never opened up to her, and she did not ask her questions. Like Hannah in *The Flat*, she herself did not ask questions; hence creating a double wall of silence. After Michla's death Etti began to work as a librarian in a center that commemorates Vilnius, Michla's hometown; her way of dealing with memories is to commemorate, yet to file them away. Unlike Etti's reluctance to deal with the past, Uwe, Peter's son, was always very curious and discovered at age twelve that his father was Jewish. As noted, when he grew up, his investigations revealed a much more tangled truth.

This part of *Farewell Herr Schwarz* also presents the similarities and differences between Etti and Peter's daughter Barbara. She says that she never asked Peter about his past, but after the revelation is extremely upset that her father never told them the truth, whereas Etti goes through a process of making peace with Peter's choice. At first, since it is hard for Etti to accept Peter's decisions, when Uwe asks whether he can place a pebble from Peter's grave on Michla's grave, Etti is appalled. It is difficult for her to accept this ritual because she identifies with her mother, who never forgave Peter. In the end, Etti decides to compromise by placing the pebble at the foot of the grave. When she does so, she asks for Michla's forgiveness out loud. As in *Aida's Secrets* and *The Flat*, *Farewell Herr Schwarz* raises ethical questions about the way the survivors' preferences should be documented and distributed by their descendants. Would Michla approve of putting stones from Peter's grave at the base of her grave?

Etti also invites Peter's grandson home and into the intimate space around Michla's grave (a space which in the first parts of the film she had shared only with daughter). Like her mother, for many years Etti refused to go to Germany, "to that cursed land." Even when her beloved daughter moves to Berlin, Etti refuses to visit her for five years. Eventually, Reuveni's choice forces her to undergo a process of change and travel there. In the struggle between mother and daughter about "validating" the German space, Etti chooses her daughter. "She visited me at home, ate off my plates, and met my friends," Reuveni says in her voice-over in scenes in which her mother is filmed in Reuveni's home laughing and enjoying the family reunion.

Wardi suggested that in families of Holocaust survivors, there is a child who functions as a "memorial candle" for the dead.[47] This child is expected—implicitly or explicitly—to act as a link between the traumatic past that must be remembered, the present, and the future, to fill their parents' emotional void caused by the Holocaust, and to construct the present and the future of the family. In some third-generation documentaries such as *Oy Mama*, *The Flat*, and *Kleiner Rudi*, it is obvious that the "memorial candle" has skipped a generation. There are cases in which members of the third generation take it upon themselves to discover and speak, whereas their parents chose to remain silent.

The part of *Farewell Herr Schwarz* entitled "Third Generation" highlights this attitude. Unlike her mother, Reuveni decides to go to Germany to find out more about Peter's life. As in many other third-generation documentaries—such as *Oy Mama*, *Kleiner Rudi*, *The Flat*, and *My German Children*—this is an *I* movie in which the director is the protagonist. The film begins from Reuveni's perspective. Her parents, Etti and Shauli, are seated in front of her camera. "Shoot," her father says (in English), meaning "film us already," but the word takes on another meaning, especially when he sits with his hands raised ("can I sit like that?") in a pose resembling surrender. As the conversation develops, it turns out that Reuveni hurt her parents psychologically. "The topic of our conversation today is that I'm leaving in a week," Reuveni says; Etti moans, "Don't remind me." "Leaving for where?" Shauli asks. "Home," Reuveni answers. Shauli resents this: "To the doleful diaspora. This is not home. Defining Germany as home is a little bit exaggerated, don't you think?" "Now my home is Germany," Reuveni tries again. "I don't think you are defining it correctly but never mind," Shauli says heavily. "I think that what she feels is what counts," Etti interferes, and they bicker over the definition of *home*. Etti explains to Shauli that Reuveni has a homeland but Germany is where she lives right now. "Ah, living is not a home," he answers. They do not seem to agree. "Are you going to stay there?" Etti asks hesitantly; Reuveni remains silent and cuts to the film's title. By the end of *Farewell Herr Schwarz*, Reuveni's father's surrender pose takes on its symbolic meaning: her parents did indeed surrender and go to Germany to meet her. "I was supposed to be the new Jew but somehow it turned out that I live in Germany, a state I was not allowed to set foot in. My grandmother's story, which haunted me as a child, is what finally brought me here [to Germany] to build my home here," Reuveni states as she is filmed on a train in Berlin. In one of the "Third Generation" section scenes, Reuveni films Berlin's rooftops and skyscrapers and a large billboard containing the words "How Long is Now?" Since Reuveni chose to insert the billboard in the film, it can be assumed that the message symbolizes the questions she is asking herself: How long will she stay in Germany? Is this her home? Will she be able to stay there for the rest of her life like Peter?

In the "First Generation" sequence, Reuveni tells her mother over the phone that she has been in Schlieben for several days, talking to people who knew Peter, and learning that his new family meant everything to him. Etti's response is heard on the soundtrack (she cannot accept it; she cannot understand how he could stay there). During this conversation, Reuveni does not show her mother or Peter, but rather herself, in her new home in Berlin, unpacking books and cookware, washing glasses, putting books on shelves. Through this editing, Etti's lack of ability to accept Peter's choice actually symbolizes Etti's inability to understand or accept Reuveni's choice either.

The third part of *Farewell Herr Schwarz* shows how the survivors' past deeply affects the third generation's identity. As in *Oy Mama* and *The Flat*, Reuveni depicts herself as someone whose identity is fused with her grandmother's identity. She embarks on a journey for her grandmother, a journey her grandmother did not dare to take because she swore she would never set foot in Germany. Reuveni deals with difficult questions about Peter with a level of pain and emotional intimacy as though it was her own brother and not a person that she had never met. Her total identification with her grandmother is also portrayed physically: toward the end of *Farewell Herr Schwarz*, Reuveni includes a scene in which a friend of her grandmother's looks at her and says that both she and her grandmother have the same eyes ("your eyes are from Łódź, not from Petach Tikva").

Farewell Herr Schwarz documents the third generation from the two sides—Germany and Israel. Stefan Kummer, Barbara's son and Peter's grandson, has found partial redemption through his Jewish identity. He works at a synagogue in Berlin and is studying Judaism and Hebrew. His library is filled with books about Judaism, and the Israeli flag hangs on the wall—a flag he was given by his German friends. "We are really connected to Israel," Kummer tells Reuveni, claiming the flag was a part of an Israeli kit that also included the Israeli Proclamation of Independence. "Guten appetit," Reuveni tells him as they sit to eat. "*Beteavon*" ("enjoy your meal"), Kummer answers in Hebrew. The camera follows Kummer as he tours Jerusalem and purchases a yarmulke in a market. At the same time, Reuveni is drawn to Germany, the forbidden place. In her voice-over Reuveni says that at the beginning of her stay there, her grandmother's Holocaust was present everywhere—in the grocery store, on the street, but gradually as she stayed longer in Berlin, the Holocaust dissolved. Reuveni, too, like Peter, has found a home there. She is studying German and does not intend to return to Israel. Unlike second-generation documentaries that represent Israel as a natural home, Reuveni finds peace in Germany. The girl who was excused from attending Holocaust Day ceremonies because they caused her nightmares tells her mother that in Berlin, her nightmares about the Holocaust have almost disappeared. "Do you know what helps the most? Living with them," Reuveni tells Etti.

In several scenes when Reuveni documents herself and her mother in the cemetery beside Michla's tombstone, Etti tells Reuveni that she is getting sunburned. Reuveni tells her that she put on some sunscreen, but it does not help, the Israeli sun still scorches her skin. The fact that Reuveni chose to insert this seemingly trivial part of their conversation on two separate occasions implies that it has a symbolic meaning. Reuveni was born in Israel but never got used to the sun, which is such a prominent Israeli feature, suggesting she never got used to Israel. In the German climate, she flourishes.

Reuveni's immigration to Berlin is a part of a familiar process that began slowly in the 1990s and intensified in the twenty-first century when Jewish Israelis began to immigrate to Berlin. In 2017 there were approximately ten thousand Israelis living in Berlin. There are larger former Israeli communities in other localities—for example, New York City, Los Angeles, Silicon Valley, etc.—but the community in Berlin has attracted the most attention given its symbolic meaning.[48] The researcher Ofri Ilani suggests that the "return" to Berlin is a return to the phase before Zionism, before the Holocaust. He sees it as an act of "undoing" the foundational events of the history of the Jewish people.[49] However, Reuveni's emigration seems to be more of a redoing than an undoing. *Farewell Herr Schwarz* takes the position that Reuveni would never have moved to Berlin if it had not been for the Holocaust, whose echoes have permeated her life. Reuveni's soul-searching as a third-generation survivor brought her to Germany so she could face her demons, and only this frontal confrontation gives her solace.

Jewish Israelis' immigration to Berlin is also documented in *Art Liberates*, directed by Solo Avital and Adam Horowitz and released in 2004. The film deals with some Israeli third-generation immigration to Berlin and the way they have integrated into the local art scene and interact with second- and third-generation Germans. Many scenes represent the lively streets, the nightclubs, and highlight the city's freewheeling atmosphere. The artists see Berlin as free, inspirational, and liberal. However, the past, the question of guilt, and the conflict between Germans and former Israelis living in Berlin, is presented as an integral part of their coexistence. The interviewees struggle with these issues, each from his/her own perspective, thus simultaneously confirming and contradicting the film's title, a paraphrase on the infamous expression—and the sign above the entrance to some concentration and exterminations camps—*Arbeit Macht Frei* ("work sets you free"), which today is one of the most well-known images of the Holocaust. They all chose to live in Berlin and devote their lives to making art, which is supposed to free them from dichotomous divisions and stereotypes, but at the same time rekindles the echoes of the past.

For Germans, the questions of guilt, heritage, and genes are always there. The interviewees are young German artists who are seemingly detached from their grandparents' era, but actually struggle with the past. Their problematic desire to let go of the past is tackled by the directors: as an interviewee talks about change in the present, she/he is filmed walking on train tracks. The contradiction between his words and the visuals subvert his desire to focus solely on the present. For the former Israelis who are documented in the film, the trains that once took Jews to their death are replaced by the toy electronic trains in a toy store; the fear of Germans is replaced by Israeli men's interest in having sex with German women (as discussed by Noam Braslewsky); disgust with the German language is replaced by a fascination with it (as described by Roni Froind), but the fact that they emphasize these topics makes it clear that the past is still there. Its echoes are apparent in the interviewees' daily behavior. For example, the Israeli painter Nir Raketz talks about how he was afraid to go to the dentist in Germany because he remembered the famous scene in the film *The Marathon Man* in which the ex-Nazi tortures the young man by chasing him with dental equipment. Michel Dan, one of the interviewees, acts as the director's mouthpiece when he says, "Twelve years of the Third Reich are stuck like a bone in the throat of the two peoples."

Similar to *Aida's Secrets*, *Oy Mama*, and *The Flat*, *Farewell Herr Schwarz* does not present the third generation as a homogenous group. Reuveni points to the considerable gap between the way the Holocaust has affected her and the way it has affected Oded, her brother. Oded has decided to let go of the past. His life echoes the model of the new Jew in that he lives on a kibbutz and works in a cowshed. Reuveni films their conversations near the cowshed, to highlight their contrasting lifestyles. Oded states that he does not understand Reuveni's obsession with the Holocaust and suggests she should focus on the present. Reuveni emphasizes Oded's detachment through editing. When she films herself and her mother discussing whether Etti can forgive Peter, Reuveni cuts simultaneously, in parallel editing, between their conversation and her brother and father watching a basketball game on TV, completely unaware of the drama the mother and daughter are experiencing.

What Might Have Happened If . . .

As noted, many second- and third-generation Holocaust documentaries are "road movies," in which the geographic journey is also an emotional one. Visiting Holocaust sites involves associating places with inherited memories. The researcher Esther Jilovsky suggests that the places survivors' descendants travel to—either physically or metaphorically—become a crucial point of access to the past, which enables them to bear witness to the effects of the Holocaust on their lives. In Jilovsky's view, for third-generation survivors, Holocaust sites also shift into the imaginary realm, and this fictionalization is the way this generation bears witness to the Holocaust.[50] Second-generation documentaries are realistic, aim to commemorate the survivors' past in the Holocaust, familiarize themselves with their lives before the atrocities, and return to the former camps to try to turn their parents' past into a coherent story. Third-generation documentaries sometimes go beyond realism, and also combine the imagined with the concrete. These films use fantasy to document what did not happen, and "what might have happened if . . ."

For example, in the short film *There*, directed by Yael Hersonski and released in 2001, the director sets out to trace her grandparents' life in Poland before and after World War II and the post–World War II films they directed. However, throughout the film, the historical-concrete reason for the journey is gradually relegated to the sidelines.

Hersonski situates these films and utilizes short sections of them in *There*, but the screen time she devotes to them is minor. The concrete search is taken up by Hersonski's fantasy, where she wonders how her life would have unfolded had there been no Holocaust, and her grandparents had stayed in Poland.

At the beginning of *There*, there is a scene showing a birth taking place in a Polish hospital. After the birth, Hersonski reverses the scene so it seems as though the infant is returning to his mother's womb. This scene reflects the theme of the film, which is a simulation—what would have happened if things had been different. To engage in an imaginary journey of what could have been, many scenes in *There* deal with Hersonski's observation of present-day Poland and include interviews with young Polish girls and women during different periods of their lives: girls and women that could have been her. Hersonski said in interviews that in her twenties she had dreamed of studying at the Łódź Film School, which has produced artists such as Andrzej Wajda, Roman Polanski, and Krzysztof Kieslowski. Hersonski's fantasy never became reality because it took several years to obtain a Polish passport. The scenes in which Hersonski interviews a student from the Łódź Film School and the scenes in which she photographs herself wandering down the long corridors of the school are a film-reflexive way of fulfilling her personal fantasy.

According to Aarons and Berger, representatives of the third generation try to uncover and expose the past and, at the same time, rewrite its ending.[51] "Every time my grandmother told me this story, I would anxiously await the end as though Feiv'ke could save her from her everlasting wait at the train station, and now eight years after she died, I'm still trying," Reuveni confesses. This attempt turns *Farewell Herr Schwarz* into a mixture of realism and fantasy. What would have happened had they met? What kind of life would her grandmother have had? These questions lead Reuveni to include scenes in the film in which she shoots the old train station in Łódź over and over again. Reuveni cinematically returns to the point where their lives went in different directions, as though filming it again would change Peter's decision, as though he would suddenly reappear. "What kind of family would we have been if this miracle [of meeting Peter] had happened [to Michla]?" Reuveni muses as she films the empty ruins of the Łódź train station. "Maybe she would have been different? Maybe we would have been different if history had opened up its jaws and brought him back to her? Maybe it is true that things can change in a minute. That one missed meeting can dictate the course of entire lives of generations."

The trauma researcher Cathy Caruth considers the return to a traumatic event as a return to the moment when things could conceivably have changed; in other words, when the horrible event could still have been prevented.[52] She suggests that the incomprehensibility of traumatic events makes it impossible to integrate the trauma into a narrative memory of the past. The inability to formulate a comprehensive story from the trauma leads back to the initial trauma in an endless cycle.[53] The return to the same space is a cinematic illustration of a repetition compulsion. As Reuveni phrases it, in the five years she has been living in Berlin, she has been constantly contemplating "these 24 hours in 1945 Łódź." The repetition compulsion is also apparent on *Farewell Herr Schwarz*'s soundtrack, in which Reuveni tells and retells the brothers' story in the form of a fairy tale: "Once upon a time, she had a beloved brother named Feiv'ke. They were separated because a war started . . ."

Reuveni states she did not want her film to tell a story about the war. She wanted a simple story about a brother and sister, about families, what constitutes a family, how family mythologies work, and how they operate the different generations. "Do you think that there is a chance he didn't want to meet her after the war?" Reuveni asks Uwe. "I don't know," he answers. There is a long silence. This question is not answered until the end of the film. "It is a question about family," Reuveni continues. She and Uwe are sitting on a dilapidated porch that symbolizes the broken family. They face each other, together after all these years, close, but visually shot like strangers, perhaps even opponents in a duel. "I think a choice was made there," Uwe finally says. "Do you think we can become a family? The Schwartz family and the Reuveni family? Me and you?" Reuveni continues. "Yes, of course," Uwe answers, "we are a family." However, the fact that the camera has to pan between them illustrates their actual distance. In the *Farewell Herr Schwarz*'s final scenes, Reuveni returns in voice-over to the story of Peter and her grandmother in the legendary style of "once upon a time." But there is disconnect between the fairy tale and the scenes depicting bulldozers destroying the old train station, flattening it, and putting an end to the fantasy. Symbolically, the destruction of the old train station may be Reuveni's way out of her repetition compulsion. Once the train station is gone, and the fantasy will never come true, she can try to work out the trauma.

Farewell Herr Schwarz, like many other autobiographical third-generation documentaries, ends with no clear answers or closure. Reuveni embarks on a journey to answer questions, but throughout the film realizes that it is not possible to obtain consistent, conclusive responses. As in *The Flat*, the question of *why* is not answered in *Farewell Herr Schwarz*. In that sense, third-generation journeys in both films fail: the directors learn more but are unable to fathom the survivors' choices. The films do not generate a definitive answer to the questions raised but rather express the force of the pull toward Germany that defies interpretation.

Between Germany and Israel in My German Children

The issue of Germany as home is represented from a different angle in *My German Children*, directed by Tom Tamar Pauer and released in 2012.[54] The psychologist and researcher Ruth Netzer argued that the camera can have therapeutic value and that filmmaking can be a form of what is termed *video therapy*. The camera has two therapeutic functions: it acts as a buffer zone between directors and the world, which enables them to touch on subjects that are hard to deal with, and the by-product—the film—enables reflection, which is one of the primary functions of the relationship between therapists and patients.[55] In *My German Children* director Tom Tamar Pauer explores her own and her family's hybrid identity in the shadow of the Holocaust. Pauer was born in Israel to a Gentile German mother and a second-generation Holocaust survivor father. All her life Pauer has gone back and forth from Germany to Israel and hoped to resolve the issue of her own and her children's identity. Two of Pauer's sisters moved to the United States. Pauer moved to Germany; the fathers of her two children are Christian, and they grew up speaking German and observing Christian holidays. After seventeen years in Munich and as the mother of Shira, age six, and Daniel, age fifteen, in 2006 Pauer decided to go back to Israel for a year. Most of *My German Children* traces Pauer's year in Israel, in which she discusses her dual identity, and her attempts to establish a firm identity for her and for her children with great openness.

A Distant Perspective in an I *Movie*

In *My German Children* Pauer repeatedly displays what she calls her "hyphenated identity." According to her, talking about a German Israeli and a Jewish Gentile woman is impossible. "It's like being fat and skinny at the same time. Both identities are quite different and share one body. And you just want to belong to something, a home, an identity."[56] To resolve this unresolvable conflict, Pauer's journey is not just from Germany to Israel but also between family members and childhood friends, from whom she tries to understand who she is and which identity she should give her children.

In many third-generation *I* movies, the autobiographic style is similar: the filmmakers place themselves at the center of the film and accompany it with voice-over through which they explore inner monologues. However, the personal dimension in *I* movies does not need to be expressed solely through the director's voice-over, but can also emerge in the way the filmmakers make their presence felt and structure the secondary voices in the documentary (voices of interviewees or events depicted in the film, which help shape the world of the filmmaker/protagonist for the viewer).[57] Pauer wrote, directed, and produced *My German Children* but did not use voice-over. In the many scenes in which she appears, Pauer is silent and mostly listens to her mother, her children, her relatives, and her friends. Pauer commented on these functions and the way she maintained a measure of distance in the editing room as follows:

> When I viewed the material, it was not easy to see myself and the people dearest to me in close up with wrinkles, with mistakes in Hebrew. But as soon as I shifted to directing, I kept my distance. I looked at the figures from the outside. I said to the editor, "The mother, the child." I did not relate to them as though it was me talking, or my daughter. I concentrated on the statements of the characters, on the message. Each character represents itself and that person's account.[58]

Through the "characters," Pauer assembles the puzzle pieces of their hybrid identity. She frequently asks her children questions from behind the camera. In other scenes she is in the frame filming them together. Many of these scenes are shot in close-up and in extreme close-up, which enables viewers to see the expressions on their faces and the looks in their eyes that mirror their pain and puzzlement.

Between Israel and Germany, Perpetrators and Victims

Fritzi, Pauer's mother, is a Christian German. She went to Kibbutz Yotvata in 1962 when she was twenty-five years old. She was a part of a group of volunteers who wanted to ease the burden of guilt. On the kibbutz, Fritzi fell in love with Danny, a second-generation Holocaust survivor. They moved to Germany, and after a few years returned to Israel, where their three daughters were born. Despite her deep connection to Israel, Fritzi refused to convert to Judaism or completely erase her German identity.

My German Children describes a chain of generations with a hybrid identity. Fritzi tells Pauer that she went to Israel to reach out, to show Israelis that "there are also other Germans." The atmosphere in Israel at that time was extremely anti-German, but Fritzi never hid her identity. On the contrary, "I presented myself as German." The members of Kibbutz Yotvata accepted Fritzi, "and those who did not like Germans kept their distance." *My German Children* shows that religion and nationality are not necessarily associated with a sense of belonging and patriotism. Fritzi, who has lived in Israel for decades, has not shed her German culture but rather has stuck to it stubbornly. She forced her children to learn German, even though it adversely affected their social life. Even though Fritzi knew that it set them apart from others she insisted on continuing to celebrate both Christian and Jewish holidays. Fritzi says that it was important for her to maintain her German Christian identity, "to be a good German, to stay German," not only for her but also for her parents and grandparents. They were not Nazis, "and it is important the world will know it." Fritzi says she knows that her daughters were ashamed of her. "I understood, but it made me sad." When Pauer chose Germany as her home and left Israel, it made Fritzi happy: "For me it was like a closure."

On the other hand, Fritzi resents German culture, and claims the Jews are much more tolerant. Her on-camera conversations reveal how complicated postmemory can be as she experiences it from the perpetrators' side. For example, she tearfully tells Pauer that often when she sees a child in the kibbutz, she thinks, "Dear God, how many children like that we have killed? And didn't just kill but killed through torture."

Danny's family perished in the Holocaust. His parents fled Germany in the 1930s, but his grandparents perished at Theresienstadt. Pauer does not elaborate on his attraction to Fritzi, but the fact that he fell in love with her echoes the attraction of Jewish Germans to Germany as reflected in other third-generation documentaries analyzed in this chapter. Zvi, Danny's cousin, is a Holocaust survivor who also straddles his two identities, which are symbolized by the fact that he has two names—in Berlin he is called Horst, but in Israel he is called Zvi—and two cultures (he plays a Hebrew song and a German folk song on the harmonica for Pauer and Daniel). Zvi tells Pauer and Daniel about the beatings and humiliation he suffered as a Jewish child in Nazi Berlin, and the moment he and his parents were taken by the SS. Unlike second-generation films, Pauer does not use Zvi's testimony to conduct an in-depth discussion about the Holocaust but rather to emphasize the features of a shattered family identity where members are on both the victims' and the perpetrators' sides. Zvi states that in spite of family history, they accepted Danny and Fritzi's relationship ("love is a sacred thing").

My German Children's teaser begins with scenes that capture the essence of the 2006 Jerusalem "Israeli" street: laundry hanging on clotheslines, a kiosk selling orange juice, Ultra-Orthodox Jews on the street while a loudspeaker mounted on a vehicle calls the Orthodox to pray. In the middle of the Israeli hustle and bustle, Pauer and her children walk down the street as though they are just another Israeli family. The next scene shows fifteen-year-old Daniel sitting in a hair salon talking to Pauer (while she is not seen), asking, "What do you want from me? There is nothing for me here . . . everything here is bad." Daniel feels that Israel is a dangerous place, and he will soon be drafted and does not see the point: "We are not religious, we are not Zionists; we are not really even Jewish." In his monologue Daniel talks about his life as in-between: "You say I was almost born here but I wasn't born here. You say I almost knew Hebrew, but you never taught me Hebrew, that I was almost born Jewish, but I'm not Jewish!" Throughout Daniel's monologue the camera often films him in extreme close-up, which highlights the frustration, anger, and sadness in his eyes. Pauer is shot only listening to him. She does not answer or react. She lets him finish his monologue and then asks, "So I have to choose between my son and my homeland?" as the scene fades to black. This scene captures the core of the family's problems and guides their trajectory throughout the film.

The conversations reveal that since her childhood, Pauer has actually been living in two opposing, colliding worlds. As a child, Pauer wore a necklace with a Star of David and a cross, and in this way sought to combine the opposing elements of her upbringing; however, she was unable to bridge the gap. Their classmates looked enviously at the tree in their home on Christmas, but also called them "Nazis" and shunned them. "Every time Holocaust Memorial Day approached, it was like our friends had forsaken us. In the stories of the Holocaust, especially as children, we make generalizations. We say Germans and not Nazis. And the blame was directed at us because we were German." Even for Pauer, German identity was problematic. "For me, Germany was the other half of my identity, and this was usually in the context of the Holocaust, Anne Frank's diary, soldiers and the like," Pauer says, and yet she chose to return to Germany after the army and live there for sixteen years. Pauer thought that a journey to Israel would not deepen the rift in her children's identity but instead would allow them to shape a complete identity, to become familiar with Israeli society "beyond the reports of terrorist attacks" and to choose freely.[59]

The cinematic language reflects Pauer's personal confusion as she jumps from topic to topic, from place to place. This confusion is shared by almost all of the characters in *My German Children*. Even though Pauer's father describes her as "confused" and states that his two other daughters "are more down to Earth with a solid grip on reality," Pauer's documentation of her sisters suggests otherwise. Her older sister, Hani, claims she has no identity problem: "I was always an Israeli. I have no conflict." However, Hani has been living in the United States for seventeen years and still defines herself as an Israeli. She married an Israeli, chose to convert to Judaism, and live in the United States while continuing to celebrate Christmas. Gudrun, Pauer's younger sister, says she never felt she belonged in Israel. She sometimes felt Israeli and sometimes invented a German accent. Sometimes Gudrun told people that she was Israeli; other times she told people that she had just immigrated to Israel from Germany, even though this was not true. "This is a part of not feeling I belong. Fooling myself and fooling others claiming I was a newcomer." Gudrun was bullied at school, where students called her a Nazi whore and bit her. "It was a difficult job being a representative of Germany and Christianity at such an early age," she says. "I don't know where my home is and I don't know what my mother tongue is." Gudrun immigrated to New York, because it was easier for her to be in a place where everybody was considered "a foreigner." Most of her conversations with Pauer are filmed in a coffee shop on a New York street and not in her home, highlighting her feeling of anomie, which can only be resolved on the streets of New York.

The scenes portray Pauer in various houses, but since the places are not mentioned by name or in the captions, none are presented as her home. The result is a series of rooms in different locations. Many times, viewers are uncertain whether they are watching scenes that take place in Israel or Germany.[60] The oscillation between identities is also expressed in the multiple scenes in parallel editing that move back and forth between situations to highlight their connection and/or contrast. For example, Pauer is filmed walking through the Carmel Market, which is symbolic of Israel, while the parallel editing portrays her son playing indoor squash (unclear where), alienated from the outdoors. The editing underscores the fact that he will never be part of the Israeli space.

Pauer characterizes Israel in 2006 through Daniel's eyes as a war zone: on their arrival, when Pauer's girlfriend gets to their new apartment she explains to Daniel that his room is "a *mamad*" (a bomb shelter). "You know what a *mamad* is?" She explains to Daniel the advantages of the room and shows him how to close the window in case of a missile attack. From there Pauer cuts to a scene in school in which a soldier talks to the students and from there to another scene in which Daniel goes to a shooting range with his grandfather. In other scenes Daniel portrays the problems he experiences in Israel. He says that in Israel he learned to value the importance of German education in comparison to the "low standards" of Israeli schools. It made him understand how lucky he was to have been educated in Germany. Daniel refuses to go to school on Holocaust Martyrs' and Heroes' Remembrance Day because he does not want to "feel accused." On that day he even refuses to talk to his mother face-to-face and unlike the other scenes in which he is filmed in close-up and extreme close-up, in this scene Pauer's attempts to talk to Daniel take place when his back is turned away from her as he plays on the computer. "I don't like living here!" Daniel shouts at his mother when he realizes that she is thinking about extending their stay in Israel a few more years, "You are holding me hostage . . . here there are only disadvantages! I just want to go back to Germany. I cannot live my life for you!" In other conversations Daniel says that he has friends in Israel, things he loves, but the Israeli part of his identity is minor. For him, Germany is home.

In 2006, when Pauer decided to live in Israel for a year, her daughter Shira was approximately nine years old. She is excited about the trip without understanding the meaning of the move. She is a little German child who packs her suitcases enthusiastically, asking her mother, "What are 'Jews'?" When Pauer explains to her that Jews believe in God but not in the divinity of Jesus and tells her the names of all her Jewish relatives, Shira immediately claims that she believes in both. "I'm two incompletes," she explains to her mother. Pauer is moved by this definition. "Two incompletes," she mumbles to the camera. While Daniel is shot in scenes that highlight the alarming, frightening aspects of being an Israeli (missile attacks, being drafted, Yad Vashem, Holocaust Martyrs' and Heroes' Remembrance Day, etc.), Shira is mostly filmed in scenes that depict the beautiful, relaxed parts of Israel (the beach, playing outside on the playground until evening, marching in an Independence Day parade in the middle of the street on a sunny day, enjoying a day at the Sea of Galilee). The decision to portray them in such different spaces is not only related to their age gap but also to the way Pauer aims to portray the way they experience Israel. However, Pauer makes it clear that Shira will never fully integrate. Thus, when Fritzi explains to Pauer that Jewish children absorb specific values like fear from childhood ("even if we convert ten times, we will never be Jews"), Pauer cuts to scenes of Shira wandering freely in the open fields of the kibbutz, feeling very confident. This contradiction between sound and visual symbolizes that the hybrid identity will always be part of Shira's life.

At the end of *My German Children*, Pauer moves from a scene of herself and her children taking a walk on the beach in 2006 to a similar composition of Shira and herself in 2012. It emerges that in 2006 Daniel decided to return to Germany and make his life there.

Shira stayed with Pauer in Israel. She is now an Israeli teenager, who speaks perfect accent-free Hebrew. While Shira is being filmed at a ceremony on Memorial Day for the Fallen Soldiers of Israel and Victims of Terrorism in an Israeli youth movement choir singing the national anthem, her voice is heard: "Sometimes I feel part of it and sometimes I feel like I'm not connected." Daniel comes back for a visit. "I feel German and Israeli. I think I belong to both places," he says calmly and with confidence. His teenage confusion has disappeared. In the final scene Shira and Pauer are at the beach. Shira tells her mother that for years she had a hard time and wanted to go back to Germany but now she is glad they stayed. Pauer smiles. Both her children have found a home in different places, but their hybrid identity will remain and so will her own identity. Germany will always be a possible home.

3

(Mis)Representations of the Past

The Complexity of the Image

Films and photographs have the power to translate past, present, and future images to the public and shape collective memory. Films and photographs convey messages that are meticulously selected and organized. Cinematic images create a collective technological audiovisual "bank," which is difficult to avoid, and shapes the perception of the past. Memory is dominated by technology, which burns a fixed set of images into the audience's memory.[1] In most second-generation documentaries, the complex role of the image was seldom addressed. Visual material was mostly used as a natural device through which pieces of the past were recollected to complete the puzzle of the family's history. Some have used Nazi footage, whereas others have combined contemporary footage and interviews with Holocaust survivors and their children with old photos and family documents.

By contrast, third-generation documentaries reflexively discuss the complexity of the image, its (mis)representations of the social actors, the advantages and disadvantages inherent to rebuilding a portrait out of historical images, and the relationship between image and viewers. This chapter analyzes the third-generation documentaries *A Film Unfinished* (Yael Hersonski, 2010), *The Green Dumpster Mystery* (Tal Haim Yoffe, 2008), *Numbered* (Dana Doron and Uriel Sinai, 2011), and *A Documentary about the Holocaust* (Itay Ziv, 2012), and compares them to the second-generation documentary *Tango of Slaves* (Ilan Ziv, 1992).

Second-Generation Documentaries: Footage as Historic Evidence

Most second-generation documentaries place survivors at the forefront so they can tell their story. They dominate most of the screen time. The visuals—old photos, documents, and/or scenes from the 1930s and 1940s—are used as devices to highlight personal stories. *Tango of Slaves*, directed by Ilan Ziv and released in 1992, is exceptional among second-generation documentaries because it combines a journey back to the Europe of the past (which appears in many second-generation documentaries) with questions regarding the images that represent it. Ziv and his brother Noam venture on a journey with their Holocaust survivor father, guided by the sole family photograph that survived the Holocaust, to trace the family's footprints throughout Europe. They try to put together a composite picture of the family's chronicles from a mosaic of testimonies, but they finally realize that the unknown is greater than the known.

During their trip, Ziv interviews historians and heads of archives who explain how difficult, if not impossible, it is to comprehend "what happened" from photographs and video footage. For instance, in the Warsaw archive, Ziv learns that there is very little visual documentation of Warsaw (since most was destroyed during the war) and the films that are available were made as propaganda and do not paint a reliable portrait of reality or provide an objective depiction of the city or the ghetto. *A Day in Warsaw* (1938), which is available in the archive, was probably made for the Association of Immigrants from Poland and aims to show the comforts of Jewish life in Warsaw. During World War II, the Nazis filmed Warsaw for propaganda purposes, and after the war it was filmed by the Allies, who wanted to accentuate the horrors inflicted by the Nazis. The director of the Warsaw archive repeatedly admonishes Ziv that "it is not a reflection of reality and the public must know that." This suggests that it may be impossible to re-create the story of Warsaw before, during, or after the war through film.

Ziv interviews the historian Stuart Ewen, who explains the problematic nature of trying to relate to the past through photographs and video footage to him as well as to viewers: "You are trapped. On one hand, the memories of the Warsaw Ghetto, its oral history, are part of your tradition. On the other hand, the problem is that in our world more and more people understand history through pictures." When Ziv and his father are seen walking through a Polish cemetery, Ewen's voice-over is heard on the soundtrack: "Even when you are travelling with your father you are trapped, you know the story and are searching for proof, because in some ways both of you are products of the generation of photography, and if there are no photographs, maybe it didn't happen."

Ewen claims that the history the public learns from images remains engraved in people's minds. Ziv and Noam's constant pursuit of photographs suggests that they accept this reasoning. However, the discussion becomes even more intricate when the images of Warsaw, whether real or staged, kindle their father's memories and take him back to the horrors. Eventually, these images are what enable him to provide historical testimony about his life to his sons. However, by the end of *Tango of Slaves*, Ziv still feels that the search for the past has led him to a dead end: the past is made-up in the sense that it had been manipulatively represented in cinema and no longer exists in the present. Ziv starts and ends *Tango of Slaves* in an empty hall to show that despite the journey and the footage he has found, no concrete memories could be found to fill the empty spaces in his family's memory.

Third-Generation Documentaries: Undermining the Image

Third-generation documentaries considerably broaden these issues of the image and its place in reconstructing the past. They reflect skepticism as regards documentation; express complex attitudes toward pictures and films; explore the complex and problematic nature of the image, the visual symbol; and debate aesthetic and historical questions regarding images, their meaning, the "truth" behind the pictures, the illusive nature of constructing the past through images, and the ability to reclaim known images and change their meaning.

The Deceptive Power of the Image in A Film Unfinished

Alongside the third-generation *I* movies, an additional group of documentaries directed by third-generation survivors engage in the Holocaust from a more distant perspective. In these documentaries, the filmmakers do not place themselves in the center, as the protagonists who present their own personal journey, but rather take a more distant approach on Holocaust-related topics. However, there are narrative similarities between these documentaries and *I* movies—in particular the fact that these films assume that debates on the national and private trauma are well known, which allows them to present new perceptions. Both groups of documentaries use the memory shaped by second-generation documentaries, but construct another layer of memory while also undermining and replacing the notions of commemoration that appeared in their cinematic "parents'" documentaries with new themes.

A Film Unfinished, directed by Yael Hersonski and released in 2010, is a reflexive film that traces the making of the Nazi film *Das Ghetto*, which was shot in the Warsaw Ghetto in 1942 but never completed or released. *Das Ghetto* was produced after the Nazi documentary *The Eternal Jew* (1940) had failed, and Goebbels realized that Germans were not interested in watching horror images of Jews. Hersonski maintains that the Nazis intended to use *Das Ghetto* as a didactic propaganda device when the Third Reich had won the war to explain and educate the world why the Jewish people had been exterminated. *Das Ghetto* was intended to depict a community running itself into the ground because of its own moral corruption and lack of humanity. It would thus be able to "prove" that the horrific deaths and hunger that prevailed in the ghetto were caused by the obstinacy of the Jewish community's upper class, which maintained a comfortable, luxurious life while other Jews were starving and dying. This is why the film crew worked so hard on directing juxtaposing scenes of Jews dying from hunger with the luxurious life of other Jews in the ghetto.[2]

Despite the meticulousness with which the film was directed to adhere to Nazi ideology, scenes released from *Das Ghetto* have become an integral part of the Holocaust's worldwide collective memory.[3] As Hersonski points out at the beginning of *A Film Unfinished*:

> Ironically, after the war, this film commissioned by the Nazis turned into a trustworthy document for any filmmaker or museum seeking to show what really happened, to tell the untellable. The cinematic deception was forgotten, and the black-and-white images were engraved in memory as historical truth. From the frenzy of propaganda, the images alone remain, concealing many layers of reality.[4]

A Film Unfinished confronts the film as visual evidence and engages with the power of the image. It forces the audience to rethink basic conceptions of history and documentation, while addressing the complex nature of the documentary genre. Similar to other third-generation-made films, Hersonski does not use *A Film Unfinished* to historically narrate the story of the ghetto but rather orients the debate toward other, wider realms, including questioning the concept of historical memory, its meaning, its relationship to reality, and the relationship between photographed images and the truth. According to Hersonski, her producers were not interested in making another documentary about the Holocaust; she wanted to make a film about the relationship between images and reality: "The Holocaust was mentioned, in general, but it was a broader question," states Noemi Schory, who produced the film with Itai Ken-Tor. "It was obvious that we were not making a film about the Warsaw Ghetto, but rather a film about the film," she says.[5]

Reality and Documentary: A Reflexive Outlook

The film researcher Garnet Butchart has argued that one of the ways of enabling ethics in documentary cinema and solving the problem of the audience's right to know the truth is to reveal the creative-interpretive process. This can take place by "doubling" the visual mechanism by declaring the existence of the camera. This shattering of the illusion, which deconstructs the "objectivity" of documentaries, was acknowledged by documentarists as early as the 1920s and later in the works of the New Wave directors in France in the 1960s, who fractured the cinematic illusion by revealing the cinematic components of the craft of filmmaking.[6] Reflexivity in a film can prevent people from projecting the typical emotions engendered by Holocaust films. Hersonski is aware of this, and in fact intentionally edits *A Film Unfinished* to confront these emotions, which have become an automatic part of viewers' response to Holocaust films. She states that this set of emotions has become flat: "Our attitude toward images has become a given," and aims to deconstruct this attitude.[7]

A Film Unfinished dismantles the power of Holocaust images by presenting the "behind the scenes" of the footage of these now famous images to comprehend the frame's manipulative nature and not just the image framed within it:[8]

> I realized that if I wanted to provide the viewers with a new opportunity to view the materials critically, from beginning to end, I couldn't show the film exactly as it was originally edited, consecutively, in the raw and without sound. This is where my manipulation came in. I tried to structure the film as a space which would allow viewers to see what they could not have seen before, even if they had looked.

Hersonski claims that there is something about this footage, or any footage from that time, that generates anxiety and awe, which precludes any attempt to understand the artistic manipulation. She confronts materials that have become sacred over the years, to dispel the aura of holiness around them and reveal their manipulative reflection of reality.

To explore the "truth" value of the documentary and reflexively question the ability of any documentary to represent reality, Hersonski shows another reel that was discovered by East German archivists forty-five years after *Das Ghetto* was found. This reel contains scenes that were left on the cutting room floor such as the outtakes rejected by the filmmakers, the frames in which the camera crew is visible, and the takes that were shot over and over again to produce a scene that satisfied the director. This enables Hersonski to highlight the manipulative nature of the editing by showing how the crew repeatedly filmed several takes until they were happy with the results. Screening these outtakes unveils the cinematic operations behind the scenes to deconstruct the "truth" and capture the artificial nature of the documentary. Hersonski shows the crew working to portray scenes that will look "real enough," taken from various angles, thus documenting themselves.

In *A Film Unfinished*'s teaser, the camera moves in a travelling shot down a dark hallway. The place is unknown and its threatening nature resembles the corridors to the gas chambers. Hersonski states via voice-over that *A Film Unfinished* is the story of an unfinished Nazi propaganda film, which generates an even stronger feeling that this is the hallway to death. Its location only becomes clear when the following scenes show an archive. Hersonski's questions as to why the Nazis decided to film the ghetto before its eradication and why they stopped working on the film remain unanswered until the end. Hersonski's film titles appear between scenes of hands going over films. Hence, from the outset it is obvious that *A Film Unfinished* is not about "the Holocaust." This reflexive attitude is maintained throughout the film in that Hersonski contradicts scenes so that they are not construed as reality. One device she uses is to show the end of a reel and a new film reel being threaded into place.

At the beginning of *A Film Unfinished*, Hersonski lets the scenes speak for themselves. She screens them as she found them, without sound, without commentary. She presents several scenes before stating in voice-over that they were shot in May 1942; two months later many of the people filmed had been sent to their death. To remind viewers of the power of cinematic manipulations and the power of the director, the frames that are frozen show the film crew in the background. Hersonski zooms in on the freeze-frame to point out their incongruity in the natural environment. According to the researcher Nitzan Lebovic, the freeze-frame—the suspension of linear movement and time, which reappears several times in *A Film Unfinished*—draws viewers' attention to the process of documentation. It emphasizes the present of filming in 1942 (the event), the present of the filmed, and the present of the director-viewers' analysis of the footage seven decades later. This stylistic intervention calls upon the audience to criticize and ponder the visuals, making it an ethical as much as a stylistic choice.[9]

In order to encourage viewers to rethink the images, the material is juxtaposed from different perspectives. Hersonski intertwines scenes from *Das Ghetto* with the commentary of five survivors from the Warsaw Ghetto who witnessed the filming in the ghetto, whom Hersonski films watching *Das Ghetto* and sharing their comments. She uses the testimony of Heinz Auerswald, the Nazi commissioner of the Warsaw Ghetto in 1942. She also adds an reenactment of an interview that was held with Willy Wist, the sole member of the German camera crew who was investigated after World War II, excerpts from the diaries of Emanuel Ringelblum, the ghetto's historian, the diaries of Adam Czerniaków, the head of the Warsaw Ghetto Judenrat (an administrative agency imposed by Nazi Germany), and the diaries of Jews from the ghetto who wrote about the filming.[10] "I tried to assemble as many perspectives as possible on the making of the film, to create a sort of incomplete puzzle, most of whose parts are necessarily missing."[11]

Czerniaków addressed *Das Ghetto* in his diary and described himself as "an actor who plays himself without knowing how his role will end." An actor reads from Czerniaków's writings that describe how the Nazi film crew staged scenes in his office with rabbis and wheeler-dealers. The juxtaposition between the visuals of

Das Ghetto and Czerniaków's diaries shatters the cinematic illusion of the footage as truth and reveal its manipulative nature. For example, in a scene showing Czerniaków's office, his voice-over is heard (an actor reading from his diary), sharing how the Nazis staged this scene, took his things off the table and walls and added their own props, including a menorah. In another instance Czerniaków writes about how a champagne ball was staged. While Hersonski shows the scenes of well-dressed young men and women drinking, eating good food, laughing, dancing, and enjoying themselves, Czerniaków reports that the film crew prepared the hall, the women were ordered to wear elegant dresses, and one Jew was ordered to play the part of the host of the ball. Auerswald prohibited Czerniaków from taking part in *Das Ghetto.* A wheelbarrow, which in daily life was used to transport the dead, was filled with flowers that were brought to the ball. Czerniaków's voice is heard saying, "There are rumors that thousands of people will be deported" when Hersonski shows the scenes of the Jews making merry. In the market scenes, a survivor who witnessed the filming says that the Nazis brought geese to the market to prove that the Jews were living well. He says that in fact "maybe twenty or fifty people" in the whole ghetto—in which approximately half a million Jews were forced to live—could afford to buy food, and that the majority were starving.

Ringelblum's notes, read by an actor, are also used in the voice-over accompanying certain scenes. He describes how he asked people to document their stories in diaries that later would be buried and hence preserved for future generations. Some entries from these diaries are read in *A Film Unfinished.* "They keep on filming in the ghetto," an unknown Jewish diary writer states, whose voice is heard (through an actor), "all the scenes are staged." He gives examples of how the film crew was ordered to assemble a large group of Jews in a square and then ordered the Jewish police to drive them out. His testimony is read as the scene is shown. "In order to make it look more real, the Nazis shot in the air to scare the Jews who ran away in panic." In another scene (whose takes are shown) of a restaurant in which Jews are seated elegantly and are served delicacies, a Jew's voice (from a diary) is heard saying, "They filmed a staged scene in Shultz's restaurant today." He notes that Jews "with a typical Jewish look" were ordered to arrive, were seated, and were given food: "This disgraceful shooting lasted hours." The Nazis ordered the waiters and waitresses to go outside and look happy and filmed them. At the same time the Nazis captured child beggars and ordered them to crowd around the elegant waitresses and beg for food, and then go away empty-handed: "This scene was filmed to show that the Jews live in luxury and give nothing to the poor." Against the backdrop of a scene of elegant women in fur coats in the ghetto, one of the survivors who watched the film commented: "So what? My mother also wore her beautiful coat. So what? It says that life goes on as usual? After the filming these people were hurled into cattle cars and sent to their deaths. Maybe they believed that being filmed would save them. But they were wrong. They ended up like all the rest." While Hersonski shows a scene from *Das Ghetto* depicting Jews standing in line to get into a theater, a voice from another diary is heard. The actor who reads from the anonymous writer's diary says that the Nazis captured people in the street for this scene, the terrible panic caused turmoil, and the Nazis beat them to make them participate. The following scenes show Jews standing in line for tickets and enjoying the show. "They were forced to shout bravo," he says as the audience is shown applauding. "They were held at the theater until the filming was over at eight p.m., without food or bathroom breaks. When one of the actors sang a happy song, the crowd was ordered to laugh."

The personal diaries and Czerniaków's diaries reveal that the film crew also ordered the community to prepare and stage scenes of Jewish religious customs, including a bris, a wedding, Sabbath at the synagogue and at home, a luxurious funeral (with a Jew buried in a casket because the Nazis were unfamiliar with Jewish customs), and a mikveh (a ritual bath). Hersonski says that as part of her research work before making *A Film Unfinished* she visited a museum in Warsaw that was presenting a Holocaust exhibit. A television screen showed a scene from *Das Ghetto* in loops, depicting women bathing in the mikveh, with the title "Ritual Bath in the Warsaw Ghetto." In fact, women were forced to go to the mikveh, take their clothes off, and bathe while the Nazi camera crew was filming them and talking about lighting problems. *A Film Unfinished* shows not only the scene itself but also the outtakes, which reveal the women trembling with fear and the camera crew discussing amongst themselves the best way to shoot the scene.[12] While Hersonski shows the mikveh scenes of men and women undressing, a voice-over of a Jew who witnessed it and wrote about it in his diary is heard: "Today they [the Nazi film crew] invented a new form of abuse. They arrested young beautiful women and made them go to the mikveh. Then men were rounded up and were taken to the same mikveh. One Nazi whipped them and the other filmed them undressing and getting in the pool."

Even though *A Film Unfinished* deals with a misrepresentation of the Holocaust, it contributes to the ongoing debate about the value of truth in documentaries in general. As noted, over the years many researchers have pointed out that documentary films are not descriptive of reality but rather represent "creative" treatment of actuality that uses ingredients from the real world to tell a story. Subjective directing, filming, and editing choices are made, and reality is compressed into a narrative.[13] However, the narrative nature of the documentary does not eliminate the kernels of truth within it. Hersonski's film highlights this complexity since aside from the manipulative aspect of the scenes, the way *A Film Unfinished* reflects true aspects of Jewish life in the ghetto is also addressed.

Several times, *A Film Unfinished* shifts from scenes in *Das Ghetto* to contemporary scenes of Holocaust survivors in a movie theater watching the film and commenting on the footage. Their tormented looks and the way they react to the scenes remind viewers that even in a propaganda documentary, there are elements of truth that makes it hard for them to watch. *Das Ghetto* documents their prison, the people who were with them, and the survivors wonder out loud how they would feel if they recognized one of the people: "Maybe I'll see my mother walking there." The scenes accompanied by Czerniaków's voice-over also underscore the complex relationship between truth and fiction. While Hersonski shows scenes of a luxurious house, Czerniaków states that in the afternoon when he returned home, he found the Nazi film crew there. They were planning to shoot a scene that involved two women and a male paramour who were enjoying their afternoon in the spacious house, smoking and laughing. Czerniaków's testimony points to the artificial directing of an invented situation, but confirms that the filmed home was his real home. In this case the Nazis did not film a rich household outside the ghetto and edited it as though it were located in the ghetto. This was Czerniaków's lifestyle. The testimony of a survivor watching the wretched conditions of the masses who were crowded together in cramped quarters, who says only "outstanding individuals" like Czerniaków had comfortable living spaces, only deepens the "truth" value of these scenes. In another sequence Hersonski shows a scene from *Das Ghetto* of a wealthy woman in her luxurious bedroom, sitting at her dressing table, applying lipstick, and looking in the mirror. Czerniaków's testimony, which accompanies the scene, says the filming crew was busy filming his neighbor's house. "They brought in a woman, who was ordered to put on lipstick in front of a mirror." Again, the staging is false, but the house is real. In *Das Ghetto* the Nazis inflated the disparities between rich and poor. This portrayal is false, but the fact is that there were classes in the ghetto and there were some who preserved a reasonable standard of living, at least in May 1942, while others were starving. "What do they want to show?" asks a survivor while watching scenes of Jews sunbathing in lounge chairs, "that there were contrasts in the ghetto? There were contrasts." She talks about the ways people tried to maintain their humanity by brushing their teeth, joking, laughing, and singing as a way to rise above the horrific every day.

Hersonski also shows the "truth" value of the filmed footage in other scenes where she does not create dissonance between sound and image but rather emphasizes the resemblance. For example, while showing scenes of Jews packing their belongings and loading them into a wagon, one of the survivors watching *Das Ghetto* talks about the day the Germans further reduced the ghetto's perimeter. She and her family were forced to leave their home and find new lodgings. Her father hired a wagon to transport their belongings, and she remembers that they were filmed. Her father was harshly beaten. The shots of hunger, cold, starvation, corpses on the street, children trying to smuggle food and getting caught document the reality the survivors who appear on camera in *A Film Unfinished* witnessed and confirmed. "It is true we had to walk by the corpses that were lying in the streets," one survivor says after Hersonski shows the staging of scenes where Jews were told to walk past corpses in the streets. "We became indifferent to the suffering of others because it was so frightening . . . the next day it could have been me."

Another testimony in *A Film Unfinished* that is incorporated in a voice-over is that of Commissioner Auerswald. He reported to his superiors every week about steps taken in the ghetto and about the filming. To provide some action to his reports, Hersonski uses illustrative scenes of a faceless Nazi officer (only his body is shown), using a typewriter while an actor's voice-over is heard. Auerswald talks about the ghetto residents who refuse to cooperate. But when he writes about the panic in the ghetto prison (people who were arrested when they tried to leave the ghetto) when they saw the Nazi crew coming (and were sure they were about to be executed), the scenes show them running in panic. The camera alternates between hungry skeletal individuals and panicked prisoners. Their condition and the panic are real. After showing a woman beggar with a screaming baby in her arms (the footage is silent but the scenes show her crying out to people in the street), one of the survivors says that he knew her; she was roaming the streets with a baby, crying out for food.

The documentary researcher David LaRocca refers to reenactment in documentaries as a creative expression, a productive intervention that "leads to the truth."[14] Wist, the photographer whose identity was only revealed in the 1960s, is the protagonist in other reenactment scenes in *A Film Unfinished.* Wist concealed his identity after the war, became a metal dealer, burned the films he made, and was only finally identified by a ghetto entry pass. The reenactment of his investigation shows the attitude of the person behind the camera. His voice is heard while the scene portrays an interrogation room where the interviewer and Wist (played by an actor) discuss his role in *Das Ghetto*. The voice heard is Wist's real voice from his interrogation. Hersonski states that she decided to reenact it because she was afraid Wist's voice would be missed in the midst of so many other testimonies and reactions heard during the film. It was very important for her to acknowledge that there was a real person behind the camera, remind her audience that this was not objective evidence, but a human who decided how to represent the ghetto. It only strengthens the dual nature of the gaze: whatever he was seeing was not the same thing viewers are seeing.[15]

From Wist's testimony it is clear that *Das Ghetto* indeed captures moments of "truth," such as the barefooted beggars in the Polish winter, the overcrowded houses, and the huge pile of garbage in front of a house. Hersonski matches Wist's words with film footage. A survivor approves the sights—when Hersonski shows a huge pile of garbage in front of a building, a survivor says that people used to throw garbage from the windows because they did not have enough strength to go down—"a hungry person becomes apathetic." "It is true, there were piles of garbage," another survivor says. Hersonski shows how Wist claimed not to have known Auerswald and stated he was never told the purpose of *Das Ghetto*, "but it was clear that it was for propaganda because we focused on the tremendous gap between the rich and the poor in the ghetto." Wist states that the SS brought him "Jews they thought were fit for the film." His emotional detachment is echoed in Hersonski's cinematic choices. As Wist talks to his interviewer about technicalities and complains about the lack of light or the fact that his superiors did not let him express himself but always told him what to film, Hersonski shows scenes he filmed of dying, starving people cramped in a dirty room.

Revealing the "behind the scenes" dismantles *Das Ghetto*'s attempt to masquerade as an authentic representation but also acts as an authentic documentation of the violence and constant intimidation Jews suffered in the ghetto, thus restoring another "truth" value to the documentary. These shifts between blunt manipulation and cinematic lies and reflections of truth attest to the complexity of documentary filmmaking in general. Hersonski made it clear in an interview that her purpose was to stimulate critical thinking about the use of images beyond the issues related to *Das Ghetto*: "Since nowadays we tend to experience reality through images, it is important to understand the essence of the image, how it is produced and our ability to understand it, in spite of its manipulative nature."[16]

The issue of the viewer's place also jolts the classical memory of the Holocaust. *A Film Unfinished* creates a feeling of discomfort, as it requires viewers to take the viewpoint of the Nazi camera crew in the "behind-the-scenes" sequences and observe the filmed victims from their point of view.[17] This raises doubts about all photographed images of the Holocaust, including the footage that often appears in other documentaries. The scholars Haim Deuelle-Luski and Oded Wolkstein suggested that in *A Film Unfinished* the audience is also lying there with the dead, in the horrendous scene of mass burial witnessed by the future victims and present victimizers, but the audience is also part of the film crew. It creates unease among the spectators and forces them to rethink conventional Holocaust visual representations.[18]

Using Nazi Footage in Contemporary Documentaries

By exploring the question of how to treat the raw material filmed by the Nazis, *A Film Unfinished* echoes a controversy that has existed since the aftermath of World War II concerning the representation of the Holocaust.[19] As noted earlier, Lanzmann's *Shoah* included numerous testimonies by Holocaust survivors, perpetrators, and bystanders, while intentionally refraining from using material taken by the Nazis and relying solely on present-day footage.[20] Lanzmann, who was against the production of fiction films about the Holocaust because they trivialize it, also disapproved of montages of archival images with voice-over commentary in documentary films, since it takes the sources out of context, and imposes a certain interpretation on the spectator. He claimed that the Holocaust can only be told, not shown. Lanzmann believed that the solution was to collect present-day testimonies, although this record is also incomplete. He is known for having remarked that if he found a reel showing what happened in the gas chambers, he would burn it.[21]

As part of his criticism of the use of material produced by the Nazis, Lanzmann set down rules governing the ethics of documentary filmmaking regarding the Holocaust. His stance was approved by some and met by opposition from others. One of Lanzmann's best-known opponents is Jean-Luc Godard, who argued that the representation of the Holocaust can be approached if the cinema highlights its filmmaking methods, is self-aware to the extent of reflexivity, and produces a type of cynical, deconstructive cinema. This kind of cinema does not allow the spectator to become submerged in the images but rather constantly engages in disillusionment by walking the fine line between cinema, a philosophical treatise, and video art.[22] Lanzmann's film was dismissed by Godard, who said *Shoah* "did not show anything." Unlike Lanzmann's opposition to using materials produced by the Nazis, Godard argued that he would have shown a Nazi reel of the gas chambers.[23]

Godard's approach to the Holocaust and the Jewish people is a complex, controversial issue. In the 1980s Godard considered that the death camps were the constitutive event of the twentieth century and embraced the view that the crisis of Western society, as symbolized by Auschwitz, also constituted a turning point that led to the emergence of modern cinema. Godard then expressed sympathy with the faith of the Jewish people, and even called himself "The Jew of the cinema"—a persecuted cinematographer who was forced to flee his home, his land, and was sentenced to eternal exile. However, this position was always accompanied by anti-Semitic statements and use of the Holocaust to make pro-Palestinian claims. For instance, the director François Truffaut ended his relationship with Godard in the 1970s and said that Godard called his producer "a dirty Jew." In his 1974 film about the Israeli-Palestinian conflict, *Here and Elsewhere*, Godard presents, inter alia, a visual analogy between the figures of Golda Meir and Adolf Hitler. In his 1995 audiovisual mass, *JLG/JLG: Self-Portrait in December*, Godard challenged the term

Musulman, the slang for living skeletons in the concentration camp, emphasizing that its etymology is derived from the word *Muslim*. This was interpreted as using the Holocaust to create an analogy between the fate of the Jews in the Holocaust and that of the Palestinians under Israeli occupation.[24]

Hersonski's interest in this controversy was kindled when she was translating an article by the film scholar Libby Saxton into Hebrew on the responses of Lanzmann and Godard to the issue of the representation of the Holocaust. Saxton attempted to demonstrate that despite their disagreements, the way both handled the memory of the Holocaust was actually similar, since both had expressed concerns about its visual representation. According to Saxton, they both opposed and even despised representations of the Holocaust in fictional narratives that turn the reality of the Holocaust into a collection of images. They both were against its commercialization in fiction films (such as Steven Spielberg's *Schindler's List*) and both concurred that the best attempts at representing the Holocaust will forever be doomed to failure, and be partial at best. These similar attitudes nevertheless led to different solutions: for Lanzmann it involved exclusion (the refusal to use Nazi material), whereas Godard implemented redundancy (claiming that the abundance of images can deny the emptiness).[25]

In one interview Hersonski described herself as closer to Godard's stance. She said that she did not accept Lanzmann's immensely sentimental attitude toward the footage, which she saw as exaggerated and blinding: "Who is Lanzmann, or any other filmmaker or anyone else, to decide to burn a reel because he feels those images should not exist?"[26] However, in another interview Hersonski said that she was inspired by Resnais, Lanzmann, and Goddard's Holocaust films and also by Péter Forgács' 1997 documentary, *The Maelstrom: A Family Chronicle*, in which he composed a film from home movie footage shot by a Jewish family and a Nazi family in the Netherlands before and during World War II. The film has no explanations in voice-over and only subtitles explain the frames. Hersonski said she consulted Lanzmann while she was working on *A Film Unfinished* and said she preferred these directors' critical rereading of the images and the way they made the frame declare its own limits and borders.[27] In that same interview Hersonski also expressed her admiration for Lanzmann's cinematic choice in *Shoah*: "It was brilliant to go against the archive, against the way its images (which were mostly produced through the Nazi lens) were used or rather misused." However, Hersonski noted that "soon there will be no more witnesses to do the remembering, and this was a very crucial point of departure for me." This is what pushed her to take a closer look at the visual archives, identify the nature of their images, and their historical veracity.[28]

In *A Film Unfinished* Hersonski appears to alternate between Lanzmann's and Godard's positions. By contrast to Lanzmann's view that the Holocaust should take place entirely outside the archive, Hersonski returns to the archive to acquire a new perspective on familiar images, thereby voiding them of their power. Hersonski accepts the problematic nature of the image and avoids trying to tell a historical story through Nazi footage by making critical observations about the footage forming the core of her film. The reflexive perspective deconstructs the power of the Nazi image and undermines the world of images the Nazis sought to produce. The use of Nazi materials and their juxtaposition with testimonies from both that time and the present draws attention to the problematic issue of Nazi footage. Hersonski adheres to Lanzmann's position by exposing the truth behind the directed scenes, which can be considered the equivalent of "burning" the image created by the Nazis. Hersonski's metaphorical burning may thus be even more potent than the destruction suggested by Lanzmann, because *A Film Unfinished* not only challenges the reliability of *Das Ghetto* as documentation but also raises questions regarding Nazi documentation and documentation in general.

In their book *Testimony*, Shoshana Felman and Dori Laub discuss Nazi deception programs in which the Nazis rewrote the narratives of history and memory by eliminating every trace of their own violence.[29] Saxton claims that by murdering its eyewitnesses and eliminating their traces, the Holocaust not only created a crisis of testimony but also (to paraphrase Felman) rendered itself an occurrence devoid of any images.[30] *A Film Unfinished*, however, takes the opposite course and revives the scenes the Nazis sought to erase and destroy, thus creating an alternative to the Nazi attempt to control the narrative of Holocaust remembrance.

Amos Goldberg criticized the film's Hebrew title, *Shtikat haarchion*, which literally translates to "the archive's silence," claiming that the Holocaust is one of the most highly discussed and studied events of the twentieth century—"A standard against which present-day individuals are required to think about the past"—thus making the notion of "silence" inappropriate.[31] According to Goldberg, the archives are not silent but rather speak incessantly about the Holocaust.[32] However, the film's Hebrew title can be interpreted in another way. The film reels found in the archive were "silent" in the sense that there was no soundtrack and the false representations were considered authentic ones. In that sense, the archival footage silences the truth. The representation of the complex truth in *A Film Unfinished* shows that despite the tens of thousands of documents and visual material in archives, there will always be parts that cannot be explained, and will remain "silent." The images obtained from the archives, whether text or photographed footage, are always partial, subjective, biased by a viewpoint with a particular agenda, and therefore do not constitute a complete story of the Holocaust.

The film's English title is *A Film Unfinished*. Hersonski said in an interview that her film is a counterreaction to the "closed historical story" of the Holocaust in Israel, which has a beginning and an end (a Zionist closure). As the granddaughter of Holocaust survivors, she realized there was a disparity between the national narrative and the personal trauma, which has no ending and no closure. The past like the present has no closure; therefore, it is a film unfinished.[33] The English title also suggests a more general conclusion. *Das Ghetto* was indeed never finished, but the choice of the words *a film* may imply that no documentary can be considered a complete representation of reality.

Remembrance and Photography in The Green Dumpster Mystery

Contrary to *A Film Unfinished*, *The Green Dumpster Mystery*, directed by Tal Haim Yoffe and released in 2008, is an ode to the importance of the image and its power in reconstructing a vanished past and the place of photography within it. Director Yoffe does not document his family but rather explores the genealogy of an unknown family through a series of old, yellowing photographs and documents he found in a dumpster. In an interview with Yoffe, he stated that:

> This film is not at all about me, it's a film about a different family, but I feel it's my personal film . . . It's a film about me, it's my film. My involvement in the film is not just to decide where the camera is placed and what questions to ask; my involvement is a much greater emotional involvement. This family moved me in such a way that even I cannot understand . . . it is about my search from the perspective of director/detective. The direct materials are not mine, but the person embarking on this journey is really me.[34]

The Green Dumpster Mystery is full of scenes of the search, and in this way Yoffe the "detective" becomes the film's protagonist no less than the family members he locates and documents. The camera follows him repeatedly scrounging through the photographs and trying to extract information from them, lingers on his computer searches and trips to put together the story of the family. The fact that this is not his own story is concealed in that throughout the film when Yoffe meets different family members, he silences their voices and summarizes the conversation for viewers in his own voice-over. This unusual cinematic choice turns the film and the family's story into an *I* movie, even though it is not Yoffe's family.[35]

Building a Familial History from Images

The Green Dumpster Mystery begins with a phrase attributed to the seventeenth-century playwright John Fletcher: "We do not fear dying, but rather dying unremembered." This is the leading theme, whereas the still pictures, the core of the film, are those which enable "remembering" to come to the fore. In the opening scene, Yoffe's voice-over describes how he discovered the visual "archive" of the family. His face is concealed behind a motorcycle helmet as he rides through the streets of southern Tel Aviv:

> In early April 2007 I was riding my scooter in the industrial area south of Florentine . . . then something caught my eye. I came to a screeching halt near a green garbage dumpster, because I had noticed an old black-and-white photograph sticking out. I got off my bike and was careful not to remove my helmet so that no one would see that this strange man digging through the trash was me. I took out the photograph and underneath it was another one, and another one and another one, and a diploma and another diploma. I took all of them, there might have been more but I was really ashamed of digging and rummaging in the garbage; a lonely old man had probably died and someone had thrown his stuff into the trash. But in this area, there were no apartments, just industrial buildings, so where did this come from?

Yoffe documents the defining moment when the mystery penetrates his world by filming the scene when he stops his scooter near the dumpster again, from a different angle. The first scene is from Yoffe's perspective, when he stops his scooter, and the second is from the dumpster's "perspective." This enables Yoffe to stress the importance of finding the photographs. This duplication also indicates symbolically that there are many ways to examine a story derived from images.[36]

After finding the album in the dumpster, Yoffe returns home, spreads the photographs out on the carpet, and tries to find out about the people in them. One of the photos has the inscription "Hella

Rosen, 1940." He goes to his computer and looks for the name in the Yad Vashem database. This is the start of his docu-detective journey, during which Yoffe is able to put together the story of the Wolkowicz family: Pola and Jacob, the Holocaust survivors, and their children, Shuah and Rivi.[37]

The story Yoffe unravels begins in Europe, continues through the Holocaust, escape to Siberia, life in Tashkent, immigration to Łódź, then to Israel, and coping with additional traumas. As in other third-generation documentaries, *The Green Dumpster Mystery* makes it clear that the Holocaust is not the only trauma that can define survivors' identity: their firstborn daughter, Sarah, died at the age of three or four, their son Shuah was killed on the first day of the Yom Kippur War (1973), their daughter Rivi died at a young age as a result of medical malpractice, and Pola died of cancer.[38]

The Green Dumpster Mystery documents the search step-by-step, showing viewers the lengthy process Yoffe engages in while conjuring up the anonymous family's history. One of the first pictures he shows is of a young man at a festive event. Another picture represents a couple dancing. Yoffe turns over the pictures and shows that from the writing on the back he finds out that the couple is Pola and Jacob Wolkowicz. The young man is their son, and it is his bar mitzvah in 1966. Yoffe then focuses on a yearbook photo of R. Wolkowicz ("Probably their daughter," he says, "I couldn't find the full name"). Yoffe documents himself checking information online while explaining to viewers, in his voice-over, his line of thought: from Shuah's high school pictures, Yoffe knows the year he graduated, and deduces that Shuah was a soldier in the 1973 Yom Kippur War. From a document he found amongst the pictures, Yoffe realizes that Shuah was killed in the war. From the Israel Defense Forces (IDF) site he finds out about Shuah's short life. He finds where Shuah is buried and when Memorial Day for the Fallen Soldiers of Israel and Victims of Terrorism arrives, Yoffe goes to Shuah's grave to see whether he can find family members there, which he does. From there the search continues in that way, slowly interweaving the threads of the family tree. Yoffe finds where they lived, worked, but beyond that, he finds out about their personalities, their happier periods, and which periods were dark.

During his search Yoffe meets Yaron Enosh of the Reshet Bet radio station, who is the broadcaster for the "search for relatives program" (*Hamador lehipus krovim*). This program has already linked thousands of people, with sixty thousand appeals pending. More than half of them are connected to the Holocaust. The program was aired in the 1950s, and "my mother says that when it was broadcast there was a total silence in the neighborhood." Yoffe asks anyone who knew Jacob and Pola to call, another confirmation of how deeply Israel is still immersed in the Holocaust. One mystery—that of the Wolkowicz family—has been solved, but so many others have not.

Yoffe shares not only his revelations but also his doubts and questions (is Hella Rosen Pola's mother?), his mistakes during the search (the Wolkowicz couple did not go to Germany after they immigrated to Israel, but rather before), thus turning them into partners in the search for revelations. In *The Green Dumpster Mystery*, Yoffe reveals that the family members he encounters do not know many branches of their own family who perished in the Holocaust. The film underscores the importance of photographs, as well as their power to mislead. According to *The Green Dumpster Mystery*, images do not represent reality fully, but help establish historical information. In Yoffe's case this enabled a stranger to reconstruct the entire history of a family he did not know, from scratch, including bringing to light familial histories of which family members were not even aware.

The photos and their importance raise broader questions concerning images and memory. Some filmmakers have argued that films and pictures preserve and perpetuate details to the point that human memory is unnecessary.[39] "I remember January in Tokyo," the director Chris Marker says, "or rather I remember the pictures I took in January in Tokyo. They replaced my memories. They were the memories. I wonder how people who are not filming, photographing, or recording remember."[40] *The Green Dumpster Mystery* adheres to this view. "Is there a meaning to life if no one remembers you?" Yoffe asks in his voice-over. He uses the individual story of the Wolkowicz family to formulate a broader statement about an entire generation of "anonymous people" who were an integral part of Israel's founding generation but are not a part of its collective memory: "A completely anonymous family represents tens of thousands of anonymous immigrants like them, . . . people who are not inscribed on the golden pages of the history of the State of Israel. This generation was underestimated. These people came and built the country and paid the most terrible price—their only son died in the war. These people deserve to have their story told."[41]

Yoffe includes scenes that seemingly do not advance the search; for instance, when he sees a sign indicating *Wolkowicz* near the dumpster, he is sure there is a connection to the family and goes into the store only to discover that this is another family whose father emigrated from Hungary. He discovers that one hundred members of that family had perished in the Holocaust. The same happens when Yoffe decides to have the text written on the back of Hella Rosen's picture translated: "Maybe that will help me to find out if she was Pola's mother." The text says, "The picture was taken in the ghetto and was found after the Holocaust." This translation does not serve Yoffe's purpose, but he inserts a scene in which he chats with Karin, the translator, and in his voice-over says that "Karin's family is also Holocaust survivors. Her grandparents were prisoners in several concentration camps. They survived but they lost most of their family members." The cinematic decision to include these encounters reinforces the pivotal argument of *The Green Dumpster Mystery* that it is important to commemorate ordinary people, whose memory is not a part of the collective memory.

"That's it. My journey is over," Yoffe says in his voice-over as he collects the photo albums to return to a member of the Wolkowicz family. Now the photos of the family members have "returned home." This is what Yoffe says while he is filmed climbing the stairs to the apartment. The camera stays in the stairway filming him climbing up, as the sun shines through the glass of the rooftop, marking a small redemption to the tragic story of the family.

The Tattoo as a Reclaimed Image in Numbered

The Holocaust researcher Oren Baruch Stier examines what he refers to as "Holocaust icons." He defines these icons as "symbolic, often visual pointers that are themselves derived directly from the events to which they refer." He considers that Holocaust icons are vehicles of Holocaust memory, intensified forms of Holocaust symbols that embody memory, model sacred engagement, mediate experience, and establish remembered relationships to the past.[42] The Auschwitz tattoo is one of these icons.

Over the years, the number tattooed on Auschwitz prisoners' left forearm has remained a poignant living symbol of its horrors. It is estimated that during the Holocaust, about four hundred thousand prisoners in Auschwitz and its satellite camps were tattooed, of whom only several thousand are still alive. The tattoo is the main protagonist of *Numbered*. The film deconstructs its well-known associations to revisualize and reclaim this image. It shifts from the tattoo as a symbol of humiliation to discuss love, laughter, relationships, and familial warmth.

Dana Doron, who is a physician, says that she was prompted to make *Numbered* after treating an elderly woman who came to the emergency room. The elderly woman complained of chest pains, but when Doron wanted to examine her, she showed her the tattoo and began to tell her about the Holocaust. Her daughter told Doron that her mother's pains were faked—that she goes to the emergency room to talk about her whereabouts during the Holocaust. "It was the first time I had been confronted with the number and not the symbol," Doron says. "It was a woman's arm talking to me. As a doctor I check people's pulse, draw blood. It felt like the ashes from Auschwitz were still burnt in her flesh seventy years later. She used this symbol to drag me into a conversation and knew it would be hard for me to refuse." After encountering two other Auschwitz survivors near death, Doron realized she had to document them quickly.[43]

Sinai is a well-known photographer. At first, he and Doron considered making a still-picture project accompanied by sound bites, but Sinai had access to movie cameras and they decided to make a documentary. As in other third-generation documentaries, Doron and Sinai did not turn the film into a collection of testimonies: "We started to talk to these people not because we wanted to know what happened to them, because we grew up on what happened. As an Israeli you grow up with testimonies and I reject the standard Israeli narrative about the Holocaust which constantly brings up voices saying, 'what was done to us' and 'we shall never forgive and forget' that leads to fears of a second Holocaust." In her attempt to dismantle the tattoo as a national symbol, Doron says she wanted to emphasize the everyday lives of individuals with this tattoo. "She [the Holocaust survivor] holds the ice cream cone in that hand, takes her grandchildren to kindergarten."[44] Sinai wanted to avoid the type of commemoration of the Holocaust he experienced as a child, not dwell on the misery of the victims, but rather to make a film people can "watch and also have a laugh."[45] The result indeed is much lighter in tone than most second-generation documentaries.

The Tattoo as the Center of the Films

The Holocaust survivor Jean Améry wrote the following about the number tattooed on his arm: "On my left forearm, I bear the Auschwitz number; it reads more briefly than the Pentateuch or the Talmud and yet provides more thorough information. It is also more binding than basic formulas of Jewish existence."[46] The Holocaust survivor Primo Levi wrote that the moment the prisoners were tattooed was the moment of their demolition, the moment when their designation as a nonhuman was carved into their flesh, reconstituting them as objects, the property of the Third Reich: "I have learnt that I am a Häftling [prisoner]. My number is 174517; we have been baptized, we will carry the tattoo on our left arm until we die. . . . And for many days, while the habits of freedom still led me to look for the time on my wristwatch, my new name ironically appeared instead, a number tattooed in bluish characters under the skin." The symbolic meaning of the tattoo, Levi writes, "was clear to everyone:

this is an indelible mark, you will never leave here; this is the mark with which slaves are branded and cattle sent to the slaughter, and that is what you have become. You no longer have a name: this is your new name."[47] Following liberation, the permanent tattoo remained a visual reminder of victimization and suffering. Just as it was imprinted in the survivors' flesh, it was stamped on the second and third generation's consciousness as well.[48]

The fact that the Auschwitz tattoo is the center of *Numbered* is obvious from the first frame. The film's teaser begins with a quotation from Primo Levi, who wrote about the tattoo as an integral part of his body and his amazement when people asked him why he did not have it removed. "Why should I?" he writes. "There are not many of us in the world to bear this witness." Before the name *Primo Levi* appears, his number (174517) appears on-screen. This focus on the tattoo, the image, the visual myth, is the lead narrative. *Numbered*'s first scene begins with a close-up of an elderly arm. The camera tilts up and focuses on the tattoo. Then it turns to the survivor Leo Luster in close-up. His voice-over is heard—"My name is Leo Luster"—the camera then moves to a medium shot of Luster, holding up his arm, displaying the number as his voice is heard, "My number is B11647." From there the directors cut to still black-and-white studio shoots of survivors looking at their tattooed arms, rolling up their sleeves to reveal their tattoo, or close-ups of their arms while they are heard in voice-over as they discuss when they were tattooed.

Whenever a new survivor appears, the camera shows a black-and-white photo and the person's name and tattoo number. This aesthetic creates cohesion between the name and the number and serves to remind viewers that for a certain time in their lives, when they were prisoners in Auschwitz, the number was their identity. Years after they were liberated, this trauma is still tattooed onto their soul, like the number carved onto their flesh. It is an integral part of their identity, even in the present. The lighting and the way their bodies and heads are tilted toward the arm make the tattoo the dominant part of the frame and forces viewers to look first at the arm and then at their faces and bodies. In some of the interviews they tell their story with their arm extended forward.

In many cases, since their names do not appear and it is not clear who is speaking, the tattoo becomes the main focus of the scenes. As in *Martin* (see chapter 4), the transition between real-life scenes and stills immediately breaks the flow of *Numbered*, preventing viewers from sinking into a cinematic illusion, and reminding the audience that this is a staged representation which forces them to take a critical perspective. The survivors' differing and even contradictory voices as they address the way they perceive the tattoo are heard—for example, one talks about the tattoo as a moment of dehumanization, whereas another says the tattoo is like a medal—enable a more complex outlook on their experiences and posttrauma. *Numbered* presents a mosaic of interviewees that reflect different ways of coping with memories and postmemory. Although they all share same general story (their arrival at Auschwitz, the tattoo, and having to cope with posttraumatic stress for the rest of their lives), the film undermines the term *Holocaust survivors* and introduces a heterogeneous group in which there are more differences than similarities. This is one way *Numbered* deconstructs the Nazi's attempt to turn them into one dehumanized unit and shows that they failed not only to exterminate them but also to deprive them of their identity. Some have talked about their whereabouts during the Holocaust with their children; others have chosen silence. For some, their way of repressing the trauma has been to forget the number; others have memorized it, along with their friends' or relatives' numbers.

Numbered empowers persons who have suffered great loss.[49] The film gives the survivors what the Nazis strove to take away from them by assigning the tattoo; namely, variety and vitality. The fact that *Numbered* is not composed of standard interviews (talking heads) but rather follows the survivors as they go about their daily lives (on the street, with family, talking to students, etc.), captures their lively spirit.[50]

As in *A Film Unfinished*, *Numbered* is also a reflexive film about creating an image. As the film titles appear, the camera focuses on the act of photographing. It moves between shots of Holocaust survivors in the studio and shots of the photographer taking their picture against a black screen. Sinai is in the foreground of the frame, his back to the camera, and is in focus, while the survivors are in the background, out of focus. The whirring sounds of the camera are heard. These scenes in the studio when the survivors pose, the camera clicks, and the flash is seen are used many times throughout *Numbered*, interspersed between the interviews, sometimes in color, sometimes in black and white. The Holocaust survivors are not "the poor victims" but rather models in a studio which reconstructs an image that has become a visual myth.

Dismantling the Tattoo as a Symbol of Shame

During the first decades of the state of Israel, perceptions of Holocaust survivors were sometimes problematic and the tattoo formed part of a negative image of victimhood, helplessness, and even immoral acts.[51] Many Holocaust survivors felt that the number on their arms led to "insensitive" questions about their past. In the 1950s healthcare clinics in Israel opened certain branches at additional specific hours in the afternoon to respond to the high demand for laser treatment to remove tattoos.[52] For example, the Holocaust survivor Ruth Bondy says in *Numbered* that when Israelis saw the tattoo, many insinuated that the survivor had managed to stay alive by being "a Kapo, maybe something else"—a reference to the common notion that women who survived the Holocaust did so through prostitution.[53] Bondy did not want to be defined by her number and in order to avoid these questions, she had the tattoo removed. Another example can be found in the documentary *Love in Auschwitz* (discussed in chapter 1), in which the Holocaust survivor Tahori, who was in a close relationship with SS officer Franz Wunsch, says in her voice-over, "I had a stain. How come I survived?" as the camera focuses on the number on her arm. As noted earlier, from the 1980s on, as Holocaust awareness changed for numerous reasons, the attitude toward survivors changed in many cultural fields, yet it still appeared in fiction cinema and other texts.[54] *Numbered* takes this change one step further by making the tattoo aesthetic and also reclaiming it by attributing other feelings, stories, and emotions to it. *Numbered* explores the many ways a tattoo has become part of the survivors' identity, and also part of their offspring's identity, while revealing other at times humorous and sympathetic reactions to the tattoo.

The survivor Dani Chanoch, for instance, uses black humor to deal with his trauma. The importance of humor in coping with post-traumatic symptoms has been studied extensively. When used as a defense mechanism, humor can take two forms: black humor and self-deprecating humor.[55] These types of humor are believed to help individuals alleviate stress, cope with negative feelings and tough situations, mitigate suffering, and dissipate feelings of anxiety, at least for a certain time. It is also thought to help those coping with unpleasant memories and aid trauma victims in reducing their tension and anxiety.[56] Chanoch describes his imprisonment in Auschwitz as "forty-four months in prestigious facilities." He discusses the death that surrounded him as an adventure: "Death is a part of life. Death is cool. To cover yourself with a dead body is like coddling in a warm blanket." Chanoch talks about the way he escaped a children's "action" in Kovno (Kaunas), claiming, "I redeemed my life, I became superior. I owe my birth to my mother's womb, but I owe my life only to myself." With a big smile Chanoch declares that he loves the Israeli summer, because he can show off his tattoo. Laughing, he says, "It's a sign of prestige today, I'm a celebrity, especially my number, so aesthetic, it gives me a kind of superiority."

Chanoch's story and his black humor were documented in the second-generation film *Pizza in Auschwitz* (Moshe Zimmerman, 2008). The film accompanies Chanoch and his two children, Shraga (Sagi) and Miri, during their six-day journey to Lithuania and Poland. The film shows how Chanoch and Miri use black humor to cope with the horrors of the past. By contrast, *Numbered* marginalizes Chanoch's life story and focuses on the humoristic implications of the tattoo. *Numbered* goes deeper in this sense than *Pizza in Auschwitz* to show that black humor and self-deprecating humor can be found in many families of Holocaust survivors and is not a unique attribute of a particular family. The deconstruction of the tattoo as a symbol of shame also emerges from other humorous scenes in which survivors and their children talk about how over the years they have used the numbers tattooed on their arms when playing the lottery or when needing passwords or codes.

The deconstruction of the negative meaning of the number is also apparent in other scenes, which show the tattoo as a symbol of love. When Zwi Steinitz and his wife, Regina, appear for the first time, they are shot in a studio in two-shot, as she asks him to do what the director and the photographer asked him, to look at the number and read it out loud. As he does so she kisses and hugs him and he giggles. Only afterward his name appears. This cinematic tactic immediately associates the tattoo and their love. This is strengthened as Zwi and Regina talk to the interviewer about their first meeting, following liberation. They talk simultaneously, holding hands, discussing the mutual love for music that brought them together, their first talk, and their instant physical attraction. Regina says that she approached Zwi first, embraced him, and he almost fainted and fell on the floor, because it was the first time he had been kissed and hugged since he was a child. "When making love, we weren't in Auschwitz," she says.

Another type of love is expressed through interviews with second- and third-generation members of other families who have chosen to have the number of their parent or grandparent tattooed on their own arms. *Numbered* presents the ways in which they upend the tattoo as symbol of humiliation by making it a symbol of continuity, family, affection, love, the bond between generations, and the victory of life. This reclaiming is represented on the body. *Numbered* shows how skin becomes a "site of memory" (*un lieu de mémoire*), a phrase coined by the French historian Pierre Nora, which relates to any significant entity, whether material or nonmaterial, which has become a symbolic element of the memorial heritage of a community.[57]

As noted, many second-generation documentaries reveal the complexity of life in the shadow of survivors' post-trauma and depict a narrative of transgenerational transfer that shapes their lives. Second-generation films portray the second generation as victims of their parents' silence (*Daddy, Come to the Fair*, *Six Million and One*) or compulsive talking (*Pizza in Auschwitz*), their toughness (*Hugo*), or their sensitivity (*Because of That War*). The families portrayed are different but the second generation's victimhood is always apparent. Third-generation documentaries reflect a different attitude. They echo many studies showing the close, warm connection between Holocaust survivors and their grandchildren in Israel. *Numbered*, like other third-generation documentaries, does not deal with the emotional baggage, but rather depicts admiration.

Hanna Rabinowitz, daughter of Leon Klinger, talks about how integral the tattoo was in their everyday lives: the family used it as the combination to their safe and the locks on suitcases. She says that when her father was dying she thought she wanted to engrave it on her flesh. Hanna is shown in her home, displaying her father's pictures, hearing his voice in a recording, as the camera focuses on the tattooed number on her leg. In these scenes none of their names are mentioned. When Hanna appears again in later scenes her name is still not mentioned as she discusses the number, and that she accidentally had the wrong number tattooed on her leg after her father's death. The camera follows her as she enters the tattoo parlor, asks them to change the number, and uses close-ups of her pain as the correct number is engraved.

Later Hanna finds out that the name of the Jew whose number she had wrongfully tattooed on her leg was Maurice Finsi. When she accessed a document containing his information, she confesses on-camera that she felt sad because she erased him. The directors immediately respond with an act of remembrance of their own as they cinematically treat Finsi as one of *Numbered*'s interviewees. They place his picture, name, and number on a black background. The use of the still picture, which inserts him into the film, again draws to viewers' attention the importance of the image in commemoration.

Another depiction of the association of love, continuity, and commemoration is presented in the scenes dealing with the Holocaust survivor Abramo Nacson and his grandson Ayal Gelles, who had his grandfather's number tattooed on his arm. They are filmed hugging, focusing on their forearms, which display the same number. McGlothlin has argued that Holocaust survivors' offspring may want to be tattooed for a number of reasons. It can be seen as an expression of difference, in which the offspring take on a familiar symbol to manifest their own feelings of stigmatization, to mark themselves as a victim, to express a sense of solidarity with the family and the Jewish tradition, and/or an attempt to understand, in the flesh, the event that cast such a long shadow on their lives.[58] The second- and third-generation members featured in *Numbered* express a sense of solidarity, an attempt to commemorate the survivors and use it as a sign of love of their parents or grandparents. Ayal says that he knows that in the future, when he has children, they will ask him what the number means and he will tell them. Tattooing his grandfather's number on his arm is thus a guarantee that his grandparents' memory will live on.

Numbered ends with a sequence in which the interviewees meet. As requested by the directors, they raise their arms toward the camera as a sign of victory. In a long scene the camera pans across them, focusing on their arms while the soundtrack records their voices talking with each other, stating their numbers. But, like many other second- and third-generation documentaries, *Numbered* does not contain closure. The symbolic triumph remains partial. During the encounter, one of the few conversations captured on-camera is between Chanoch and Zoka. "Have you gone back to Auschwitz?" Zoka asks. "Many times," Chanoch replies. "Then you were never really released from there," Zoka replies. However, earlier scenes in *Numbered* show that although Zoka has never returned to Auschwitz, she is not released from her memories either. In the film she says that her compulsive shopping, especially for warm clothes, is her posttraumatic reaction ("I buy myself confidence"). When Holocaust Martyrs' and Heroes' Remembrance Day approaches, Zoka's compulsive shopping increases. She says on-camera that she cannot forgive herself because when her mother stood in one line, she asked

Zoka whether she should escape. Zoka, who saw that others who tried to escape were beaten and did not want her mother to suffer, advised her to stay in line, not knowing that this was the group of people who would be sent to the gas chambers. Thus, Chanoch is not the only one who "was not really released."

As in other third-generation documentaries, the Holocaust is not mentioned as the only trauma in life. After Zoka talks about her compulsive shopping and the camera follows her in a mall, she says that she responded the same way when her son was in a coma. She does not explain what happened to him. The fact that this is not explained suggests Zoka may find this trauma more difficult to work through than her memories of the Holocaust. She simply says that the neighbors whispered, "Her son is badly hurt and look how she dresses." According to Zoka, at that time, "I was in a shopping stupor. A new outfit every week . . . I wanted to cover something up, so no one would see." As Zoka walks home with bags full of clothes, her voice is heard saying, "A mother's grief is the most terrible of all." In another scene the camera follows Gita Kalderon as she goes to visit her late husband Shmuel (Simo) Kalderon's grave. In previous scenes Gita spoke about their love, and their lovemaking, which changed her life. At Shmuel's graveside Gita talks to him in the first person, "Simo, I hope you can hear me. I want to tell you so many things." She tells him that she talks to many people. They listen, "but they are not you," Gita says and kisses the tombstone. The proximity of these scenes, and the long scene in the graveyard, remind viewers that life is more complicated than simple definitions of *Holocaust survivors*.

By the end of *Numbered*, after the survivors are shot in a group shot in a studio, as they raise their tattooed arm, the directors cut to still black-and-white pictures of the survivors who were interviewed in the film showing their arms. This time, the headlines don't mention the number, and attach to their name a family name, which didn't appear before. As if the film's ending offers a small, aesthetic, cinematic redemption to a trauma that cannot have a closure.

"Master Paradigm" Deconstruction in A Documentary about the Holocaust

Tobias Ebbrecht claims that the many cultural representations of the Holocaust in popular Western culture have turned the Holocaust into a "master paradigm"—that is, a series of well-known, repetitive Holocaust narratives and visuals.[59] *A Documentary about the Holocaust*, directed by Itay Ziv and released in 2012, summarizes this saturation. This twenty-minute documentary/video works critically and cynically deconstructs Holocaust documentaries. Its title lumps Holocaust documentaries into one category (implying they are all the same), and its reflexive scenes point to the inability to produce another Holocaust documentary, since Holocaust images and Holocaust documentary narratives have become a series of clichés. Ziv's attitude toward yet another Holocaust documentary is immediately apparent at the beginning of the film, with its utility poles shadowing a brick wall and the melancholic music playing in the background. This simple manipulation sums up the director's attitude. To illustrate how everything has already been said visually, Ziv overloads *A Documentary about the Holocaust* with frames taken directly from the pool of images and illustrations associated with Holocaust films, such as talking heads, dramatic music, black-and-white shots of staircases, dark skies, a chimney, a brick wall, wire-fence graphics, the "Partisan Song" in Yiddish, and transitions from black and white to color (symbolizing life must go on). These shots are exaggerated, preposterous, with no logical connection between the soundtrack and the visuals. When in the deliberately overly long final scene a cat crosses the frame behind a young couple kissing (symbolizing new beginnings), the comic effect is clear. This is Ziv's way of exposing how Holocaust documentaries have become a checklist designed to evoke emotions. By exposing his attempts to find the "right" Holocaust images that should accompany his grandmother's story, he deconstructs Holocaust commemoration as shaped in many Holocaust documentaries.[60]

Ziv deliberately focuses on the technical sides and shares technical questions bothering him with viewers: What constitutes a good opening scene? What kind of music is appropriate for a Holocaust film? Should he make the film in black and white or in color? What colors should be used? ("Red," the child interviewee replies with confidence, "because it's blood.") How should the script be written? Is it important to interview Holocaust survivors? How long should the final scene be? What is the appropriate length of a Holocaust film? The discussion of the technicalities renders the eventuality of representing the Holocaust in a documentary meaningless. Ziv pulls the rug out from under a documentary film's ability to capture or commemorate once the "behind-the-scenes" is revealed to viewers. The cinematic "recipe" undermines the status of such documentaries as representations.[61]

Part of the deconstruction of typical Holocaust documentaries involves interviews with second-generation family members. Through the obvious, even banal, things they say, Ziv undermines familiar perspectives. He films his father, who says that the Jewish people have to make sure that the next generation has learned from the Holocaust, and his mother, who starts by saying that the way the family coped in the years after World War II should also be discussed. Unlike most second-generation documentaries, which focus on personal stories, Ziv does not allow his mother to continue discussing her feelings but rather cuts the scene as she speaks. This stop illustrates the feeling that Ziv, who has already heard these statements before in many documentaries, is trying to find a new direction.

Unlike the many second-generation films that have dwelled on Holocaust survivors and dedicated most of their screen time to their stories, in *A Documentary about the Holocaust*, Ziv approaches his grandmother, but is unable to interview her. He records a phone call in which he asks whether he can come over to film an interview with her and his grandfather. She, sounding upset, tells Ziv that there is no reason. Numerous films have already been made about the Holocaust, and there is nothing unique about their story. "Leave us alone," she decisively dissuades her grandson. "Your grandfather is so mad he turned purple . . . and we have nothing to tell!" Then she asks, "Aren't you working today? What are you doing picking on us? . . . What's gotten into your head with this film?" Ziv's grandmother scolds him ("What do you want, some kind of model?") and briefly informs him that during the Holocaust they hid in a Gentile's house. "And that's it." She claims the "trendiest" survivors are those from Auschwitz, and they have already been the subjects of vast numbers of films. She suggests that he leave it alone and use the money for something else ("Isn't it a shame to waste money on a film? Go get yourself some warm clothes instead!").

By inserting his grandmother's (comic) refusal, Ziv raises three issues that relate to the memory of the Holocaust: First of all, she hints at the quantification of suffering, a hierarchy among Holocaust survivors that is well-known among families of Holocaust survivors and researchers, but is hardly ever discussed within the Israeli Holocaust narrative, apparently in order not to hurt the survivors. She then points to the problem of how the Holocaust has flooded popular culture, an issue that has been widely discussed and also widely criticized.[62] Many researchers have engaged in what they perceive as the trivialization of the Holocaust in popular culture. For example, Gavriel D. Rosenfeld argued that until the turn of the millennium, the Nazi era was viewed as an exceptional period in history.[63] In the last two decades, however, this view has been challenged by what he calls a powerful wave of normalization. Rosenfeld suggests that in contemporary intellectual, political, and cultural life, the Nazi era is being relativized, universalized, and aestheticized in the United States and Europe. Rosenfeld defines this as a move away from moralizing approaches. In his opinion, normalization threatens to blunt the horrors, and annul the singularity of the Nazi past and World War II. Alan Rosenfeld sees the dominance of the Holocaust in American popular culture as destructive and wrong. He feels that these representations make the memory of the trauma shallow, blunt the possibility of feeling empathy toward the victims of the Holocaust, and trivialize mass murder.[64] Ziv's grandmother also raises another weighty argument; namely, that since popular culture is flooded with Holocaust images, there is nothing more to say. It is her version of "the end of the Holocaust."

Finally, in the Western world, which encourages talking and sharing as part of the healing process, Ziv's grandmother chooses silence as the approach that works best for her and sticks to it. She does not pour her heart out by sharing difficult stories—she refuses to return to the trauma and prefers focusing on the present. Unlike second-generation documentaries in which survivors dwell on the past, she suggests an alternative. Making such a statement in Israel—a country that has made the Holocaust one of its most important facets of identity—is controversial and unusual, especially coming from a Holocaust survivor. The last time a Holocaust survivor spoke like this publicly was in 1988. The Holocaust survivor Yehuda Elkana wrote an open letter to *Haaretz*, asking to "forget" the Holocaust, because of its politicization in Israel. He claimed that the memory of the Holocaust in Israel was being manipulated for political reasons and was being used to turn Jewish Israelis into eternal victims, a view that fuels the Israeli-Palestinian conflict. Thus, Ziv's usage of his grandmother's statements subverts canonical aspects of Holocaust commemoration in Israel.

In the American documentary *Nobody's Business* (1996) director Alan Berliner attempts to make a documentary about his father. Throughout the film, the father is surly and resistant, and cannot understand why the world should take any interest in the mundane life of an ordinary man. But throughout the film, the audience learns that the father was wrong and his son was right. The father's life story is not boring, but indeed fascinating and reflects important periods in the history of American Jews in the twentieth century. *Nobody's Business* proves that there is no such a thing as a boring life of an ordinary man—there is drama everywhere. In *A Documentary about the Holocaust*, Ziv's grandmother, who is against the film, wins in the end. Ziv learns that all the images have already been exhausted, his grandmother remains adamant that she will not deliver what he wants, and at the end of the film he seems to understand that her views that one should focus on the present and future are probably correct.

Thus, many years after Adorno's claim that the Holocaust cannot be represented through art, and after the Holocaust has been represented in thousands of various texts, Ziv goes back to the beginning, to the problem of the inability to represent, but this time from a different direction. *A Documentary about the Holocaust* suggests that it is impossible to make a documentary about the Holocaust, not because the trauma cannot be represented, but because a selected bank of images and narratives have taken over Holocaust commemoration and have been overused. Thus, directing "a documentary about the Holocaust" is impossible since the event itself has already become a worn-out series of visual metaphors. In a way, third-generation documentaries constitute a response to Ziv's frustration. They neglect the "usual" bank of images and narratives and address the Holocaust from new perspectives while questioning the "classic" images, undermining them, and looking at them critically while expanding Holocaust commemoration in other visual and narrative ways.

4

The Elusiveness of Memory

Second-generation documentaries were the first to turn Holocaust survivors into protagonists and devote the lion's share of the screen time to their testimonies. The second-generation filmmakers were the observers who questioned, interviewed, but never disputed the testimony.[1] However, research since the 1950s has questioned personal remembrance and has shown that victims have subjective and partial recollections. This chapter discusses the ways in which, in contrast to the depiction of survivor testimony-as-fact in second-generation films, the aesthetic, rhetorical, and thematic presentations of survivors in third-generation documentaries view survivor testimonies in more complex ways that acknowledge these issues of veracity. The third-generation documentaries examined are *Martin* (Ra'anan Alexandrowicz, 1999), *The Cahana Sisters* (Gilad Melzer, 2006), and *Shalom Italia* (Tamar Tal-Anati, 2016), which are contrasted with *Because of That War* (Orna Ben-Dor, 1988) and *Choice and Destiny* (Tsipi Reibenbach, 1994).

Second-Generation Documentaries: The Survivors' Stories as Facts

Because of That War, directed by Orna Ben-Dor and released in 1988, tells the story of two families of Holocaust survivors: Halina Birenbaum and her son Yaacov Gilad (a songwriter and musical producer), and Jacko Poliker and his son Yehuda Poliker (a singer and musical producer as well). In the film, Jacko describes his deportation from Thessaloniki to Auschwitz in cattle cars and his futile attempts to save his family. Halina talks about the deportation of Warsaw's Jews to Treblinka and Auschwitz, and the death that awaited them at every turn. In addition, they discuss their relationship with their children, two musicians who grew up in the shadow of their parents' trauma and the producers of the 1988 album *Ash and Dust* (*Efer veAvak*). In this album they deal with their parents' trauma and in particular its influence on them and their experiences as members of the second generation. This was the first documentary in which the survivors primarily told their story and spoke on-camera with their children about the way the trauma affected their lives. When the survivors talk, no one interferes. The children, the director, and viewers are the listeners.

Orna Ben-Dor, the director of *Because of That War*, herself a second-generation survivor, stated in interviews that she did not want to film her parents and herself and preferred to maintain "an aesthetic distance." She chose to film Gilad's and Poliker's families, and even though she is not filmed she identifies with their stories.[2] Contrary to the assumption that most Holocaust survivors chose to remain silent, *Because of That War* depicts two individuals who engage in compulsive talking and are bursting with tales to tell. Both engage in the continual exposure of their children to Holocaust stories without weighing the ability of the child listener to comprehend, understand, and contain these stories.

The scenes documenting the survivors reveal how they transition from acting out to working through. For example, Halina is a skilled lecturer, who frequently addresses high school students. When she faces them in the auditorium, she performs her life story. She creates a mental barrier between herself in the present and the past trauma, so she can tell it from a distance, act it (sometimes she reenacts herself as a little girl, while at others she imitates the screams at the Nazi officers and so on),[3] and does not cry. But after these lectures, when Halina returns home, she tells Ben-Dor that the present disappears and the ghetto "swallows" her: "It is not a past; it will never be a past for me."

Jacko Poliker's story presents the tragic fate of the Greek Jews, especially the Thessaloniki community that perished in the Holocaust.

Unlike Halina, Jacko is not a professional witness. He is filmed in his modest home, sitting at the dining room table. He does not speak Hebrew fluently, and returning to the tragedy makes it even harder for him. He pauses occasionally and is silent while trying to find the right words.[4] Jacko shifts from acting out to working through. He started a new family, worked, and raised his children, but the trauma is acted out in his actions. Jacko says that every day when he would come home from work, he would go out to see where his children were. They were used to his sudden arrivals at basketball practice, would wave to him, and he would move on. When the four interviewees sit together, Jacko talks about the way his past ruined his son Mordechai's bar mitzvah. After everything was all set and the guests had arrived, his murdered family members (who could not be with him to celebrate) took over his mind and he began to rant, yelling and throwing dishes on the floor: "The whole event was ruined."

Because of That War presents the survivors' and the second generations' stories in minimalistic cinematic language. Ben-Dor does not use archival footage or illustrations but rather only dwells on four interviewees who are mainly shot in their homes—or in the studio for Gilad and Poliker. Most of the interviews are in medium shots, to which Ben-Dor adds a few old photos. The scenes that do not depict conversations document Poliker and Gilad's rehearsals for the album. Film critics suggested that the film's success was due to its asceticism, and argued that it is strong because it is simple. Ben-Dor could convey the atrocities without speeches by Hitler or shots of mass graves filled with corpses, since the memories were allowed to speak for themselves and the style remained direct and restrained.[5]

In *Choice and Destiny*, directed by Tsipi Reibenbach and released in 1994, Reibenbach documents her parents, Fruma and Yitzhak Goldberg, who are in their seventies. Reibenbach films family reunions, intimate moments, and different ways of coping with trauma. Fruma and Yitzhak are antiheroes in the sense that they are simple people, and the film's minimalism reinforces its antiheroic stance. Reibenbach records the everyday life of "regular people": their routines and habits that repeat themselves.[6] Reibenbach is the listener, and the interviewer, who asks and documents her father's stories.

Throughout *Choice and Destiny* Reibenbach questions Yitzhak about his faith during the Holocaust and he speaks fluently, in a remote manner, about day-to-day survival in the camps. He describes taking the belongings of people who had been sent to the crematorium, buying tobacco and selling it for bread, throwing the dead off their beds to make room for the living, etc. Most of the time Yitzhak's stories are told in such a detached manner that he seems to be talking about someone else. At times Yitzhak even giggles when describing the surrealist and incomprehensible reality of the Holocaust. For example, he talks about having to move the camp fence in Płaszów where he was imprisoned. When the workers finished, they discovered that they were outside the perimeter. They began discussing whether to run away but then decided that there was nowhere to go. When they asked the guards to let them in, the guards refused. After all, they had not registered when they left the camp (since they had not left), so the guards did not want to let them enter. The guards only agreed to let Yitzhak and the other prisoners back into the camp after much pleading and explaining. Reibenbach listens in astonishment and asks, "Why didn't you run away?" "We had nowhere to go," Yitzhak answers. "You could have escaped into the woods, hid with the partisans," she tries again. "Nonsense"; Yitzhak interrupts her questions: "Polish partisans also killed Jews."

Fruma is unable to talk about the past. Dominick LaCapra has suggested that silence reflects acting out—or, more precisely, an inability to work through trauma while creating an emotional distance from it.[7] Fruma's long faces highlight the fact that inside she is about to burst. Her body language tells a story of turmoil, fear, and restlessness.[8] She frowns when she hears Yitzhak's stories and sometimes is unable to listen, gets up, and leaves the room. At other times the only way she can ease her soul after hearing these stories is by obsessively cleaning. Reibenbach documents Fruma polishing the spotless kitchen, preparing food, and carefully shutting the multiple locks on the front door when Yitzhak goes out shopping for food.

But Fruma's silence can be also interpreted otherwise. Naomi Mandel states that language has limits and there are inherent problems in "speaking the unspeakable." It can be "an inevitable reduction of infinite complexity to a limited concept," and thus silence can sometimes be a compelling choice.[9] Paraphrasing on Mandel's notions, Fruma's character in *Choice and Destiny* might not be representing only acting out but, following the film's title—a choice. As opposed to LaCapra, Yohai Ataria claims that a survivor can choose silence. It is a rational choice and not an uncontrollable acting out. It is an understanding that every use of words is a normalization of the trauma by turning it into a narrative. Words might be a step on the way to healing, but in that sense healing is creating a story/narrative that never was. Silence is a rebel in a world where words arrange everything—a choice not to take part in the game.[10]

Fruma finally relents at the end of *Choice and Destiny* and tells bits and pieces of her life story. Standing in front of the camera she talks about the wife of an SS officer who abused her, and about the daily activities of her fellow inmates. Her stories provide viewers with insights into other ways of acting out. Fruma says that when she lies in bed, all the traumatic sights from the Holocaust appear in front of her eyes, preventing her from falling asleep. When she is home alone she calls out the names of the dead, those who perished without leaving a trace, without knowing what really happened to them, "without a tomb to put a stone on." She tells Reibenbach about Hashik, another family member who also did not talk about the Holocaust, and wonders whether it was the fact that he did not talk about the past that made him so ill.

Choice and Destiny's aesthetic structure is based on these opposing modes of dealing with trauma. Reibenbach uses parallel editing to emphasize the differences between her parents. Cinematically, their screen time is unequal since Reibenbach's father constantly talks about the past while her mother is silent. Fruma's silence turns Yitzhak into the film's protagonist. The audience travels back with him into the past and accompanies the storyteller from one domain of memory to another—from one concentration camp to the next.[11]

Viewers do not undergo the same process with Fruma. Even the film's title, *Choice and Destiny*, refers to Yitzhak's life philosophy: everyone has his/her own faith and make choices within this framework. This is the manifesto he presents in the film, whereas none of Fruma's beliefs are revealed. Thus, apparently, it seems that Yitzhak's way of dealing with the trauma, the working through, dominates *Choice and Destiny*. But it is not so.

Choice and Destiny moves in two timelines: the past as depicted in Yitzhak's stories of the war years from beginning to end, and the present in the form of Yitzhak and Fruma's life in contemporary Israel. The narrative of the past is linear in that Yitzhak's stories are ordered chronologically. The scenes in which Reibenbach listens to his stories and documents them present a linear chronology from 1939 to 1945. By contrast, the timeline that deals with the present is circular: Yitzhak and Fruma are documented as they carry out their daily routines: they wake up, buy food, cook and clean, Yitzhak sets the big grandfather clock, they watch some TV, and go to sleep.[12] The film's pace is slow, and in that sense, reflects the couple's life in their old age. The precise routine, which gives the couple reassuring comfort, contrasts sharply with their chaotic past as recollected in Yitzhak's stories.[13] Yitzhak and Fruma's routine in Israel is submerged in the past. Amongst themselves they speak Yiddish, use very old cutlery (including a spoon that Yitzhak took as a souvenir from one of the camps in which he was imprisoned); when Yitzhak leaves the house to go shopping, Fruma tells him to watch out. Even when they watch TV, Reibenbach shows the couple watching Polish prime minister Lech Walesa, who apologizes for the Poles' deeds during the Holocaust.

The merging of past and present is also highlighted by the cinematic editing since Reibenbach edits Yitzhak's stories in a way that blends past and present. When Yitzhak is documented playing with his grandchildren in a park in Israel, Reibenbach embeds his voice-over on the soundtrack telling her about his family in Poland; when Yitzhak is filmed in the shower washing his face, the soundtrack is made up of his stories about the showers in Auschwitz; when Reibenbach documents a conversation between them over dinner, she asks him on-camera specific questions about food in the camps. At the end of each major sequence, Reibenbach returns to the same scene where Yitzhak climbs the ladder and winds up the big grandfather clock.[14] This repeated movement and the tick-tock of the pendulum, which is a central part of the film's soundtrack, turn the clock into a symbol of the fusing of past and present. It suggests that for Fruma and Yitzhak, time stands still. The Holocaust is not part of the past and will never be for either of them.

In this atmosphere, there is no redemption, only the small comforts of the family, and the ability to sleep. Reibenbach's perspective on the need to talk is reflected in her cinematic choices. After Fruma's outburst, Reibenbach documents her parents again in their bed as they get ready to go to sleep. In all the previous scenes, which depicted the sameness of the routine, Reibenbach showed Yitzhak falling asleep easily, while Fruma stares at the darkness, unable to close her eyes. Now, after Fruma's emotional outburst, Reibenbach focuses on her mother's face—the eyes that are closing, and the way she falls asleep. The subtext is clear: it is the outburst, the ability to testify, which gives her some peace.[15]

Third-Generation Documentaries: Furtive Memory

Over the years, research has dealt with the importance of oral history in general and the importance of Holocaust survivors' testimonies but has also made its reservations heard. Oral history studies have stressed the importance of oral history to historical accounts. For example, the historian Dan Sipe claims that filmed testimonies constitute not merely supplemental, but central, evidence. They add layers of expression since they capture human interactions and settings.[16] The historian Michael Frisch sees many advantages in oral history, which can act as an "alternative to imposed orthodoxy and officially sanctioned versions of historical reality."[17] The historian and culture researcher Alessandro Portelli has argued that oral sources may not add much to the historical facts, but contribute a great deal to their psychological impact, thus making oral history more than simply a support for traditional written sources. Oral sources are credible, but in a different way: "Once we have checked their factual credibility with all the established criteria of philological criticism and factual verification which are required by all types of sources anyway, the diversity of oral history consists in the fact that 'wrong' statements are still psychologically 'true' and that this truth may be equally as important as factually reliable accounts." According to Portelli, the subjectivity of interviews and the need to verify the witnesses' stories does not invalidate their historical significance since they can provide elements to better understand historical processes since "subjectivity is as much the business of history as are the more visible 'facts.'"[18]

Alongside these positive qualities of oral history, and the acknowledgment of the problematic and nonobjective nature of written documents,[19] research has also examined the problematic issue of false memories and the ways the human memory alters reality, and in particular the many "intrusions" of personal memories, although witnesses are certain that what they described actually happened.[20] Portelli argues that memory is not a passive depository of facts but rather an active process of creation of meanings that reflects the narrators' efforts to make sense of the past and to give form to their lives. Personal memories change as the person grows older and as a function of personal subjective consciousness or socioeconomic status. Oral history "tells us less about events than about their meaning. . . . Oral sources tell us not just what people did, but what they wanted to do, what they believed they were doing, and what they now think they did."[21]

Michael Frisch made the point that oral history does not describe the past accurately. Interviewees often combine the past with their later experiences. Their stories are not pure history but rather a selective interpretation. Their view on their experiences depends on many other factors than the events themselves. Frisch suggests that memory is also "manipulated in a host of direct and indirect ways."

Recollections are doubly filtered by time and subsequent experience: "Contemporary pressures and sensitivities encourage people to screen their memories in a selective, protective and above all didactic fashion."[22] Elizabeth Luftus, an American cognitive psychologist and expert on human memory, claims that personal memories can be manipulated and false. A memory is not a transcription of the past, but a rebuilding of the past based on how the memory has been coded in the mind, and information obtained after the event occurred. Hence, people may "remember" experiences they never went through.[23] Research shows that testimony is also affected by interviewers through their questions, their knowledge of the topic, the nature of the interview, the emotional connection, and the interaction between the listener and the speaker.[24] Frisch claims that these influences turn oral testimony through interviews into "a shared authority."[25]

These critiques are also found in studies specifically addressing Holocaust survivors' testimonies. The Holocaust memory scholar James Young claims that "it is not the experiences that are being transmitted in testimony but the special understanding of them that only survivors can have." This special memory must be preserved.[26] The Holocaust historian Boaz Cohen notes that Holocaust testimonies are invaluable because they discuss dilemmas, questions, and feelings. Their historical facts are not the main issue because they supply evidence that cannot be found in documents.[27] The Holocaust survivor and historian Saul Friedländer talked about the integration of the so-called mythic memory of the victim within the overall representation of the past. He reasoned that Nazi attitudes and policies cannot be fully assessed without knowledge of the lives and feelings of Jewish victims. Their voices are essential for a real grasp of the past in that their voices place the Nazi policies and philosophy in full perspective.[28] When Friedländer consulted diaries kept by Jews he was not looking for historical details but for the emotions—the way they understood and captured the situation—"Their way of seeing the events, their emotional state . . . not at all the documentation of the situation but small details which say a lot about the situation without being an overview of the situation," all of which are elements that are not to be found in documents.[29] The Holocaust researcher Paul B. Jaskot considered that the survivor's story is important, and historians must not lose sight of it in the vast abstraction of a systemic analysis of the concentration camp network. Each record has its side of the story, each remains distinct, and each is crucial to explaining the Holocaust.[30] According to the philosopher and Holocaust scholar Berel Lang, Holocaust survivors' personal testimonies provide a sharp edge to what happened, and what should have happened, thus constituting a counterfactual history that is also factual. Testimonies make the Holocaust more intelligible. They make an immense contribution to history but should also be questioned.[31] The historian Omer Bartov incorporated the testimonies of over two hundred Holocaust survivors in his book *Anatomy of Genocide: The Life and Death of a Town Called Buczacz*, without which, in his view, the biography of the town would have been incomplete.[32]

Alongside these observations, the Holocaust survivor and novelist/chemist Primo Levi noted as regards survivors' testimonies that human memory is a marvelous but fallacious instrument. The memories that lie within us are not carved in stone; not only do they tend to fade as the years go by, but they often change, or can increase by incorporating extraneous features.[33] Researchers who have interviewed Holocaust survivors as early as the 1950s claimed that "we all know how misleading human memory can be. For this reason, we need to confront the interviewee with written documents . . . and verify the interviewee's testimony by comparing it with other testimonies of people who were also present at these events."[34] The historian Tim Cole calls this "a different kind of truth," which reveals individual perspectives and the connections between the individual and the systemic.[35] Research focuses on the subjective meaning of the events for the witnesses since the survivors build their behavior and lives around this interpretation.[36] The Holocaust historian James Young suggested that this history integrates both the factual truths of the historians' narrative and the contingent truths of the victim's memory. This narrative and counternarrative generate a "frisson of meaning in their exchange."[37] The psychologist and psychoanalyst Dori Laub stated that the survivors are not always testifying "empirical historical facts," but feelings and emotions, their ways "of being," "of surviving." Their silence talks, and their body language, the way they tell their stories, are all components that cannot be found in written documents and hence enrich historical knowledge.[38]

The complexity of survivors' testimonies is not only related to their personal memories but to the way these are mediated. The media and Holocaust memory researcher Jeffery Shandler have raised pointed questions about the relationships between media practices and memory. He argues that readers, viewers, and listeners should be alert to narrative themes, language, and spectacle while watching, reading, or listening to Holocaust survivors' testimonies. Shandler notes that some survivors are in fact telling their story for the first time whereas others have related their life stories repeatedly (thus enabling them to hone their narratives); often survivors are affected by what they have read or watched about the Holocaust over the years. Holocaust projects designed to ensure the preservation of memory through filmed interviews may inadvertently provide guidelines for a certain narrative form that is also dependent on the interaction between interviewer and interviewee. However, in Shandler's view the fact that these are mediated, performed narratives does not diminish the value of this testimony.[39]

For many years, these astute observations remained within the realm of Holocaust research and did not enter into the public debate or popular commemorations of the Holocaust, which simply accepted survivors' testimonies without question. Third-generation documentaries, however, associate research and popular memory and for the first time address this topic in their films. They often question Holocaust survivors' stories and the position of the survivor as a witness, and examine the relationship between testimony and fact. They dare to touch on subjects that were considered taboo and gently reveal the complex nature of memory and testimony, without invalidating its importance.

What Happened in Dachau? *The Survivor as a Witness in* Martin

In *Martin*, directed by Ra'anan Alexandrowicz and released in 1999, Alexandrowicz traces the life of Martin Zaidenstadt, a Jewish Polish soldier during World War II who was imprisoned in Dachau from 1942 to 1945. He hid his Jewish identity and survived. After the war, Martin married a Gentile German from the town of Dachau, settled there, and decided to become a self-appointed guide to the former concentration camp. Every day he goes to Dachau and presents an alternative to the canonic story of the museum. The museum's official narrative states that the gas chamber in the camp was never activated and fails to discuss a hanging tree in the camp. However, Martin claims the camp had a hanging tree that was cut down following liberation, and that the gas chamber was active. The museum employees know him, but cannot do anything to stop him. "He acts as if he has rights here," one of them complains. His assistant says that they cannot take any steps to prevent Martin's private tours and that he respects him since he was taught to respect the elderly. Simultaneously, his facial expression clearly shows his rejection of Martin, and he later refers to him as a "nag." Barbara Distel, director of the Dachau Concentration Camp Memorial Site, expresses her dissatisfaction with the fact that Martin lets visitors take his picture for money. She thinks it is highly inappropriate, and suggests that Martin pressures visitors to pay him, that they have received complaints, and that there have been several incidents they could do nothing about. "I think he is part of this place, with all its problematic aspects," Distel says. Alexandrowicz uses his documentation of Martin and his encounters with him to raise questions about memory, commemoration, and Holocaust survivors as witnesses. Alexandrowicz did not plan to make this documentary. He met Martin by accident and filmed him with a home video camera without the prior research that typically characterizes most documentaries. He thus spontaneously presents Martin's feelings and his story for the first time. This gives *Martin* its raw quality and supports the feeling of a revelation to the director.

According to Laub, bearing witness is composed of two main components: (1) being a witness to a trauma, such as the victims who experienced the Holocaust and can testify to what happened to them; and (2) witnesses to the trauma witnesses. Laub discusses the strong emotional influence of testimony on the listener: "Through his very listening he [the hearer] comes to partially experience trauma in himself."[40] This may account for the power of Holocaust survivors' oral testimony over written documents that do not elicit the same emotional response. *Martin* deals with these two forms of testimony.

The Witness to the Trauma: An Embellished Memory

Martin is presented as a memory agent who was physically, but not mentally, liberated from Dachau. The repetitive use of still photos in the film symbolizes that for Martin, time has stood still. "Everybody has left [the camp]. Only he [Martin] is still there," Alexandrowicz states in his voice-over. He documents Martin in his home in Dachau and in the former camp so that the camera reflects the way he is locked, geographically and mentally, in the past. Martin is aware of the differences between past and present, but relives his trauma every day, because he feels compelled to tell the next generations his story and the camp's chronology over and over again.

Similar to *The Flat*, *Goodbye Herr Schwartz*, and *Address: Germany*, Alexandrowicz also deals with Germany as home for Holocaust survivors after World War II. "Where else could I go?" Martin asks. "In the USA there is the KKK [Ku Klux Klan]," and in Israel the rabbis would cause him trouble because he married a Christian. "I've come to terms with the fact that the whole world is bad," he says. The camera follows Martin as he gets up and "goes to work" in the camp every morning, looking for tourists to guide. He approaches tourists, and tells them in broken English about his imprisonment in the camp. They take Martin's photo as though he is an item in the exhibit. In exchange Martin promises them that if they write him, he will send them a photo of the gas chambers and guides them through the camp. He hands out his business cards and says that he needs money to print more cards, and they pay him a small sum. Martin's story becomes more complex when he tells Alexandrowicz he cannot talk about the Holocaust with his children, saying, "I wanted to but I was afraid," and begins to cry.

The Holocaust researcher Lawrence Langer sees Holocaust survivors' testimonies as a main source of information since there are things that only survivors have seen. Additionally, they are the only source of what they felt, what they thought, and their coping mechanisms, "the human dimension," that cannot be verified historically. This is why they are so essential. Langer simultaneously discusses testimonies' problematic features and says that survivors' testimonies should be listened to carefully and cross-checked. He differentiates between two sorts of misinformation that can be found in testimonies. The first is *misremembering* and involves inaccurate recollections of details in the past, nurtured by misinformation, and rumors that turn into "facts." The second is *embellished memory*, where crucial mistakes are made in testimonies. One example is a survivor's testimony in which she claims that she was pushed into the gas chambers in Birkenau with others, but instead of gas, water came out. However, there was no water in the gas chambers at Birkenau. According to Langer this statement is not false and it is not lying because the survivor truly believes what she is saying.[41]

Café Nagler, directed by Mor Kaplansky and released in 2015, is an example of the way young directors deal with *embellished memory* regarding the past in pre–World War II Germany, this time documenting a familial embellished memory and not a personal one.[42] Director Kaplansky's grandmother, Naomi, is not a Holocaust survivor. Her family, who owned Café Nagler in Moritzplatz, Berlin, emigrated from Germany to Eretz Israel in 1925. Naomi grew up listening to stories about the café, and passed them on to her granddaughter. Kaplansky grew up listening to her grandmother's stories about the family's legendary café, which according to Naomi was the hottest place in Berlin in the 1920s. It was the place for the bohemians ("everybody went there: from Einstein to Bertolt Brecht to Kafka"). The family still has elegant plates and dinnerware with *N* imprinted on them, and some family photos and postcards showing the three-story café. Kaplansky embarks on a journey to find out what remained of the family's café. She hopes to make a documentary that will satisfy her grandmother's sentimental yearning for a past long gone. Her grandmother, who was a documentarist herself, waits in Israel with anticipation.

To Kaplansky's amazement, in Berlin she learns that in fact the real Café Nagler pales in comparison to her grandmother's glamorous recollections. Her search reveals that the café was probably no more than a nice neighborhood coffeehouse. The scholars she meets explain that her grandmother's story that swing dancing was invented in the café was not possible historically. An elderly man who recalls that he spent many wonderful evenings with his parents at the café seems to be an important witness to Naomi's stories. Kaplansky meets him and listens to him reminisce about the good old times, but later it turns out that he was just one year old at that time. Kaplansky documents her failures and disappointments. Because she is afraid to break her grandmother's heart, she looks for a creative solution.[43] She finds the answer in a cultural phenomenon in Berlin: young people who are obsessed with the 1920s. On-camera she tells them about her failure, her fear of disappointing her grandmother, and asks them to tell their family stories of the 1920s and embed them in fake stories about how important Café Nagler was at that time, and they agree to do so. They talk about the way their family members always mentioned the wonderful times at the café. It turns *Café Nagler* into a combination documentary and mockumentary. Thus, the film emphasizes the problematic aspects of memory, testimony in documentaries, and illustrates the disparities between recollections and truth and the ways embellished memories replace reality.

Martin's stories also correspond to a clear case of what Langer terms *embellished memory.*[44] Martin claims that the gas chamber in Dachau was operational. He heard the shouts of the dying. When the US Army liberated the camp, they forced the SS soldiers to demonstrate how the gas chamber worked. In the museum, Alexandrowicz watches scenes from a documentary filmed by the Allies after liberation, in which the commentator states the gas chambers were never used. He also interviews Distel, the museum's director, on the subject. She states that there could have been experiments with gas in the camp ("there is contradictory evidence"), but it is clear that there were no mass murders in the gas chamber. Alexandrowicz initially attempts to confront Martin with this discrepancy. Martin denies its accuracy. He states he has pictures that prove his claims, but refuses to show them. Eventually he agrees and shows the camera a photo of a crematorium, but this photo nevertheless does not confirm the existence of an active gas chamber. Alexandrowicz returns to Israel and continues to research the subject. Against the backdrop of a documentary that was filmed in Dachau in 1949, Alexandrowicz shows that there was a hanging tree, which was probably later cut down. But the staff of the Yad Vashem archive confirm that the gas chamber was not active.

Confronting the "Bystanders"

There is an ongoing debate on the terminology that most appropriately describes patterns of behavior during the Holocaust of individuals who were neither victims nor perpetrators. Holocaust historiography up to the 1990s tended to employ the term *bystanders* to describe the international community and citizens who failed to stop the Holocaust (including world leaders, international banks and corporations, diplomatic and humanitarian circles, and local populations). Since the 1990s, however, scholars tend to define the behavior of local populations, individuals, and institutes in new ways. In *Perpetrators, Victims, Bystanders: The Jewish Catastrophe, 1933–1945* Raul Hilberg categorized bystanders into *helpers*, *gainers*, and *onlookers*, and more recently scholars have followed in his footsteps and showed that the category of *bystander* in fact encompasses a wide range of actors and behaviors.[45] Certain terms refer to people who remained passive (*onlookers*, *observers*, *witnesses*). Some refer to the fact that certain individuals benefitted from these crimes and gained materially—for example, by acquiring Jewish property (*gainers*)—or depict the ways local populations engaged in the crimes (*collaborators* and *perpetrators*). Others rebelled against the Nazis, were part of the local resistance, helped Jews momentarily, or risked their lives to provide safety and refuge ("The Righteous Among the Nations").[46]

The theme of bystanders in the Holocaust was mostly disregarded in previous Israeli documentaries. This issue was, however, dealt with by second-generation director Boris Maftsir, who made a series of documentaries to commemorate the Holocaust in the Soviet Union, a topic that for many years was erased from the collective memory because of the Iron Curtain and because the USSR did not acknowledge the Holocaust. Maftsir's documentaries, which aim to provide a broad historical picture, involve interviews with survivors, local historians, museum curators, artists, and local witnesses.[47] Third-generation documentaries broaden the analysis of bystanders by presenting deeds and conduct that range from passive observers to gainers, collaborators, and perpetrators (*Martin*, *Shalom Italia*, *Kleiner Rudi*, *Lerner's Revenge*, *The Dark Side*, and *Out of the Forest*. The latter four will be analyzed in chapter 5).

Alexandrowicz underscores the importance of the survivor as witness when he and his friends visit the town of Dachau and meet those who remained passive. As in other third-generation documentaries, Alexandrowicz does not use Dachau as a backdrop to discuss the victims but rather to interact with the locals. In the present, the people seem nice, and there is a traditional Christmas market with beer and sausages. When a local is asked to talk about Dachau he describes a city of artists but says, "We also have our past. There is a concentration camp." He clears his throat. "We knew there was a gunpowder factory there and that people were working there. By the end of the war there were several corpses there but they were not from Dachau. They were brought in from Auschwitz to be burned in Dachau. But Dachau's beauty is that it is a 1,200-year-old artists' town. We've had very famous painters here . . ." He goes on and on about the beautiful paintings, the old houses, the wonderful scenery. "We knew nothing about it," an elderly woman smiles. "It was off-limits for us. We were only told when the war ended that there was a concentration camp in Dachau. Before that, we had no idea." Another elderly man claims that "Dachau had to cope with it, even though its inhabitants are not guilty at all. We don't deny it or try to renounce it, but it bothers us that people are picking on us because of it." He says that he was fifteen years old when the war ended. The American soldiers forced them to see what happened in Dachau. "It was horrendous. Until then I had no idea what was going on there." Alexandrowicz does not identify these respondents by name. Their lack of specific identity hints that they are not alone and represent the general attitude. "The townspeople detest the memory of the camp," Alexandrowicz concludes in his voice-over. In other scenes in which Alexandrowicz and his friends engage in discussions with the museum employees, they talk about the lack of interest in knowing. Many people who live in Dachau have never visited the Dachau Concentration Camp and Memorial Site. School classes come because it is part of the curriculum but the children's behavior suggests they have very little interest in what happened ("They would have been better off taking them to the pool in the summer than bringing them here"). However, Alexandrowicz shows that even the museum's staff is detached from the emotional aspects: "It is a job like any other job . . . like working in the ER and wallowing in patients' blood. That is not so pleasant either." This atmosphere strengthens the importance of testimony by "witnesses to the trauma."

The Witness to the Witness

Dori Laub noted that listeners exposed to testimony of extreme human pain and suffering needs to deal with a unique situation.[48] They engage in the traumatic event in that they feel the hurt, helplessness, and horror that torment the victim. They need to deal with these feelings so they can fulfill their role as listeners, so the trauma can surface, and that the unspeakable testimony can emerge. The listeners become part of the victim's struggle with memories. Simultaneously, however, the listeners are also separate individuals, who undergo their own struggles as they fulfill their role as witnesses to the witness. Only in this way can they enable the testimony to emerge. Indeed, in *Martin*, Alexandrowicz commits to this process.

The film's title is *Martin*, and it follows the man, but nonetheless Alexandrowicz, the witness to the witness, is the protagonist who undergoes a change. Like many other third-generation documentaries, the film is the director's personal story. *Martin* discusses a process of disillusionment with regard to what Alexandrowicz considered to be Holocaust commemoration. He says that "Martin is also the story of a confused encounter that testifies to the relationship between the first generation [survivors] and the third, my generation, whose ignorance regarding the Holocaust, although this doesn't really appear in the film, is to a certain extent a result of how we're educated in Israel."[49]

Viewers' first encounter with Martin, which is supposed to represent the first time Alexandrowicz saw him, is filmed in voyeuristic extreme long shots showing an old man yelling and arguing with another man and calling him a Nazi. Alexandrowicz's camera tracks Martin from behind, filming him walking slowly with his cane. "The old man that shouted felt that we were looking at him and came closer," Alexandrowicz's voice is heard while in the visuals he is thumbing through still pictures of Martin. "He said, 'If you like, I'll tell you a little bit about what happened here.'" Alexandrowicz dissolves from the still photos to scenes of Martin as he explains the camp. This is the first time that an inner glimpse of the camp is not presented as a dry litany of facts, but as a description of life.

Martin's personality attracts Alexandrowicz's attention and he returns to Dachau a second time. His camera follows Martin again in voyeuristic shots ("He didn't pay any attention to us") as he explains to an American visitor about the camp, repeating the story of the gas chamber and the hanging tree. "The tourist was apparently moved," Alexandrowicz states. He films Martin and the

American tourist in extreme long shot as they say farewell: "The tourist gave him something. We didn't see what." Later Alexandrowicz discovers that Martin tells the same story to all the visitors in the camp, and asks to be compensated for his services. This discovery changes Alexandrowicz's attitude toward Martin from a hero to a greedy old man. He leaves Dachau without saying good-bye to Martin. He reveals his feelings in the voice-over, as the scene presents still photos of him and his friend Artemis in the train, sitting apart, angry at each other. Alexandrowicz feels that Martin "scammed us. Twice we've returned to Dachau for him and now it turns out that he is no better than the museum." Artemis, who also serves as the translator, is upset about Alexandrowicz's superficial perspective of Martin, his quest for black-and-white reality. In *Martin*, she scolds him ("You're asking all the wrong questions"), and helps him to look at Martin in a different way as a man who needs to earn a living. "When you needed a hero, you turned him into a hero, and now you cannot accept that he is simply a human being, and that he needs money for the bus." Alexandrowicz confirms Artemis's perception when his camera, which enters Martin's home in later scenes, shows a very modest lifestyle and discovers that his guide work at the camp has not made him rich but rather only helped him survive financially. Alexandrowicz decides to go back to Dachau one more time. Again, he observes Martin from afar, showing the old man walking with tourists in the camp in freezing weather, telling them about the hanging tree and the gas chambers. His perspective on Martin has changed: he understands that Artemis was right.

Unlike second-generation documentaries, but consistent with many third-generation films, *Martin* is not about the Holocaust, but about memory. The film does not provide a historical account of the Dachau concentration camp or the various incarnations and perpetuations of Martin's life as a prisoner. On the contrary, cinematically, Alexandrowicz makes it clear that this is not the subject of the film. For example, Alexandrowicz documents himself and Artemis in Martin's home, listening to his Holocaust stories. However, Alexandrowicz does not insert long minutes of testimony into the film, but cuts them into a montage of very short sentences, which do not enable viewers to construct the chronology of his life as a prisoner. "Martin talked and talked as though he had waited a long time to be heard. His memories burst out and flooded us: the American soldiers, the SS soldiers, the friends who died in the camp, the friends from the Yeshiva, the children in the rabbi's classroom were all blurred together," Alexandrowicz summarizes in his voice-over while in the visuals he is shown browsing through stills of Martin as he tells his stories. Meeting Martin in person, acknowledging his efforts to maintain collective memory, and his stubborn fight to challenge the museum's official stories, turn Alexandrowicz into a witness to the witness and lessens his detachment from the topic of the Holocaust.

Garnet Butchart writes that one of the ways of empowering ethics in documentary cinema and resolving the problem of the audience's right to know the truth is to reveal the creative-interpretive process. This can involve "redoubling" the visual mechanism; in other words, by creating a documentary about the making of the documentary. These reflexive documentaries help the audience understand the way cinema constructs narratives, and enables viewers to develop a critical and more sophisticated perspective. It allows them to see the photographed world not as "it is" but as it is represented. It suggests that "truth" in documentaries is always a question of perspective. This "behind-the-scenes" presentation means the filmmaker cannot be accused of misrepresenting the facts. It shows that a documentary is a representation that reflects the director's perspective more than it represents reality, and that creating a documentary is an interpretive process.[50] The way Alexandrowicz inserts himself, his doubts, and revelations into the scenes and sharing the production process with viewers enables the audience to develop a complex perspective on the value of "truth," the concept of "facts," their role in Holocaust commemoration, and the chasm between historical facts and emotional responses to testimony.

The reflexive mode of *Martin* is apparent from the first sequence, which begins with a close-up of a package. Hands open the package and take out a stack of photos. The hands start to go through photos of Alexandrowicz and his friends as they travel to Munich. "It all began during my first visit to Germany." Alexandrowicz's voice-over is heard telling the story as the visuals show his hands going through the still pictures of their journey. "I toured Munich. I met Artemis, a Greek woman who lived there, and Christoph, her German friend who had a small video camera." Artemis suggested they should go to Dachau. None of them had been there before. Alexandrowicz notes that "I felt sorry that idea was not mine." Artemis asked him if he knows something about the camp, and Alexandrowicz replied that he only knows the name. He continues to describe their visit to Dachau through still pictures, but this time they fill the frame. Instead of scenes showing them touring the camp, Alexandrowicz shows the central places in the camp and himself in the stills, while in his voice-over he laconically relates what is there to see. There is no real interest in his voice, nor any kind of feeling. Alexandrowicz reads the text as though it were an inventory list, even when he talks about how he entered the gas chamber, which according to the signs never functioned. "I was disappointed with the whole thing," Alexandrowicz continues in the same indifferent voice. "Artemis said that what I'm looking for cannot be found here. You cannot understand hunger in a museum. I wanted to get away and go back to Munich. But Christoph wanted to take some more pictures of Dachau." The first live scene is the encounter between Alexandrowicz and Martin, which changes the rest of the visit.

This aesthetic choice has several implications. The first involves the transition between live scenes and still photos that ruptures the cinematic illusion and prevents viewers from sinking into the cinematic world. This deliberate tactic is intended to create a critical viewer. Second, it hints that Martin is the only one who injects some life into the memory of the camp. Before meeting him, the Dachau Concentration Camp Memorial Site provided Alexandrowicz with dry facts that meant nothing to him; they were simply numbers and empty spaces that failed to convey a sense of what it was like to be a prisoner in Dachau. Martin is the only one who changes this. He takes a frozen, dry collection of facts and turns them into real live history of atrocities and suffering. In so doing he is much more important to Alexandrowicz than the museum's collection of objects, which are historically more correct but have no emotional meaning. Alexandrowicz thus deals with very important themes that had never been dealt with in Israeli documentaries before. He questions Holocaust survivors' testimonies and simultaneously strengthens the importance of survivors as witnesses for the next generation in spite of the risks of *embellished memory*. The message of *Martin* is that whether there was an operational gas chamber in the camp and a hanging tree or not is less important to the common person than the survivors' ability to elicit feelings and kindle emotional responses in the listener. The film's many questions regarding memory, truth, facts, and the survivors' role as witnesses intensifies because, according to Alexandrowicz, Martin actually taught him more than any history book or the Israeli education system through/despite his embellished narrative. As Alexandrowicz tells viewers, he came to Dachau like many other Jewish Israelis with a specific concept of history instilled by the Israeli education system and received a lesson in memory and commemoration that brought him closer to the subject in a way no official visit could have done.

The Holocaust scholar Sharon Kangisser Cohen suggests that meeting a witness in person is more important for students than the specification of details. In surveys, students mention that direct encounters constitute an overwhelming event that makes them look at the Holocaust from a different perspective. The personal link creates an emotional experience they do not get from history books.[51] *Martin* echoes these perceptions by underscoring the importance of Martin's and Holocaust survivors' testimonies in a world controlled by a lack of knowledge, indifference, forgetfulness, and denial as reflected in the film. Martin and his fellow Holocaust survivors are the only way to combat this loss of interest. In this atmosphere that wants the past to remain the past, does it really matter to the common person whether the gas chamber was active or not? For the general public, this atmosphere is very dangerous, and Martin's resistance to this "amnesia" is priceless. A sequence devoted to the letters of appreciation and thanks Martin receives from tourists around the world provides yet more proof. These emotional letters point to the important work Martin does, and his enormous contribution to memory by eliciting feelings in his listeners. His testimony, his stories, his insistence on touring the camp and passing on the atrocities of history to the next generation are priceless. By the end of *Martin*, Alexandrowicz joins those who write Martin to thank him after they return home. Over the visuals of the 1949 documentary of Dachau shot by the Allies, Alexandrowicz's voice is heard in the form of a letter: "Dear Mr. Zaidenstadt, I hope you and your wife are well. I wanted to tell you about the pictures that were photographed in Dachau in 1949. I found them in a Holocaust archive in Israel. When I looked at the photos, I suddenly saw the tree you told me about, the tree you said they cut down." The camera shows documentary scenes of a tree with the words *hanging tree* on it. Alexandrowicz writes Martin that the Yad Vashem archive scholars told him the gas chamber did not work: "They told me that Holocaust survivors are considered problematic witnesses for these kinds of issues, and in case of doubt the formal version should be accepted. I tried to explain them that if I had not met you, I would not have been interested at all in what happened or did not happen in Dachau, and I would never have visited the archive. They only looked at me and smiled."

Martin thus demonstrates that despite the problematic aspects of Holocaust survivor's testimonies, they remain extremely important. One person can make a difference and attract more attention than twelve years in the Israeli education system, living in a society flooded with Holocaust awareness, or visiting a camp, listening to official guides. The film suggests that all types of historical memory are manipulated, subjective, and partial. Personal testimony, with all its flaws, can still create an emotional effect that other historical devices cannot.

The Clash of Testimonial Misremembering in The Cahana Sisters

The Cahana Sisters, directed by Gilad Melzer and released in 2006, is a group portrait that tells the dramatic life story of four sisters from Romania: Sara, Riko (Rivka), Rachel, and Esther. They were teenagers at the time World War II broke out. Sarah was seventeen, Rachel was thirteen, Rivka was sixteen, and Esther was twelve. They managed to stay together and survive Auschwitz, Bergen-Belsen, and Theresienstadt. Their parents and two younger brothers were separated from them in a selection at Auschwitz and murdered. Whereas *Martin* deals with *embellished memory, The Cahana Sisters* deals with *misremembering*. It represents four stories of the four sisters, who survived the Holocaust together but remember the details differently.

The Subjectivity and Selectivity of Personal Memories

Director Gilad Melzer constructs *The Cahana Sisters* as two types of interviews: in some scenes, the sisters tell their story while sitting together around the table. In other scenes, each sister is interviewed alone in her home. The personal interviews are composed of identical questions, as Melzer tries to fit the puzzle pieces together. In between scenes he inserts old photographs of the family and the deportation to camps to illustrate the events the sisters describe. However, the sisters' different recollections of the past prevent him from presenting a coherent story. The comparisons of the testimonies in parallel editing, and the constant bickering as to who is right and who is not, interfere with the presumably linear narrative and turns *The Cahana Sisters* into a discussion about memory and not an account of Holocaust chronology. Melzer divides *The Cahana Sisters* into chapters. Each chapter focuses on one sister and in between he tells their story of joint survival. However, the narrative is fragmented and confusing since the sisters not only talk about themselves but also about their relationship with the other sisters, and instead of focusing in each chapter/sequence on one sister, the editing veers to scenes in which the other sisters are interviewed. In addition, the sisters' testimonies are often heard while Nazi photographs of deportation and arrival at Auschwitz are presented, such that viewers are unable to understand whose voice they are hearing, which further blurs the perspective.

The sisters agree on the frame story and some central issues such as the various camps in which they were imprisoned; the traumatic farewell and separation from their mother; the relatively good conditions in the ammunition factory in which they were forced to work; the fact that Sarah, the oldest sister, took them under her wing, sheltered them, helped them, and saved them; and their sobbing when they returned to their empty home in Romania in the aftermath of World War II. But their recollections of the details that form the larger picture are different, even though they were together and experienced the same events. Their conversations and the individual interviews reflect their lack of agreement. One remembers that in the mornings they were given "plain tea"; another remembers black coffee; a third recalls oatmeal. One claims that at Auschwitz they were given a uniform and underwear; the other only remembers the uniform. The sisters constantly bicker over whether at Auschwitz they were sent left or right; whether the person they spoke to on the train was a German officer or a Jewish *kapo*; whether Mengele ordered their father to go left or right; whether Rachel and Esther returned to the camp after another selection by Mengele or not; whether Sarah rescued Rachel and Esther from the group of women who were supposed to be exterminated, or whether Rachel and Esther managed to infiltrate the group of women Mengele selected to live; whether the food at Bergen-Belsen was worse than the food at Auschwitz; and whether they were imprisoned at Auschwitz for five months or a year. Statements such as "you are talking nonsense," "no way," and "it didn't happen like this" are often heard in their conversations.[52] Melzer frequently uses voyeuristic shots to track the sisters—his camera watches them from a window, as they take a walk, from a crane when they sit in the backyard and argue. This aesthetic choice strengthens the authenticity of the disagreements between the sisters who were so united during the war.

These scenes reflect research that acknowledges that Holocaust survivors can interpret the same reality in different ways. "We are four sisters. Each of us has her own perception, different memories, other pains," Rachel says in her voice-over as Melzer films a cake being cut in close-up. The pieces are seemingly the same, from the same cake, but are in fact shaped differently. The film and media researcher Janet Walker uses the term *disremembering* to describe the complexity of memory—the forgetting of events that are too hard to deal with, which are therefore "cut off." According to Walker this selective form of memory is related to traumatic events. It is not a "whimsical practice, but a survival strategy," in which the victim "chooses" what to remember and what to omit from his or her narrative. Disremembering can become a vital necessity when events such as the Holocaust are personally unfathomable.[53] Laub, who recorded oral testimony from many survivors while collecting material for the Fortunoff Video Archive for Holocaust Testimony at Yale University, discusses the controversy that arose when a group of historians, psychoanalysts, and artists viewed a videotaped interview with a woman in her late sixties. This woman was narrating her experiences at Auschwitz, and in particular, her memories of the Auschwitz uprising. "All of a sudden," she said, "we saw four chimneys going up in flames, exploding. The flames shot into the sky, people were running. It was unbelievable." In fact, only one chimney was blown up, not four. Because of this error, the historians in the group were loath to give credence to the woman's testimony, claiming her memory was fallible. Others took the view that every survivor of the Holocaust has a different story to tell, not because people's experiences varied, but because the ways in which they as victims grasped and related to their experiences comprise the actual core of their story. They argued that the woman was testifying not to the number of chimneys that were destroyed, but to something more crucial: she was testifying to an event that momentarily shattered overwhelming oppression.[54]

The Cahana sisters' representations appear to be a case of misremembering and disremembering in that memory is not always reliable. It cannot be totally accurate, but it does not change the larger picture. As in *Martin*, the fact that *The Cahana Sisters* captures the problematic aspects of testimony does not undermine the significance of the Cahana sisters' role as witnesses. Melzer's aesthetic-cinematic choices question the truth value of the documentary mode. As the sisters tell their story, he integrates still photos from World War II, which indicate certain specific events, such as their arrival at Auschwitz. However, the arrival he shows in the photos is not the sisters' (which was not photographed). Thus, Melzer himself subverts the truth value of the documentary and highlights its problematic nature in trying to build a historical portrait. By using this visual footage, he shows that every "historical truth" is partial.

Melzer not only questions memory but dares, as in other third-generation documentaries, to challenge the place of the Holocaust in the Holocaust survivors' life in ways that depart from second-generation documentaries. As in *The Cemetery Club*, *The Green Dumpster Mystery*, *Numbered*, and *Shalom Italia*, Melzer reminds viewers that Holocaust survivors are people who went through other disasters in their lives that hurt and affected them. According to Laub, "survivors will experience tragic life events not as mere catastrophe, but rather as a second Holocaust." In his opinion, "the trauma of the second Holocaust bears witness not just to a history that has not ended, but, specifically, to the historical occurrence of an event that, in effect, does not end."[55] In *The Cahana Sisters*, Esther, the youngest sister, who manifests emotional difficulties while recalling the events, talks about her eldest son, Ben-Ami, who for her was the symbol of new life in Israel. He was killed in the Yom Kippur War in 1973. "This is the real Holocaust and not Auschwitz," Esther says, her voice trembling. These scenes broaden the term *survivor's guilt*, which relates to the way survivors torment themselves with the question of why they survived while others perished. These scenes make it clear that similar guilt is applicable to other tragedies the survivors undergo. It is a part of the third generation's attempt to show the person behind the survivor, and to remind viewers that those who were perceived only in terms of the Holocaust in fact live a much more complex life.

Recollections of the Past in Shalom Italia

Shalom Italia, directed by Tamar Tal-Anati and released in 2016, is a fairytale-like documentary that records the exploits of three brothers: Emmanuel (Meme), Reuven (Boobi), and Andrea, who survived the Holocaust by fleeing with their parents and grandmothers from city to city in Italy, finally hiding in a cave.[56] Even though the search for the cave is the main plotline of *Shalom Italia*, it deals with broader issues than attempts to find a specific location. The film reflects the limits of memory, perceptions of disremembering and misremembering, and the disparity between facts and subjective recollections.

Shalom Italia's teaser starts with a close-up of a wet motorcycle side mirror. Someone wipes it, and his face is mirrored through the drops. He revs up the motorcycle but puts it in reverse. Later we find out that the person in the mirror in Boobi, the youngest brother. As the titles come up he reverses again, and then drives forward. The camera follows him in a traveling shot as he rides alone down an unknown road. This teaser symbolizes Boobi's initiative in *Shalom Italia*: to go back, return to the past, in order to continue to the future.

Boobi, a seventy-four-year-old science park planner, initiates the search. He was four years old when the family went into hiding; Andrea was twelve, Meme was fourteen. Boobi remembers bits and pieces and is not sure which memories are real and which are the result of family stories. He remained attracted to Italy even after they immigrated to Israel in 1945. Currently he lives half the year in Israel and half in Italy. "I've always wanted to come back to Italy," is the first sentence of the film, which viewers hear (Boobi's voice-over), as director Tal-Anati pans over the Italian scenery. "After almost seventy years I became Italian again. Half Italian, to be precise." As Boobi packs a suitcase his voice-over is heard: "For many years I have wanted to find that cave. The place that saved us from death. The only ones who can help me are my brothers." As Boobi talks

Tal-Anati shows the three brothers standing with their backs to the camera, with Andrea pointing to the Italian landscape. On the back of Boobi's T-shirt there is a big question mark, the leitmotif of the story. The aesthetic choice not to show the three brothers' faces when they first appear conveys what Tal-Anati sees as identity issues. The answer to the questions of the past, the missing part of Boobi's identity, may lie somewhere in the Italian surroundings.

Originally, they were a family of four brothers. Dada died. Meme, the older brother, at the time eighty-four years old, is a world-renowned anthropologist, archeologist, and specialist in prehistoric art. He does not want to take part of the search and only agrees to go to Italy because Boobi pressures him. "Six years of misery," he says. Thus, this archeologist, who digs into cultural history, is reluctant to take the same step when it comes to his own history. This is an expedition he does not want to join. "I accepted Boobi's need to go search for the cave, so Boobi would be pleased," Meme says in voice-over as he sadly closes a suitcase. "I don't understand why we should look," he adds. "I don't want to remember." Symbolically, Meme's attempt to close the door on the past is disrupted by his brother.

Andrea, the middle brother, is eighty-two and the complete opposite of his older brother. Meme's first scenes were shot over the course of cloudy, rainy days, which contributed to the extremely serious, gloomy atmosphere he exudes. Andrea's first scenes are shot on a sunny day, in lush woods. The camera follows him as he rides his bike and climbs rocks in the desert. Andrea is an enthusiastic sportsman, and a physics professor who looks twenty years younger than he is, and seems content all the time, as he laughs, sings, and hums. "My little brother Boobi told me, 'Let's go find the cave,' and I immediately said, 'Let's go for it,'" Andrea says excitedly in voice-over as he packs his suitcase. Unlike Meme, Andrea says that the Holocaust years were "a wonderful time," as he mimes playing an imaginary violin and whistling. "We were in the forest, played Robin Hood, I picked mushrooms. We were all together. I had fun during the Holocaust." As in other third-generation documentaries, which show how other disasters affected the survivors, Andrea claims that the real trauma in his life was the death of his wife, Edna, who was assaulted when she was seventy-three years old. A mugger beat her, her memory deteriorated, and she passed away. When roaming the woods in Italy, Andrea carves their names on a tree like a teenager in love. The only time in the film he looks grim is when he describes this event.

The facts presented in *Shalom Italia* regarding the family's fate during the Holocaust are not the center of the story. Bits and pieces recalled by the brothers are mentioned, including that they fled from one place to another, then hid in the cave, and hence were saved. The crux of the film however, is their vastly different recollections of the past.

Since immigrating to Israel in 1945, the brothers have never traveled anywhere together and their current trip together generates numerous humorous scenes. The bickering between the brothers, which is deliberately given a great deal of screen time, is presented in a very light, comic fashion. Tal-Anati deliberately accentuates the irrelevant moments of the search, such at getting to the villa they will share, their small concerns. It is these minor things that reveal the tremendous differences between the brothers: Meme complains (the room is too cold, there is no stereo, is there Wi-Fi?); happy Andrea puts his clothes away and exercises; Boobi helps Meme resolve the accommodation problems. "Great place," Boobi and Andrea say. "If it were heated better it would have been ideal," Meme replies. "Fantastic," Andrea says joyfully in another scene in which after breakfast, Boobi explains the itinerary for the day. "If we keep on chitchatting, we'll eat lunch at home," Meme replies as he turns to go. Their arguments about who is supposed to make breakfast, when are they supposed to start out for the day, or what happened in the cave are often accompanied by circus-like music. Tal-Anati inserts "comic relief" scenes between the scenes of the search, thus giving *Shalom Italia* a light tone, like other third-generation documentaries. For example, after a scene in the car in which the brothers argue about being hungry in the cave, Tal-Anati cuts to a scene in a delicatessen with close-ups on cheeses and sausages and documents their gastronomic grocery list as they buy the finest products.

Boobi drives the car since he is the one leading this expedition. Because *Shalom Italia* is a film about memory, Tal-Anati combines superimposition (old photos of the brothers) with black-and-white scenes from documentaries that illustrate what they remember of the past. These superimpositions are short and fragmented, as are the brothers' memories. During the trip they travel down roads they remember are near the cave and should lead toward it. They cannot remember its exact location. "Try to remember, how did you get down to the village?" Boobi says to Meme but he does not remember. Claiming he is tired, Meme asks to stop climbing the mountain. His tiredness is logical but he also uses it as an excuse not to continue seeking the past. Even though Andrea assures Meme that there are outcroppings he can use to support himself, Meme refuses. Since it is a joint journey they all stop for the day.

As in *The Cahana Sisters*, Meme and Andrea agree on the frame story, but disagree on everything else when it comes to details. They agree that their family escaped death several times: the first time they fled Florence, afterward they escaped from Campoli, and the third time they escaped from the house the family had rented in a village to the cave their father built, where the two parents, four children, and two grandmothers hid during the winter of 1943. But Meme and Andrea disagree on the details that make up the story. Meme recalls that they were constantly hungry in the cave. Andrea does not remember they suffered from hunger. They answer Boobi's questions with contradictory answers: "Who went down to the grocery to buy food?" he asks them. "We ourselves did," Andrea answers. "No. We never went down to the grocery," Meme claims. "We went to the farmers to buy eggs and flour. That's it." Andrea recalls, "We had a wonderful life, me and Meme," and nostalgically remembers the bows and arrows they played with. "We've made our own arrows," Meme says. "No!" Andrea states decisively, "The arrows were bought." "No," Meme insists, trying to show Andrea how wrong he is when asking where they bought them and whether he believes that when they had to flee Florence they packed bows with them. "No doubt. Two arrows. My memory about it is not vague. I have a clear-cut memory of it," Andrea answers. During the journey their bickering continues: Did the Italian family who helped them get jewelry or money? What was the name of the house they were born in? Was the cave covered in tarpaulin or tiles? When they get to their old house in Campoli, Andrea walks around, remaining his cheerful self, while Meme looks sad and his misery is clear while in his voice-over he says that when they fled it was rainy and muddy; he lost a shoe but they could not stop, and even though it hurt him, he would not let himself cry. Andrea and Boobi open a bottle of wine, and a picnic basket filled with bread, cheese, and sausage. Meme sits alone on the side. They ask him to join them and he does so reluctantly. "It [this visit] doesn't help me in any way. It only reminds me of the suffering, the confusion." "Oh, oh, what suffering," Andrea mocks him, "I had a wonderful time here." Meme tries to explain that this is exactly the difference: Andrea was a child, "and I became an adult before my time."

The brothers not only contradict each other but also the stories of the villagers. Boobi says that when he walked into the village at the foot of the cave, an old woman approached him and asked if he was Emmanuel. She took him to a house, showed him a hole leading to a small cellar, and claimed that this is where her family helped his family hide their goods. Now and then her father sold something to a pawnbroker and used the money to buy food for them. Meme and his father used to come at night and take the food. Meme and Andrea reject that story: "I think this is a fairytale invented by the villagers," Meme claims. "We didn't have any silver or gold, only cash, that father got by selling his business. Him and mom kept it on their bodies." Andrea recalls the same.

During most of their disagreements and bickering Boobi is silent and listens, but the cinematic language points to the fact that he leans more toward Andrea. For example, in Campoli he and Andrea sit on one side of an outcropping while Meme is at a distance. In the following scene Boobi and Andrea are presented taking a nap together in the car, their body postures in the exact same position, while Meme is shot alone outside. "You take life too seriously. Lighten up," they tell Meme. "Life is beautiful. Go with the flow." But Meme cannot. At one point, after they bicker over whether a family in the village "saved them" or just "didn't hand them over to the authorities," and Meme states again that "there will always be doubts," Boobi bursts out: "Again you doubt the doubt and question, and contradict again and again, leave it like that. Maybe it is true, maybe it is not." "Okay," Meme agrees. "This is why I use the words 'doubt.' We will accept the story as a story." "I accept it as fact," Boobi states. Amazingly, in their encounter with the family in which the grandmother repeats the story of the hidden gold, Meme is the one to tell them that his only positive memory from those troubled times is in fact that this family "saved us," thus accepting the story he and Andrea resisted at the beginning of the journey.

Tal-Anati uses Meme as a mouthpiece to represent *Shalom Italia*'s main point, which has been acknowledged in Holocaust research: each historical chronology, whether historical writing or testimony, is always partial, subjective, and constitutes a narrative. "Everything that is written in history books is filled with lies," Meme tells his brothers as they eat dinner together. "What really happened we don't know and we will never know." Andrea is upset: "No, no, no! Don't say it didn't happen." Meme maintains his opinion and calmly replies that there are and will always be different versions.

In the end, the three brothers find the cave. Since Meme has problems climbing, he and Boobi rest while Andrea roams the woods and finds the location. Boobi shouts excitedly because he remembers that as a child, they were not allowed to shout or cry. The following scene is of the family celebrating Passover. The combination of the two scenes hints that finding the cave is an act of liberation, and is symbolic of the way they were liberated after hiding in the cave during the Holocaust. The final scenes show the brothers bringing their families there, preparing a plaque to commemorate the place, and placing it near the entrance. The fact that *Shalom Italia* is not only about a search is reflected in the cinematic choice of the last scene, which does not end with this happy family reunion near the cave. Instead, Tel-Anati concentrates on Meme's words and images in which he contradicts notions that appear in second-generation documentaries. He is filmed in an extreme long shot in the open desert and his voice is heard. He talks about human memory a thousand years from now when World War II and the Holocaust will only be an instant in time. The extreme long shot reflects human insignificance against the vastness of nature. The fact that Meme does not treat the Holocaust as the most important event in his life or in history contrasts with second-generation films, which concentrate almost entirely on it. The final sentence of *Shalom Italia* is Meme's final sentence: "We are made of memory." This cinematic choice deliberately sabotages the closure near the cave and reminds viewers that even though the brothers have found the cave, they have not resolved their disputes, and the past will never be completely recovered. Tal-Anati states that it did not matter whether they found the cave since "this is a film about coping with childhood trauma and the decisive essence of memory."[57] Even though the cave is found, the brothers, the director, and viewers will never be able to determine what really happened during those years. Each brother has his own contradictory memories and Boobi, who was very young, will not be able to find "the truth" because there is no such thing, only subjective partial memories.

"Testimonial injustice" is a fairly recent concept in ethics and epistemology. The philosopher Miranda Fricker defines it as the prejudice-driven discounting of a speaker's or writer's credibility. She argues that such discounting affects testifiers primarily in their capacity as knowers, and that it is often accompanied by secondary damage such as mockery or diminished self-confidence.[58] The documentaries analyzed in this chapter appear to reflect this ethical problem because they seemingly discount the survivors' credibility and undermine their perception as knowers. However, documenting the problems of memory and disclosing to the public what Holocaust researchers have been discussing since the 1950s does not constitute "testimonial injustice" in these films. Rather, it is an important way of dealing with the complex nature of testimonies that the general public should be aware of. This complexity does not deny survivors' importance as witnesses. On the contrary, these films represent the survivors in a loving, respectful manner, giving central stage to their perspectives and their pain while showing that there is an important story each and every one of them can tell even though the details may be historically incorrect. Documents alone cannot supply a historical account, and testimonies are not enough without documents. These documentaries substantiate researchers' claims that testimony is composed of pieces of memory. It does not make a complete statement, nor a comprehensive report of the events, but it leads to a broadly distributed authority for making new sense of the past in the present.[59]

5

Looking beyond the Victims

Nazis, Bystanders, and Their Descendants

For many years, Israeli culture mostly recoiled from dealing with perpetrators, their descendants, or bystanders. Israeli documentaries focused on Holocaust survivors, their stories, their posttraumatic reactions, and the transgenerational transfer of the trauma. Historical TV films dealt with the rise of the Third Reich and historical accounts of Nazism. This chapter discusses the ways in which third-generation documentaries deal with "the other side" by exploring the perspectives of perpetrators, bystanders, and both these groups' descendants. It analyzes how directors have begun to paint an in-depth portrait of themes not previously represented, such as the private lives of the SS, the ways in which the perpetrators' offspring cope with their families' pasts, the complexity of the term *bystanders* and its many facets. The chapter analyzes the third-generation documentaries *Kleiner Rudi* (Michelle Stein-Teer, 2006), *The Flat* (Arnon Goldfinger, 2011), *Hitler's Children* (Chanoch Ze'evi, 2011), *The Most Beautiful Woman* (Maya Sarfaty, 2016), *The Decent One* (Vanessa Lapa, 2014), and *Out of the Forest* (Yaron Kaftory Ben-Yosef and Limor Pinhasov Ben-Yosef, 2004), and compares them to the second-generation TV documentary *Healing by Killing* (Nitzan Aviram, 1996).

Second-Generation Documentaries

As noted, most second-generation documentaries address the victims. Few TV documentaries have discussed the chronology of Nazi atrocities and prominent Nazi figures. The TV documentary *Healing by Killing*, directed by Nitzan Aviram and released in 1989, is exceptional because it does not solely deal with the Holocaust but also discusses the Nazi euthanasia program, which laid the groundwork for the extermination of the Jews. The film portrays two major doctors, Dr. Irmfried Eberl and Prof. Carl Clauberg, high-ranking Nazi physicians who betrayed the Hippocratic oath. Eberl was the director of several euthanasia institutes and, for a period, the commander of the Treblinka extermination camp. Clauberg, a gynecologist, was a member of the medical experiments team in Auschwitz (in Block 10). Through a combination of in-depth investigations, multiple locations, interviews with euthanasia survivors, doctors who operated at that time, the doctors' assistants, psychiatrists, and researchers, director Nitzan Aviram portrays the first large-scale mass murder in Germany. The first half of *Healing by Killing* (fifty minutes) is devoted to Eberl, the second to Clauberg, but the story concerns many more individuals—"two of many" who turned killing into a form of healing, says Aviram in his narration.

Aviram presents Eberl's and Clauberg's lives chronologically as he films different places where they lived and describes the way they climbed the Nazi ladder and became prominent figures in the Nazi death industry. Aviram's camera roams the empty institutes and the Auschwitz barracks while narrating every detail of the process. While a historian outlines the nature of the injections Clauberg tested on female prisoners (what they contained, how they were chosen, the way they felt, the pain and suffering of the victims from the moment they arrived at the institute until they were gassed), Aviram follows the route with the camera, goes down to the basement, films the gas chamber door opening and closing, the fake shower heads in close-up, and ends by showing the false death certificates issued by the doctors. Aviram also briefly mentions other doctors who conducted experiments in Auschwitz, including Josef Mengele. He interviews Wilhelm Brasa, a Jew who was an inmate at Auschwitz and was ordered to photograph the experiments. Aviram's camera wanders through the halls of Block 10 as Brasa describes what it looked like during the war and the horrific experiments done on twins, triplets, and Gypsies, as well as Jewish women.

Using photos, documents, and present-day scenes, Aviram makes it clear that euthanasia involved numerous doctors (patient selection, examination, paperwork, delivery to the gas chamber, signing false death certificates, collecting body parts for further medical experiments), nurses, and staff (secretaries, drivers, gas-chamber operators), thus clarifying that it was a vast enterprise. The interviews with accomplices highlight the fact that many "ordinary" Germans took a part in these killing operations.[1] Heinrich Hermans, a transport supervisor at Bedburg-Hau, sits facing the camera and talks very laconically about transporting patients to their death, and the train carriages he was in charge of. When one patient tried to escape, Hermans pushed him in, and the patient was severely hurt: "It was very good for me," Hermans smiles, "he was already finished." Aviram also interviews Dr. Hans Münch, a former Auschwitz staff member who supervised the employees who experimented on ways to prevent epidemics in the concentration camps. His narrative expresses admiration—"It was fascinating. They were the best professionals in Europe and their attitude was exceptional." He describes Mengele as the only person he could "have a normal conversation" with. Aviram highlights the self-deception mechanism of Nazis, when Hermans states that he was not part of the killing machine because he refused to take an active part in the selections.

Aviram films researchers who show how the euthanasia programs prepared the infrastructure for the Holocaust. The killing methods developed was the beginnings of the operations developed in the extermination camps. These methods—including misleading victims, killing by gas, and burning the bodies—were all based on the euthanasia system. "Treblinka, Sobibór, and Bełżec were exactly like the Brandenburg and Bernburg euthanasia centers only on a larger scale. Without their work and the eagerness of these doctors, the Holocaust might not have happened." To stress his point, Aviram alternates between close-ups of the gas chamber in Brandenburg and the gas chambers in Majdanek and Auschwitz.[2]

Throughout *Healing by Killing* Aviram questions how these doctors could betray their Hippocratic oath. The well-known psychiatrist and academic Robert J. Lipton suggested that these individuals transformed their actions into a therapeutic process where a doctor provided treatment. Professor Benu Miller-Hill, of the Genetics Institute at Cologne University, claims that at that time, the notion of *volk* (*Ein Volk, ein Reich, ein Führer*, "One people, one nation, one leader") was far more important than the individual and hence enabled the euthanasia of those who were considered aliens. Aviram does not only deal with the past. The interviews he conducts with German medical students today suggests that these future doctors are uncertain as to the nature of ethics or the Hippocratic oath. One student is aware of its value in general. Another student states that their heavy course load does not give them the time to study ethics since they need to absorb so much to become "reasonably good doctors." *Healing by Killing* thus suggests that a present-day lack of concern for ethics could lay the groundwork for past horrors to return.

Third-Generation Documentaries: Perpetrators, Bystanders, and Their Descendants

Third-generation films broaden this initial outlook to "the other side" and ask to explore it by addressing questions and topics that have been marginalized in Israeli documentary and Israeli Holocaust commemorations. They deal with four generations of Germans, in a sense entering the "heart of darkness" by exploring the way the German nation, past, and present is coping with Nazi ideology, the Holocaust, and its aftereffects and by exploring bystanders in other nations and their offspring.

Dealing with the Nazi Past in Germany and Israel

Third-generation documentaries provide Israeli audiences with a cinematic exploration of the ways Nazis dealt with their deeds and the way their offspring deal with the past. These themes had appeared in research in Germany and Israel, but until the last few decades were rarely discussed in Israeli culture, which has tended to emphasize victims and their offspring.

Even though there are some conservative German historians who claim that Germany dealt bravely with its past as of the aftermath of World War II, most historians have documented a narrative of silence, repression, denial, and self-victimization in Germany up to the 1960s.[3] Rarely was the Holocaust mentioned in public addresses. Roger Frie claims that blame was apportioned to the Nazi leaders, such that the public's interpretation of the outcome of the Nuremberg trials was that most "ordinary" Germans could remain silent about their role in the Nazi horrors.[4] Those who were adults during World War II mostly remained silent because they were part of the Nazi regime or backed it with their silence. Younger people who made up the Hitlerjugend generation remained silent because their world had collapsed.[5] Alongside this silence, a discourse of victimization emerged. In this narrative, most Germans saw the Nazi leaders as guilty, which enabled them to portray Germans as victims of the Nazis. They cite the four million Germans who were killed in World War II, the millions who were expelled or uprooted from their homes in the East, the approximately four hundred thousand who were killed in the Allied bombings, and those killed and raped by the Red Army.[6] In this narrative, the German public is represented as being helpless in the grips of a terrorist regime. By claiming that only a small group of criminals (the Nazis) were responsible for the Holocaust, the victimization approach constructed a difference between "us" and "them."[7] From the 1950s until 1989, when Germany was reunified, the discourse of victimization existed in East and West Germany, but the identity of the victimizer was different. In East Germany, Hitler and his cohorts were described as imperialists, whereas in West Germany they were considered Stalin's henchmen.[8]

The descendants of Nazis began to attract research attention in Germany in the 1960s. West Germany was witnessing a new generation of Germans who were met with silence when attempting to seek answers about the past. The German media coverage of Adolf

Eichmann's trial in Jerusalem in 1961 and the Frankfurt Auschwitz trials in 1963–65, the renewal of diplomatic relations with Israel in 1965, and Willy Brandt's 1969 slogan *Mehr Demokratie wagen* ("Let's dare more democracy") began to change families' and the public's way of grappling with the past.[9]

In 1959 the German journalist Norbert Lebert interviewed the adult children of prominent Nazis and published them as a series in the magazine *Weltbild*. As a result, Lebert was showered with hate mail from Germans who did not appreciate him breaking the taboo.[10] But from the 1960s onward, many broke the silence and hammered their parents with inconvenient questions, and, as Mary Fulbrook states, "began to scratch the surface of convenient post-war myths."[11] Collective guilt was manifested symbolically when it became fashionable to give children Jewish names or volunteer on Israeli kibbutzim. One of the best-known enactments of this ritual guilt was when German chancellor Willy Brandt knelt before the monument to the victims of the Warsaw Ghetto uprising in 1970.[12] In 1987 German television networks screened a series of interviews with the descendants of Nazis. *Born Guilty: Children of Nazi Families*, published in 1987 by the Austrian journalist Peter Sichrovsky, also provided a forum for monologues and dialogues with Nazis' offspring.[13] In 1988 the English translation of *Born Guilty* was published. In 2000 a number of German empirical studies were conducted.[14] Second-generation perpetrators have been publishing their memoirs and prose that present their ways of handling the familial legacy.[15] Katrin Himmler's book on the Himmler brothers was published in Germany in 2005 and in England in 2007.[16] The 2013 French TV documentary *Descendants of Nazis: An Infernal Heritage* features Nazi descendants who converted to Judaism and/or moved to Israel. The documentary examines the dichotomy between the German collective acknowledgment of the Holocaust and the personal silence within families.

However, this change in mentality was neither rapid nor absolute. The book *The Inability to Mourn: Principles of Collective Behavior* (1967, English trans. 1975) by Margareta and Alexander Mitscherlich is considered to be the most incisive introspection on the Nazi past in Germany on the eve of the 1968 revolution. The Mitscherlichs claim that Nazi history was deliberately silenced by the German state and its institutions, and that the younger generation of the 1960s embraced the denial and repression that had been cultivated in the German public sphere since 1945.[17] In addition, the perception of the suffering of "innocent Germans" during World War II did not disappear.[18] The 1978 American miniseries *Holocaust*, which was broadcast in Germany in 1979, is considered to be another turning point.[19] After the reunification of Germany in 1989, commemorating the Holocaust, public remorse and debates about the Nazi atrocities, and publications revealing the extent of crimes "ordinary Germans" were capable of became a part of the public discourse (e.g., Thomas Kohuts's 2012 book *A German Generation: An Exceptional History of the Twentieth Century*).[20] Simultaneously there was, nevertheless, a growing trend to accentuate the suffering of German civilians as victims of Nazism and then as the victims of the liberating armies.[21] For example, the traveling exhibition *Crimes of the Wehrmacht* aroused controversy in the mid- to late 1990s. It drew attention to "ordinary grandfathers," and raised questions about the complicity of far wider circles among the German people, undermining the earlier, convenient circumscription of the perpetrators to the demonized circles of Hitler and his henchmen, the SS, and the Gestapo. Others point out that there is widespread indifference and even hostility toward Holocaust remembrance.[22]

Israelis' relationships to post–World War II Germany and descendants of Nazis were and are very complex. Since the 1950s, there are continued debates in the Israeli sphere whether Germany after 1945 was different from Nazi Germany. The term *another Germany* was first coined in the early 1950s during the stormy public controversy over financial reparations from Germany whether to differentiate between Nazi Germany and Chancellor Konrad Adenauer's Germany (1949–63). In the 1950s many Israelis identified Adenauer's Germany with Hitler's Germany, and the undeclared but official policy was to boycott West Germany completely. However, in fact, immediately after the war, formal and informal relations were established between

Jewish organizations and representatives of the left-wing Mapai Party (which governed Israel) and Germans regarding reparations. The proponents advocated a rational approach to the harsh economic conditions facing the state of Israel and put the good of the country first.[23]

The issue of reparations generated an outcry from the right-wing Herut opposition party but also from within Mapai itself and other left-wing parties, which was accompanied by demonstrations and public debates. The left-wing opponents included Mapam (the United Workers' Party), which claimed that negotiations would desecrate the memory of the resistance heroes that Mapam saw itself as representing. Maki (the Israel Communist Party) opposed negotiations with West Germany and favored relations with the East. The right-wing Herut movement headed by Menachem Begin rejected negotiations with the perpetrators. Members of Herut claimed that there could be no compensation for Jewish blood; that the reparations were humiliating, a symbol of the "disgrace of exile," and would be a stain on the national honor. They argued that German money would be impure; that the concept of *another Germany* was phony and had no basis in reality. Even within Mapai, whose members spearheaded the process, some opposed any contact with Germany.[24]

After extremely heated sessions, the Knesset voted to initiate negotiations with Germany. In the end, the reparations agreement between Israel and Germany—the Luxembourg Agreement—stated that Israel would receive reparations for "the resettlement of uprooted and destitute Jewish refugees," and in the form of individual reparations to Holocaust survivors (under certain conditions related to their imprisonment and/or forced labor).[25] Although the reparations were paid, the question of "another Germany" remains contentious even today, and opinions are divided as to whether Germany after 1945 can be considered different from Nazi Germany, and whether Jewish Israelis can create some sort of "normalcy" with Germans and the German space.

Na'ama Sheffi argued that as of the late 1960s, and especially in the 1970s and 1980s, there was a change in the way the Israelis treated Germany and Nazism, where contempt and estrangement gave way to huge interest. During this time numerous translations of postwar Germany literature, including works by authors such as Günter Grass, Heinrich Böll, and Siegfried Lenz appeared in Hebrew. Sheffi suggested that responses to German films also reflected curiosity about Germany.[26] Despite this interest, there was uproar in Israel when diplomatic ties were established with Germany in the 1960s and it was discovered that Israel was selling arms to Germany. This issue made the headlines again in 1972 when Israeli athletes were murdered at the Munich Olympics. The combination of a terror attack on German soil and the ongoing debates regarding German conduct during and after the massacre contributed to the already complex relationship between Israel and Germany. In 1976 this was further aggravated when an Air France plane on its way from Ben Gurion Airport to Paris was hijacked with about one hundred Jewish Israeli passengers aboard. During the hijacking and the negotiations with the hijackers, who flew the plane to Uganda, it was discovered that some of the crew were radical German leftists who had joined Palestinian terrorist groups.

This complexity was further fueled by a debate between historians in the 1990s as to whether Germans have specific traits that make them an anti-Semitic nation (as was claimed by Daniel Goldhagen)[27] or whether the Holocaust could happen anywhere and to any nation, and was carried out by "ordinary people" who obeyed authority and not by individuals with a special legacy and characteristics different from other nations (as was claimed by Christopher Browning).[28] The fall of the Berlin Wall in 1989, the reunification of Germany, and the recent rise of neo-Nazis in Germany have continued to make the relationship of Jewish Israelis to Germany a complex one. These mixed attitudes toward Germans and Germany are reflected in surveys.[29] Although Israeli Jews still express curiosity which is apparent in cultural texts and writings in Hebrew about Germany and Nazism, suspicion and hard feelings are there as well.[30] This curiosity, however, was on the margins of Holocaust commemoration. Third-generation documentaries were the first to explore this complex topic and present its range of issues.

The way the offspring of Nazi Germans deal with their families' pasts is also a complex subject in Germany and in Israel. Before the third-generation documentaries, only a few Jewish Israelis dared to touch on the subject. In the 1960s the historian Shlomo Aronson interviewed the son of former senior Nazi officer Reinhard Heydrich, one of the chief architects of the Holocaust. He argued that "as early as the 1960s, a number of descendants of the Nazis were willing to talk. Heydrich's son was three years old when his father was killed by British special operations commandos in 1942, so he does not feel responsible for his actions . . . There were some people in Israel who objected to the fact that I had interviewed the son of a Nazi . . ." Aronson was similarly criticized when he conducted another interview with a former senior Nazi official, Albert Speer, which was published in *Haaretz* in 1964.[31] In 1972 an interview with Manfred Rommel, the son of Field Marshal Erwin Rommel, the commander of the Nazi Western Desert Force, was published in the Israeli newspaper *Davar*. Although Rommel was not a Nazi war criminal per se, he held a key position within the Nazi war machine, and an interview with his son was unusual in the Israeli press. In the interview, Rommel claimed that disillusionment and the exposure of lies and misconceptions at the end of the war prompted him and many of his contemporaries to get involved in more democratic forms of politics.[32]

Another turning point came in 2011, when certain descendants of Nazis visited the Knesset and proclaimed that even their deepest apologies could not make up for acts of the past. They emphasized their dedication to the fight against anti-Semitism.[33] Since 2016 the Israeli media have occasionally published stories on the March of Life, a German movement of third-generation Nazi offspring who want to atone for their families' crimes by commemorating the Holocaust and establishing a strong connection to Israel.[34] A few books dealing with Nazi offspring have been translated into Hebrew,[35] and stories of Nazi descendants who converted to Judaism and immigrated to Israel have appeared in the last decade several times in the Israel media.[36]

One of the first people to try and include Nazi descendants in Israeli Holocaust commemorations was the psychologist Dan

Bar-On. His research dealt with the implications of the Holocaust on the perpetrators' offspring in Germany.[37] When Bar-On began his work in the 1980s, he was surprised how little literary and academic research had been done on the coping mechanisms of the children of perpetrators, as opposed to the dozens of articles on second generation Holocaust survivors. Bar-On stated that he intentionally avoided interviewing the children of famous Nazi perpetrators, such as the sons of Rudolf Hess and Joseph Mengele, who had already received public attention, because he feared that they had developed an "external self" to discuss their fathers and the Third Reich. Instead, Bar-On sought out, and located, people whose feelings about the past and the participation of their fathers in the genocide had until then been part of an internal dialogue.

In interviews Bar-On conducted between 1985 and 1987, out of the fifty-eight sons and daughters of Nazis he approached, nine refused to meet him. Only one descendant agreed to reveal his name. Bar-On discovered that the coping mechanisms of the interviewees were multifaceted. Some denied the facts, while others acknowledged them; some continued to admire their fathers, and others developed an antagonism toward their parents; some accepted the "collective silence," while others tried to break it. Beginning in 1992, Bar-On also initiated and facilitated meetings between offspring of Holocaust survivors and offspring of Nazi perpetrators. During these meetings, which were held once a year, he attempted to broaden the ways the Holocaust had been examined in Israel.[38]

Bar-On and Israel Charny's analysis of interviews with the children of Nazis enabled them to identify seven moral excuses cited by Germans: (1) the Holocaust did not take place; (2) the Jews did it to themselves; (3) Auschwitz was not a death camp; (4) the Germans suffered as well; (5) my family members did not take part in the atrocities; (6) my family members were forced to do it; and (7) my family members took part in the atrocities, or my family members were part of the horrors, but I am not sure I would have done something different.[39] Bar-On and his colleagues' work did not reach the general public. Third-generation documentaries that deal with the first-generation and second-generation perpetrators' perspectives have reached wider publics and have added another layer to the Israeli Holocaust commemoration.[40]

The Encounter/Confrontation with Four Generations of Germans in Kleiner Rudi

At the beginning of *Kleiner Rudi*, which presents director Stein Teer's journey with her grandfather Rudi, back in his hometown of Norden, Germany (parts of which were analyzed in chapter 2), she says that she always refused to go to Germany, but she acquiesced when her grandfather asked her to come along. "I wanted to see Germany through his eyes." However, the film shows that the journey, which Stein Teer depicts as her grandfather's journey into the past, is in fact her own attempt to deal with it. Since Rudi had gone back to Norden many times, the film focuses on Stein Teer's first trip and encounters with four generations of Germans—from the elderly who lived under the Nazi regime to high school students. Throughout *Kleiner Rudi*, Stein Teer films herself in many of the scenes, accompanies her encounters with her voice-overs, and expresses her complex feelings about the generations of Germans. The film is not only a geographic journey but also a mental one that tries to make sense of the varied and complex ways of dealing with the past in contemporary Germany.

As noted in chapter 4, third-generation documentaries are the first to address the many facets of bystanders in-depth. Instead of focusing solely on victims, the directors hear and document the local population. They address various deeds and behaviors that range from passive observers to those who benefitted, the collaborators and the perpetrators—see *Martin*, *Shalom Italia*, *Kleiner Rudi*, *Lerner's Revenge*, *The Dark Side*, and *Out of the Forest*. When representing Germans who lived under the Third Reich, *Kleiner Rudi*, like *Martin*, presents individuals who remained passive. On his trips, Rudi renewed relationships with people he knew as a child, such as Hans Karl Kortman, a priest. The close friendship between the two ("I've lived in Israel for seventy years, and I don't have a friend as close as he is," Rudi says), which is illustrated in the film, shows that as in *The Flat*, the grandparents' path to forgiveness was sometimes easier than that of the grandchildren.

In *Kleiner Rudi* the European landscape is not the backdrop for familial dialogue (by contrast to many second-generation documentaries) but rather a space that allows for encounters and/or confrontations with the locals regarding the Holocaust, its echoes, and the way they live in its shadows. Rudi himself is not concerned with questions such as who knew at the time what was happening or the way his German friends deal with the past. Stein Teer, however, enters her grandfather's world and asks four generations of Germans the questions he did not and does not ask, but are of interest to her. In one scene, when Rudi and his friend Lena, who is his age, are talking, Stein Teer interrupts the conversation to inquire why Lena is so interested in Jews and Israelis. Rudi, who translates her question into German, is embarrassed, and tells Lena, "It's her question, not mine." In another scene, Rudi lectures high school students and tells them that he does not blame the postwar generation. They are silent. Unlike her grandfather, Stein Teer does not accept this silence. She rushes into the frame and demands to hear their opinions. Her conversations with Germans create a transgenerational outlook on the trauma from both sides, not only from victims' perspective.

Kleiner Rudi is a cinematic documentation of the Germans' multifaceted struggle to come to grips with their past. On her journey Stein Teer discovers that in a lecture about Norden, the lecturer conveniently jumps from the 1930s to the 1950s, and does not mention World War II at all; Rudi's former classmates detach themselves from the events and choose to repeat clichés, including, "we couldn't have known" and "it was an awful era." Some Germans from Rudi's generation research the Holocaust to find out as much information as they can, whereas others confess to what they knew, saw, and thought: in one scene Ursula, who is Rudi's age, asks Stein Teer to sit with her in her car. The closed car becomes a confession booth.

Only there, for the first time in her life, does Ursula confess that as a child she saw the town's synagogue being burned down. She says that what she saw remains engraved in her mind, but she has never mentioned it to anyone. Although Ursula was only ten years old at the start of World War II, she admits that she too was influenced by Nazi propaganda and believed that the Jews might devour her. While Ursula tells Stein Teer these stories, she is distraught and emotional, and has trouble breathing. The frames are closed, which increases the audience's identification with the feelings and memories that are suffocating Ursula. Thus, even though Ursula tells a story that Jewish Israelis may find difficult to accept, the aesthetic cinematic staging is aimed to create identification with her.

From Stein Teer's conversations with second-generation Germans, she realizes the extent of silencing in Germany. A tour guide who takes them around town tells her that the first time she heard about the Holocaust was at the age of twelve or thirteen, when a teacher showed them scenes from films of the liberated camps. She and her classmates were shocked. She says that even though she was born after World War II, she feels guilty. However, alongside this silence, it is clear that Stein Teer and her grandfather only came to Norden because in 1985 a group of residents decided to commemorate the Jews of Norden and worked hard for many years to build a memorial. Third- and fourth-generation Germans take a variety of stances ranging from interest in investigating the past and learning more, to shame, a lack of interest in knowing, difficulties handling the emotional burden, and a feeling that in Germany the Holocaust is discussed so much that it has become "boring." The scenes presenting these voices in contemporary Germany echo the debate in Israel since the 1950s regarding the question of "another Germany."

The interviews in *Kleiner Rudi* encourage viewers to abandon clichés such as the "other Germany," and do not enable another generalization, which was common in Israel, to view all Germans, past and present, as anti-Semites who have repressed their nation's atrocities. The film rejects these binary divisions and forces viewers to acknowledge the complexity and multiple facets of this topic.

Kleiner Rudi does not address the question of whether it is possible to forgive the Germans. Neither Rudi's perspective nor that of his granddaughter can provide definitive answers. "This is the first time I have felt a stronger atmosphere of goodwill," Rudi says to Stein Teer. However, the interviews Stein Teer conducts and the questions she asks people she encounters reveal the broad spectrum of ways that Germans cope with the past. These scenes negate Rudi's statement and prompt viewers to see his feelings as subjective. "I understand the magnitude of the loss and the courage of my grandfather who, at the age of eighty-five, must deal with a wound that will never heal," Stein Teer concludes. "His greatness is his ability to reconcile, accept that you cannot change history," she declares while filming Rudi in Israel with their large family. However, Stein Teer's perspective tells a much more entangled story of a nation that alternates between commemoration, guilt, shame, and denial.

Denial among Second-Generation Germans in The Flat

Kleiner Rudi dealt with the responses to the past of four generations of Germans, but none of the interviewers were offspring of high-ranking Nazis. *The Flat* (parts of which were analyzed in chapter 2) not only deals with the question of memory in Israel but also with the issue of memory in Germany through conversations Goldfinger has with Edda, the daughter of Leopold von Mildenstein, a high-ranking Nazi who befriended his grandparents before and after the Holocaust. Through these encounters, *The Flat* breaks the code of silence in Israeli documentary regarding the "other side" and presents the difficulties faced by the perpetrators' offspring in dealing with their parents' past.

One quarter of the film (twenty-five minutes) is devoted to Edda, Leopold von Mildenstein's daughter. The scenes present a complex portrait of a sweet "auntie," who is also the daughter of a Nazi who refuses to acknowledge her father's past and proclaims, "my father did not do it." Edda clings to the perception that her father was a journalist who left for the United States during World War II. Even when Goldfinger presents Edda with the facts, she maintains her denial. For example, she shows Goldfinger a newspaper article entitled "Goebbels' People Help Nasser," which claims that after World War II von Mildenstein was a member of a group of former Nazis who helped produce a series of violent stories against Jews for an Egyptian radio station. Edda tells him proudly about the successful libel suit filed against the journalist by her father.

In a highly charged scene, Goldfinger, who shares his dilemmas with the audience via voice-over, decides to confront Edda with the details he reveals later during his investigations. He shows her von Mildenstein's curriculum vitae, written in his own handwriting, stating that he served as head of department in the SD (1935–36) and head of department in Goebbels's ministry of propaganda (1938–45). As opposed to Edda's notions, her father was abroad only for one year in 1937 and not during the entire war, and he was not a journalist. Edda refuses to accept this. Goldfinger, who states this is one of the most important scenes in *The Flat*, is aware of the fact that this confrontation is controversial and says that it was resented by both German and Israeli audiences: "I felt I should do it," he says.[41] The scene highlights the power of repression and denial since even after Goldfinger's clear revelations, Edda refuses to face reality. Her husband, Harold, supports her and tries to undermine the historical facts from a different angle and explain to Goldfinger that not all Nazis were "bad" and many belonged to the party because they had to, and they did nothing "except wearing a pin showing their party membership."

Edda and Harold are not alone in their denial. From 1997 to 2000 the German social psychologist Harald Walzer surveyed forty-one second- and third-generation German families and showed how family members in twenty-six of these cases altered the history of their families during the Nazi period. In what Walzer called "cumulative heroization," they only remembered stories that were not related to the atrocities, although they knew them from their parents' and grandparents' depictions. They cling to every shred of evidence to invent their own versions of the past in which family members who lived during the Nazi era were good and innocent.[42] Other German historians have suggested that the process of transgenerational transfer is more complicated. Alexander von Plato wrote that transgenerational discourse also reveals much more indifference, suspicion, and disbelief.[43] Norbert Frei indicated that many of the perpetrators' children were those who turned against the silencing of the Holocaust in their parents' generation and demanded changes in Germany's collective memory of the Holocaust.[44] Erin McGlothlin's research on second-generation literature points to the various contradictory ways that descendants of perpetrators have written about their complex relationship with their family's Nazi past. She suggests that their parents' rejection of guilt, which takes the form of amnesia, puts a tremendous burden on the children and creates an inherited guilt that resists resolution.[45]

According to Anna Ornstein, for many children of perpetrators, their parents' stories conflicted with what they had learned about the Holocaust. Few confronted their parents. The majority engaged in "a psychological compromise: in order not to bring their love and loyalty into question, they joined their parents in their silence."[46] As suggested by the researcher Eric L. Santner, who claimed that people can acknowledge the historical facts of the Holocaust but continue to disavow its existential and experiential impact, the researcher Gabriele Schwab refers to the complex dynamic between knowing and not knowing. For those who grew up in post–World War II West Germany, as she did, the facts were not hidden. Schwab's generation learned about the Holocaust in their early teens in high school. They were given factual knowledge about historical events, yet "the silence was not broken" because there was no kind of emotional engagement at either the personal or collective levels. The open politics of acknowledgement of war crimes did not address responsibility, guilt, or shame. Thus the historical account did not break through the politics of silencing, denial, and disavowal. Santner argues that breaking this "emotional silence" is a collective responsibility. Consistent with McGlothlin she considers that the legacies of the descendants of victims and perpetrators are intertwined, and that the Holocaust is a "stain on the soul" on both sides of the barricade, but for different reasons.[47]

In his book *Not in My Family: German Memory and Responsibility After the Holocaust* (2017) the psychologist Roger Frie reveals the complicated attempts of Nazi descendants to deal with their familial past, but above all his personal journey into his own family's unspoken Nazi past. As a member of the third generation of a Nazi family, Frie has dealt openly and bravely with his history without "sitting in judgment" or "assigning blame" but also without concealing or embellishing the Nazi familial history.[48] "As a third generation German I have a responsibility to know about my family's history, an obligation that grows more relevant with time, not less. Current generations of Germans are not guilty for what took place long before they were born, but they have a responsibility to grapple with memory and avoid the kind of ambiguous and facile remembering that is really a form of forgetting."[49] In Frie's journey into the past, he had to overcome his parents' silence. He differentiates between two kinds of Holocaust memories in Germany: the public and the private. In Frie's view, the public memory (which appears in statements, memorials, high school curricula, etc.) assumes guilt and responsibility for the horrors of the Holocaust. However, private memory is more problematic, and families often know very little about their familial history during the Third Reich. Frie himself comes from a family of perpetrators—"I learned about the Holocaust early in life from my parents. It was important to them that I hear it at home, yet my grandparents' role in the Nazi era remained gray and murky."[50] He, too, acknowledges the similarities between descendants of perpetrators and victims, although acknowledges the vast differences between them.[51]

Edda's "cumulative heroization," her unwillingness to ask questions or acquire knowledge, resembles Hannah's (Goldfinger's mother) refusal to investigate the past. According to the cinema researcher Yael Munk, Goldfinger also uses cinematic language to highlight the similarities between Hannah (second-generation victim) and Edda (second-generation perpetrator), who both grew up in families that are silent about the past, each for a different (opposite) reason. Edda's response is cinematically visualized, as is Hannah's realization of the truth using the same shooting angle, the half-shadowed close-up, and the same silence (no background music) that accompanies the scene.[52] This hinted comparison blurs the binary divisions between the two sides and suggests a much more nuanced attitude toward the trauma than in the past.

This resemblance echoes researchers' arguments that despite the differences between children of victims and children of perpetrators, there are also similarities. For example, Dan Diner suggested that the German and Jewish lives are intertwined because traumatic histories in both groups affect their descendants.[53] McGlothlin states that both groups grew up in the shadow of the trauma they were not part of, but that shaped their lives. Even though their parents played completely different roles in the Holocaust, on both sides, the second generation is marked by their parents' experiences and shares the problem of feeling marked by the continued presence of the Holocaust. "Despite the gulf that separates the legacy of perpetrators from the legacy of survival and the qualitative differences in their perspectives, the children of survivors and the children of perpetrators are like two sides of the same coin, both must confront the aftermath of an event that they have not experienced." The critical difference between these two groups is guilt.[54]

Goldfinger notes that wherever *The Flat* was screened in Germany, the depiction of Edda was reviewed the most critically. Viewers saw her refusal to acknowledge the past in a very negative way. "Does it imply that today in Germany there is guilt? Shame? It is hard to say," Goldfinger says. Surprisingly, in Israel, Edda was viewed sympathetically, as someone who needed to be shielded from the director, who confronts her with her father's past. Goldfinger thinks that perhaps this is because she represents the general fear of facing the past: "What would happen if you learned things about your family history that you did not want to know? This fear does not only intimidate Nazi offspring." Hence even the responses to *The Flat* underscore its role in undermining stereotypes, blurring boundaries, and representing Holocaust commemoration in a more complex way that challenges perceptions of Israelis and Germans.

The Flat was very successful worldwide, including in Germany. Many viewers, especially third-generation Germans, told Goldfinger that the film encouraged them to start asking questions in their own family circles. In 2015 the film was officially made part of the German high school curriculum to encourage younger generations to look critically at their families' histories.[55]

"Cumulative Heroization" in The Most Beautiful Woman

Maya Sarfaty's short documentary, *The Most Beautiful Woman* (parts of which were discussed in chapter 1), presents the relationship between Helena Citronova, an inmate at Auschwitz, and the SS officer Franz Wunsch. Like many other third-generation films, *The Most Beautiful Woman* seeks out the voices of the perpetrators and their offspring that were marginalized in Israeli culture for so many years. The film discusses the relationship from various perspectives. Some of the voices that are heard in this Rashomon-like film are of Wunsch himself, and his daughter Dagmar. In an interview, Sarfaty claims that what drew her attention is that in spite of the dichotomy between victim and perpetrator, there is no black and white. She notes the disparity between "our perception of the Holocaust commemoration and the certain repression of the other side."[56] These attitudes are reflected in the film.

The historian Mary Fulbrook distinguishes between "communities of experience" (perpetrators) and "communities of connection" (perpetrators' relatives). She claims that "communities of experience" among perpetrators were not founded on shame and guilt as they were among the victims. Officially, the public cultures of both West Germany and East Germany allowed for the effective disappearance of guilt on the part of the vast majority of perpetrators, beyond the few vilified monsters at the top. Most of the perpetrators seem to have been able to live relatively undisturbed postwar lives and evade public view. Perpetrators' stories frequently rely on strategies of distancing themselves from evil. These include claims that they accomplished morally "good" deeds, which must be weighed in the balance, such as having allegedly given assistance or sustenance to prisoners, or having supposedly "tried to save a Jew." The perpetrator community thus denied responsibility and rejected guilt. Some of these perpetrators continued to sustain a Nazi world view; others transitioned seamlessly into the new postwar societies, and became conformist citizens of the new states. The past appears to have disturbed them most when there was a risk of being brought to court. Only rarely have perpetrators been personally troubled by memories of their misdeeds.[57]

In one scene, the camera moves from a still picture of young Wunsch to an interview which looks like a home movie from 2003 in which he tells his daughter about how he met Citronova at Auschwitz. Wunsch's dialogue with his daughter shows similarities. He expresses no remorse or regret. Wunsch talks about how he helped Citronova mentally and saved her when she suffered from typhus. The home-movie quality highlights his "humanity" by showing an elderly man, in shorts, sitting in his backyard discussing the past with his daughter in a very relaxed atmosphere. Wunsch does not refer to his role in the SS or to any other aspect of his work, only his kind relationship with Helena. The parallel editing between an interview with Helena, Wunsch's documentation, and parts of his diary, which is shown while his voice is heard, emphasize the complexity of the relationship and how a victim and a perpetrator could see the human side of each other. It also shows that an SS officer could be kind to one woman while mistreating and abusing others. This is intensified when Helena testifies that those who abused her were Jewish inmates who did not accept her well-known connection with Wunsch, and would beat and curse her. When Wunsch helped her when Helena was sick with typhus, a woman denounced him to the Gestapo, and he was sentenced according to the Nuremburg Laws, which prohibited contacts between Germans and Jews; however, the judge did not charge him.

Communities of Connection's Ambivalence toward the Past

According to Fulbrook, the "communities of connection" took on the burden of shame, but there are different attitudes toward the past. Some children of perpetrators simply deny the guilt of their parents and continue not to "see." Another widespread response is the vicarious shame often associated with attempts to work this through by more thorough exploration and understanding of the past. Some have engaged in extraordinary efforts to "make good again" through campaigns for compensation, restitution, or other good deeds. Identification with the victims was and is often a twisted emotional situation for individuals who continue to love but can no longer respect parents with compromised pasts.[58]

Dagmar represents the second generation's puzzled, ambivalent attitudes toward perpetrators. She does not reject or repress her father's deeds, but does not fully admit them. She is interviewed while in the background there is a large photograph of her as a teenager with her father. They are both happy, smiling, and give the impression of a normal family. Her stories back up this close relationship. Dagmar says that when she was seventeen her father gave her a locket with a picture of himself and Citronova. She was embarrassed that her father chose to give her a picture of Citronova and not her mother ("it should have been my mother in there"). In his obsession with Citronova, Dagmar's father made reproductions of her picture and even doctored photographs on a different body in a farm scene. This was apparently his way of creating a visual fantasy of the way he wanted their lives together to look like ("he took that away a little bit, the reality").

According to Dagmar, Nazism was always a part of their lives while she was growing up. Adolf Hitler's book *Mein Kampf* was on their bookshelves, as well as other Nazi books dealing with the SS. Her words are heard as the camera shows pictures of the family in the countryside, contradicting Wunsch's role in the past. Dagmar says that when she got older she went to Auschwitz to understand the scope of the camp, but still cannot grasp what happened and the fact that her father was a part of it. "I don't really know what he must have thought when he came to Auschwitz. If he thought what was going on there was right." She was shocked to see "the scale of it. How big it was. How organized it was." This complexity is intensified as Sarfaty discusses his trial in 1972, in which Helena was asked by his wife to testify on his behalf. Helena says that she told "the good and the bad" knowing that, as she says, "before they met," Wunsch was responsible for killing several people. The court records attest that Wunsch "was involved in ramp duty during acts of mass murder. He would drag the weary and those unable to walk straight to the gas chambers and the crematorium, during which time he would lie to them about their true fate. In cases of resistance he would forcefully shove them into the gas chambers." In spite of this, Wunsch was acquitted. As the court records are shown and translated, there is no soundtrack. The silence emphasizes the essence of the revelations, the horrible facets of the man who saved Helena and her sister, and emphasize Dagmar's inability and unwillingness to face the true nature of her father's deeds. "He was declared innocent," Dagmar says in the following scene, "and he was innocent. As innocent as you can be under these circumstances." However, court records prove that even though Wunsch was acquitted, he was surely not innocent. "He is not a saint or a monster, he is a war criminal," summarizes Israel, Helena's son.

Helena's children and her niece are interviewed in the same way—this time Helena's pictures as a young mother with each and every one of them is screened behind them. In addition, after Helena's relatives talk about the difficulties of growing up in a house of Holocaust survivors, Sarfaty interviews Dagmar, who talks about her own upbringing. The similarities in the cinematic language point to the similarities between second-generation victims and perpetrators. This is also reflected in the interviews themselves since both sides find it difficult to comprehend the relationship.

Following Dan Bar-On's initiative of encounters between Jews and Germans, Schwab suggests that Germans and Jews should create a dialogical relationship with one another, and develop collective practices of mourning that cross the divide between victims and perpetrators.[59] *The Most Beautiful Woman* shows how complicated this can be. In a charged scene the director initiates an encounter between Dagmar, Helena's children (Israel and Billy), and Micky, Helena's niece. In the conversation between them Dagmar is asked whether her father ever told her what he did. She replies that his part in the SS was never a secret. They had books; he met colleagues from the past. When Dagmar turned fifteen Wunsch told her about Helena and described her as "the love of my life." Both sides show pictures on a large screen, and when a picture of Wunsch in his SS uniform appears, they realize that it was taken at Auschwitz and there is a swastika on his belt, silence ensues. "Disturbing picture," Israel whispers to his sister. When Micky asks Dagmar whether she ever confronted her father, she avoids giving a clear answer and says her father always talked about "Canada," and "he saw it as a work camp. In his eyes it was a work camp; or that's what he would tell me." "But he knew it wasn't," Micky insists. "Of course he did," Dagmar confesses. The scenes are shot in the dark, with cold lighting, thus even though the welcome is warm as is their willingness to meet each other, the cinematic language tells a much more complex story.

At the end of *The Most Beautiful Woman*, Dagmar and Helena's offspring and relatives sit together in the garden, in the open air, drinking wine. But the final shot is older footage of Helena swimming in a pool. In the previous scene her relatives talked about Helena swimming. "She used to scream in the water," Israel says. Thus, the film deliberately does not provide viewers closure or a happy ending. Wunsch, who probably never stopped loving Helena, also never distanced himself from his former colleagues or his Nazi identity. The interviews reveal that there was not silence in all houses, and that Dagmar is a prototype of what Walzer called "cumulative heroization," because she clings to the good, acknowledges the bad, but suppresses it at the same time. "Just as the traumas of the past continue to affect the lives of Holocaust survivors and their descendants, contemporary Germans must struggle to understand the hidden histories," claims the psychologist Roger Frie, the third generation in a family of Nazi perpetrators.[60] Dagmar did not go through this process. Her defense mechanism can also characterize the way her father dealt with his own past.

Shame, Inherited Guilt, and Confessions in Hitler's Children

Hitler's Children, directed by Chanoch Ze'evi and released in 2011, is the first Israeli documentary centered on the testimonies of the descendants of perpetrators. Descendants of Hans Frank, Rudolf Hess, Heinrich Himmler, Hermann Göring, and Amon Göth reveal to the camera the ways in which they cope with shame and responsibility for acts they did not perform. *Hitler's Children* also provides a glimpse into the everyday lives of the perpetrators and the way in which the second generation learned of their parents' Nazi past. The film raises tough questions about the impact of the issue on present-day Germany and the dialogue between Israelis and Germans. What was perceived in Israel until recently as the "absolute evil" is discussed in an Israeli film by the absolute evil's offspring.[61]

Chanoch Ze'evi, the director of *Hitler's Children*, is not a biological grandchild of Holocaust survivors, but states that he feels he belongs to the third generation in every sense of the word. He humorously describes himself as "Holocaust-crazed," and says that the Holocaust is very present in his life, although his grandparents immigrated to Israel and started a family before World War II.[62] In 1998 Ze'evi directed the film *The Disappearance of Martin Bormann* (alternate title, *In the Fuhrer's Shadow*), which revolved around Martin Bormann's mysterious disappearance. As part of the film, Ze'evi interviewed Traudl Junge, Hitler's secretary, and Bormann's son Martin, who became a priest to atone for his father's acts. "Even then, there were people who struggled with the very idea of having the son of a Nazi official interviewed in a film made by an Israeli Jew."[63] *The Disappearance of Martin Bormann* was the catalyst for the making of *Hitler's Children*, which Ze'evi devoted fully to interviews with descendants of Nazis.

Ze'evi was aware that telling the stories of Nazi offspring and presenting their dilemmas and pain in all their complexity would be problematic, especially in Israel: "I've had sleepless nights wondering if it was the right thing to do, whether the time had come and whether I was ready to tell the story from a new perspective."[64] However, he felt that it was vital to include the voices of the perpetrators and their descendants in Holocaust debates despite the emotional and ethical difficulties involved.[65] Ze'evi felt that by presenting the perpetrators and their offspring, he was actually telling the Jewish story, because

> I wanted to tell their story to better understand our own story . . . I think that trying to give evil a face—not turning the Nazis into demons and monsters but rather showing them as they are, people who made a decision to do something and did it, that's important . . . This is not at the expense of the victims. We need to find more stories and document them in films and books. But this story has two sides. It did not happen in a vacuum. Somebody did it, made decisions, carried them out . . . this realization that someone did this, consciously, has to be part of the story.[66]

Ze'evi was very apprehensive about reactions to *Hitler's Children*, which was broadcast on Channel 2 in 2011 on the eve of Holocaust Martyrs' and Heroes' Remembrance Day, but he was pleasantly surprised: "I expected the responses to be 50-50, with one half saying, 'Why in the world put them in front of the camera?' and the other half saying, 'The time has come, 66 years later, the story can be told from other angles.' In fact, it was 80-20 in favor of those who said it was time. I was preparing to have to explain myself and I was really surprised. There was no harsh criticism whatsoever."[67]

When Ze'evi began searching for descendants of Nazis and requesting interviews, many were pressured by their families to refuse. "The usual response I got was 'leave me in peace, let me rebuild my life without the demons of the past and without reliving this thing.'"[68] Eventually, he located five offspring who agreed to be interviewed. Apparently, for some, talking to the camera was also part of their attempt to come to terms with their troubled identities.[69]

In his book *Legacy of Silence*, Dan Bar-On integrated his own difficult personal experiences (such as the death of his son) and his ordeals during his trips to Germany during and after his interviews with the children of Nazis. Ze'evi, by contrast, leaves himself out of the frame. Nichols uses the phrase *observational mode* to define documentaries that attempt to capture reality, and stresses the non-intervention of the filmmaker, who is a "neutral" observer, and not part of the scenes.[70] In *Hitler's Children* Ze'evi is a "fly on the wall," and his voice is not heard. The only subjects seen and heard are the descendants themselves, and the Jewish Israeli journalist Eldad Beck, who lives in Germany and accompanies Rainer Hess on his visit to Auschwitz. Ze'evi explains that he deliberately chose to remain off-frame, because the descendants' stories were so powerful that he did not want to "waste time" on the dynamics of their interchanges. Had he inserted himself into the film, he would have had to tell two stories, "and one always comes at the expense of the other." Ze'evi felt that in a story as big as the Holocaust, he did not see his own story as worthy.[71] *Hitler's Children* is a third-generation product of "after postmemory."[72] In turning the spotlight on the families of Nazis, Ze'evi assumes that viewers are familiar with the history of the Holocaust. He therefore only sketches out the atrocities committed by each perpetrator and instead focuses on the offsprings' responses.

Cinematic Confessions

Hitler's Children begins with scenes that depict the opening of an archive. A box in a coffin-like image is taken by elevator to an upper floor. From these archive scenes, Ze'evi cuts to an interview with Bettina Göring, Herman Göring's niece. The first thing she says is "Yes. I resemble Herman Göring." This editing hints at Ze'evi's attempt to open the Pandora's box of his subjects' lives. The mysterious box dragged from the basement and into the light mirrors his efforts to bring the sensitive topic of dealing with the Nazi past into the open.

The distinction between confession and other modes of expression or self-disclosure has to do with the existence of guilt.[73] The origins of confession are religious. In its traditional sense, confession took place in a private booth, with the priest and congregant sitting next to each other, separated by a small wall. The priest, as a representative of God, granted the penitent atonement and forgiveness. Voluntary secular confession does not require forgiveness, but the relief it provides may be considered equivalent to the forgiveness offered by the clergy. Unlike religious confession, which takes place privately, filmed confessions expose the penitent to the world. The camera serves as a catalyst for confession, both encouraging it and turning it into a cathartic and exhibitionistic act at the same time.[74]

The monologues in *Hitler's Children* are confessions by the offspring, who talk about the ways in which they deal with their pasts. Researchers have argued that the desire to recover the lost love of the outside world and a way to reconcile guilt are strong motivations.[75] The confessions by perpetrators' offspring are even more complex than ordinary secular confessions because the interviewees are not confessing to their own wrongdoings, but what McGlothlin calls "inherited guilt" for acts they did not commit.[76]

After each interview begins, Ze'evi inserts slides that briefly explain the role each speaker's Nazi relative played during World War II. This cinematic choice is an attempt by the filmmaker to create empathy with the confessor. Viewers "meet" the interviewees on-screen before they are introduced to their infamous relatives. In this way, they are not "judged" for their forefathers' actions. The first impression is of affable, polite, sometimes miserable, individuals, which creates instant empathy. Most of the confessions are filmed in medium shot and close-up, which draws viewers closer to the stories. Ze'evi's decision to use this cinematic minimalism strengthens the stories themselves. There are no props, no reenactments, no shots of cattle cars, gas chambers, or Holocaust atrocities. Instead, there are mainly scenes of "talking heads," combined with scenes of their daily life. By doing so, Ze'evi embraces the

Lanzmann perspective of cinematic minimalism in his avoidance of voice-over and archival footage and his concentration on presenting interviewees' stories.

In *Hitler's Children* the differences between interviewees can be seen in the ways they deal with the inherited guilt: Bettina Göring changed her last name to that of her first husband and moved to a secluded place in the United States, where she lives an isolated life.[77] Monika Hertwig and her brother decided to be sterilized so that they would not "give life to other Göths."[78] Katrin Himmler, Himmler's great-niece, married a Jewish Israeli from a family of Holocaust survivors and lives with him in the United States. She writes about Himmler's murderous brutality and also lectures around the world. Rainer Hess, Rudolf Hess's grandson, is shown touring the Auschwitz-Birkenau Memorial and Museum and his grandfather's house looking shocked and tearful. Niklas Frank, the son of Hans Frank, who was the governor general of occupied Poland, has dedicated his life to lecturing throughout Germany about his father, and his life as his father's son. In the meetings, Frank reads from the books he wrote about his family, and deliberately uses foul language when describing his Nazi parents.

The representation of these ways of dealing with the past echo McGlothlin's definition of Nazi descendants for whom the Holocaust represents a mark of Cain—an unresolvable force that remains an ever-present shackle, binding the children of perpetrators to their parents' crimes.[79] Even though the descendants have committed no crimes, their familial pasts will never be forgotten. Their penance will not offer familial absolution, but it helps them manage their guilt.

Ze'evi's choice of interviewees, and the empathetic cinematic language that he uses, draws viewers' attention to the descendants' remorse, and projects a fairly positive and homogenous perspective on the shame and guilt of Nazi descendants. The interviewees do acknowledge that other attitudes toward the past still thrive in Germany and in their families. Rainer Hess says he bears the burden, not only of his grandfather's history but also of his father's, a harsh and brutal man who never abandoned Nazi ideology, and continued to believe in the Third Reich. Hess notes that since his parents' divorce, he has had no contact with his father. Bettina Göring and Monika Hertwig discuss the silence that their families have chosen as a response to their pasts. Katrin Himmler relates that her marriage to a Jew resulted in the termination of contact with some family members. Niklas Frank speaks about the different ways in which his siblings coped with their father. His sister, who is a Holocaust denier, immigrated to South Africa because she was enamored with the apartheid regime, and supported her father throughout her life. Another sister did not want to become any older than their father at his death and committed suicide at the same age. Another brother declared Niklas a liar. The only brother who supported Niklas stated that he did not want to have children, so that the Frank name would vanish from the earth. Niklas has a very negative opinion of the German people. He maintains that he is "lucky" because he knows the full truth about his father, while other Germans his age, whose family members were "less notorious" have to live with doubt about their families. "All the Germans were part of it . . . unfortunately I don't trust us Germans," Niklas remarks bitterly. His determination to discuss the past with audiences throughout Germany is a weapon in the war against what Niklas sees as specific German personality traits. In his view, these characteristics are still embedded within German society and make him fearful of what his compatriots are capable of doing today, especially with regard to minorities.

Even though the interviewees discuss contradictory responses of other family members, the fact that *Hitler's Children* is dedicated to the visual remorse of these five descendants without visually representing other responses ultimately marginalizes other attitudes. The Germans mentioned as having other responses are never interviewed nor represented, even in still pictures. They remain nameless, faceless people. This minimizes the complexity of the responses, especially for an Israeli audience, since viewing the Holocaust from the perspective of the perpetrators' children is still marginal in Israeli culture.

Dialogue between the Perpetrators' Children and Jewish Israelis: No Closure

One charged scene in *Hitler's Children* presents the issue of dialogue between the descendants of the perpetrators and the victims. Hess goes to Auschwitz, accompanied by the Israeli journalist Eldad Beck. During his exploration of the camp, Hess encounters a group of Israeli high school students who are on an educational tour. The Israeli guide introduces the group to Hess and encourages the students to ask him questions. One student asks how Hess deals with his familial past, and what he would do if he were to meet his grandfather. Hess's emotional answer, "I would kill him myself," brings him to tears. The person who reaches out to comfort Hess is the Holocaust survivor accompanying the high school group. The survivor tells him that he has been lecturing to German youths for years, explaining to them they are not to blame for their forefathers' sins. Young Israeli students who approach Hess after the conversation are shown hugging and comforting him. The German members of the production team wanted to end *Hitler's Children* with this scene, or a scene in which Beck and Hess go to an Israeli beach together (a scene that was shot but ultimately remained in the editing room), but Ze'evi refused:

> There are stories that don't have an end . . . There are people who are still suffering from this story, and I certainly don't have the right to tell them the story is over. There were very humane people here in Israel too, who desperately want to show that we love everyone and also wanted the film to end there [at Auschwitz], but for me it was important for the end to be different.[80]

Instead of ending *Hitler's Children* on a saccharin note, Ze'evi uses Beck as a mouthpiece, and ends the film with the following words: "We Jewish Israelis crave these people who feel guilty, who ask our forgiveness because we want to find a happy end to this historical period. But not every story has a happy end and sometimes there is no closure. This specific story has no closure." This scene echoes

Ze'evi's view that he does not object to empathy toward the descendants of Nazis because they themselves have done nothing wrong. The fact that fate chose them to be the "children of" cannot be held against them—"There is something in the way they do not dispute the facts and express remorse which makes things easier to take in. They have not done anything. I think an intelligent viewer can cope with this complexity."[81] These notions are indeed reflected in *Hitler's Children*. The cinematic confessions alongside discussions of the long-term effects of Nazism on contemporary Germany acknowledge a complex reality in which redemption exists alongside denial and the resurgence of neo-Nazism. But the emphasis on the interviewees' torment turns *Hitler's Children* into stronger evidence for shame and remorse in contemporary Germany.

The Representation of the Nazi Perspective in The Decent One

As noted earlier, some second-generation TV documentaries have reviewed the chronology of prominent Nazi figures—for example, *The Hunt for Adolf Eichmann* (1994), *Mengele: The Final Account* (1995), and *The Disappearance of Martin Bormann* (1998). These films are "classical" observation-mode documentaries in which the narrator uses a combination of historical information, documents, pictures, film footage, etc., to chart the biographies of the high-ranking Nazis. *The Specialist* (Eyal Sivan, 1999) is composed of scenes from Eichmann's 1961 trial in Jerusalem. *The Specialist* relies on Hannah Arendt's *Eichmann in Jerusalem: A Report on the Banality of Evil* (1963), in which she referred to Eichmann as a "desk murderer." Several hundred hours (350) of filmed trial are contracted into a two-hour film, which aims to draw the portrait of the gray clerk, who obeys orders, while also criticizing the Israeli category.

The Decent One, directed by Vanessa Lapa and released in 2014, is the first Israeli documentary devoted solely to the perpetrator's perspective. Chanoch Ze'evi said that during the preproduction of *Hitler's Children*, there was a phase in which he wanted to talk to a number of perpetrators, because one of the reasons for making the film was to combat Holocaust deniers. No one agreed to be interviewed, and many slammed down the phone.[82] Director Vanessa Lapa dealt with the issue in a different way. In *The Decent One* she depicts Heinrich Himmler's identity, thoughts, and feelings through hundreds of private personal letters and diaries. Throughout the film Lapa concentrates on the documents that were revealed and shed light on Himmler's life, his relationship with his wife, his daughter, his mistress, and his activities in the Nazi leadership.

Like many others, Lapa requested an interview with Himmler's daughter Gudrun, who was then eighty-six years old, but was turned down. Gudrun remained an admirer of her father. She founded the organization Silent Help, which supports former Nazi criminals by sending money, Christmas presents, providing psychological assistance to convicted Nazis, and helping former Nazis escape trial and live outside Germany.[83] However, Lapa was able to work with Himmler's grand-niece, Katrin Himmler (who was interviewed in *Hitler's Children*).[84]

Even though the perpetrators' deeds have been discussed extensively in research and literature since the aftermath of World War II, the perspective of the perpetrators, their subjectivity, motivations, thoughts, and desires still elicit unease. One of the key fears is that representing the perpetrators' interiority could be construed as legitimating or exonerating the perpetrators.[85] *The Decent One* proves that a perpetrator's life can be explored without creating identification. It illustrates what the perpetrator researcher James Waller called "the ordinariness of extraordinary evil" so that viewers "will be less likely to be unwitting contributors to evil, and perhaps better equipped to forestall evil."[86]

Behind-the-Scenes: The Cinematic Creation of Himmler's Perspective

Lapa is a Belgian Jew who immigrated to Israel in 1994 at the age of nineteen. She studied at Tel Aviv University, became a researcher for

Channel 1, a reporter on Channel 10, and in 2006 started her own production company.[87] The story behind *The Decent One* sounds like a Hollywood blockbuster: the Holocaust survivor Haim Rosenthal kept a suitcase filled with Himmler's personal letters and documents under his bed for forty years. It is unclear how he came to possess these documents, which were stolen from Himmler's home by American soldiers in 1945. Rosenthal said that he bought them at a flea market in the 1960s.[88] In 2006 he decided, on his son's advice, to give it to someone "who would do something important with it."[89] Rosenthal contacted Netanel Laor, a professor of psychiatry and philosophy at Tel Aviv University, and Laor contacted Lapa to ask whether she would be interested, as a filmmaker, in using the material. After few weeks of reading, Lapa decided to accept the challenge and make a documentary.

The suitcase contained 350 personal letters, 135 photos, and 20 diaries from 1927 to 1945. Lapa worked on the material for seven years. She and her colleagues transcribed the texts into modern German and then translated them into English and Hebrew. They also traveled extensively to collect visuals to fit the descriptions in the texts, including, for example, German home movies from the first decades of the twentieth century. Lapa and her crew were careful in selecting the visual material for *The Decent One*:

> We wanted to remain faithful to the text so we looked for material that was not propaganda. We went to locations in Europe where Himmler had been to trace footage from home videos of families, schools, etc. It was an artistic choice to remain faithful to the text. . . . A team spent three years searching in Europe and the USA. The Himmler family gave the German research team home videos but they withdrew the rights when they found out it was an Israeli production just before production.[90]

In the end, the visuals came from 151 different sources and film materials. To cope, Lapa and her colleagues started a restoration studio and worked with an expert. They were able to remove dust and scratches from many frames, to make the visuals viewable without impinging on the authenticity of the material. The choices for the sound were an integral part of the restoration of the footage as well.[91] Most of the films they wanted to use were silent. So they added soundtracks that fit the time periods in the film (for example, the noise of carriage wheels, street sounds from the 1930s, and so on), to enable viewers to have a fuller experience of the era. Every sound bite was verified by historians and only approved sound sequences were included on *The Decent One*'s soundtrack.

Lapa feels that the third generation as compared to earlier generations has the required remoteness to work with these materials and listen to the perpetrators' side: "If my mother had access to these documents, she couldn't have touched it, because her father lived through Auschwitz."[92] Like Ze'evi in *Hitler's Children*, Lapa also takes the perspective of an outside observer. She never films herself or inserts her voice-over. As a member of the third generation Lapa was strongly affected by the power of the Himmler documents. Thus, in her opinion, documenting herself would have been a waste of screen time.

The result is ninety minutes of original footage and narration by actors who read from Himmler's letters and diaries in the first person (they act out Himmler as a teenager, Himmler as an adult, his wife Margarete Boden, his father, his mother, his daughter Gudrun, and his mistress Hedwig). Lapa says that this cinematic choice was deliberate. She wanted to avoid narration and informative voices (psychologists, historians, and Holocaust survivors) to allow viewers to reflect on what they saw, decide what they thought, and draw their own conclusions as to "what will they bear in mind in the future."[93]

Himmler's World

The Decent One was the first time an Israeli film provided access to the mind of a high-ranking Nazi. Unlike Goebbels's diaries, Himmler's documents and diaries were not written for purposes of publication, and hence they give tremendous new insights into the man, his thoughts, and his deeds.[94] The film traces Himmler's life starting from his childhood. He began keeping a diary when he was thirteen years old and kept on writing until the end of World War II.

Lapa uses two major cinematic editing choices to accompany Himmler's writings. She associates his words with visuals aimed at depicting his beliefs and the way he saw the world. The other is deliberate discrepancies between visual and sound, which are meant to emphasize the lies Himmler told himself, his relatives, and his subordinates, which highlight the twisted way Himmler understood the world, the Nazi regime, and his deeds.

The choice to associate words and visuals dominates the first part of *The Decent One*, when Lapa presents Himmler's earlier writings. The materials show that as early as World War I, when Himmler was in high school, he was enthralled by war, wrote diatribes against citizens of south Bavaria who surrendered, calling them cowards and stupid, and envied his seventeen-year-old brother, who was drafted. In his writings, the young Himmler protested against what he saw as the weakness of Germans who were afraid of defeat. His personal diaries reveal low self-esteem and a lack of sociability ("People don't like me. Why? Because I talk too much"), the dream of becoming a soldier, and an admiration of Nordic beauty. Himmler felt humiliated in gym class and became depressed when the girls he was interested in turned him down. His social relations were strained, and Himmler apparently considered the solution to be to take on the persona of a soldier.

In 1918, when he was eighteen years old, Himmler enrolled at the University of Munich. He joined a nationalistic fraternity that debated the "homosexuality problem" and the "Jewish problem." Whenever Himmler met a girl who seemed nice he would add, "but she is Jewish." When Himmler was upset that he lost the fraternity elections, he relaxed by going to a shooting range, flogging himself if he did not get up on time ("What kind of soldier am I? Such weak character. I wish there would be another war. How I want to fight, risk my life"). Himmler's diaries indicate that he was still a virgin in his twenties, speak about his disappointment with the undisciplined young generation in Germany, the lack of modesty (after seeing his friend's three-year-old daughter jumping naked on her bed), and his disappointment with women's so-called promiscuity ("It is troubling that German women do not want to be mothers anymore," Himmler writes after going to a bar with his friends). He writes about "living space" as early as his twenties ("The East is the most important place for us. We should fight and settle there"), and the need to be pure, superior, and elevated, "like our forefathers." In all these scenes, Lapa uses visuals that tally with Himmler's thoughts. For example, when he argues that Nordic individuals are the most talented and beautiful and praises the Nordic bone structure and muscles ("indeed a royal race"), Lapa shows blonde, healthy-looking women exercising in the fresh air. From the books he reads and writes about, Himmler appeared to be looking for a leader who could encourage the German people to be braver: "A man we need so much in our era." Himmler hopes for a revolution, even if it is bloody, and joined the Nazi Party on August 1, 1923. "I believe Hitler was exactly the leader Himmler was looking for. He was the most dominant person in his life. The correspondence between Himmler and his father and wife make it clear that Hitler took the place of everyone else in Himmler's life," Lapa says.[95]

By contrast to the claim that dealing with Nazi leaders' personal lives humanizes Nazis in a way that condones their crimes and violates the memory of the Holocaust, the scenes that describe Himmler's youth do nothing to turn him into a loveable character. They supply the psychological background that accounts for Himmler's attraction to the Nazi Party and his position. Lapa also consulted with psychiatrists during her documentary work to get a better idea of Himmler's personality ("The more I learned, the more I was disgusted with him").[96]

Lapa says that during production she kept on asking Laor, who handed her the documents, "If you had not known Himmler wrote these letters, could you predict what this young boy would become?" Laor said he could not: "I could have said that this young boy would turn out to be very dangerous and problematic but not to the extent of the real Himmler." Laor suggests that there is no Dr. Jekyll and Mr. Hyde within Himmler because all of his relationships were twisted, perverted, sadomasochistic mind games with his soldiers, his wife, and his mistress.[97]

In *The Origins of Totalitarianism* (1951) Hannah Arendt defined the characteristics of totalitarian regimes, their origins, their universal aspects, and their danger to the world. She listed a number of key features of totalitarianism, which include a unique hierarchical structure that disconnects the masses from reality and common sense. The leader is at the top and represents the ultimate source of power whose wishes are the supreme law. Under him are the high-ranking officials, and the most secret and exclusive organizations controlled by the most powerful individuals in the hierarchy. These people have no personal life independent of the regime. Each facet of their lives is wrapped up in totalitarian ideas, which make them completely disconnected from reality and the outside world. Under them are the party members and supporters. The totalitarian structure prevents citizens from recognizing reality as it is, and produces a fake world based on constant disinformation, with internal moral norms of conduct. Ordinary people living in a totalitarian state, let alone the regime's officials and executioners, lose the ability to think independently, to see reality, to differentiate between fact and fiction, true and false. They are neutralized by false propaganda that feeds the false world that surrounds them and normalizes "mob mentality."[98]

This fake world establishes extreme control over the masses, who become unable to exercise free will. It eliminates any human activity independent of the regime and creates obedient party members, for whom the leader's words are moral principles that cannot be challenged. Criminal norms are proclaimed to be normal, which makes the very act of extermination seem completely reasonable. Since it destroys the essence of freethinking, monstrous and totally new evil can be enacted by normal persons.[99] Totalitarianism turns crime into a banal act, not in the moral sense, but in the ordinary, almost casual manner in which it is performed. Arendt considered that the Nazi regime created conditions in which the moral anchor was eliminated, awareness was stifled, and doing good became almost impossible.[100]

Himmler's portrait in *The Decent One* can be analyzed in terms of Arendt's definition of totalitarianism. It highlights the process by which a normal man becomes a mass murderer, lives in a false world of self-deception based on criminal acts, and is sure that he is committing normal and even moral deeds.[101] *The Decent One* emphasizes the way a totalitarian regime shapes the individual into a submissive subject that observes the laws of the totalitarian state with unwavering loyalty and blind obedience to its leader. Himmler's diaries show how he becomes a representative of the rise of a new kind of evil, where perpetrators are not even aware of the criminal and immoral nature of their acts, and carry them out diligently and naturally.[102]

According to *The Decent One*, Himmler is, as Arendt claimed, a "normal bourgeois," who was interested in status symbols such as a new car, and writes to his wife at length about the house he is building and describes details such as the color of the walls chosen for every room, including the maid's room:

> You good sweet little wife. Dear darling, how lovely our home will be. How fine. The trees and shrubs have grown, I'll handle the details with the painter and electrician tomorrow. I left you a note with the window measurements. The kitchen I specified "yellowish," the stairs "blue-gray," the bedroom light green, the maid's room, a lighter color, and the guest room a lighter color too. How marvelous our life will be.

On one occasion, when the Himmlers invited twenty-four people for a dinner party, Margarete writes that the servants were awful "and Heini was furious." After their marriage, they go on family vacations with their children to resorts, and Himmler goes hunting.

In order to explain the way he developed an alternative moral world, Lapa uses visuals. In 1924 Himmler keeps on talking about the greatness and importance of the Middle Ages, the German forefathers, and laments the current estrangement from them. "I wish we were like them, with their practices and their healthy approach to life." Lapa inserts these sentences while showing Nazi parades from the 1920s. The personal letters in which Himmler and Margarete discuss their love, trivialities, their wonderful future ("how great our lives will be") are also read while screening Nazi parades. Himmler considered Nazism to be healthy, pure, and romanticized. When the actors read Himmler and Margarete's letters to each other in which they express their fascination with the infant Gudrun, Lapa shows Nazi marches and salutes. In the following scene Lapa shows a baby playing while Himmler's letter describing SS training is heard. This cinematic presentation echoes Arendt's analysis that all facets of life are united under the leader, such that the newborn baby (personal life, innocent) and the SS (career, killers) constitute a homogenous unit of something proud, important, and pure that will improve society. From both of these worlds Himmler "expects total obedience in all times." Arendt's argument that the totalitarian regime includes every component of life is also reflected in Himmler's statement that the SS is a community, not just of men. Women are also part of the SS; therefore, women and children must obey. Thus, when Himmler talks about the need for order, "which is the foundation of our nation," Lapa shows scenes of children. When Himmler talks about teaching the SS commanders to "eat properly," Lapa shows laughing teenagers and young children saluting, again demonstrating that Himmler's rules, morals, and perceptions of the SS are applicable to a totalitarian culture as a whole, as Arendt pointed out.

In her reporting on Adolf Eichmann's trial, Arendt made the point that language is a crucial factor when accounting for the Nazis' actions. She argued that the Nazis' ability to become mass murderers involved a change in the meaning of words, resulting in the double-speak that justified the totalitarian world. Himmler was, in Arendt's terms, "the member of the Nazi hierarchy most gifted in solving problems of conscience." He coined slogans, catchphrases, watchwords, and kept repeating them. *Decent* was an integral part of the new language Himmler disseminated. What stuck in the minds of the men who had become murderers was the notion of being involved in something historic, grandiose, and unique. The new terminology helped overcome people's conscience as Himmler turned the animal instinct of pity around by directing it toward the self: "Instead of saying: 'what horrible things I did to people!' The murderers would be able to say: 'what horrible things I had to watch in the pursuance of my duty, how heavily the task weighs upon my shoulders.'" The attempt to reconstruct humanity after Nazism is therefore a battle over the reconstruction of language.[103]

The reversal of moral norms in a criminal regime that turns mass murder into something necessary and natural as well as this "loss of language" is highlighted in *The Decent One* through Himmler's definition of morality. "Only those with unclean consciences are those who should fear us," Himmler stated after the Nazis came to power in 1933. "We will never be cruel and heartless without necessity," Himmler proclaimed in 1941 after the invasion of the Soviet Union. "We Germans . . . will treat human beings in a decent way . . . The most I will demand of you is to be strict in education . . . so I demand of you human kindness," Himmler writes to SS soldiers. "We have a moral responsibility to our people to kill the people who want to kill us." When Albert Speer agreed to supply Himmler with one thousand tons of iron so Himmler could expand the concentration camps—Auschwitz in particular—Himmler writes him, "Your letter reinforced my belief that there is still justice in the world."

Lapa says that in the material, Himmler uses the word *decent* more than one thousand times and in the ninety-minute film it appears thirteen times. "For me *The Decent One* reflects the various facets of this man. For him it was what he strongly believed and that's how he educated his family, his subordinates. He truly believed he was a decent man."[104] Himmler refers to SS soldiers as "decent men." In Poznan in 1943 Himmler gave a four-hour speech in which he explained how decency is important and how one can kill and murder in a decent way. In his letter to Gudrun in 1941 Himmler says that in life one must be always "decent, brave and kindhearted." In his letters, when he tries to explain his recruitment methods, Himmler insists: "When recruiting SS men, I demand the following criteria: a minimum age of twenty three, minimum height 1.70, 1 year of party membership, written testimony of two witnesses willing to vouch for the man, he must also be a good and decent person. Out of 100 men we can take no more than ten to fifteen." While this letter is being read, Lapa does not show the crimes of the SS but rather scenes of mustering the troops, maneuvers, and so on, thus staying with Himmler's perspective. Lapa says that this was her cinematic way of showing viewers that "what is considered decent to me, to us, was totally different from what he considered to be 'decent' and whatever is decent for Himmler is in no way decent for us, so this world is totally perverted by him."[105] In his letters to Gudrun, Himmler also reveals his interpretation of *decent*: "We Germans are the only ones with a decent approach towards animals, and we treat human beings with the same decency, but worrying about them is a crime against our own blood." "He [Himmler] was not a psychopath," Lapa says. "He knew he was killing, he knew he was a murderer." Lapa's decision to use the phrase *decent man* in the film's title also refers to Arendt's reasoning that the moral values within a totalitarian regime turns "normal" people into murderers who believe their actions are just and correct.

The historian Moshe Zimmermann considers that Himmler saw himself as a decent man, wanted the "job" to be done in a decent way, and, as he saw it, murdering Jews was decent because, as Himmler perceived it, his people were fighting to survive. This survival justified perceptions such as "it is either me or you." Zimmermann suggests that these letters ("ordinary letters of a man writing to his family, writing to his mistress, writing to his family circle on everyday matters") are so difficult to grasp because they show viewers that an average individual does not need to be the incarnation of evil to become a mass murderer. "These perceptions are disturbing, because no one wants to think that he/she could become this type of person."[106] In interviews Lapa highlights the combination of mass murder and family life. When she compared dates, she saw that the day on which hundreds of thousands of Jews were murdered, the Himmler family spent their day at a spa and enjoyed massages. "Even if you spend seven years on it you are shocked every time you read it."[107] The writer Nir Baram says that this duality is not surprising, and that the Israeli narrative has failed to grasp "the fact that a man can be in charge of mass murder in concentration camps in the morning, and in the evening to be upset because some boy at school pulled his daughter's pigtails; it is obvious, but we Jewish Israelis have a hard time dealing with this duality." Baram suggests that the Israeli narrative is primarily aimed at defining a monster, to show that Nazi officers were deranged, but in fact, in daily life, at least some of them were normative individuals, and Himmler saw himself as a decent man who contributed to society.[108]

Lapa, who decided to base *The Decent One* on Himmler's materials and was interested in representing his twisted approach toward "decency," faced the problem of how best to represent Jews and the Holocaust, since in his personal letters Himmler rarely addressed the murderous brutality of the SS. The fraternity he joined as a student discussed "the Jewish problem"; when Himmler and his wife write to each other about buying a new car, he does not want to buy a Hanomag (Hannoversche Maschinenbau AG) because the car company is run by "Jewish cheats"; when a patient owes Margarete money, she complains, "The bastard hadn't paid me yet. A Jew stays a Jew! Sometimes I'm alarmed with people's wickedness. Are they all bad like my Jewish riffraff?" "My sweet darling wife," Himmler replies, "money is a necessity. How annoying and upsetting this behavior is. Don't get too upset because of your Jew." After the invasion of Poland, Margarete visits several cities and notes, "The Jewish riffraff, the Poles do not look like humans at all." In another letter Margarete queries, "Regarding the Jews . . . when will those scoundrels finally leave, so we can enjoy life again?"[109] These letters are read while the visuals describe everyday life in Germany, thus highlighting how "natural" these perceptions were.

In scenes after 1933, Lapa makes use of material shot on the streets of Germany where people held signs with slogans such as "The Jews are our disaster" and "It is forbidden to shop in Jewish stores." The soundtrack airs one of Himmler's speeches: "A small group of rootless people creates panic and makes mischief between nations, travels from place to place and does business everywhere." Himmler talks about Jews, but does not use the word *Jew*, so Lapa uses visuals to explain what he is talking about. When Himmler writes, "As long as there are people in the world, there will always be war between humans and sub-humans. . . . A sub-human is a creature that seemingly resembles humans . . . but mentally and physically is inferior to animals," Lapa shows scenes of Jewish young people (children with yarmulkes, girls with dark hair). After pictures of synagogues burned to the ground during Kristallnacht, Lapa quotes from a speech on the "master race" that must "eliminate people who undermine the whole."

Lapa solved the problem of the absence of direct mention of the Holocaust by creating an intended dissonance between the sound (Himmler's writings read by an actor) and visuals in several scenes. For example, when Himmler talks about "an interesting" visit to the Baltic states, is happy to hear that his daughter Gudrun does not understand the meaning of war, and joyfully tells her that he had bought "something sweet" for her, the camera shows scenes of Jews being executed. The incompatibility between sound and picture pinpoints Himmler's distorted values and world view. "Dear mommy, I'm sorry that for the first time I forgot our wedding anniversary," Himmler writes his wife while the camera shows scenes of Nazis abusing Jews. He describes his morning routine (gets up, drinks coffee, reads the mail) while the camera shows a Jew being beaten with a stick. "Despite all the hard work I feel good and sleep well," Himmler writes as Lapa shows the famous scenes where the Einsatzgruppen squads shoot Jews into mass graves, "Many kisses. With love, Heini." When Himmler sends his wife and daughter expensive gifts, which he specifies, "Basket . . . silk . . . our daughter will get the golden bracelet and the sports outfit," the camera pans over the plundered suitcases of Jews who were sent to their death. The disparity between a man writing to his wife how much he longs to see her "when the work day is over," who promises her that the paradise they built together cannot be destroyed, apologizes that he forgot their wedding anniversary "because of my workload," discusses their children's education, and signs the letter "Heini" contrasts with the fact that the audience knows about his "workload," and what Himmler means when he uses the word *filth*. This underscores what Arendt referred to as the capacity of a totalitarian regime to create a world dissociated from reality based on lies and deceptions that change and distort norms and values.

"Himmler is the most brutal man I have ever encountered. He was brutal in his career but also in his private life," Lapa says. "Outwardly, Himmler seemed to be a good husband, and a good father, but the brutality was there. When he writes his wife-to-be that he loves her very much but there is something he loves more and that is the nation, that is brutal."[110] In another letter Himmler writes to Margarete he says, "I won't always be able to be as good as you will want me to be," perhaps implying he has a mistress. At first, when Himmler's father asks him to help German friends who were arrested, he helps, but when he is asked to help another friend whose son was arrested, and even writes him how difficult these requests are for him to handle, Himmler says that the arrest was necessary. He also fails to send his father birthday wishes shortly before his death.

To portray Himmler as a liar who lies to himself and his family when he writes, "I'm working harder than ever," Lapa shows him playing tennis. Three weeks before the end of the war, Himmler still believes in Germany's ability to win, and when his daughter writes in her diary, "Daddy doesn't believe that the German people will despair," the visual shows the Nazi flag trampled on the sidewalk and a Hitler doll in a noose. When Himmler writes to his wife and daughter, "In spite of the difficult situation I'm completely convinced of our victory," Lapa shows Berlin in ruins after being bombed. When Himmler recites a poem entitled "Redemption," the camera shows Red Army soldiers in Berlin capturing Nazis, raising their hands in surrender.

Himmler was captured by the British army and committed suicide on May 23, 1945. While showing a British soldier standing over Himmler's corpse, Lapa inserts segments from his 1943 speeches to the commanders of the Einsatzgruppen and the Higher SS and Police Leaders: "I'm not a bloodthirsty man . . ." She cuts to films of the concentration camps shot by the Allied armies. Lapa shows scenes of hundreds of corpses that were found when the camps were liberated as Himmler's voice is heard: "When I think something needs to be done, I do it without compromising." When Himmler says, "To have remained decent, that is what has made us hard," Lapa again screens the piles of corpses and the *muselmen* (slang for the starved, exhausted concentration camp inmates) who were discovered at liberation. *The Decent One* begins and ends with Margarete's interrogation by the Allies. Against a background of scenes of people loading corpses found in the concentration camps onto wagons, Margarete is asked whether she and her husband ever talked about the concentration camps. She says she knew he was in charge of them, but they never talked about it: "I knew nothing about it." "Why didn't you ask him?" "I don't know," Margarete answers, the wagon drives away, and the film ends.

As in *Hitler's Children*, where Ze'evi refused to finish his film with a closure, Lapa also argued that she wanted to end *The Decent One* with a sense of continuity. Himmler's end is not the end. The Holocaust is the handiwork of human beings, and because it happened, it can happen again.[111] The message Lapa wants to convey is that Himmler was a human being and not a monster.

> It would have been much easier if we had discovered that he was mentally ill, or that he was a monster, that he was not human. Unfortunately, he was mentally sound and made a choice—he

> chose evil and we must be aware that there are people like this everywhere and in a certain geo-political environment and with a strong leader it can lead to the murder of millions.[112]

The Decent One has been distributed in seventeen countries. The only place where it was poorly accepted was in Germany. Lapa believes this is because Himmler is portrayed as an individual who made conscious choices. When Nazis are shown as human beings, acceptance is difficult, especially for Germans, because what they see in the film is themselves—their language, their landscape, their culture, their families. "There was a lot of anger and it was a huge failure as opposed to Israel and the USA where the film was screened for many months and it was acclaimed."[113]

Representing "Bystanders" in Out of the Forest

Kleiner Rudi and *Martin* represented Germans who remained passive during World War II, who saw Jews in their town deported and did nothing. *Shalom Italia* discusses the resistance of local bystanders and how they assisted Jewish families. Other third-generation documentaries address the darker sides of bystanders by representing gainers, collaborators, and bystanders who became perpetrators. They discuss the complexity of the term *bystanders* in occupied countries—in which, as Barnett points out, populations were under foreign military occupation during the war years and could (and still do) argue that they also were victims of Nazi violence.[114] For example, *The Dark Side*, directed by Natalie Assouline Travilio and released in 2015, tells a story of revenge. The Holocaust survivor Moshe Knebel, now eighty-five years old, returns to Poland with his three children. The family tour enables the director to represent a complex portrait of the term *bystanders* in Poland. Knebel's family's friends and neighbors denounced his family to the Nazis. He managed to escape and survive the war by joining Russian partisans. He discusses the Polish towns he passed on his way, the town mayor who saw him and did not tell on him, and his fear of Polish informers who were everywhere. When Knebel returned home after the war, he realized that Poles had taken over Jewish property, wore their clothes, and some of them tried to kill him when he tried to recover his family's possessions. Knebel decided to take revenge on those responsible for killing his family and trying to kill him by murdering them. *The Dark Side* represents parts of Knebel's memoirs and his revenge on the Poles by using animation depicting the Poles' evildoings. The TV documentary *Lerner's Revenge*, directed by Gila'ad Tokatly and released in 2006, discusses the offspring of the Lerner family, who return to Poland and meet with the Poles who hid their family for money and killed them when the money ran out. The Israeli offspring meet with the bystanders-turned-perpetrators, their offspring, and other onlookers who knew what happened and remained silent. This spectrum of bystanders, ranging from onlookers who are still alive and remember the murder of the town's Jews, to gainers and perpetrators, provides a complex picture of 1940s Poland and contemporary Poland. *Only God Is Allowed*, directed by Gad Aizen and released in 2018, follows Tsafrir, a third-generation Holocaust survivor who knew there was a story of revenge in his family but did not know the details. He decides to investigate and unearths the story of Henek, his grandfather. Henek and his sister Mirka hid from the Nazis. A Polish woman handed Mirka over to the Nazis for money. She was taken to the woods and was shot. Henek found her dying and promised to avenge her death. He fled, and survived the war with a group of partisans. When the war ended, Henek returned to the village and killed the Polish woman and her daughter. These films address the bystanders for the first time, but their main focus is the perspectives of the victims and their offspring.

Out of the Forest, directed by Yaron Kaftory Ben-Yosef and Limor Pinhasov Ben-Yosef and released in 2004, is the first Israeli documentary dedicated to bystanders. Yaron Kaftory Ben-Yosef and Limor Pinhasov Ben-Yosef are a couple who make films together. *Out of the Forest* brings to the forefront the perspectives of the people of Ponary, Lithuania, who witnessed the mass murder in the Ponary forest of over seventy-five thousand people, roughly 95 percent of whom were Jews, many from the Vilnius Ghetto. At first, the directors wanted to make a film about Kazimierz Sakowicz, who lived in Ponary and wrote a diary describing what he heard and saw from the summer of 1941, when the mass shooting began, to July 1943, when the mass killing was over and he was murdered. The more Kaftory and Pinhasov researched, the more they realized that the most critical story was that of the villagers' responses to what they heard and saw.[115] Surprisingly, the locals who were children at the time or young adults were eager to talk.[116]

Out of the Forest is not a historical account of what happened in Ponary but rather an attempt to reveal the bystanders' points of view and their various responses and behaviors. It approves the contemporary research that dismantles the term *bystanders* to different attitudes, by representing a range of behaviors from passive indifference to perpetrators.

Even though its subject is dramatic, *Out of the Forest* is very restrained and its cinematic language is minimalistic.[117] There are no images of dead bodies or mass graves. The film is divided into three parts corresponding to the years in Sakowicz's diary. In each part, diary pages are shown as an actor reads parts in Hebrew with a Russian accent. Dr. Rachel Margolis, who translated the diary, is interviewed, as are the people of Ponary and survivors. At the end of each sequence pre–World War II photos of some of the murdered are shown while the soundtrack plays a song in Yiddish. From the first scenes of the countryside houses and the woods, the gloomy light and the stark silence which, at times, accompany the scenes of the woods, create an atmosphere suggesting a cursed, depressing place.[118] The combination of colors and the lack of music emphasize the chilling effect of the interviews and the simple, emotionless way in which the locals talk about how they witnessed mass killings. The interviews are conducted, Lanzmann-style, without any photos of the atrocities or extradiegetic soundtrack. As in Lanzmann's *Shoah*, the survivors are interviewed on location, sometimes reenacting their past (for example, walking toward the killing pits). The interviews with locals reflect how problematic the term *bystanders* is and manifest its various facets, especially the different ways of collaboration and cooperation.[119]

Sakowicz documented what he saw and heard. He also mentions the close ties between the locals and the killers, the economic boom in Ponary after the mass killing began, names the accomplices, and describes their trade in murdered belongings. He then stuffed his diary in lemonade bottles and buried them in the garden. According to Margolis, Sakowicz rebels at first in his writings against what he sees, but in time gets used to it, "like the rest of the people . . . he is indifferent as well." Margolis claims she did not find materials that show Sakowicz was anti-Semitic. In her opinion Sakowicz documented the events because he wanted to use them after the war for scientific or journalistic purposes. Albeit, Margolis also claims that Sakowicz's writing can be seen as a memorial to the Jews who were murdered in Ponary. Another woman from a neighboring village tells how in the middle on the night, a young woman, who succeeded to get out of the shooting pits alive, knocked on her door, asked for clothes (because her cloths were covered with blood), and asked for directions to the partisans. The woman helped her. These are the two rebel acts that *Out of the Forest* represents. Most of the screen time is dedicated to indifferent onlookers and witnesses (interviewees who were teenagers and saw various stages of the executions), gainers, collaborators, and perpetrators. *Out of the Forest* shows that although Sakowicz was the only one who documented the atrocity, all the people in the village and the surrounding villages were aware of what was happening, did nothing, and did not think they should do something. One woman laconically states that when a young Jew who had escaped came to their house and asked for help, her mother refused, and he was caught and killed. She justifies her mother's actions and, like other interviewees, accuses the Jews, the victims, of their passivity. When she and others are asked, "Why didn't you do something?" they insist that they could not. The interviews reflect the onlookers' indifference. The locals complain how they were adversely affected by the smell of the burning bodies and how afraid they were of the fires. This indifference continues to the present. The memorial site custodian talks about the youngsters who come there at night to party and drink. In addition, the interviews suggest that the people do not care that they are living in a place where the ground is soaked with blood: "I don't mind living here . . . it is beautiful . . . pleasant." However, Yaron Kaftory Ben-Yosef and Limor Pinhasov Ben-Yosef use the interviews and the cinematic language to suggest otherwise: the children who were witnesses to the atrocities and grew up in Ponary lived in poverty, did not create families of their own, could not provide for their family, or lost their families. From the first scenes of the countryside houses, which are accompanied by a soundtrack more appropriate in a horror movie, along with the gloomy lighting and stark silence often used for scenes in the woods, an atmosphere suggesting a cursed, depressing place is created.

As noted earlier, research since the 1990s has deconstructed the term *bystanders*.[120] Contemporary research shows how the differentiation between the terms *victims*, *bystanders*, and *perpetrators* is problematic since a bystander who helped victims could have become a victim, and a bystander could have become a perpetrator. Scholars have revealed various degrees of complicity and pointed to a more fluid process in which people started out as onlookers and became more involved as time passed.[121] Others claim that the term *bystanders* should be deconstructed because the local population was always complicit in these crimes in various ways—some participated by turning a blind eye; others by doing nothing; others occupied Jewish property; and others took an active part in the killings.[122] *Out of the Forest* reveals that many locals not only maintained their distance but became gainers. Interviewees speak freely about the way they were and are completely aware of the fact that the villagers began to steal clothes belonging to the murdered ("carts filled with clothes"). People saw their neighbors wearing the Jews' clothes. "I think they treated it as 'secondhand clothes,' says a woman from a village near Ponary, who witnessed the trading. "People give clothes to secondhand stores even if it belonged to a person who is already dead. You give it to dry cleaning and then you wear it. This is the way it was." As in the indifference documentation, Yaron Kaftory Ben-Yosef and Limor Pinhasov Ben-Yosef connect between past and present as parts of her testimony are added in parallel editing with a clothes street market that takes place there in the present.

Locals also gained financially by yanking gold teeth and gold crowns from victims' mouths and trading them, selling, or replacing for alcohol. Villagers in the surrounding areas were also indifferent and active gainers at the same time. They knew what was going on and took an active part in trading in the belongings of the dead.

According to local testimonies, villagers also gained from another perspective—in interviews they talk about how they cooked for the Nazis and Lithuanian killers, who came to eat lunch in the village in between mass executions, and also met them at night and partied with them. "The relationship between them, and Ponary's youth was very close," Sakowicz writes. According to *Out of the Forest*, collaboration took other forms as well—when Jews tried to escape or wanted to hide in the village, they were extradited to the shooters. Sakowicz mentions a Jew who escaped, knocked on a villager's door, asked for their help, but was turned down. The shooters caught up with him and killed him. One of the interviewees remembers this scene—it was her house and her mother refused to hide him. She justifies her mother and blames the victims for not running away, as do other villagers.

Similarly, interviewees speak freely about the way they were and are completely aware of the fact that some Lithuanians took an active part in the killings, thus becoming active collaborators and perpetrators. One woman interviewee tries to claim that there were only few of them, but a local standing next to her, other interviewees, and the extracts from Sakowicz's diary that are read confirm that there were many Shaulisti (Lithuanian nationalists who helped the Nazis murder Jews on many occasions).

As in *The Flat*, the responses of descendants of perpetrators in *Out of the Forest* show that they refuse to acknowledge their parents' deeds. The directors confront Edward, the son of Yanovsky, a

Lithuanian who is mentioned by the interviewees and in Sakowicz's diary as a killer and the head of the clothing trade. In previous scenes Edward spoke freely about Lithuanian perpetrators, mentioned their last names, admitted he knew them because his father worked at the "transit point" where Jews were led to the killing site, and discussed the close rapport between his father and the killers who came to get warm in his guardhouse. However, the way Edward deals with his father's past does not acknowledge that he took part in these crimes. He refuses to accept that his father was a perpetrator. When standing in front of the camera reading this part of Sakowicz's diary, Edward claims his father probably sold a pair of boots that were indeed too small for his feet. "My father had nothing to do with that. This is Sakowicz's assumption. He only assumes." Yanovsky's daughter also claims she knows nothing about her father's involvement: "I was a child at the time . . . he was a kind-hearted man. Maybe he sold a couple of things to buy vodka."

The interviews with Dr. Margolis extend the issue and pose difficult questions for the first time in Israeli documentaries. She describes the villagers, not only in Ponary, but "everywhere there were concentration camps" as passive and indifferent—"If it doesn't affect them, they'll do nothing." However, she does not only blame them and states, "It is human nature. I don't know how the Jews would have reacted if things were reversed." These statements completely subvert the binary divisions that appear so strongly in Israeli Holocaust commemorations. This statement turns *Out of the Forest* from an indictment against the people of Ponary into a reflection on human nature.

Out of the Forest presents the disparity between this dark outlook on human nature and an (almost desperate) attempt to believe that there is still a modicum of good out there, and that people can behave differently. This is reflected in the way the directors stage the scenes in the film. Margolis's dark statement appears thirty minutes into the film. However, the final testimony in this ninety-minute film is that of a woman who says she gave clean clothes to a female survivor and directed her to a partisan hideout. "I hope she is happy if she is still alive," this villager says sadly as she looks into the woods. This appears after an interview with another local woman, who blames the victims for not escaping and claims the locals could not do anything. "How could we help? How?" she asks. The following scene, which depicts a helping hand, is the directors' answer. They could help. There were many ways the locals could help. The closing scene shows a memorial ceremony for the dead at the Ponary memorial site, where the few survivors pay their respects to the dead. The soundtrack that accompanies the memorial scene—the song "Ponary" sung in Yiddish—begins in the final minutes of the preceding testimony, thus turning a small act of help into another tribute to the Jews. Choosing to insert the testimony of the villager who helped toward the end, after so many testimonies that present indifferent onlookers and witnesses, gainers, collaborators, and perpetrators who blame the victims, reflects the need to believe that there is always a choice.

Epilogue

In the battle over collective memory, cinema plays a significant role in affecting popular memory as well as consensual beliefs and knowledge.[1] Documentary researchers claim that the twenty-first century is a "new documentary age" in which documentary cinema is enjoying unprecedented levels of public attention and is a significant category in the media industry.[2] Documentary cinematic representations of the Holocaust in Israel have been influenced by the changes in Holocaust awareness in Israel, and have simultaneously influenced these changes by taking an active part in altering perceptions. Since the late 1990s, third-generation survivors have joined other Israeli collective memory agents and have become the new "custodians of memory."[3] Their documentaries are an important medium through which their experiences, thoughts, and perceptions are articulated to larger publics.[4]

Dan Bar-On and Tal Litvak-Hirsch noted that in terms of Holocaust awareness, the Israeli society in which the third generation lives differs considerably from the Israel of their parents.[5] The third generation has been educated in a society that had already modified its stance toward Holocaust survivors. The divisive perceptions commonplace in the first decades of the state of Israel, such as the dichotomy between the European Jews who had rebelled against the Nazis and those who had not (and the question of how/why they survived), were replaced by the view of survivors as heroes who had proven their immense ability to overcome atrocities. This cultural atmosphere may have facilitated their closeness to the survivors. Additionally, the grandchildren of Holocaust survivors, unlike their parents, who lived in close contact with Holocaust survivors, grew up in a sheltered atmosphere with a generation separating them from direct trauma. They are able to see their grandparents in a more intimate light than their parents. From the survivors' point of view, grandchildren represent a return to "normalcy"—they are proof that they indeed succeeded in rebuilding their lives after the World War II.[6] Research indicates that grandchildren perceive their grandparents as figures who can help them, and they express interest in their past. The grandparents, in turn, often contribute to their grandchildren's development and have a positive impact on their values.[7] These differences have influenced the thematic and aesthetic ways in which the trauma, the survivors, and their stories are represented in third-generation documentaries as compared to second-generation documentaries.

Another key feature affecting the differences in documentary representations between the two generations is the contemporary fatigue with Holocaust representations. Second-generation rhetoric, aesthetic, and thematic key factors (whose Israeli characteristics were analyzed in this book), which were revolutionary when they appeared, have become an integral part of Holocaust collective memory in Israel and the Western world. The third generation thus grew up into a world in which these representations were considered a given. Many third-generation directors make it clear that they deliberately did not want to make "another Holocaust documentary." What was once a novelty, for them was trivial and even overly familiar. They do not want to recirculate earlier representations but rather use them to expand Holocaust commemoration in other ways. Therefore, many third-generation directors deliberately neglect the usual bank of images and narratives and address the Holocaust from new perspectives while challenging these classic representations. As shown in this book, third-generation documentaries draw on second-generation documentaries as "realms of memory"—that is, what Pierre Nora described as basic texts that code, summarize, and constitute the national memory, in order to create a new layer of commemoration.[8]

The films analyzed in this book reveal that prosthetic memory is not a uniform perception of the past by the victims' descendants, and it highlights the various ways in which postmemory differs from after-postmemory. It shows how these differences govern cinematic trends as well as aesthetic choices and impact the moral recollection of the past. The in-depth exploration of these documentaries, most of which were analyzed for the first time in *Remaking Holocaust Memory*, shed light on the ways third-generation directors relate to the existing documentary commemoration, and maintain it while dealing with new notions such as the representation of gender, Germany as home, historical versus emotional perspectives, victims and victimhood, the veracity of victims' testimony, photographic and cinematic visuals, additional traumas, perpetrators, bystanders, both these groups' descendants, and ethics.

Gender: Unlike the marginalization of the unique aspects of women's life and death during the Holocaust in second-generation documentaries, third-generation documentaries make it clear that women's and men's trajectories ending in death or survival have similar but also different characteristics. They show how Jewish women suffered as Jews, but also as women, as a result of social, psychological, and physical differences. Third-generation films deal with pregnancies, abortions, childbirth, sexual abuse, and motherhood.

Germany as Home: In second-generation films, Germany is hardly ever mentioned. The survivors, their children, or both, are described as traveling back to other places in Europe to retrace the past before and during the Holocaust. Third-generation documentaries turn Germany into a key arena. They undermine the Zionist narrative by presenting Germany as a beloved homeland, a place where the postwar rehabilitation of survivors occurred, and as a possible home in the present for survivors and their descendants.

Historical/Emotional Perspectives: Many second-generation documentaries present a personal historical account of the atrocities, and chart the hunt for stories that will produce facts about the survivors' lives during the Holocaust. By contrast, many third-generation documentarists orient the debate toward other realms. They do not aim to produce a historical account of the Holocaust, and in interviews often state that they did not want to produce a documentary centering on testimonies and reflecting historical events. They are more interested in other topics, such as emotions, subjective perceptions, or in specific life choices.

Victims and Victimhood: Despite debates in the psychological literature on whether the second generation constitutes a separate group with their own psychopathological characteristics, second-generation documentaries tend to consider the children of survivors as a separate group that suffers from secondary traumatic stress. Research claims that third-generation survivors in Israel have attempted to find another mode of remembering—one that preserves the Holocaust's significance, but avoids creating a new generation of victims.[9] Third-generation documentaries discuss the influence of the Holocaust on them, but marginalize aspects of victimization and represent a range of reactions to the past. The complex and difficult relationships of children of survivors with their parents are marginalized. The films appear less involved in processes of dealing with emotional burdens or judgments and depict Holocaust survivors with more admiration and closeness.

Testimonies and Historical Truth: Many second-generation documentaries devote considerable screen time to survivors' testimonies. The evidence they provide is presented as historical fact. The second-generation filmmakers are the listeners, the observers who question, and interview, but do not dispute these testimonies.[10] However, as early as the 1950s, research on the complex aspects of personal testimonies showed that victims have subjective and partial recollections. Third-generation documentaries address this complexity of survivors' testimonies by drawing attention to the problems of personal recollections and simultaneously to their importance for historical accounts of the past.

Reexamining the Image: Second-generation documentaries mainly operate in a realistic mode and refrain from reflexive discussions. The complex role of the image is rarely addressed directly and images are used as a natural device through which pieces of the past are recollected. Some use Nazi footage, although most avoid it and deal with the past by combining old photos and family documents with interviews. Third-generation documentaries challenge the veracity, exploitation, and importance of photographs, Nazi footage, and Holocaust symbols. They discuss the complexity of the image as well as the advantages and disadvantages inherent to rebuilding a portrait out of historical images, and the relationship between Holocaust images and collective memory.

Additional Traumas: Most second-generation documentaries deal with Holocaust survivors solely through the perspective of the Holocaust as the trauma that shaped their lives. In third-generation documentaries the depiction of the victims is also intended to remind the audience that Holocaust survivors are people who went through other traumas and disasters in their lives, which, at times, hurt and affected them even more than the Holocaust. In so doing third-generation filmmakers represent the "people" behind the label *Holocaust survivors*. They broaden the depiction of the victims by showing that the posttraumatic effects of the Holocaust cannot account for all their actions.

Perpetrators and Bystanders: Second-generation documentaries focus on the victims and their descendants. The personal perspectives and perceptions of perpetrators, bystanders, and both these groups' offspring are marginalized. Third-generation documentaries do not shy away from that once-taboo topic. For the first time they dare to look beyond the victims, and grapple with the behavior, motives, objectives, and characteristics of perpetrators, bystanders, and both these groups' offspring. These films reveal varied and complex ways of dealing with the past from "the other side."

Ethics: Third-generation documentaries raise new ethical problems that did not appear in second-generation films—primarily the clash between the filmmaker's right of expression and the rights of the filmed subjects to privacy, information, and preservation of their reputation. Second-generation documentaries were mainly directed when the survivors were alive and completely aware of the documentation. In the cases of documentaries filmed after the survivors' death, their children, eager to understand the historical route to hell, did not damage their reputations. By contrast, certain third-generation documentaries have been made when the survivors are elderly or after they have passed away. These films reveal hidden secrets or violate familial hidden truths at a time when the survivors can no longer defend themselves.

Overall, in the transition from second-generation documentaries to third-generation documentaries, the "absolute truths" that appeared in the majority of second-generation films are deconstructed and disputed in third-generation documentaries. The latter reject dichotomic divisions between people, places, and perceptions of narratives and visuals. They do not dismiss their "cinematic parents'" approach but rethink fixed notions, focus on marginalized topics, and pose questions where previously there were exclamation marks.

Third-generation documentaries make use of the important commemoration layer established in second-generation documentaries, but at the same time criticize its main configurations. They do not construct a competitive memory or a demolition model of memory, in which a new memory eradicates the previous one and emerges at the expense of the other. They adhere to the notion of *multidirectional memory*, which allows different forms of commemoration to coexist simultaneously and different representations to merge and meld together.[11] In a world that is unsure how Holocaust awareness will evolve in the twenty-first century, and wonders how Holocaust remembrance will be shaped after the Holocaust survivors—the direct witnesses to the trauma—will no longer be with us, *Remaking Holocaust Memory* shows how third-generation documentaries provide new ideas and concepts to commemorate and preserve the memory for future generations.

Appendix

Notes

Filmography

Bibliography

Index

APPENDIX

Festivals and Awards

Third-Generation Documentaries

A Film Unfinished [*Shtikat haarchion*], Yael Hersonski, 2010

Festivals

Academy of Film & Multimedia Marubi, Albania, 2011
Bangkok International Film Festival, 2010
Belarusian Confederation of Creative Unions, 2010
Beldocs International Documentary Film Festival, 2011
Biblioteca di Storia Moderna e Contemporanea, Italy, 2011
Bucharest Jewish Film Festival, 2011
Cinémathèque/Ville de Luxembourg, November 2011
Copenhagen Jewish Film Festival, 2011
EDOC: Ecuador Documentary Film Festival, 2011
Embassy of Israel, Dublin, November 2011
Exile Film Festival, Greece, November 2011
Filmoteca de Catalunya, 2010
Holocaust Fund of Jews from Macedonia, 2011
Hong Kong Independent Film Festival, 2010
Hong Kong Jewish Film Festival, November 2011
IndieLisboa Film Festival, 2011
Jerusalem Film Festival, 2010
Jewish Historical Museum, Netherlands, March 2011
Makedox International Film Festival, 2011
Melbourne International Film Festival, 2010
Memorial de la Shoah, France, 2011
Memorimage Barcelona, 2010

Moscow Israel Film Festival, September 2011
One World Film Festival, Prague, March 2011
One World Film Festival, Romania, March 2011
Pitigliano Rome Film Festival, 2010
PKF Milano Film Festival, 2011
Planete Doc Review, 2010
Rio de Janeiro Jewish Film Festival, 2011
Rio International Film Festival, 2010
Saarbrücken Israeli Film Festival, 2010
Sao Paulo Jewish Film Festival, 2011
Split Film Festival, Croatia, 2011
Taiwan International Film Festival, 2010
This Human World, Vienna, 2011
UK Jewish Film Festival, 2010
Verzio International Human Rights Documentary Film Festival, 2010
Zagreb Jewish Film Festival, 2011

Awards

Berlin Film Festival; Full-Frame Documentary Film Festival, 2010
HOT Docs: Best International Feature
Jerusalem Film Festival: Van Leer Best Documentary and the Forum for the Preservation of Audio-Visual Memory
Shanghai International TV Festival: Magnolia International Documentary Award
Silverdocs Festival: WGA (Writers Guild of America) Award for Documentary Screenplay, 2010
Sundance Film Festival: Best Editing

Aida's Secrets [_Hasodot shel Ida_], Alon Swartz, 2016

Festivals and Awards

Austin Jewish Film Festival, 2017.
HOT Docs, Toronto, 2016
Jerusalem Film Festival, 2016
Official selection, New York Jewish Film Festival, 2017

Official selection, Palm Springs International Film Festival, 2017
Official selection, Warsaw Film Festival, 2016
Philadelphia Israeli Film Festival, 2017
San Francisco Jewish Film Festival, 2017
True Stories Selection—Palm Springs International Film Festival, 2017
Winner, Audience Award, Miami Jewish Film Festival, 2017
Winner, Jury Prize for Best Documentary, Atlanta Jewish Film Festival, 2017
Winner, Audience Award, DocAviv Film Festival, 2016

Aida's Secrets was bought for distribution in twenty locations in the United States, and it is still making the rounds at festivals.

Café Nagler, Mor Kaplansky, 2015

Festivals and Awards

AICE (Australia Israel Cultural Exchange) International Film Festival, 2016
All Lights India International Film Festival, 2016
Calgary Jewish Film Festival, 2016
City Food and Film Festival, Netherlands, 2016
Detroit Jewish Film Festival, 2016
Devour! The Food Film Festival, Wolfville, Canada, 2016
DOK.Fest München (Munich International Documentary Film Festival), 2016
Filmmor Women's Film Festival on Wheels, Turkey, 2016
Filmmor Women's International Film Festival, Turkey, 2016
La Costa International Film Festival, 2016
Minsk International Film Festival, 2016
Molodist International Film Festival, 2016
Official selection, Berlinale Culinary Cinema, 2016
Philadelphia Jewish Film Festival, 2016

The Cahana Sisters [*Ha'ahayot Cahana*], Gilad Melzer, 2006

Festivals

7th Festival of Israeli Cinema, Paris, 2007
East European Docs

Haifa Film Festival, 2006
Holocaust Center of Northern California

The Cemetery Club [Moadon beit hakvarot], Tali Shemesh, 2006

Festivals and Awards

Allentown (Pennsylvania) Film Series
Boston Jewish Film Festival
Brussels Jewish Film Festival
Cannes International Film Festival
DocAviv Film Festival, Tel Aviv, Promising Filmmaker Award and Best Photography Award
DOK Leipzig International Film Festival, Leipzig, Golden Dove Award for Best Documentary
European Film Academy Nomination for Best Documentary, 2006
Hartford Jewish Film Festival
HOT Docs International Film Festival, Toronto, Official Competition
International Documentary Festival Amsterdam, Reflecting Images, Best of Fests
International Women's Film Festival, Israel, Best Film Award
Jewish Community Center on the Palisades (New Jersey)
Miami International Film Festival, Official Competition
New York Israeli Film Festival
One World, Human Rights Documentary Film Festival, Prague, Best Director
Palm Beach Jewish Film Festival
Portland Jewish Film Festival
Rome Israeli Film Festival
San Francisco Jewish Film Festival, 2007
Sao Paulo Jewish Film Festival
Shanghai International Film Festival, Magnolia Award for Best Asian Documentary
Staten Island Jewish Film Festival
Tucson Jewish Film Festival
Washington Jewish Film Festival

The Decent One [*Adam hagun*], Vanessa Lapa, 2014

Festivals and Awards

Bergen International Film Festival, 2014
Berlin International Film Festival, 2014
DocumentaMadrid, Madrid Documentary Film Festival, 2014
FOCAL International Awards nominee for Best Use of Footage in a Cinema Release and Jane Mercer Footage Researcher of the Year Award, 2015
International Documentary Film Festival, Amsterdam, 2015
International Documentary Film Festival, Zagreb, 2015
Israeli Academy Awards, Ophir Prize nominee, 2014
Jameson CineFest, Miskolc International Film Festival
Jerusalem International Film Festival, Van Leer Group Foundation Award for Best Israeli Documentary, 2014
Munich International Documentary Film Festival, 2014
Planete and Doc Film Festival, Warsaw, 2014
Reykjavík International Film Festival, 2014
Rio de Janeiro International Film Festival, 2014
Telluride Film Festival, 2014

Farewell Herr Schwarz [*Heye shalom, Peter Schwartz*], Yael Reuveny, 2013

Festivals

Berlin Jewish Film Festival, 2014
Cottbus Film Festival, 2013
Dok Leipzig, 2013
First Film Fest, 2014
Haifa International Film Festival, 2013
Israeli Filmmaker Forum Competition, 2014
Schleswig Holstein Film Festival, 2014
Toronto Jewish Film Festival, 2014
Women's Film Festival, Cologne, 2014

Awards

Winner, Audience Award, Women's Film Festival, Cologne, 2014
Winner, Best Debut Film, Israeli Filmmaker Forum Competition, 2014
Winner, Best Documentary Film, Haifa International Film Festival, 2013
Winner, Best Film, Schleswig Holstein Film Festival, 2014
Winner, Best German Film, Berlin Jewish Film Festival, 2014
Winner, DEFA Award, DOK Leipzig Film Festival, 2013
Winner, DIALOGUE Award, Cottbus Film Festival, 2013
Winner, Outstanding Storytelling Award, First Film Fest, 2014
Winner, Promising Director Award, Toronto Jewish Film Festival, 2014

The Flat [_Hadira_], Arnon Goldfinger, 2011

Festivals and Screenings

Antenna International Film Festival, Official Competition, Australia, 2012
Athens Israeli Film Week, Greece, 2014
Athens Jewish Film Festival, Georgia, 2013
Banff Centre, Canada, 2014
Barcelona Jewish Film Festival, 2013
BelDocs International Film Festival, Official Competition, Serbia, 2012
Berlinale, 2013, Best of Best German Films for 2013, preselected for the LOLA Film Prize
Boston Jewish Film Festival, 2012
Budapest Israeli Film Festival, 2013
Chicago Israel Film Festival, 2013
Cleveland Jewish Film Festival, 2012
Copenhagen Jewish Film Festival, 2012
Denver Film Society, 2012
DocEst International Film Festival, Romania, 2013
Documentary Edge Film Festival, New Zealand, 2012
DokuFest International Documentary Film Festival Kosovo, Official Competition, 2012
East Bay Jewish Film Festival, California, 2012
Edmonton Jewish Film Festival, Canada, 2013
EIDF (EBS International Documentary Festival) South Korea, 2012

European Psychoanalytic Film Festival, London, 2015
Gainesville Jewish Film Festival, Florida, 2013
Geneva Jewish Film Festival, Switzerland, 2013
Hamptons International Film Festival, New York, 2012
Harrisburg Jewish Film Festival, Pennsylvania, 2013
IDOCS (International Documentary Film Festival), Beijing, 2016
Jerusalem International Film Festival, 2011
Jewish Motifs Film Festival, Poland, 2013
Krakow International Film Festival, Official Competition, 2012
Louisville Jewish Film Festival, Kentucky, 2013
Mediterranean Film Festival, Bosnia, August 2012
Midland Center for the Arts, Michigan, 2013
Minneapolis International Film Festival, 2012
Montreal Israeli Film Series, 2013
Movies at War International Film Festival, Norway, 2012
DOK.Fest München (Munich International Documentary Film Festival), 2012
New Jersey Israeli Film Series, 2013
Palm Beach Jewish Film Festival, 2013
Philadelphia Israeli Film Festival, 2013
Rhode Island Jewish Film Festival, 2013
Rockland Jewish Film Festival, New York, 2013
San Antonio Jewish Film Festival, 2013
Sao Paulo Israeli Film Festival, 2012
Sedona International Film Festival, Arizona, 2013
Silicon Valley Jewish Film Festival, California, 2012
Spokane Jewish Film Festival, 2012
Stockholm Jewish Film Festival, 2012
Temple Beth Shalom Jewish Film Series, Needham, Massachusetts, 2013
Temple Isaiah Film Festival, Lafayette, California, 2014
Toronto Jewish Film Festival, 2012
Traverse City International Film Festival, Michigan, 2012
Tribeca International Film Festival, New York, Official Competition, 2012
University of Wisconsin Israeli Film Series, 2013
Vancouver International Film Festival, 2012
Watch Docs International Human Rights Film Festival, Warsaw, 2012

Winnipeg Jewish Film Festival, 2012
Zagreb Israeli Film Festival, 2012

Awards

Bavarian Film Award for Best Documentary, 2012
Best Documentary, Minneapolis-St. Paul International Film Festival, 2012
Best Editing, Tribeca International Film Festival, 2012
Best Documentary Director, Jerusalem Film Festival Award, 2011
Best Documentary nominee, LOLA German Filmprize Awards, 2013
Best Film, Best Director, and Best Research, Israeli Documentary Filmmakers Forum's Awards, 2011
David A. Stein Memorial Award for Best Documentary, Toronto Jewish Film Festival, 2012
FIPRESCI (International Federation of Film Critics) Jury Award, 52nd Krakow Film Festival, 2012
Gilde-Filmpreis, German Art Cinemas Guild Award for Best Documentary in German Cinemas, 2012
Golden Phoenix Award, Jewish Motifs Film Festival, Poland, 2013
Israeli Academy Award ("Ofir") for Best Documentary, 2011
Special Jury Mention, New Zealand International Documentary Film Festival, 2012
Special Jury Prize for a Foreign Film, Traverse City International Film Festival, Michigan, 2012

The Green Dumpster Mystery [_Hata'aluma bamechola hayeruka_], Tal Haim Yoffe, 2008

Festivals, Screenings, and Awards

Calgary Jewish Film Festival, 2008
Chicago Festival of Israeli Cinema, 2008
International Documentary Film Festival, Amsterdam, 2008
Jerusalem International Film Festival, 2008
National Center for Jewish Film Annual Festival, Boston, 2008
Palm Beach Jewish Film Festival, 2008
Palm Springs International Film Festival, 2008

Syracuse International Film Festival, 2008
Toronto Jewish Film Festival, 2008
Washington Jewish Film Festival, 2008
Yad Vashem Award, Jerusalem International Film Festival, (Chairman's Award for Artistic Achievement in a Holocaust-Related Film), 2008

Hitler's Children [*Yaldei Hitler*], Chanoch Ze'evi, 2011

Festivals and Awards

Atlanta Jewish Film Festival, 2013
Boston Jewish Film Festival, 2012
Documentary Edge Film Festival, New Zealand, 2012
Hartford Jewish Film Festival, 2013
Houston Jewish Film Festival, 2013
IDFA (International Documentary Film Festival Amsterdam), Netherlands, 2011
Jewish International Film Festival, Australia, 2012
Jewish Motifs International Film Festival, Poland, 2013
Moscow International Film Festival, 2012
DOK.Fest München (Munich International Documentary Film Festival), 2012
One World, Prague, Czech Republic, 2012
Rutgers Jewish Film Festival, New Jersey, 2012
San Diego Jewish Film Festival, 2013
Santa Fe Film Festival, New Mexico, 2012
Sevastopol Film Festival, Ukraine, 2012
Silicon Valley Jewish Film Festival, California, 2012
Teaneck International Film Festival, New Jersey, 2012
Thessaloniki International Film Festival, 2012
Vancouver International Film Festival, 2013
Vilnius Documentary Film Festival, 2012
Warsaw International Film Festival, 2012
Zagreb Jewish Film Festival, 2013

Hitler's Children also won the Warsaw Phoenix Prize for Best Documentary Film at the 9th annual Jewish Motifs International Film Festival in 2013.

Kleiner Rudi, Michelle Stein Teer, 2006

Festivals

Chicago Israeli Film Festival, 2006
Jerusalem Jewish Film Festival, 2006

Kleiner Rudi was broadcast in educational cinematic meetings all across Germany.

Martin, Ra'anan Alexandrowicz, 1999

Selected Festival Screenings and Awards

Berlin Film Festival, 2000 (Forum for Young Cinema)
Best Film Israeli Competition, 1999
Jerusalem International Film Festival, 1999
New Directors, New Films Festival, 2000 (MoMA/Lincoln Center)
Second Place Winner, DocAviv Film Festival, 2000
Sheffield International Documentary Film Festival, 2000
Wolgin Award for Best Documentary, 1999

Martin was also purchased by the Museum of Modern Art in New York City for permanent collection.

My German Children [_Yeladim Germanim sheli_],
Tom Tamar Pauer, 2012

Festivals

Astra International Film Festival, 2013
Australia-Israel Cultural Exchange, 2013
Documentary Film Fest, Saratov, Russia, 2013
DOK.Fest München (Munich International Documentary Film Festival), 2013
Gold Coast Arts Center, Great Neck, New York, July 2014
International Documentary Film Festival, Amsterdam, 2016

Jerusalem Jewish Film Festival, 2012
Religion Today International Film Festival, 2013
Shanghai International TV Festival, 2013
University of Denver, November 2013
University of Florida, May 2014

Awards

Aliza Shagrir Fund Prize, Israel, 2012
Audience Award at the International Documentary Film Fest, Saratov, Russia, 2013
First Prize at the International Documentary Film Fest, Saratov, Russia, 2013

Numbered [_S'furim_], Dana Doron and Uriel Sinai, 2011

Festivals and Screenings

Atlanta Jewish Film Festival, February 2013
Austin Jewish Film Festival, April 2013
Australia Jewish Film Festival, November 2013
Brandeis University Festival, April 2013
Calgary Jewish Film Festival, November 2012
Charlotte Jewish Film Festival, North Carolina, November 2014
Cherry Hill Jewish Film Festival, April 2013
Chicago Festival of Israeli Cinema, October 2013
Chicago International Film Festival, October 2012
Cincinnati Jewish Film Festival, Mayerson Jewish Community Center, February 2013
Cleveland Jewish Film Festival, October 2013
Detroit Jewish Film Festival, April 2013
East Bay Jewish Film Festival, California, March 2013
Edmonton Jewish Film Festival, May 2014
Greenwich Jewish Community Center, Connecticut, January 2014
Hangzhou Asian Film Festival, October 2013
Hartford Jewish Film Festival, April 2013
Holocaust Museum and Learning Center, St. Louis, November 2013

Hong Kong Jewish Film Festival, November 2012
Houston Jewish Film Festival, March 2013
Israeli Cultural Institute, Budapest, Hungary, April 2013
Ithaca College, April 2013
Jacob Burns Film Center, Pleasantville, New York, April 2013
Jerusalem International Film Festival, July 2012
Jewish Community Center Manhattan, January 2013
Kingsway Jewish Center, August 2014
Los Angeles Israeli Film Festival, April 2013
Miami Jewish Film Festival, January 2013
Michigan State University, May 2014
Museum of Jewish Heritage, New York, April 2013
New Haven Free Public Library, Canada, November 2014
New Jersey Israeli Film Series, March 2013
New Jersey Jewish Film Festival, April 2013
New York Jewish Film Festival, January 2013
Nuremberg Human Rights International Film Festival, May 2014
Palm Beach Jewish Film Festival, January 2013
Pittsburgh Jewish Film Festival, April 2013
Rutgers Jewish Film Festival, October 2013
Sao Paulo Jewish Film Festival, August 2013
Seattle Jewish Film Festival, March 2013
Stockholm Jewish Film Festival, October 2013
Tartu International Film Festival, Estonia, March 2013
Temple Concord, Syracuse, New York, January 2014
Thessaloniki Jewish Community, April 2013
This Human World, Vienna, December 2013
Toronto Jewish Film Festival, April 2013
University of California, March 2013
University of Florida, May 2014
University of Massachusetts, April 2013
University of Toronto, October 2013
Warsaw Jewish Film Festival, October 2013
Washington Jewish Film Festival, January 2013
Vancouver Holocaust Education Centre, January 2015
Young Israel of Great Neck, November 2013
Zagreb Jewish Film Festival, May 2013

Awards

Best Debut Film Award, Israeli Documentary Forum Awards, 2012
Best Documentary, Religion Today Film Festival, Italy, 2013
Silver Hugo Award, Chicago International Film Festival, 2012
Special Jury Mention, Religion Today Film Festival, Italy, 2013

Out of the Forest [_M'kivun hayaar_], Yaron Kaftori Ben-Yosef and Limor Pinhasov Ben-Yosef, 2004

Festivals

Bangkok International Film Festival
Berlin Film Festival
Chicago International Film Festival
Human Rights Film Festival, Amsterdam
London International Film Festival
Sao Paulo International Film Festival
Toronto Jewish Film Society
Vilnius International Film Festival

Oy Mama, Noa Maiman, 2010

Festivals, Screenings, and Awards

Band Film Festival, Oregon, 2010
Documentary Forum Film Festival and Competition, 2010
History and Biography Award nominee, Shanghai International TV Festival, 2010
Religion Today Film Festival, Italy, 2010
Winner of Best Documentary, Go East Film Festival, Germany, 2010

Shalom Italia [_Shloshah ahim v'me'ara_], Tamar Tal-Anati, 2016

Festivals and Awards

Australian Jewish International Film Festival, 2016
Calgary Jewish Film Festival, Opening Night, 2016

Cleveland International Film Festival, 2017
DocAviv Film Festival, Tel Aviv, 2016
HOT Docs, Toronto, 2016
Israeli Film Festival, Los Angeles, 2016
Jerusalem Film Festival, 2016
Official Selection, American Film Institute Docs Film Festival, Los Angeles, 2016
Official Selection, Festival Dei Popoli, Florence, 2016
Official Selection, IDFA (International Documentary Film Festival Amsterdam), Amsterdam, 2016
Philadelphia Jewish Film Festival, 2016
Rochester Jewish Film Festival, 2017

Shalom Italia is being screened at various events in Europe, the United States, and Canada, and is still making the rounds at festivals.

Notes

Preface

1. Dina Porat, *Café haboker b'reach ha'ashan* [Smoke-Scented Morning Coffee] (Jerusalem: Yad Vashem: Am Oved, 2011); Liat Steir-Livny, *Shtei panim bamar'a* [Two Faces in the Mirror] (Jerusalem: Eshkolot-Magnes, 2009).

2. This book uses these terms to refer not only to the biological offspring of Holocaust survivors but also to Jews born in Israel after 1945 who grew up in an environment that considers the Holocaust to be one of the key features of Jewish-Israeli identity. See Iris Milner, *Kirei avar* [A Torn Past] (Tel Aviv: Am Oved, 2004), 19–35.

3. See the introduction to this volume.

4. See notes 7–8 and the introduction to this volume.

5. Oren Meyers, Motti Neiger, and Eyal Zandberg, *Communicating Awe: Media Memory and Holocaust Commemoration* (Basingstoke, UK: Palgrave Macmillan, 2014).

6. Liat Steir-Livny, *Har hazikaron yizkor bimkomi* [Let the Memorial Hill Remember] (Tel Aviv: Resling, 2014). To date, there are only a few Holocaust fiction films directed by third-generation Holocaust survivors, such as *The Debt* (Assaf Bernstein, 2007), *Pension Pracht* (Tamar Yarom, 2014), and *Sand Birds* (Amir Wolf, 2014).

7. Nitzan Lebvovic, "Freeze-Framing: Temporality and the Archives in Forgacs, Hersonski and Friedländer," in *Probing the Ethics of Holocaust Culture*, ed. Claudio Fogu, Wulf Kasteiner, and Todd Presner (Cambridge, MA: Harvard Univ. Press), 257–76; Odeya Kohen-Raz, "Arnon Goldfinger's 'The Flat' (2011): Ethics and Aesthetics in Third-Generation Holocaust Cinema," *Studies in Documentary Film* 6, no. 3 (2012): 323–38; Yael Munk, "Arnon Goldfinger's 'The Flat': Holocaust Memory, Film Noir, and the Pain of Others," *Jewish Film and New Media: An International Journal* 4, no. 1 (Spring 2016): 25–42; Dalia Markowitz and Kziaa Alon, "Moadon beit hakvarot" [The Cemetery Club], in *Documentally*, ed. Maayan Amir (Tel Aviv: Am Oved, 2007), 199–206. The films *Martin*, *The Flat*, and *A Film Unfinished*

were analyzed as parts of chapters in Brad Prager, *After the Fact: The Holocaust in Twenty-First Century Documentary Film* (London: Bloomsbury, 2015).

8. Moshe Zimmerman, *Al tigu li bashoah* [Don't Touch My Holocaust] (Haifa: Haifa Univ. Press, 2002); Nurith Gertz, *Makhela aheret: nitzolei shoa zarim v'aherim* [A Different Choir: Holocaust Survivors, Aliens, and Others in Israeli Cinema and Literature] (Tel Aviv: Am Oved and Open Univ., 2004); Steir-Livny, *Shtei panim bamar'a*.

9. See, for example, Yosefa Loshitzky, *Identity Politics on the Israeli Screen* (Austin: Univ. of Texas Press, 2002), 32–71; Michal Friedman, "The Double Legacy of Arbeit Macht Frei," *Prooftexts* 22, no. 1/2 (Winter/Spring 2002): 200–220; Michal Friedman, "Witnessing for the Witness: Choice and Destiny by Tsipi Reibenbach," *Shofar: An Interdisciplinary Journal of Jewish Studies* 24, no. 1 (Fall 2005): 81–93; Hagai Dagan and Gidi Dishon, "Nostalgyat shoah: iyun mehudash betrauma ubenostalgia leor hamikre shel 'pizza beauschwitz'" [Holocaust Nostalgia: Rethinking Trauma and Nostalgia in Light of "Pizza in Auschwitz"], *Teoria v'Bikoret* (Winter 2011): 185–209; Limor Bar-Ilan, "The Representation of Holocaust Survivors in Israeli Documentaries," Yad Vashem, http://www.yadvashem.org/yv/he/education/newsletter/24/survivors_films.asp; and analysis of specific films in Omer Bartov, *The Jew in Cinema* (Bloomington: Indiana Univ. Press, 2005).

10. Bill Nichols, *Introduction to Documentary* (Bloomington: Indiana Univ. Press, 2001), 99–138.

11. Michael Renov, "Introduction: The Truth about Non-Fiction," in *Theorizing Documentary*, ed. Michael Renov (London: Routledge, 1993), 1–11.

12. Marianne Hirsch, "Past Lives, First Memories in Exile," *Poetics Today* 17, no. 4 (1996): 659–67.

13. Gerd Bayer, "After Post-Memory: Holocaust Cinema and the Third Generation," *Shofar: An Interdisciplinary Journal of Jewish Studies* 28, no. 4 (2010): 116–32.

14. Alison Landsberg, *Prosthetic Memory: The Transformation of American Remembrance in the Age of Mass Culture* (New York: Columbia Univ. Press, 2004).

15. The complexity of this term, its many facets, and other terms relating to the bystander question will be discussed in chapters 4 and 5.

16. Since these films reflect two main topics, their other facets are analyzed in chapter 5.

Introduction

1. There is an extensive debate on these questions. See, for example, Theodor W. Adorno, *Negative Dialectics* (London: Routledge, 2000); Naomi Mandel, *Against the Unspeakable: Complicity, the Holocaust, and Slavery in America*

(Charlottesville: Univ. of Virginia Press, 2007); Mark Godfrey, *Abstraction and the Holocaust* (New Haven, CT: Yale Univ. Press, 2007); Shoshana Feldman and Dori Laub, *Edut* [Testimony] (Tel Aviv: Resling 2008); Libby Saxton, "Shneihem sonim et Spielberg" [They Both Hate Spielberg], *Mita'am*, December 2007, 106–24.

2. Paul Rotha, "Some Principles of Documentary," in *A Paul Rotha Reader*, ed. Petrie Duncan and Robert Kruger (Exeter: Univ. of Exeter Press, 1999), 148.

3. Hardy Forsyth, ed., *Grierson on Documentary* (London: Faber and Faber, 1966); Erik Barnouw, *Documentary: A History of the Non-Fiction Film* (Oxford: Oxford Univ. Press, 1993); Richard Barsam, *Nonfiction Film: A Critical History* (Bloomington: Indiana Univ. Press, 1992); John Corner, *The Art of Record: A Critical Introduction to Documentary* (Manchester: Manchester Univ. Press, 1996); Nichols, *Introduction to Documentary*; Bill Nichols, "Documentary Reenactment and the Fantasmatic Subject," *Critical Inquiry* 35 (Autumn 2008): 72–89; Michael Renov, *The Subject of Documentary* (Minneapolis: Univ. of Minnesota Press, 2004); Charles Warren, ed., *Beyond Document: Essays on Nonfiction Film* (Lebanon, NH: Univ. Press of New England, 1996); Judith Aston and Sandra Gaudenzi, "Interactive Documentary: Setting the Field," *Studies in Documentary Film* 6, no. 2 (2012): 125–39.

4. Hayden White, "The Historical Text as Literary Artifact," in *Tropics of Discourse: Essays in Cultural Criticism*, ed. Hayden White (Baltimore: Johns Hopkins Univ. Press, 1978); *The History and Narrative Reader*, ed. Geoffrey Roberts (London: Routledge, 2001), 221–36; Peter Novick, *That Noble Dream: The "Objectivity Question" and the American Historical Profession* (Cambridge: Cambridge Univ. Press, 1988), 573–629.

5. Steir-Livny, *Shtei panim bamar'a*, 1–5.

6. Igal Burstein, *Tiud: Seret tiudi bdia* [Documentation: Fiction Documentary] (Tel Aviv: Sal Tarbut Artzi, 2004); Ron Goldman, "Emet v'ziuf al shulhan ha'aricha" [Truth and Deceit in the Editing Room], *Panim* 32 (2005), http://www.itu.org.il/Index.asp?ArticleID=4926andCategoryID=762andPage=1.

7. Robert Rosenstone, *Revisioning History: Film and the Construction of a New Past* (Princeton, NJ: Princeton Univ. Press, 1995).

8. David LaRocca, "Introduction: Representative Qualities and Questions of Documentary Film," in *The Philosophy of Documentary Film: Image, Sound, Fiction, Truth*, ed. David LaRocca (Lanham, MD: Lexington Books), 7.

9. Bill Nichols, *Representing Reality: Issues and Concepts in Documentary* (Bloomington: Indiana Univ. Press, 1991), 32.

10. Nichols, *Introduction to Documentary*, 20.

11. Nichols, *Representing Reality*, 8, 27.

12. Brian Winston, *The Documentary Film Book* (London: British Film Institute, 2013).

13. Stella Bruzzi, *New Documentary: A Critical Introduction* (London: Routledge, 2000), 4.

14. Bruzzi, *New Documentary*, 125.

15. Elizabeth Cowie, *Recording Reality, Desiring the Real* (Minneapolis: Univ. of Minnesota Press, 2011), 118–34.

16. Agnieszka Piotrowska, *Psychoanalysis and Ethics in Documentary Film* (London: Routledge, 2014), 193.

17. Nichols, *Representing Reality*, 32.

18. Nichols, *Representing Reality*, 32–75; Nichols, *Introduction to Documentary*, 142–211.

19. Michael Renov, "Towards a Poetic of Documentary," in *Theorizing Documentary*, ed. Michael Renov (London: Routledge, 1993), 12–36.

20. Renov, "Towards a Poetic of Documentary," 21.

21. LaRocca, "Introduction," 24–25.

22. Prager, *After the Fact*, 1–26.

23. See the analysis of this film in chapter 3.

24. Stuart Liebman, "Documenting the Liberation of the Camps: The Case of Alexander Ford's *Vernichtungslager Majdanek: Cmentarzysko Europy* (1944)," in *Lesson and Legacies VII: The Holocaust in International Perspective*, ed. Herzog Dagmar (Evanston, IL: Northwestern Univ. Press, 2006), 333–51; Mimi Ash and Assaf Tal, "Total Horror Is Not Representable," Yad Vashem, http://www.yadvashem.org/yv/he/education/film_reviews/shoah.asp#04. According to Urzula Jarecka, at the time, the film was met in the Western world with disbelief and was treated as a tool of the USSR's anti-German propaganda. See Urzula Jarecka, "Wounded Memory: Rhetorical Strategies Used in Public Discourse on the Katyn Massacre," in *The Long Aftermath: Cultural Legacies of Europe at War, 1936–2016*, ed. Manuel Braganca and Peter Tame (New York: Berghahn Books, 2016), 302–15, esp. 311.

25. Toby Haggith, "How the German Concentration Camps Factual Survey (1945/2014) Became the World's First Holocaust Documentary," *Archive Zone*, n.d., http://s2s.focalint.tv/Publications/AZ_articles/az2015winter_iss96_german_concentration_camps_factual_survey_part_2.pdf. The story behind this film is the topic of the documentary *Night Will Fall* (2014). The film itself was restored by the Imperial War Museum in 2014.

26. Barry Trachtenberg, *The United States and the Nazi Holocaust: Race, Refuge, and Remembrance* (London: Bloomsbury, 2018), 134–36. Eleven official films on this subject were produced by the Allies in 1945. See Kay Gladstone, "Separate Intentions: The Allied Screenings of Concentration Camp Documentaries in Defeated Germany in 1945–1946: Death Mills and Memory of the Camps," in *Holocaust and the Moving Image: Representations in Film and Television since 1933*,

ed. Toby Haggith and Joanna Newman (London: Wallflower, 2005), 50–64; Toby Haggith, "Filming the Liberation of Bergen-Belsen," in *Holocaust and the Moving Image: Representations in Film and Television since 1933*, ed. Toby Haggith and Joanna Newman (London: Wallflower, 2005), 33–49; Haggith, "German Concentration Camps Factual Survey"; John J. Michalczyk, *Filming the End of the Holocaust: Allied Documentaries, Nuremberg and the Liberation of the Concentration Camps* (London: Bloomsbury, 2014).

27. Films shot by the Allies were also screened to German locals to confront them with the atrocities. See Ulrike Weckel, "Shamed by Nazi Crimes: The First Step Towards Germans' Re-Education or a Catalyst for Their Wish to Forget?" in *Reverberations of Nazi Violence in Germany and Beyond: Disturbing Pasts*, ed. Stephanie Bird et al. (London: Bloomsbury, 2016), 33–46.

28. Tobias Ebbrecht, "Migrating Images: Iconic Images of the Holocaust and the Representation of War in Popular Film," *Shofar: An Interdisciplinary Journal of Jewish Studies* 28, no. 4 (Summer 2010): 86–103; Gladstone, "Separate Intentions," 50; Haggith, "Filming the Liberation," 33.

29. Example of another film that was screened in Nuremberg is *The Nazi Plan*—a film composed of Nazi footage that described the Nazis' rise to power from the 1920s until 1944. See Michalczyk, *Filming the End of the Holocaust*, esp. 65–112.

30. Prager, *After the Fact*, 1–3.

31. Lawrence Baron, "Statuettes of Limitations: Oscar-Winning 'Holocaust' Films 1945–1948," Paper presented at the Conference on Film and History, Milwaukee, WI, November 4, 2017.

32. Baron, "Statuettes of Limitations."

33. Richard Raskin, Nuit et Brouillard *by Alain Resnais: On the Making, Reception, and Functions of a Major Documentary Film* (Aarhus, Denmark: Aarhus Univ. Press, 1987); Griselda Pollock and Max Silverman, eds., *Concentrationary Cinema: Aesthetics as Political Resistance in Alan Renais's* Night and Fog (New York: Bergham Books, 2011); Shlomo Sand, *Hakolnoa kehistoria: ledamyen velevayem et hameah haesrim* [Film as History: Imagining and Screening the Twentieth Century] (Tel Aviv: Am Oved and Open Univ. Press, 2002), 229.

34. Sand, *Kolnoa v'historia*, 236–37.

35. Sand, 249–51.

36. Shoshana Felman, "Film as Witness: Claude Lanzmann's Shoah," in *Holocaust Remembrance: The Shapes of Memory*, ed. Geoffrey Hartman (Oxford: Blackwell, 1994), 90–103; Felman and Laub, *Edut*; Stuart Liebman, ed., *Claude Lanzmann's* Shoah*: Key Essays* (Oxford: Oxford Univ. Press, 2007); Yosefa Loshitzky, ed., *Spielberg's Holocaust: Critical Perspectives on* Schindler's List (Bloomington:

Indiana Univ. Press, 1997), 104–18; Ron Rozenbaum, *Hitler: masa el shorshei haro'a* [Hitler: A Journey to the Roots of Evil] (Tel Aviv: Matar, 1999), 247–67.

37. Felman and Laub, *Edut*, 80. For more on the importance of the Holocaust witness, his emergence as a cultural hero, and the relationship between formal documents and testimony and the conflicts revolving around testimony, see Amos Goldberg, "Hashoah vehahistoria: netaqim beidan postmoderni" [The Holocaust and History: Disconnections in a Postmodern Age], *Theory and Criticism* 40 (Summer 2012): 121–54.

38. Prager, *After the Fact*, 1–26.

39. Friedman, "Witnessing for the Witness," 81–82.

40. Post-traumatic stress disorder (PTSD) was first included in the *Diagnostic and Statistical Manual of Mental Disorders*, published by the American Psychiatric Association, in 1982. It is considered an extremely common disorder in individuals who have experienced traumatic incidents, in which they continue to relive the trauma in the form of intrusive, recurrent recollections of the past. See Judith L. Herman, *Trauma v'hachlama* [Trauma and Healing] (Tel Aviv: Am Oved, 1994); "PTSD," in *Diagnostic and Statistical Manual of Mental Disorders*, 5th ed., ed. American Psychiatric Association (Arlington, VA: American Psychiatric Publishing, 2013), 271–80.

41. Aaron Kerner, *Film and the Holocaust* (London: Bloomsbury, 2001); Oleksandr Kobrynskyy and Gerd Bayer, eds., *Holocaust Cinema in the Twenty-First Century: Images, Memory, and the Ethics of Representation* (New York: Wallflower Press, 2015).

42. Nichols, *Representing Reality*, 10.

43. Hanna Yablonka, "Nitzolei hashoah b'yisrael: sikumim rishonim" [Holocaust Survivors in Israel: First Summary], *B'shvil hazikaron* 27 (1998), http://lib.cet.ac.il/Pages/item.asp?item=16227.

44. Porat, *Café haboker b'reach ha'ashan*, 379–96; Hannah Yablonka, "Z'huyot sotrot, z'huyot mashlimot: nitsolim, zichron hashoah vehazehut hayehudit" [Conflicting Identities, Complementary Identities: Holocaust Survivors, the Memory of the Holocaust, and Israeli Identity], *Massuah* 28 (2000): 301–17; Anita Shapira, "Hashoah: zikaron prati v'zikaron tziburi" [The Holocaust: Private Memory and Public Memory], in *Yehudim Yeshanim, Yehudim Hadashim* [New Jews, Old Jews] (Tel Aviv, Am Oved, 1997), 103–86; Tom Segev, *Hamillion hashvi'i: haisraelim vehashoah* [The Seventh Million: The Israelis and the Holocaust] (Jerusalem: Keter, 1991), 101–69.

45. See, for example: Yablonka, "Z'huyot sotrot, z'huyot mashlimot"; Shapira, "Hashoah"; Daniel Gutwein, "The Privatization of the Holocaust: Memory, Historiography, and Politics," *Israel Studies* 14, no. 1 (2009): 36–64; Porat, *Café*

haboker b'reach ha'ashan, 379–96; Dalia Ofer, "Sheerit hapleta bahistoryografya haisraelit" [The Holocaust Survivors in Israeli Historiography], *Iyunim B'tkumat Israel* 17 (2006): 465–511.

46. See, for example, Shabtai Beit Zvi, *Hazionut hapost ugandit bemashber hashoah* [Post-Ugandan Zionism on Trial (Tel Aviv: Bronfman, 1977); Segev, *Hamillion hashvi'i*; Yosef Grodzinsky, *In the Shadow of the Holocaust: The Struggle between Jews and Zionists in the Aftermath of World War II* (Monroe, ME: Common Courage Press, 2004); Idith Zertal, *Ha'uma v'hamavet: historia, zikaron, politiqa* [Death and the Nation: History, Memory, Politics] (Or-Yehuda, Israel: Kinneret Zmora-Bitan Dvir, 2002).

47. Batya Brutin, "Min hahulayim el hamerkaz: hashoah baomanut haisraelit" [From the Margins to the Mainstream: Israeli Art and the Holocaust], *Massuah* 33 (2005): 110–38; Zimmerman, *Al tigu li bashoah*, 215.

48. See, for example, Hannah Yablonka, Bella Guterman, and Avner Shalev, eds., *Anahnu po: nitzolei hashoah b'medinat Yisrael* [We Are Here: Holocaust Survivors in Israel] (Jerusalem: Yad Vashem, 2008).

49. Zimmerman, *Al tigu li bashoah*; Ella Shohat, *Mizrah v'ma'arav bakolnoa hayisraeli* [East and West in Israeli Cinema] (Ra'anana, Israel: Open Univ. Press, 2007).

50. The "new Jew" model was expressed extensively in other cultural fields. See Michael Gluzman, *Haguf hatzioni* [The Zionist Body] (Tel Aviv: Hakibbutz Hameuchad, 2007); Oz Almog, *Hatzabar: dyukan* [The Sabra: A Portrait] (Tel Aviv: Am Oved, 1997); Yael Zerubavel, "The 'Mythological Sabra' and Jewish Past: Trauma, Memory, and Contested Identities," *Israel Studies* 7, no. 2 (2002): 115–44.

51. Hanna Yablonka, *Medinat Israel neged Adolf Eichmann* [The State of Israel vs. Adolf Eichmann] (Tel Aviv: Yediot Aharonot, 2001); Liat Steir-Livny, "Hakambeck shel hagalut: meyehudi galuti leyahudi hadash ubehazara" [The Comeback of the Jewish Diaspora in Israeli Culture], in *Identity in Transition in Israeli Culture: A Festschrift for Prof. Nurit Gertz*, ed. Sandra Meiri, Yael Munk, Adia Mendelson-Maoz, and Liat Steir-Livny (Ra'anana, Israel: Open Univ. Press), 461–81.

52. Gertz, *Makhela aheret*; Liat Steir-Livny, *Har hazikaron yizkor bimkomi* [Let the Memorial Hill Remember] (Tel Aviv: Resling, 2014).

53. Jacky Feldman, *Above the Death Pits, Beneath the Flag: Youth Voyages to Poland and the Performance of Israeli National Identity* (New York: Berghahn Books, 2008), xv.

54. For more on these issues, see, for example: Porat, *Café haboker b'reach ha'ashan*, 357–78; Steir-Livny, *Shtei panim bamar'a*, 96–204; Milner, *Kirei avar*, 19–35; Loshitzky, *Identity Politics on the Israeli Screen*, 32–71; Dalia Ofer, "The

Past That Does Not Pass: Israelis and Holocaust Memory," *Israel Studies* 14, no. 1 (Spring 2009): 1–35; Gulie Ne'eman Arad, "Israel and the Shoah: A Tale of Multifarious Taboos," *New German Critique* 90 (Autumn 2003): 5–26.

55. Friedman, "Witnessing for the Witness," esp. 82–86.

56. Friedman, 81–82, 86.

57. Loshitzky, *Identity Politics on the Israeli Screen*, 32–71.

58. Ilan Avisar, "The Holocaust in Israeli Cinema as a Conflict between Survival and Morality," in *Israeli Cinema: Identities in Motion*, ed. Miri Talmon and Yaron Peleg (Austin: Univ. of Texas Press), 151–67; Gertz, *Makhela aheret*, 78–102; Zimmerman, *Al tigu li bashoah*, 250–334; Steir-Livny, *Shtei panim bamar'a*, 96–127, 148–65.

59. Ofer, "The Past That Does Not Pass"; Steir-Livny, *Har hazikaron yizkor bimkomi*.

60. Yuval Bogiinski, "A Historical Overview of the Concept of a Holocaust Survivor," Knesset, January 24, 2014, http://www.knesset.gov.il/mmm/data/pdf/m03154.pdf.

61. Nathan Kellermann, "Ha'avar shel traumat hashoah" [Transmission of the Holocaust Trauma], in *Yaldut b'tzel hashoah: yeladim-nitsolim vedor sheni* [Childhood in the Shadow of the Holocaust: Child Survivors and Second Generation], ed. Zehava Solomon and Julia Chaitin (Tel Aviv: Hakibbutz Hameuchad, 2007), 286–303.

62. Dina Wardi, *Nosei hahotam* [Memorial Candles] (Jerusalem: Keter, 1990), 14.

63. Carol Kidron, "Hahavnaya hahevratit shel hador hasheni lashoah" [The Social Construction of Second-Generation Survivors: Support Group Narratives of Wounded Carriers of Memory], in *Yaldut b'tzel hashoah: yeladim-nitsolim vedor sheni* [Childhood in the Shadow of the Holocaust: Child Survivors and Second Generation], ed. Zehava Solomon and Julia Chaitin (Tel Aviv: Hakibbutz Hameuchad, 2007), 261–85.

64. Julia Chaitin, "Yeladim v'nechadim shel nitzolim mitmodedim im hashoah" [Children and Grandchildren of Holocaust Survivors Deal with the Holocaust], in *Yaldut b'tzel hashoah: yeladim-nitsolim vedor sheni* [Childhood in the Shadow of the Holocaust: Child Survivors and Second Generation], ed. Zehava Solomon and Julia Chaitin (Tel Aviv: Hakibbutz Hameuchad, 2007), 304–36.

65. Yoram Hazan, "Dor sheni lashoah: musag besafek" [The Second Generation of the Holocaust: A Questionable Concept], *Sihot: Israel Journal of Psychotherapy* 1 (1987): 104–8.

66. Hillel Klein, "Hipus nitzolei hashoah ahar mashma'ut v'zehut" [The Survivors' Search for Meaning and Identity], in *Nazi Concentration Camps: Lectures and Discussions at the 4th Yad Vashem International Historical Conference of Holocaust*

Researchers, ed. Israel Gutman and Rachel Manber (Jerusalem: Yad Vashem, 1980), 543–53.

67. Abraham Sagi-Schwartz, Marinus van IJzendoorn, and Marian J. Bakermans-Kranenburg, "Does Intergenerational Transference of Trauma Skip a Generation? No Meta-Analytic Evidence for Tertiary Traumatization with Third-Generation Holocaust Survivors," *Attachment and Human Development* 10, no. 2 (June 2008): 105–21.

68. Milner, *Kirei avar*, 19–35.

69. Eva Hoffman, *After Such Knowledge: A Mediation of the Aftermath of the Holocaust* (New York: Vintage, 2005), 28.

70. Dan Bar-On, *Bein pahad letikva: sipurei haim shel hamesh mishpahot nitsolei shoah shlosha dorot bamishpaha* [Fear and Hope: Three Generations of the Holocaust] (Tel Aviv: Beit Lochamei Haghetaot and Kibbutz Hameuchad Press, 1994).

71. Perihan Aral Rosenthal and Stuart Rosenthal, "Holocaust Effects in the Third Generation: Child of Another Time," *American Journal of Psychotherapy* 34, no. 4 (1980): 572–80.

72. Miri Scharf and Ofra Mayseless, "Adolescents' Attachment Representations and Their Capacity for Intimacy in Close Relationships," *Journal of Research on Adolescence* 17, no. 1 (2007): 23–50.

73. Miri Scharf and Ofra Mayseless, "Disorganizing Experiences in Second- and Third-Generation Holocaust Survivors," *Qualitative Health Research* 21, no. 11 (2011): 1539–53; Miri Scharf, "The Trace of Trauma: Third-Generation Holocaust Survivors," *Development and Psychopathology* 19, no. 2 (2007): 603–22.

74. Eve Fogelman, "Third-Generation Descendants of Holocaust Survivors and the Future of Remembering," Jewcy, May 1, 2008, http://jewcy.com/jewish-religion-and-beliefs/third_generation_descendants_holocaust_survivors_and_future_remembering.

75. Sagi-Schwartz, van IJzendoorn, and Bakermans-Kranenburg, "Does Intergenerational Transference of Trauma Skip a Generation?"

76. Dan Bar-On, *Bein pahad letikva*.

77. Tal Litvak-Hirsch and Dan Bar-On, "Livnot et hahaim m'hadash: mehqar ma'qav 'l ha'vara bein droit shel traumat hashaoh" [Rebuild Your Life: A Follow-Up Study on Intergenerational Transference of Trauma of the Holocaust], *Megamot: Journal of Behavioral Sciences*, 45, no. 2 (2007): 243–71; Tal Litvak-Hirsch and Alon Lazar, "Bein avar l'atid: zikaron hashoah ketrauma qoleqtivit tarbutit vehantsahato be'einei bnei hador hashlishi beisrael" [Between the Past and the Future: Holocaust Memory as a Collective Trauma and Its Commemoration by Third-Generation Holocaust Survivors in Israel], Moreshet, n.d., http://www.moreshet.org/?CategoryID=414andArticleID=1388.

78. Esther Jilovsky, Jordana Silverstein, and David Slucki, eds., *In the Shadows of Memory: The Holocaust and the Third Generation* (London: Vallentine Mitchell, 2016); Victoria Aarons, ed., *Third-Generation Holocaust Narratives: Memory in Memoir and Fiction* (Lanham, MD: Lexington Books, 2016); Victoria Aarons and Alan L. Berger, *Third-Generation Holocaust Representation: Trauma, History, and Memory* (Evanston, IL: Northwestern Univ. Press, 2017).

79. Milner, *Kirei avar*, 19–35.

80. Ron Eyerman, *Cultural Trauma: Slavery and the Formation of African American Identity* (Cambridge: Cambridge Univ. Press, 2002).

81. Jeffrey C. Alexander, "Toward a Theory of Cultural Trauma," in *Cultural Trauma and Collective Identity*, ed. Alexander C. Jeffrey et al. (Berkeley: Univ. of California Press, 2009), 1–30.

82. Dominick LaCapra, *Writing History, Writing Trauma* (Baltimore: Johns Hopkins Univ. Press, 2000), 37–74.

83. Charles Figley, ed., *Compassion Fatigue: Secondary Traumatic Stress Disorders from Treating the Traumatized* (New York: Brunner/Mazel, 1995), esp. 1–20.

84. See the preface to this volume.

85. Amos Goldberg, "Introduction," in *Writing History, Writing Trauma*, by Dominick LaCapra (Baltimore: Johns Hopkins Univ. Press, 2000), 7–28.

86. Steir-Livny, *Har hazikaron yizkor bimkomi*, 17–36.

87. On these films and the complex debate on whether the persecutions in North Africa should be defined as part of the Holocaust, see Hanna Yablonka, *Harhek m'hamesila: mizrahim v'hashoah* [Off the Beaten Track: The Mizrahim and the Holocaust] (Tel Aviv: Yediot Aharonot, 2008); Yvonne Kozlovsky Golan, *Masach shel shichecha: al header chavayat hashoah shel yehudei hamizrach bimedia vebaomanut beisrael* [Forgotten from the Frame: The Absence of the Holocaust Experience of Mizrahim from the Visual Arts and Media in Israel] (Tel Aviv: Resling, 2017).

1. Depicting Women's Gendered Experiences in the Holocaust

1. See, for example, Lawrence Langer, "Gender Suffering? Women in Holocaust Testimonies," in *Women in the Holocaust*, ed. Dalia Ofer and Lenore Weitzman (New Haven, CT: Yale Univ. Press, 1998), 351–63, esp. 351; Na'ama Shik, "Kavim merkazim bahistoriografia shel heker nashim bashoah" [Central Themes in the Historiography of Research of Women in the Holocaust], *Zika* 12 (Autumn 2007), https://www.yadvashem.org/he/articles/general/women-holocaust-historiography.html; Ronit Lentin, "Lichbosh m'hadash et territoriot hashtika: sofrot vekolnaniyot yisraeliot k'banot l'nitzolei shoah" [To Recapture the Territory of Silence], in *Zikaron Galu'i, Zikaron Samu'i* [Overt Memory and Covert Memory], ed. Yoel Rappel (Tel Yitzhak, Israel: Massuah, 1998), 169–95.

2. Ronit Lentin, *Israel and the Daughters of the Shoah: Reoccupying the Territories of Silence* (New York: Berghahn Books, 2000), 14.

3. To name a few published in the last forty years: Renate Bridenthal, Atina Grossmann, and Marion Kaplan, eds., *When Biology Became Destiny: Women in Weimar and Nazi Germany* (New York: New Feminist Library, 1984); Joan M. Ringelheim, "The Unethical and the Unspeakable: Women and the Holocaust," *Simon Wiesenthal Center Annual* 7 (September 1983): 1–24; Marlene E. Heinemann, *Gender and Destiny: Women Writers and the Holocaust* (New York: Greenwood Press, 1986); Gizla Bock, "Challenging Dichotomies: Perspectives on Women's History," in *Writing Women's History*, ed. Karen Offen, Ruth Roach Pierson, and Jane Rendall (Bloomington: Indiana Univ. Press, 1991), 1–24; Carol Rittne and John Roth, eds., *Different Voices: Women and the Holocaust* (St. Paul, MN: Paragon House, 1993); Dalia Ofer and Lenore J. Weitzman, *Women in the Holocaust* (New Haven, CT: Yale Univ. Press, 1998); Judy Tydor-Baumel Schwartz, *Double Jeopardy: Gender and the Holocaust* (London: Vallentine Mitchell, 1998); Esther Herzog, ed., *Nashim bashoah* [Women and Family in the Holocaust] (Netanya, Israel: Otzar Hamishpat, 2006); Janet Jacob, "Gender and Collective Memory: Women and Representation at Auschwitz," *Memory Studies* 21, no. 1 (2008): 211–25; Myrna Goldenberg and Amy H. Shapiro, eds., *Different Horrors, Same Hell: Gender and the Holocaust* (Seattle: Univ. of Washington Press, 2013).

4. Dalia Ofer and Lenore J. Weitzman, "Tafkid hamigdar b'heker hashaoah" [Gender and the Study of the Holocaust], Matah, n.d., http://lib.cet.ac.il/pages/item.asp?item=20458; Judith Tydor-Baumel Schwartz, "Heker ha'isha, hamigdar v'hamishpaha b'tkufat hashoah: hitpatchuta shel disciplina historit" [The Study of Women, Gender, and Family during the Holocaust: The Development of an Historical Discipline], in *Nashim bashoah* [Women and Family in the Holocaust], ed. Esther Herzog (Netanya, Israel: Otzar Hamishpat, 2006), 1–26.

5. Myrna Goldenberg, "Women Remembering the Holocaust," in *Thinking the Unthinkable: Meanings of the Holocaust*, ed. Roger S. Gottlieb (New York: Paulist, 1990), 150–66.

6. Shik, "Kavim merkazim bahistoriografia"; Lentin, *Israel and the Daughters of the Shoah*, 10–12.

7. Gertz, *Makhela aheret*, 78–102; Zimmerman, *Al tigu li bashoah*, 250–334; Steir-Livny, *Shtei panim bamara'a*, 96–204.

8. The documentary *The Darien Dilemma* (2006) depicts the attempts of Jews from the Yishuv who dealt with illegal immigration to help one thousand Viennese Jews who escaped the Nazis and were waiting to be rescued on the banks of the Danube. Originally, the filmmaker Nachum Laufer intended to tell the story of how he fled from Europe with his mother. However, during his research, he and his son came across the story of Ruth Klüger-Aliav, a prominent figure in the Mossad L'aliya

Bet (Organization for Illegal Immigration), and the film describes her attempts to help these Jews.

9. Lentin, *Israel and the Daughters of the Shoah*, 1–26.

10. The documentary *Memories from the Eichmann Trial* (David Perlov, 1979) was the first to dedicate a lengthy segment to interviews with survivor Henryk Ross, the photographer of the Łódź Ghetto who testified in the trial, and second-generation Holocaust survivors who discussed the effects of the trial on their parents and on them. The film was screened once in what was then the only Israeli TV broadcast channel. *Because of That War* was the first documentary dedicated to the survivors' and their children's stories. The film garnered national and international success and was screened in cinemas, on TV, and at festivals.

11. Friedman, "Witnessing for the Witness," 81–93.

12. White, "The Historical Text," 221–36; Renov, *The Subject of Documentary*, 219.

13. In *Because of That War* Halina discusses the ways the Holocaust affected her behavior as a parent, but these themes are discussed in detail in Israeli Holocaust documentaries that deal with male Holocaust survivors as well. See Steir-Livny, *Shtei panim bamara'a*, 96–204; Gertz, *Makhela aheret*, 78–102; Zimmerman, *Al tigu li bashoah*, 250–334.

14. Lentin, *Israel and the Daughters of the Shoah*, 73.

15. Lentin, 72–73.

16. See Steir-Livny, *Shtei panim bamara'a*, 96–204; Gertz, *Makhela aheret*, 78–102; Zimmerman, *Al tigu li bashoah*, 250–334.

17. For example, the love story between Rivka and Yosef Bau, who even got married in Płaszów concentration camp. Bau recounted the story in his memoirs, and it was turned into an Israeli TV documentary, *Yosef and Rebecca: A Love Story* (Tzipi Baider, 2015), and was later adapted as one of the scenes in Steven Spielberg's *Schindler's List* (1993).

18. Yvonne Kozlovsky Golan, "Cinematic Love and the Shoah: Abnormal Love during Abnormal Times," *Post Script* 30, no. 3 (Fall 2011): 40–57.

19. See, for example, Nirit Anderman, "Nashim sheyeholelu et hamahapecha bakolnoa hayisraeli" [Women Who Are Revolutionizing Israeli Cinema], *Haaretz*, September 19, 2013, https://www.haaretz.co.il/gallery/cinema/.premium-1.2120655?=andts=_1531469829692.

20. Anat Tanner, "Hayot b'seret shelahen" [Living in Their Own Movie], YNet News, March 17, 2017, https://www.ynet.co.il/articles/0,7340,L-4936703,00.html.

21. Esther Namer, "Nashim nitsolot shoah bakolnoa haisraeli" [Women Holocaust Survivors in Israeli Cinema], seminar paper for the course Holocaust Survivors in Israeli Cinema, Open University, Ra'anana, Israel, 2018.

22. Bill Nichols, *Blurred Boundaries: Questions of Meaning in Contemporary Culture* (Bloomington: Indiana Univ. Press, 1994), 92–106.

23. On the dominance of subjectivity in documentary since the late 1980s, see Brian Winston, Gail Vanstone, and Wang Chi, *The Act of Documenting: Documentary Film in the 21st Century* (London: Bloomsbury Academic, 2017), 127–50.

24. Jim Lane, *The Autobiographical Documentary in America* (Madison: Univ. of Wisconsin Press, 2002); Shmulik Duvdevani, *Guf rishon matzlema* [First-Person Camera] (Jerusalem: Keter, 2010); Rosemary Marangoly George, *The Politics of Home: Postcolonial Relocations and Twentieth-Century Fiction* (Cambridge: Cambridge Univ. Press, 1996); Carmel Gottlieb Kimhi, *Hapoetica shel habayit: yezug habait vahabait haleumi bekolnoa otobiografy doqomentary israeli* [The Poetics of the Home: Representation of Home and National Home in Autobiographical Documentary in Israeli Cinema] (Jerusalem: Carmel, 2009).

25. Renov, *The Subject of Documentary*, 216.

26. Renov, 176–77, 216–18.

27. Marianne Hirsch, "Past Lives, First Memories in Exile," *Poetics Today* 17 (Winter 1996): 659–67.

28. Hilene Flanzbaum, "The Trace of Trauma: Third-Generation Holocaust Survivors," *Phi Kappa Phi Forum* (Spring 2012): 32–35.

29. Landsberg, *Prosthetic Memory*, 28.

30. Landsberg, 26–28, 33.

31. Landsberg, 34.

32. Dalia Ofer, "Estrategiot shel nashim bama'avak l'haim b'tkufat hashoah" [Women's Strategies in the Struggle for Life during the Holocaust], in *Women and Family in the Holocaust*, ed. Esther Herzog (Netanya, Israel: Otzar Hamishpat, 2006), 27–44.

33. For more on abortions in the Warsaw Ghetto, see Miriam Ofer, *Haluk lavan bageto* [White Coats inside the Ghetto] (Jerusalem: Yad Vashem, 2015), 366–71.

34. Langer, "Gender Suffering?"

35. Interview with Yehudith Inbar, Yad Vashem, n.d., http://www.yadvashem.org/he/articles/interviews/yeudit.html.

36. Interview with Yehudith Inbar.

37. Eva Fogelman, "Psychological Dynamics in the Lives of Third-Generation Holocaust Survivors," *Hidden Child* 16 (2008), http://www.drevafogelman.com/_psychological_dynamics_in_the_lives_of_third_generation_holocaust_survivors__94110.htm; Nicole Fox, "Their History Is Part of Me: Third-Generation American Jews and Intergenerational Transmission of Memory," *Trauma and History: Yalkut Moreshet Journal for the Study of the Holocaust and Anti-Semitism* 4, no. 87 (2010): 9–35.

38. Victoria Aarons and Alan L. Berger, *Third-Generation Holocaust Representation: Trauma, History, and Memory* (Evanston, IL: Northwestern Univ. Press, 2017), 35–37.

39. Marianne Hirsch, "Surviving Images: Holocaust Memories and the Works of Postmemory," *Yale Journal of Criticism* 14, no. 1 (2001): 5–37.

40. Renov, *The Subject of Documentary*, 216–18.

41. Winston, Vanstone, and Chi, *The Act of Documenting*, 1–3.

42. Gilad Natan, "Yaldei ovdim zarim um'vakshei miklat b'ma'arechet hahinuch" [Children of Foreign Workers and Asylum Seekers in the Education System], Knesset, December 12, 2010, http://www.knesset.gov.il/mmm/data/pdf/m02716.pdf.

43. See, for example, http://www.ovdimzarim.org/.

44. "Nitzolei shoah l'netanyahu: al tigaresh yaldei ovdim zarim" [Holocaust Survivors to Netanyahu: Don't Deport the Children of Foreign Workers], YNet News, August, 8, 2010, https://www.ynet.co.il/articles/0,7340,L-3931953,00.html.

45. Ruth Gavison, ed., *Coping with Global Migration: A Strategy for Immigration Policy in Israel* (Jerusalem: Metzilah Center for Zionist, Jewish, Liberal, and Humanist Thought, 2009).

46. Dana Weiler Polak, "Noa Maiman, bito shel Yosi Maiman, nilhemet" [Noa Maiman, Yossi Maiman's Daughter, Fights against the Deportation of Foreign Workers in the Name of Her Grandmother], *Haaretz*, October 14, 2009, https://www.haaretz.co.il/news/education/1.1285079.

47. Ne'eman Arad, "Israel and the Shoah," 5–26.

48. The two topics are also connected in *Valentina's Mother* (Matti Harari and Arik Lubetzki, 2008).

49. On the Righteous Among the Nations, see Naima Barzel, *Al hab'hira batov: maasei hazala b'polin u'b'holand b'milhemet haolam hashniya* [Choosing the Good: The Righteous among the Nations in Poland and the Netherlands during World War II] (Tel Aviv: Hakibbutz Hameuchad, 2007).

50. Liron Habia, "Yitzug nitzolot hashoah bakolnoa hadocomentary bashanim 1980–2010" [The Representation of Women Survivors of the Holocaust in Documentaries between 1980 and 2010], seminar paper for the course Holocaust Survivors in Israeli Cinema, Open University, Ra'anana, Israel, 2012.

51. Nichols, *Representing Reality*, 44–56.

52. *The Cemetery Club*, directed by Tali Shemesh (Jerusalem: Israeli Films, 2016), http://www.israelifilms.co.il/The-Cemetery-Club.html.

53. Agnieszka Piotrowska, *Psychoanalysis and Ethics in Documentary Film* (London: Routledge, 2013), 45–53.

54. Renov, *The Subject of Documentary*, 216–29, esp. 218–19.

55. One exception is *Café Europa* (Tzipi Trope, 2012), which follows Holocaust survivors who meet at Café Europa in the Israeli town of Ramat Hasharon.

Their stories reveal the traumas they experienced in Israel: children who were killed in Israeli wars, children who left Israel, or captivity in war and death.

56. Dan Bar-On, *Hapsychologia shel hashoah* [The Psychology of the Holocaust] (Ra'anana, Israel: Open Univ. Press, 2006).

57. See the introduction to this volume.

58. Nomi Levenkron, "Ha'alamot v'hamavet: znut, oness v'avdut minit b'milhemet haolam hashniya" [Death and the Maidens: Prostitution, Rape, and Sexual Slavery during World War II], *Theory and Criticism* 32 (2009): 15–44.

59. Levenkron, 15–44; Elizabeth D. Heineman, "Sexuality and Nazism: The Doubly Unspeakable?" *Journal of the History of Sexuality* 11 (2002): 22–66; Eve Fogelman, "Sexual Abuse of Jewish Women during and after the Holocaust," in *Sexual Violence against Jewish Women during the Holocaust*, ed. Sonja M. Hedgepeth and Rochelle Saidel (Hanover, NH: Univ. Press of New England, 2010), 255–74.

60. Hannah Pollin-Galay, *Ecologies of Witnessing: Language, Place, and Holocaust Testimony* (New Haven, CT: Yale Univ. Press, 2018).

61. Golan, *Masach shel shichecha*, 42, 45.

62. Na'ama Shik, *Haguf hamisken haze: hitnasut nashit al pi autobiografiot shel nitzolot Auschwitz-Birkenau 1946–2000* [That Pitiful Body: Women's Experiences in Autobiographies of Women Survivors of Auschwitz-Birkenau 1946–2000] (master's thesis, Tel Aviv University, 2004); Tydor-Baumel, "The Study of Women," 10.

63. Hedgepeth and Saidel, *Sexual Violence against Jewish Women during the Holocaust.*

64. See the introduction to this volume.

65. Segev, *Hamillion hashvi'i*, 101–69; Porat, *Café haboker b'reach ha'ashan*, 381–415.

66. Sharon Geva, *El ha'ahot halo yedua* [To the Unknown Sister] (Tel Aviv: Hakibbutz Hameuchad, 2010), 271–83.

67. Levenkron, ""Ha'alamot v'hamavet"; Shapira, "Hashoah", 103–86.

68. Steir-Livny, *Shtei panim bamara'a*, 52–53; Zertal, *Ha'uma v'hamavet*, 233–34; Omer Bartov, "Kitsch vesadism baplaneta ha'aheret shel kazetnik" [Kitsch and Sadism in Ka-Tzetnik's Other Planet: Israeli Youth Imagine the Holocaust] *Alpayim* 17 (1999): 148–75.

69. Itai Lev, "Hataboo ha'acharon" [The Last Taboo], *Globes*, April 15, 2015, https://www.calcalist.co.il/consumer/articles/0,7340,L-3656861,00.html; Nir Guntag, "Tohar hashoah" [The Purity of the Holocaust], *7th Eye*, April 15, 2015, http://www.the7eye.org.il/155119.

70. Zion Nanus, "Hasodot m'ahorey hatmuna" [The Secrets behind the Photo], *Mako*, May 5, 2016, https://www.mako.co.il/news-channel2/Channel-2-Newscast-q2_2016/Article-95c284fdcf18451004.htm.

71. In moshav Yedidia in the late 1940s and the early 1950s, families adopted thirty-four orphans from Bergen-Belsen. See Alon Schwartz, "A Talk at the Lev Cinema," Shoham, Israel, December 20, 2016.

72. Renee Ghert-Sand, "After 70 Years, Man Born in DP Camp Meets Unknown Brother(s)," *Times of Israel*, May 22, 2016, http://www.timesofisrael.com/after-70-years-man-born-in-dp-camp-meets-unknown-brothers/.

73. Ghert-Sand, "After 70 Years."

74. Schwartz, "A Talk at the Lev Cinema."

75. Garnet Butchart, "Al etica v'kolnoa t'udi: al emet mamashit v'ma'asit" [On Ethics and Documentary Cinema: Practical Truth], *Takriv*, August 2015, http://takriv.net/wp-content/uploads/2015/09/PDF-translatedarticle-updt.pdf; Brian Winston, "The Tradition of the Victim in Griersonian Documentary, in *New Challenges for Documentary*, ed. Alan Rosenthal (Berkeley: Univ. of California Press, 1988), 269–87; Brian Winston, *Lies, Damn Lies, and Documentaries* (London: British Film Institute, 2000).

76. In *Shoah* Claude Lanzmann filmed former Nazis with a hidden camera, without their knowledge or consent. He argued that ethical principles of documentary do not apply to them because of the acts they committed. See Winston, Vanstone, and Chi, *The Act of Documenting*, 164.

77. Butchart, "Al etica v'kolnoa ti'udi"; Winston, Vanstone, and Chi, *The Act of Documenting*, 151–72; Calvin Pryluck, "Ultimately We Are All Outsiders: The Ethics of Documentary Filming," in *New Challenges for Documentary*, ed. Alan Rosenthal (Berkeley: Univ. of California Press, 1988), 255–68; Larry Gross, John Stuart Katz, and Jay Ruby, eds., *Image Ethics: The Moral Rights of Subjects in Photographs, Film, and Television* (New York: Oxford Univ. Press, 2000).

78. See, for example, Dan Stone, *The Liberation of the Camps: The End of the Holocaust and Its Aftermath* (New Haven, CT: Yale Univ. Press, 2015), esp. 139–77; Irith Keinan, *Lo nirga hara'av: she'arit hapleita v'shlihei eretz yisrael b'germania 1945–1948* [Holocaust Survivors and Eretz Israeli Delegations in Germany 1945–1948] (Tel Aviv: Am Oved, 1996); Hagit Lavsky, *New Beginnings: Holocaust Survivors in Bergen-Belsen and the British Zone in Germany, 1945–1950* (Detroit: Wayne State Univ. Press, 2002).

79. Liat Steir-Livny, *One Trauma, Two Perspectives, Three Years* (Haifa: Herzl Institute for the Study of Zionism, Univ. of Haifa, forthcoming).

80. Steir-Livny, *One Trauma, Two Perspectives, Three Years.*

2. Back to the *Heimat*

1. See Gertz, *Makhela aheret*, 89–101; Steir-Livny, *Shtei panim bamara'a*, 103–27, 150–65; 250–334; Loshitzky, *Identity Politics*, 32–71; Avisar, "The

Holocaust in Israeli Cinema," 151–67. Germany was not represented in Israeli fiction films until the 1980s. From then onward, a few directors began to touch on the subject while dealing with the complexity of the term "another Germany." For example: *The Silver Platter* (Judd Ne'eman, 1984), *Streets of Yesterday* (Judd Ne'eman, 1989), *Walk on Water* (Eitan Fox, 2004), and *Metallic Blues* (Danny Verete, 2004). The film *Transit* (Daniel Waxman, 1980) deals with an elderly Holocaust survivor's wish to return to Germany, but focuses on his aimless wandering in Israel; the film *Tel Aviv-Berlin* (Tzipi Tropez, 1987) takes place in the 1950s and presents the Jewish-German bubble in Tel Aviv, but it does not represent Germany.

2. On the connection in Israeli culture and public debates between sexuality and the Holocaust, see chapter 1.

3. See also chapter 5.

4. This chapter discusses the representations of Germany as a home for Jews and former Israelis. Chapter 5 examines representations of Germans in other third-generation films that deal with perpetrators, bystanders, and their offspring.

5. Nirit Anderman, "Ta'amula nazit ba'aron shel savta: hadira, sirto hatiudi shel arnon goldfinger" [Nazi Propaganda in Grandmother's Closet: The Flat, Arnon Goldfinger's Documentary Film], *Haaretz*, May 9, 2011, http://www.haaretz.co.il/gallery/1.1447794.

6. Prager, *After the Fact*, 171.

7. Hagit Lavsky, *The Creation of the German-Jewish Diaspora: Interwar German-Jewish Immigration to Palestine, the USA, and England* (Berlin: De-Gruyter, 2017); Fred Behrend and Larry Hanove, *Rebuilt from Broken Glass: A German-Jewish Life Remade in America* (West Lafayette, IN: Purdue Univ. Press, 2017).

8. Moshe Zimmermann and Yotam Hotam, eds., *Bein hamoladot: hayekim bemehozoteihem* [Between Homelands: The Yekkes in Their Districts] (Jerusalem: Zalman Shazar Center, 2005); Aviva Halamish, *B'merutz kaful neged hazman: mediniyut ha'aliya hazionit beshnot hashloshim* [The Double Race against Time: The Zionist Immigration Policy in the 1930s] (Jerusalem: Yad Ben Zvi, 2006); Amnon Ramon, *Doctor mul doctor gar: shcunat rehavia beyerushalyim* [A Doctor in Every House: Jerusalem's Rehavia Neighborhood] (Jerusalem: Yad Ben Zvi, 1998).

9. Osnat Roth-Cohen and Yehiel Limor, "The German (Fifth) Aliyah and the Development of Israel's Advertising Industry," *Israel Studies Review* 33 (2018): 126–45; Boaz Neumann, Ronny Hirsch-Ratzkovsky, and Shahar Galili, eds., *Historia belo nahat: bein yehudim legermanim* [History and Discontent: Between Jews and Germans] (Tel Aviv: Am Oved, 2012); Hagit Lavsky, "Then and Now: Immigration and Absorption of Jews in Germany, between History and Historical

Consciousness," in *Culture, Memory and History, Volume 2: Israeli's Culture and Memory*, ed. Meir Hazan and Uri Cohen (Jerusalem: Zalman Shazar Center and Tel Aviv Univ., 2010), 251–74; Joachim Schlor, "Ha'aretz 'kan' ha'aretz 'sham': hirhurim al shiva" [The Land 'Here,' the Land 'There': Reflections on Returning], Association of Israelis of Central European Origin, December 25, 2012, http://www.irgun-jeckes.org/?CategoryID=373andArticleID=1280.

10. "Yekke," The Yekke, December 20, 2012, http://lib.yeke.cet.ac.il/pages/item.asp?item=19602.

11. Michel Callon, "Some Elements of a Sociology of Translation: Domestication of the Scallops and the Fishermen of St. Brieuc Bay," in *Power, Action and Belief: A New Sociology of Knowledge*, ed. John Law (London: Routledge and Kegan Paul, 1986), 196–233; Bruno Latour, *Reassembling the Social: An Introduction to Actor-Network-Theory* (Oxford: Oxford Univ. Press, 2005); John Law, "Notes on the Theory of the Actor Network: Ordering, Strategy, and Heterogeneity," *Systems Practice* 5 (1992): 379–93.

12. Barbara Mann, *Space and Place in Jewish Studies* (New Brunswick, NJ: Rutgers Univ. Press, 2012), 13–16; Jeffrey Haus, "The Younger Generation: Jews and Diaspora in Frank Capra's America" (forthcoming).

13. Guy Miron, "Lately, Almost Constantly, Everything Seems Small to Me: The Lived Space of German Jews under the Nazi Regime," *Jewish Social Studies* 20, no. 1 (Fall 2013): 121–49, esp. 123.

14. Guy Miron and Dorit Yosef, "Burganut v'tzionut b'hayei habayit shel yoyzot merkaz europa b'yisrael" [Bourgeoisie and Zionism in the Domestic Lives of Immigrants from Central Europe in Israel], *Iyunim b'tkumat Israel* 28 (2017): 197–224; Miron, "Lately, Almost Constantly," 122–23.

15. Clare Cooper Marcus, *House as a Mirror of Self: Exploring the Deeper Meaning of Home* (San Francisco: Conari Press, 1995), esp. 11–12, 49–80.

16. Carmel Gottleib Kimhi, "Teivat pandora b'gordon shtrasse" [Pandora's Box on Gordon Shtrasse"], *Takriv* 16 (2015), https://takriv.net/.

17. Ofer Ashkenazi, "Homecoming as a Dead End: Place and Displacement in the New Israeli Documentary Film," *Jewish Culture and History* 15, no. 3 (2014): 212–33.

18. Na'ama Sheffi, "Review of Guy Miron's 'German Jews in Israel: Memories and Past Images,'" *Journal of Israeli History* 25, no. 2 (2006): 377–81.

19. Schlor, "Ha'aretz 'kan' ha'aretz 'sham.'"

20. Steir-Livny, *Shtei panim bamara'a*; Orna Ben-Dor documented her own difficult relationship with her Holocaust survivor mother in 2009 in the film *Say Mother*.

21. See the introduction to this volume.

22. The film *Shadows* (2017) is exceptional in that sense. It discusses second-generation Holocaust survivors talking about the way they were abused by their parents.

23. Milner, *Kirey avar*, 19–35.

24. Aharon Hess, *B'tzel hashoah: hador hasheni* [In the Shadow of the Holocaust: The Second Generation] (Or Yehuda, Israel: Hed Artzi, 1990).

25. Bar-On, *Bein pahad letikva*.

26. Kohen-Raz, "Arnon Goldfinger's 'The Flat,'" 323–38.

27. Prager, *After the Fact*, 170.

28. Idit Gil, "The Shoah in Israeli Collective Memory: Changes in Meanings and Protagonists," *Modern Judaism: A Journal of Jewish Ideas and Experiences* 32, no. 1 (2012): 76–101.

29. Fogelman, "Psychological Dynamics."

30. Neumann, Hirsch-Ratzkovsky, and Galili, *Historia belo nahat*; Lavsky, *Then and Now*, 251–74; Zimmermann and Hotam, *Bein hamoladot*; Schlor, "Ha'aretz 'kan' ha'aretz 'sham.'"

31. Anita Shapira, "Le'an halcha shlilat hagalut: sugiyot bazehut haisraelit" [Where Did the Exile Go: Issues in Israeli Identity], *Shvut* (2004): 13–61.

32. For more details on how these changes influenced the return of the second and third generations from the East and the West, see Steir-Livny, "Hakambeck shel hagalut," 461–81.

33. Irgun yotsei merkaz eropa (Association of Israelis of Central European Origin), http://www.irgun-jeckes.org/?CategoryID=200andArticleID=461.

34. Reiter Hoppe, "The Next Generation of Young Yekkes in Preserving the Yekke Heritage," Facebook group, http://www.facebook.com/groups/HoppeHoppeReiter.

35. Irgun yotsei merkaz eropa (Association of Israelis of Central European Origin), http://www.irgun-jeckes.org/?CategoryID=200andArticleID=461.

36. Avner Shavit, "Bamai 'hadira' metzig: Ma saba shelachem asa bashoah?" ["The Flat's" Director Presents: What Did Your Grandfather Do during the Holocaust?], Walla, September 5, 2011, https://e.walla.co.il/item/1856747.

37. Bar-On, *Bein pahad letikva*.

38. Nichols, *Representing Reality*, 32–75; Nichols, *Introduction to Documentary*, 142–211.

39. Avner Shavit, "Hadira: shalosh perspectivot al haseret" [The Flat: Three Different Perspectives on the Film], Walla, April 19, 2012, http://e.walla.co.il/?w=/267/2524988.

40. Anderman, "Ta'amula nazit ba'aron shel savta."

41. This special connection between Holocaust survivors and their grandchildren, as opposed to the problematic connection of second-generation Holocaust

survivors with their parents, is also reflected in Jewish American documentaries. See Lawrence Baron, "Imagining the Shoah in American Third-generation Cinema," in *The Impact of the Holocaust in America, An Annual Review*, vol. 6, ed. Bruce Zuckerman et al. (West Lafayette, IN: Purdue Univ. Press, 2008), 103–18.

42. Shavit, "Bamai 'hadira' metzig."

43. Aarons and Berger, *Third-Generation Holocaust Representation*, 11–12.

44. Aarons and Berger, 7–8.

45. LaCapra, *Writing History, Writing Trauma*; Saul Friedländer, "Trauma, Memory, and Transference," in *Holocaust Remembrance: The Shapes of Memory*, ed. Geoffrey Hartman (Oxford: Basil Blackwell, 1994), 252–64; Henry Greenspan, "Lives as Text: Symptoms as Modes of Recounting in the Life Histories of Holocaust Survivors," in *Storied Lives: The Cultural Politics of Self-Understanding*, ed. George C. Rosenwald and Richard L. Ochberg (New Haven, CT: Yale Univ. Press, 1992), 14–65; Milton E. Jucovy, "Telling the Holocaust Story: A Link between the Generations," *Psychoanalytic Inquiry* 5 (1985): 31–50.

46. Ronen Schneidman, "A Holocaust Survivor's Confounding Choices," Forward, January 7, 2015, http://forward.com/schmooze/212162/a-holocaust-survivors-confounding-choices.

47. Dina Wardi, *Nos'ei hahotam*.

48. Gad Yair, *Ahava ze lo praktish* [Love Is Not Practical] (Tel Aviv: Hakibbutz Hameuchad, 2015).

49. Ofri Ilani, "Medinat ashkenaz" [The Ashkenazi Country], *Haaretz*, October 13, 2017, 1–2. For more on Israeli immigration to Berlin, see Fania Oz-Salzberger, *Israelim, Berlin* [Israelis, Berlin] (Tel Aviv: Keter, 2001); Shuki Shtauber, *Yisraelim b'berlin* [Israelis in Berlin] (Tel Aviv: Yediot Aharonot, 2017).

50. Esther Jilovsky, *Remembering the Holocaust: Generations, Witnessing and Place* (London: Bloomsbury, 2015), 57–120.

51. Aarons and Berger, *Third-Generation Holocaust Representation*, 25–26.

52. Cathy Caruth, *Unclaimed Experience: Trauma, Narrative, and History* (Baltimore: Johns Hopkins Univ. Press, 2016), 13.

53. Cathy Caruth, "An Introduction: Recapturing the Past," in *Trauma: Explorations in Memory*, ed. Cathy Caruth (Baltimore: John Hopkins Univ. Press, 1995), 151–57.

54. The film is an Israeli German coproduction.

55. Ruth Netzer, *Hakolno'a metapel banu: yihasei metapel-metupal bakolno'a* [Cinema Takes Care of Us: The Rapist-Patient Relationship in Cinema] (Tel Aviv: Resling, 2013), 42–48. See also Hadas Levi, "Pianuach hasod shel hatzofe: hashimush bamedium hakolno'i k'kli avoda im kvutzot" [Revealing the Viewers' Secret: Cinema as a Tool of Group Therapy], *Mikbatz* (2003): 77–98.

56. Bat-Chen Epstein Elias, "Germany tov" [A Good German]. *Israel Today*, August 2, 2013, http://www.israelhayom.co.il/site/newsletter_article.php?id=26709andhp=1andnewsletter=08.02.2013.

57. Jim Lane, *The Autobiographical Documentary in America* (Madison: Univ. of Wisconsin Press, 2002); Kimhi, *Hapoetica shel habayit.*

58. Epstein Elias, "Germany tov."

59. Epstein Elias.

60. On the issue of place, see Zali Gurevitch and Gideon Aran, "Al hamakom" [About the Place], *Alpaim* 4 (1991): 9–44.

3. (Mis)Representations of the Past

1. Robert Rosenstone, *Revisioning History: Film and the Construction of a New Past* (Princeton, NJ: Princeton Univ. Press, 1995).

2. Yael Hersonski, "Witnessing the Archive," in *Probing the Ethics of Holocaust Culture*, ed. Claudio Fogu, Wulf Kasteiner, and Todd Presner (Cambridge, MA: Harvard Univ. Press), 277–82, esp. 281–82.

3. For example, scenes from *Das Ghetto* were inserted as historical visual footage of the ghetto in the Israeli documentary *Kapo*, directed by Dan Setton and Tor Ben-Mayor and released in 1999 (see chapter 5).

4. "Colloquium: 'shtikat ha'arkhiyon'" [Colloquium: 'A Film Unfinished'], *Theory and Criticism* 40 (Summer 2012): 269–87.

5. "Colloquium: 'shtikat ha'arkhiyon.'"

6. Butchart, "Al etica v'kolnoa ti'udi," 427–52.

7. Kobi Meidan, "Reayon im Yael Hersonski" [An Interview with Yael Hersonski], *Hotzei Israel*, April 23, 2012, http://www.youtube.com/watch?v=87uq16cV1lI.

8. "Colloquium: 'shtikat ha'arkhiyon.'"

9. Lebovic, "Freeze-Framing," 263, 276.

10. Ariel Krill, "Shoah 2:0 al shtikat ha'archiyon shel yael hersonski" [Holocaust 2.0: On 'A Film Unfinished' by Yael Hersonski], Walla, November 16, 2010, http://e.walla.co.il/?w=/267/1756326; Ariel Krill, "Haemet hi lo du meimadit: reayon im naomy shcory veitai ken-tor mefikey shtikat ha'archiyon" [The Truth Is Not Two-Dimensional: An Interview with Noemi Schory and Itai Ken-Tor, producers of 'A Film Unfinished']" Walla, January 21, 2011, http://e.walla.co.il/?w=//1783133; Yuli Novak and Yaniv Ron-El, "Colloquium: hakdama" [Colloquium: Introduction], *Theory and Criticism* 40 (Summer 2012): 263–68. Hersonski's grandmother was a survivor of the Warsaw Ghetto, and she says that while watching the raw material filmed by the Nazis, in various scenes she saw figures that reminded her of

her grandmother. Her mother told her she was only imagining them. Even though *A Film Unfinished* does not directly revolve around Hersonski's family, the family ties are present. Hersonski said in interviews that she was aware that the memory of her grandmother had a major effect on her film. See Meidan, "Reayon im Yael Hersonski."

11. "Colloquium: 'shtikat ha'arkhiyon.'"

12. Meidan, "Reayon im Yael Hersonski."

13. See the introduction to this volume.

14. David LaRocca, "Introduction: Representative Qualities and Questions of Documentary Film," in *The Philosophy of Documentary Film: Image, Sound, Fiction, Truth*, ed. David LaRocca (Lanham, MD: Lexington Books), 1–54, esp. 6–7.

15. Hersonski, "Witnessing the Archive," 280–81.

16. An interview with Yael Hersonski, Channel 8, n.d.

17. Novak and Ron-El, "Colloquium."

18. Haim Deuel-Lusky and Oded Wolkstein, "Al shtikat ha'archiyon" [On A Film Unfinished], *Takriv* 4 (n.d.), http://www.takriv.net/index.php?option=com_contentandview=articleandid=27:2011-07-20-13-49-24andcatid=10:2011-08-14-09-14-03andItemid=15.

19. Deuel-Lusky and Wolkstein, "Al shtikat ha'archiyon." For more information on the various genres of international Holocaust films and the problematic nature of the various representations, see Kerner, *Film and the Holocaust*.

20. See the introduction to this volume.

21. Schweitzer claims that paradoxically, since *Shoah* was filmed more than thirty years ago, and many of the interviewers are dead, the film itself is archival material. See Ariel Schweitzer, "Archiv, bidyon, ta'amule: America bemilhama" [Archive, Fiction, Propaganda: America in War], *Takriv* 4 (2012), https://takriv.net/.

22. For more on this issue, see, for example, Hagai Levi, "Habuz: hagai levi neged Jean-Luc Godard" [The Contempt: Hagai Levi versus Jean-Luc Godard], Walla, November 12, 2010, http://news.walla.co.il/?w=/227/1754877; Danny Warth, "Hamusika shelanu" [Our Music], Danny Warth's blog, January 24, 2010, http://www.dannywarth.co.

23. Saxton, "Shneihem sonim et Spielberg."

24. Ariel Schweitzer, "The 'Jew' of Cinema," *Haaretz* (English edition), December 17, 2010, http://www.haaretz.com/israel-news/the-jew-of-cinema-1.331109.

25. Saxton, "Shneihem sonim et Spielberg."

26. "Colloquium: 'shtikat ha'arkhiyon.'"

27. Lebovic, "Freeze-Framing," 262; Hersonski, "Witnessing the Archive," 279.

28. Hersonski, 279, 280.

29. Felman and Laub, *Testimony*.

30. Saxton, "Shneihem sonim et Spielberg."

31. Amos Goldberg, "Hashoah vehahistoria: netaqim beidan postmoderni" [The Holocaust and History: Disconnections in a Postmodern Age], *Theory and Criticism* 40 (Summer 2012): 121–54.

32. "Colloquium: 'shtikat ha'arkhiyon.'" A Nazi propaganda film about the seemingly comfortable life of the Jews in the Theresienstadt concentration camp and ghetto was made in 1944: *Terezin: A Documentary Film from the Jewish Settlement Area*.

33. Hersonski, "Witnessing the Archive," 277, 282.

34. Anat Or, "Sinema balash" [Cinema Detective], *Haaretz*, June 27, 2008, http://www.haaretz.co.il/misc/1.1333472.

35. Shmulik Duvdevany, "Nichnas latmuna" [Getting into the Frame], YNet News, August 3, 2008, http://www.ynet.co.il/articles/0,7340,L-3576843,00.html; Or, "Sinema balash."

36. Anat Lachowitz, "Megamot hadashot beyetsug hashoah bakolnoa hatiudi beshnot haalpaim" [New Trends in Holocaust Representation in Documentary Filmmaking of the 21st Century], seminar paper for the course Holocaust Survivors in Israeli Cinema, Open University, Ra'anana, Israel, 2012.

37. Or, "Sinema balash."

38. "All possible types of death in Israeli society—in one family" as defined by the editor Anat Lachowitz. See Or, "Sinema balash."

39. Anton Kaes, "History and Film: Public Memory in the Age of Electronic Dissemination," *History and Memory* 2, no. 1 (Fall 1990): 111–29; Rosenstone, *Visions of the Past*.

40. Steir-Livny, *Shtei panim bamara'a*, 2.

41. Or, "Sinema balash."

42. Oren Baruch Stier, *Committed to Memory: Cultural Mediations of the Holocaust* (Amherst: Univ. of Massachusetts Press, 2013), 25, 32, 45–47.

43. Gili Izikovichz, "B'zroa hazaka" [With a Strong Arm], *Haaretz*, April 4, 2013, https://www.haaretz.co.il/gallery/television/.premium-1.1985164.

44. Izikovichz, "B'zroa hazaka."

45. Izikovichz.

46. Jean Améry, *At the Mind's Limits: Contemplations by a Survivor on Auschwitz and Its Realities* (Bloomington: Indiana Univ. Press, 2009), 94.

47. Primo Levi, *Survival in Auschwitz* (New York: Simon & Schuster, 1996), 27–28.

48. Erin McGlothlin, *Second-Generation Holocaust Literature: Legacies of Survival and Perpetration* (New York: Camden House, 2006), 22.

49. Mieke Bal, "Intimacy, Modesty, Silence," in *The Philosophy of Documentary Film: Image, Sound, Fiction, Truth*, ed. David LaRocca (Lanham, MD: Lexington Books, 2017), 261–86, esp. 263.

50. Lawrence Baron, "The Wandering Review: 'Numbered.'" *San Diego Jewish World*, December 25, 2012, http://www.sdjewishworld.com/2012/12/25/the-wandering-review-numbered.

51. See the introduction to this volume and chapter 1.

52. Hanna Yablonka, "Nitzoleu hashoah v'hayeshuv hayisraeli: mitos v'metziut" [Holocaust Survivors and the Jewish Yishuv: Myth and Reality], YouTube, February 10, 2015, https://www.youtube.com/watch?v=QpxKv8nVnj0.

53. See chapter 1. For more on this topic, see Liat Steir-Livny, "Hagalut hameshuleshet: dimuya shel nitsolat hashoah bakolnoa' haisraeli haalilaty" [The Threefold Exile: The Female Holocaust Survivor in Israeli Cinema], in *Gender in Israel: New Studies on Gender in the Yishuv and the State*, ed. Margalit Shilo and Gideon Katz (Beersheba, Israel: Ben-Gurion Univ. of the Negev, 2011), 497–520.

54. Steir-Livny, *Shtei panim bamara'a*, 96–204.

55. On the importance of self-deprecating humor and black humor, see, for example, Avner Ziv, *Humor veishiyut* [Personality and Sense of Humor] (Tel Aviv: Papyrus, 1996); Itamar Levin, *Mi'ba'ad la'dmaot: humor Yehudi that hashilton hanatsi* [Through the Tears: Jewish Humor under the Nazi Regime] (Jerusalem: Yad Vashem, 2004); Haya Ostrower, *L'lo humor hayinu mitabdim* [Without Humor We Would Have Killed Ourselves] (Jerusalem: Yad Vashem, 2009); Liat Steir-Livny, *Is It OK to Laugh about It? Holocaust Humour, Satire and Parody* (London: Vallentine Mitchell, 2017).

56. Levin, *Mi'ba'ad la'dmaot*, 13–36; Ostrower, *L'lo humor hayinu mitabdim*, 63–104.

57. Pierre Nora, "Between Memory and History: Les Lieux de Mémoire," *Representations* 26 (Spring 1989): 7–24.

58. McGlothlin, *Second-Generation Holocaust Literature*, 23.

59. Ebbrecht, "Migrating Images," 86–103.

60. Maya Galina Sela, "Hashoa: niputz mitosim bakolnoa haisraeli vebaomanut bishnot hashmonim" [The Holocaust: Shattering Myths in Israeli Film and Art as of the 1980s], seminar paper for the course Holocaust Survivors in Israeli Cinema, Open University, Ra'anana, Israel, 2014.

61. Galia Yahav, "Parodia meshubahat hosefet et habanalya shel teud hashoah" [A Great Parody Exposes the Banality of Holocaust Documentation], *Haaretz*, January 23, 2012, http://www.haaretz.co.il/gallery/art/1.1623550.

62. Mark Godfrey, *Abstraction and the Holocaust* (New Haven, CT: Yale Univ. Press, 2007); Elie Wiesel, "Art and the Holocaust: Trivializing Memory,"

New York Times, June 11, 1989, http://www.nytimes.com/1989/06/11/movies/art-and-the-holocaust-trivializingmemory.html?pagewanted=all.

63. Gavriel D. Rosenfeld, *Hi Hitler: How the Nazi Past Is Being Normalized in Contemporary Culture* (Cambridge: Cambridge Univ. Press, 2015).

64. Alan Rosenfeld, *The End of the Holocaust* (Bloomington: Indiana Univ. Press, 2013), 11, 243–44.

4. The Elusiveness of Memory

1. Friedman, "Witnessing for the Witness," 81–82, 86.

2. Steir-Livny, *Shtei panim bamara'a*, 123–24.

3. Zimmerman, *Al tigu li bashoah*, 257.

4. Gertz, *Makhela aheret*, 93; Zimmerman, 259–60.

5. Steir-Livny, *Shtei panim bamara'a*, 124.

6. Steir-Livny, 61.

7. LaCapra, *Writing History*, 37–74.

8. Loshitzky, *Identity Politics on the Israeli Screen*, 54.

9. Mandel, *Against the Unspeakable*, 5–6, 11.

10. Yohai Ataria, "Truyma: ne'emanut lashtika" [Trauma: Loyalty to Silence], *History and Theory* 29 (n.d.), http://bezalel.secured.co.il/zope/home/he/1376936935/1388333556.

11. Ataria, "Truyma," 47.

12. Gertz, *Makhela aheret*, 90–93.

13. Friedman, "Witnessing for the Witness," 87–88.

14. Friedman, 87–88.

15. Gertz, *Makhela aheret*, 90–93; Steir-Livny, *Shtei panim bamara'a*, 126–27.

16. Dan Sipe, "The Future of Oral History and Moving Images," in *The Oral History Reader*, 2nd ed., ed. Robert Perks and Alistair Thomson (London: Routledge, 2006), 379–88, esp. 382.

17. Michael Frisch, *A Shared Authority: Essays on the Craft and Meaning of Oral and Public History* (Albany: State Univ. of New York Press), xxiii.

18. Alessandro Portelli, "What Makes Oral History Different," in *The Oral History Reader*, ed. Robert Perks and Alistair Thomson (London: Routledge, 1998), 63–74, esp. 67–68.

19. See the introduction to this volume.

20. "Az'akat emet" [A True Alarm], *Dyukan*, July 14, 2017, 36–40.

21. Portelli, "What Makes Oral History Different," 66–67.

22. Portelli, xxiii.

23. Marit Slavin, "Bnei adam zochrim gam havayot shelo havu" [People Also Remember Events They Did Not Experience], Walla, June 12, 2005, https://news.walla.co.il/item/730398.

24. Zvi Baron and Dov Levin, "Be'ayat hashe'eilon l'heker hashoa" [The Problem of Questionnaires on the Holocaust], *Yad Vashem Studies* 3 (1959): 87–108; Dori Laub, "Bearing Witness on the Vicissitudes of Listening," in *Testimony: Crises of Witnessing in Literature, Psychoanalysis and History*, ed. Shoshana Felman and Dori Laub (London: Routledge, 1992), 57–74.

25. Frisch, *A Shared Authority*, 1–13.

26. James E. Young, *Writing and Rewriting the Holocaust: Narrative and the Consequence of Interpretation* (Bloomington: Indiana Univ. Press, 1988), 171.

27. Boaz Cohen, "Early Holocaust Testimonies of Child Survivors: Historical Sources or Anecdotes?" Paper presented at the Emerging Questions in Holocaust Testimonies Research Conference, University of Virginia, Charlottesville, VA, November 6, 2017.

28. Saul Friedländer, "Trauma, Transference, and Working Through in Writing the History of the Shoah," *History and Memory* 4 (1992): 39–59.

29. An interview in the documentary *When Memory Comes: A Film about Saul Friedländer* (Frank Diamond, 2013).

30. Paul B. Jaskot, "Architecture of the Holocaust," 2015, Joseph and Rebecca Meyerhoff Lecture, USHMM, cited in Tim Cole, "Please Mind the Gap: Integrated Histories and Geographies of the Holocaust and Holocaust Memory," paper presented at the Beyond Camps and Forced Labor Conference, Birkbeck, University of London, January 10–12, 2018.

31. Berel Lang, "Imagining the Past, Remembering the Future," paper presented at the Emerging Questions in Holocaust Testimonies Research Conference, University of Virginia, Charlottesville, VA, November 6, 2017.

32. Omer Bartov, *Anatomy of Genocide: The Life and Death of a Town Called Buczacz* (New York: Simon & Schuster, 2018), esp. 232–64.

33. Primo Levi, *Hashokim vehanitzolim* [The Drowned and the Saved] (Tel Aviv: Am Oved, 1991).

34. Baron and Levin, "Be'ayat hashe'eilon l'heker hashoa," 87–108.

35. Tim Cole, "Please Mind the Gap: Integrated Histories and Geographies of the Holocaust and Holocaust Memory," paper presented at the Beyond Camps and Forced Labor Conference, Birkbeck, University of London, January 10–12, 2018.

36. Bartov, *Anatomy of Genocide*; Browning, *Remembering Survival*; Dan Bar-On, *Hapsychologia shel hashoah* [The Psychology of the Holocaust] (Ra'anana, Israel: Open Univ. Press, 2006).

37. James E. Young, "Toward a Received History of the Holocaust," *History and Theory* 36, no. 4 (1997): 37–39.

38. Laub, "Bearing Witness on the Vicissitudes of Listening," 62.

39. Jeffrey Shandler, *Holocaust Memory in the Digital Age: Survivors' Stories and New Media Practices* (Stanford, CA: Stanford Univ. Press, 2017), esp. 43–86.

40. Shandler, *Holocaust Memory in the Digital Age*, 57–74.

41. Lawrence Langer, "Holocaust Testimonies," paper presented at the Emerging Questions in Holocaust Testimonies Research Conference, University of Virginia, Charlottesville, VA, November 5, 2017.

42. *Café Nagler*, Go 2 Films, http://www.go2films.com/Family-Social-issues/Cafe-Nagler.

43. *Café Nagler*, Israeli Film Center, http://www.israelfilmcenter.org/israeli-film-database/films/cafe-nagler.

44. Interview with Lawrence Langer at the Emerging Questions in Holocaust Testimonies Research Conference, University of Virginia, Charlottesville, VA, November 7, 2017.

45. Raul Hilberg, *Perpetrators, Victims, Bystanders: The Jewish Catastrophe, 1933–1945* (New York: HarperCollins, 1992).

46. See a summary of the historiography of the term in Victoria J. Barnett, "The Changing View of the 'Bystander' in Holocaust Scholarship: Historical, Ethical, and Political Implications," *Utah Law Review* 4 (2017): 633–47; "The Righteous Among the Nations," Yad Vashem, http://www.yadvashem.org/righteous.html.

47. Since 2014 the following documentaries in his *Searching for the Unknown Holocaust* series have been released: *Guardians of Remembrance*, *Holocaust: The Eastern Front*, *Beyond the Nistru*, *We Allow You to Die*, *Until the Last Step*, *Drawers of Memory*, and *Gotenland*. The series is slated to consist of nine documentaries.

48. Laub, "Bearing Witness on the Vicissitudes of Listening," 57–74.

49. Tal Ran and Even Anat, "Ra'ayon im Ra'anan Alexandrowicz" [An Interview with Ra'anan Alexandrowicz], *Takriv* 4 (2012), https://takriv.net/.

50. Butchart, "Al etica v'kolnoa ti'udi." See also Jay Ruby, *Picturing Culture: Explorations of Film and Anthropology* (Durham, NC: Duke Univ. Press, 2000).

51. Sharon Kangisser Cohen, "The Survivors and Their Stories," paper presented at the Beyond Camps and Forced Labor Conference, Birkbeck, University of London, January 10–12, 2018.

52. Ella Schneider, "Sho'ot mishelahen" [Their Own Holocausts], *Ma'ariv*, November 1, 2006, 14.

53. Janet Walker, *Trauma Cinema: Documenting Incest and the Holocaust* (Berkeley: Univ. of California Press, 2005), 17–19.

54. Laub, "Bearing Witness on the Vicissitudes of Listening," 59–60. See also Naomi Rosh White, "Holocaust Testimony and History," in *The Oral History Reader*, ed. Robert Perks and Alistair Thomson (London: Routledge, 1998), 172–82, esp. 175–76.

55. Laub, "Bearing Witness on the Vicissitudes of Listening," 65.

56. *Shalom Italia* is an Israeli German coproduction. See Orit Merlin Rosenzweig, "Shlosha ahim v'me'ara: hazru l'hapess et hamakom bo histatru bashoah" [Shalom Italia: Went Back to Search for Their Hiding Place during the Holocaust], Xnet, August 9, 2016, http://xnet.ynet.co.il/articles/0,7340,L-4839222,00.html.

57. Rosenzweig, "Shlosha ahim v'me'ara."

58. Paul Morrow, "In the Matter of Testimony," paper presented at the Emerging Questions in Holocaust Testimonies Research Conference, University of Virginia, Charlottesville, VA, November 3, 2017.

59. Frisch, *A Shared Authority*, xv–xxiv.

5. Looking beyond the Victims

1. A term used by the historian Christopher Browning. See Christopher R. Browning, *Ordinary Men: Reserve Police Battalion 101 and the Final Solution in Poland* (New York: HarperCollins, 1992).

2. See this observation in Hannah Arendt, *Eichmann in Jerusalem: A Report on the Banality of Evil* (New York: Viking Press, 1963), 107.

3. Moshe Zimmermann, "Georgrafia shel asiyat din" [Geography of Justice], Weiner Lectures 2015–2016, January 14, 2016, https://www.youtube.com/watch?v=__kESqNUgxIandt=3440s.

4. Roger Frie, "Historical Trauma and Lived Experience: An Introduction," in *History Flows Through Us: Germany, the Holocaust, and the Importance of Empathy*, ed. Roger Frie (London: Routledge, 2018), 1–14, esp. 5.

5. Bernhard Giesen, "From Denial to Confessions of Guilt: The German Case," in *Remembering the Holocaust: A Debate*, ed. Jeffrey C. Alexander (Oxford: Oxford Univ. Press, 2009), 114–34; Mary Fulbrook, "Guilt and Shame among Communities of Experience, Connection and Identification," in *Reverberations of Nazi Violence in Germany and Beyond: Disturbing Pasts*, ed. Stephanie Bird et al. (London: Bloomsbury, 2016), 15–32.

6. Alon Gan, *Korbanutam omanutam: mesiach korbani lesiach riboni* [From Sovereignty to Victimhood: An Analysis of the Victimization Discourse in Israel]

(Jerusalem: Israel Democracy Institute, 2014), 104–13; Gilad Margalit, *Ashma, sevel v'zikaron: Germania zocheret et meteiha b'milhemet ha'olam hashniya* [Guilt, Suffering, and Memory: Germany Remembers Its World War II Dead] (Haifa: Haifa Univ. Press, 2007); Samuel Salzborn, "Hamitus hagermani: l'hargish k'uma shel korbanot: hatzaga v'yetzug shel hagermanim k'korban bapulmus hahadash al briha v'girush" [The German Myth: To Feel Like a Nation of Victims], *Dapim l'heker hashoa* 21 (2007): 239–60.

7. Margarete Mitscherlich, "Hayecholet shel hagermanim l'hitabel: ashlaya o tikva?" [The Germans' Ability to Mourn: An Illusion or Hope?], in *The Germans 1945–1990*, ed. Oded Heilbronner and Moshe Zimmermann (Jerusalem: Magnes Press, 1997), 440–48; Alf Lidtka, "Hitmodedut im ha'avar: ashlayot shel zcira, drachim l'shchichat hanazism begermania hamiaaravit" [Ways to Deal with the Past in West Germany] in *The Germans 1945–1990*, ed. Oded Heilbronner and Moshe Zimmermann (Jerusalem: Magnes Press, 1997), 417–39.

8. Gan, *Korbanutam omanutam*, 104–13; Oded Heilbronner and Moshe Zimmermann, "Introduction: Dealing with the Past," in *The Germans 1945–1990*, ed. Oded Heilbronner and Moshe Zimmermann (Jerusalem: Magnes Press, 1997), 415–16; Gilad Margalit, "Toda'at ha'ashma hagermanit v'hashlachoteiha acharei 1945" [German Guilt and Its Implications after 1945], in *Zikaron v'shichicha: germania v'hashoah* [Memory and Amnesia: Germany and the Holocaust], ed. Gilad Margalit and Yifat Weiss (Tel Aviv: Hakibbutz Hameuchad, 2005), 228–66; Lidtka, "Hitmodedut im ha'avar."

9. Richard J. Evans, *In Hitler's Shadow: West German Historians and the Attempt to Escape from the Nazi Past* (London: I. B. Tauris, 1989).

10. Some forty years later, his son Stephan interviewed the same offspring on their lives in the shadow of Nazism. His book, *My Father's Keeper*, was published in 2013.

11. Fulbrook, "Guilt and Shame among Communities of Experience, Connection and Identification," 15–16.

12. Giesen, "From Denial to Confessions of Guilt," 117.

13. Elad Hopper, "Lo miflazot, bnei adam: Izogey hanazim veyaldehem bakolnoa hadocomentary haisraeli" [Not Monster, Human Beings: Representations of Nazis and their Offspring in Israeli Documentary Cinema], seminar paper for the course Holocaust Survivors in Israeli Cinema, Open University, Ra'anana, Israel, 2016.

14. For example, Gertrud Hartmann, "Children of Nazis: A Psychotomimetic Perspective," in *International Handbook of Multigenerational Legacies of Trauma*, ed. Yael Danieli (New York: Plenum Press, 1998), 85–96.

15. McGlothlin, *Second-Generation Holocaust Literature*, 16.

16. Katrin Himmler, *The Himmler Brothers: A German Family History* (Basingstoke, UK: Palgrave Macmillan, 2007).

17. Margareta and Alexander Mitscherlich, *The Inability to Mourn: Principles of Collective Behavior* (New York: Grove Press, 1975), 440–48.

18. Nitza Harel, "Yetzugam shel hanazism v'hashoah bakolnoa hama'aravi: diyun b'shlosha narrativim kolno'in: hanarrativ hakolno'i hagermani" [Representation of the Holocaust and Nazism in Western Cinema: Three Cinematic Narratives: The German Narrative], in *Kolnoa v'zikaron: yahasim mesukanim*? [Cinema and Memory: A Dangerous Relationship?], ed. Haim Bresheeth, Moshe Zimmermann, and Shlomo Zand (Jerusalem: Zalman Shazar Center, 2004), http://lib.cet.ac.il/pages/item.asp?item=15911.

19. Lidtka, "Hitmodedut im ha'avar."

20. Frie, "Historical Trauma and Lived Experience," 5.

21. Gan, *Korbanutam omanutam*, 104–13; Salzborn, "Hamitus hagermani, l'hargish k'uma shel korbanot"; Margalit, *Ashma, sevel v'zikaron*; Frank Jordans, "Germania: hasidra shesho'elet ma hahorim asu bashoah" [Germany: The Series That Asks What the Parents Did during the Holocaust], YNet News, March 28, 2013, http://www.ynet.co.il/articles/0,7340,L-4361823,00.html; Aviva Lory, "Ho, kama savalnu" [Oh, How Much We Suffered], *Haaretz*, August 6, 2007, http://www.haaretz.co.il/misc/1.1431956; Alon Confino, "From Psychohistory to Memory Studies: Or How Some Germans Became Jews and Some Jews Nazis," in *History Flows Through Us: Germany, the Holocaust, and the Importance of Empathy*, ed. Roger Frie (London: Routledge, 2018), 17–30, esp. 23–24.

22. Fulbrook, "Guilt and Shame among Communities of Experience, Connection and Identification," 15–32, esp. 28.

23. Yaakov Sharett, ed., *Pulmis hashilumim* [The Reparations Controversy] (Tel Aviv: Moshe Sharett Heritage Society, 2007).

24. Sharett, *Pulmis hashilumim*; Segev, *Hamillion hashvi'i*, 171–236.

25. Yechiam Weitz, "Haderech l'vasenar: keitsad ushra hahahlata al masa umatan yashir bein Israel legermania" [The Way to Wassenaar: How the Decision for Direct Negotiations between Israel and Germany Was Approved], *Yad Vashem Studies* 28 (2000): 275–47; Yaacov Toby, *Hahurban v'haheshbon: medinat Yisrael v'hashilumim migermanua 1949–1953* [The Reparations Agreement between Germany and Israel 1949–1953] (Ramat Gan and Tel Aviv: Bar Ilan Univ. and Tel Aviv Univ., 2015).

26. Avner Shapira, "Ma oseh Dudu Topaz b'kenes al kolnoa nazi?" [What Is Dudu Topaz Doing at a Conference on Nazi Cinema?], *Haaretz*, November 3, 2016, http://www.haaretz.co.il/gallery/cinema/.premium-1.2153857.

27. Daniel Jonah Goldhagen, *Hitler's Willing Executioners: Ordinary Germans and the Holocaust* (New York: Vintage, 1996).

28. Browning, *Ordinary Men*.

29. Alon Tal, "Hamechkar shehosef ma be'emet hoshvim hagermanim al hayisraelim," *Spitz*, January 15, 2015, http://spitzmag.de/issues/spitz_15/5759.

30. For example, for depictions of Israeli German encounters in contemporary fiction films, see Steir-Livny, *Shtei panim bamara'a*, 181–89.

31. Hartmann, "Children of Nazis."

32. Hartmann.

33. Arik Bender, "Tzatzaei nazim baknesset: ne'avek b'antishemiyut" [Nazi Descendants in the Knesset: We Will Fight Anti-Semitism], NRG, November 22, 2011, http://www.nrg.co.il/online/1/ART2/309/033.html.

34. Itay Ilany, "K'she tzatzaei hanazim sharim hatikva berap lifney nitzolim" [When Nazis' Descendants Sing Hatikva Rap-Style in Front of Survivors], YNet News, December 18, 2016, http://www.ynet.co.il/articles/0,7340,L-4894262,00.html; Liron Nagler-Cohen, "Shovrim Shtika: Nazi Descendants Sing Hatikva" [Breaking the Silence: Nazis' Descendants Sing Hatikva], YNet News, August 16, 2016, http://www.ynet.co.il/articles/0,7340,L-4842043,00.html.

35. See, for example, Norbert Lebert and Stephan Lebert, *Harei ata nosei et shmi: hamoreshet hamara shel yaldei hanazim hab'chirim* [You Bear My Name: The Bitter Legacy of High-Ranking Nazis' Offspring] (Tel Aviv: Am Oved, 2014); Jennifer Teege and Nikola Sellmair, *Amon: saba sheli haya yore bi* [Amon: My Grandfather Would Have Shot Me] (Tel Aviv: Hakibbutz Hameuchad, 2014).

36. "Tzatzaei hanazim: moreshet stanit" [Nazis' Descendants: A Diabolical Heritage], *Erev Hadash*, June 12, 2013, https://www.youtube.com/watch?v=juVyDqx7Mws; "Hagermanim shehechlitu la'alot v'l'hitgayer: dor sheni lashoah" [Germans Who Decided to Immigrate to Israel and Convert to Judaism: Second Generation of the Holocaust], *Channel 2 News*, April 25, 2012, https://www.youtube.com/watch?v=4nEv1_Iuk6Q; "Tzatzaei hanazim hahaim b'yisrael" [Nazis' Descendants Who Live in Israel], *Orly and Guy: The Morning Show*, June 20, 2013, https://www.youtube.com/watch?v=4nEv1_Iuk6Q.

37. Tal Litvak Hirsch and Julia Chaitin, "Hakdama" [Introduction], in *Drachim Miztalvot* [Intersecting Roads], ed. Tal Litvak Hirsch and Julia Chaitin (Beer Sheva, Israel: Ben Gurion Univ. of the Negev, 2011), 2–13.

38. See, for example, Dan Bar-On, *Legacy of Silence: Encounters with Children of the Third Reich* (Cambridge, MA: Harvard Univ. Press, 1989); Dan Bar-On, "Descendants of Nazi Perpetrators: Seven Years after the First Interview," *Journal of Humanistic Psychology* 36, no. 1 (1996): 55–74; Dan Bar-On, "The Use of a Limited Morality to Rationalize Horrendous Evil: Interviews with an Auschwitz Doctor and His Son," *Journal of Traumatic Stress* 3, no. 3 (1990): 415–27; Dan Bar-On and Amalia Gaon, "We Suffered Too: Nazi Children's Inability to

Relate to the Suffering of the Victims of the Holocaust," *Journal of Humanistic Psychology* 31, no. 4 (1991): 77–95; Dan Bar-On, Tal Ostrovsky, and Dafna Fromer, "Who Am I in Relation to My Past, in Relation to the Other? German and Israeli Students Confront the Holocaust and Each Other," in *International Handbook of Multigenerational Legacies of Trauma*, ed. Yael Danieli (New York: Plenum Press, 1998), 97–118.

39. Dan Bar-On and Israel Charny, "The Logic of Moral Argumentation of Children of the Nazi Era," *International Journal of Group Tensions* 22, no. 1 (1992): 3–20.

40. See chapter 4.

41. Shavit, "Bamai 'hadira' metzig."

42. Harald Walzer, "Heroizatzia mitztaberet: hafihat 'haomdim menegd' veposhim legiborei hahitnagdut lanatsism basiach habein dori" [Cumulative Heroization: Turning Bystanders and Criminals into Heroes of Nazi Resistance], in *Zikaron v'shichecha: germania v'hashoah* [Memory and Amnesia: Germany and the Holocaust], ed. Gilad Margalit and Yifat Weiss (Tel Aviv: Hakibbutz Hameuchad, 2005), 198–215.

43. Alexander von Plato, "Eifo hayeladim shelo m'aminim l'horeihem? Bikoret 'l kama tezot min haproyeqt 'hanhala shel mudut historit'" [Where Are the Children Who Don't Believe Their Parents? Critique of a Few Theses from the Endowment of Historical Awareness Project], in *Zikaron v'shichecha: germania v'hashoah* [Memory and Amnesia: Germany and the Holocaust], ed. Gilad Margalit and Yifat Weiss (Tel Aviv: Hakibbutz Hameuchad, 2005), 221–27.

44. Norbert Frei, "Y'kumim makbilim? madua yesh lahkor et nekudot hamaga shabein hahistoryografya lezichronot mishpahtiyim" [Parallel Universes? Why Should We Examine the Touch Points between Historiography and Familial Memories?], in *Zikaron v'shichecha: germania v'hashoah* [Memory and Amnesia: Germany and the Holocaust], ed. Gilad Margalit and Yifat Weiss (Tel Aviv: Hakibbutz Hameuchad, 2005), 216–20.

45. McGlothlin, *Second-Generation Holocaust Literature*, 1–42.

46. Anna Ornstein, "Foreword," in *Not in My Family: German Memory and Responsibility after the Holocaust*, ed. Roger Frie (Oxford: Oxford Univ. Press, 2017), ix–xiii, esp. xi–xii.

47. Gabriele Schwab, *Haunting Legacies: Violent Histories and Transgenerational Trauma* (New York: Columbia Univ. Press, 2010), esp. 11–13, 67–91.

48. Roger Frie, *Not in My Family: German Memory and Responsibility after the Holocaust* (Oxford: Oxford Univ. Press, 2017), 199–200.

49. Frie, "Historical Trauma and Lived Experience," 5.

50. Frie, 5.

51. Frie, 1–14.

52. Munk, "Arnon Goldfinger's 'The Flat,'" 37.

53. Frie, "Historical Trauma and Lived Experience," 7.

54. McGlothlin, *Second-Generation Holocaust Literature*, 15.

55. Hopper, "Lo miflazot, bnei adam"; Avner Shavit, "Hadira: re'ayon im Arnon Goldfinger al hatzlahato hamadhima b'germania" [The Flat: An Interview with Arnon Goldfinger on His Tremendous Success in Germany], Walla, April 7, 2013, https://e.walla.co.il/item/2630758.

56. Itay Stern, "Haseret hayisraeli 'hayafa banashim' zacha b'taharut hastudentim shel haoscar ha'amerikani" [The Israeli Film "The Most Beautiful Woman" Wins the Student Competition of the American Oscars], *Haaretz*, June 29, 2016, https://www.haaretz.co.il/gallery/cinema/1.3052773.

57. Fulbrook, "Guilt and Shame among Communities of Experience, Connection and Identification," 15–32, esp. 15–16, 27.

58. Fulbrook, 15–16, 28.

59. Schwab, *Haunting Legacies*, 25.

60. Frie, *Not in My Family*, 200.

61. Gili Izikovich, "Tzatzaeihem shel b'chirei hamishtar hanazi nechsafim baseret 'Yaldei Hitler'" [Descendants of Prominent Nazi Officials Are Represented in the Film "Hitler's Children"], *Haaretz*, May 1, 2011, https://www.haaretz.co.il/gallery/1.1172643.

62. Izikovich, "Tzatzaeihem shel b'chirei hamishtar hanazi."

63. Hopper, "Lo miflazot, bnei adam."

64. Hopper, 5.

65. Chanoch Ze'evi, "Yaldei Hitler" [Hitler's Children], Yaldut avuda: yeladim sordei shoah (Lost Childhood Association), n.d., http://www.ylas.org/117983/%D7%99%D7%9C%D7%93%D7%99-%D7%94%D7%99%D7%98%D7%9C%D7%A8.

66. Izikovich, "Tzatzaeihem shel b'chirei hamishtar hanazi."

67. Hopper, "Lo miflazot, bnei adam."

68. Izikovich, "Tzatzaeihem shel b'chirei hamishtar hanazi."

69. Izikovich.

70. Nichols, *Representing Reality*, 38–42.

71. Hopper, "Lo miflazot, bnei adam."

72. Bayer, "After Post-Memory."

73. Gurevich and Arev, "Trauma, ashma, mehila"; Duvdevani, *Guf rishon matzlema*; Matan Aharoni, "Hatiud ha'ayzmi v'mishtar hamabat batelevizia" [Self-Representation and the Governing of the Gaze in Television], *Panim* (2005): 68–69, http://www.ruvik.co.il/.

74. Duvdevani, *Guf rishon matzlema.*

75. Duvdevani.

76. McGlothlin, *Second-Generation Holocaust Literature*, 1–42.

77. According to Schwab, self-hatred and a sense of not wanting to belong (to Germany) is a widely shared sentiment among second-generation Germans and is prominent among descendants who left their country. See Schwab, *Haunting Legacies*, 92–117.

78. The fear of inherited sin, transfer of evil, and the will to stop it by not having children is also expressed in literature by the children of perpetrators. See McGlothlin, *Second-Generation Holocaust Literature*, 26–27.

79. McGlothlin, 26.

80. Hopper, "Lo miflazot, bnei adam."

81. Izikovich, "Tzatzaeihem shel b'chirei hamishtar hanazi."

82. Hopper, "Lo miflazot, bnei adam."

83. Hopper.

84. "New Jewish Cinema: Vanessa Lapa, Director of 'The Decent One,'" YouTube, October 9, 2014, https://www.youtube.com/watch?v=aledk49EM1g.

85. McGlothlin, *Second-Generation Holocaust Literature*, 1–42; Jenni Adams, "Introduction," in *Representing Perpetrators in Holocaust Literature and Film*, ed. Jenni Adams and Sue Vice (Portland, OR: Vallentine Mitchell, 2013), 1–12, esp. 2.

86. James Waller, *Becoming Evil: How Ordinary People Commit Genocide and Mass Killing* (Oxford: Oxford Univ. Press, 2002); Adams, "Introduction," 3.

87. "New Jewish Cinema."

88. "Vanessa Lapa: Charney Report," YouTube, January 15, 2015, https://www.youtube.com/watch?v=94VhOq1TekQ.

89. "Vanessa Lapa: Charney Report."

90. "New Jewish Cinema."

91. "'The Decent One': A Behind-the-Scenes Look," YouTube, September 26, 2014, https://www.youtube.com/watch?v=FAbhWUnRcII.

92. "Vanessa Lapa: Charney Report."

93. "New Jewish Cinema."

94. "Arise America: Documentary Film 'The Decent One.'" YouTube, October 9, 2014, https://www.youtube.com/watch?v=UD_6z-2R80A.

95. "Vanessa Lapa: Charney Report."

96. Hopper, "Lo miflazot, bnei adam."

97. "New Jewish Cinema."

98. Hannah Arendt, *The Origins of Totalitarianism* (London: Andre Deutsch, 1951), 305–482.

99. Arendt, *The Origins of Totalitarianism*, 305–482.

100. Ayala Paz, "In the Shadow of Dark Times: A Reading of Hannah Arendt's *Eichmann in Jerusalem* through the Lens of *The Origins of Totalitarianism*" (forthcoming); Arendt, *The Origins of Totalitarianism*, 665.

101. Arendt, *The Origins of Totalitarianism*, 305–482; Arendt, *Eichmann in Jerusalem*, 290–91.

102. Paz, "In the Shadow of Dark Times."

103. Arendt, *Eichmann in Jerusalem*, 105–6.

104. "Vanessa Lapa: Charney Report."

105. "Vanessa Lapa: Charney Report."

106. "Himmler: harotzeach hanazi ahshav shehu ish tov" [Himmler: The Nazi Murderer Who Thought He Was a Good Person], YouTube, January 27, 2014, https://www.youtube.com/watch?v=q2NiWfvUQwk.

107. "New Jewish Cinema."

108. "Himmler: harotzeach hanazi ahshav shehu ish tov."

109. "Vanessa Lapa: Charney Report."

110. "Vanessa Lapa: Charney Report."

111. "Vanessa Lapa: Charney Report."

112. "New Jewish Cinema."

113. Hopper, "Lo miflazot, bnei adam."

114. Barnett, "The Changing View of the 'Bystander' in Holocaust Scholarship," 637–39, 644–45.

115. Hannah Brown, "Out of the Forest: Movie Review," *Jerusalem Post*, May 4, 2004.

116. "Lizkor: Ein matzav lishkoach," *Reiting*, May 26, 2004.

117. Uri Klein, "M'kivun haya'ar" [Out of the Forest], *Haaretz*, June 10, 2004; Stav Yehuda, "Ya'ar hazvaot" [Forest of Horrors], *Yediot Aharonot*, May 13, 2004.

118. Meir Schnitzer, "Bata'ar baya'ar" [In the Forest, in the Forest], *Ma'ariv*, April 30, 2004.

119. See chapter 3.

120. See chapter 4.

121. For example: Victoria Barnett, *Bystanders: Conscience and Complicity during the Holocaust* (Westport, CT: Greenwood Press, 1999); Robert Ehrenreich and Tim Cole, "The Perpetrator-Bystander-Victim Constellation: Rethinking Genocidal Relationships," *Human Organization* 64, no. 3 (Fall 2005): 213–24.

122. Bartov, *Anatomy of Genocide*, esp. 265–88.

Epilogue

1. For a summary of studies on this topic, see, for example: Steir-Livny, *Shtei panim bamara'a*, 1–6; Kozlovsky Golan, *Masach shel shichecha*, 13–17.

2. Winston, Vanstone, and Wang, *The Act of Documenting*, 1–3.

3. Victoria Aarons, "Introduction," in *Third-Generation Holocaust Narratives: Memory in Memoir and Fiction*, ed. Victoria Aarons (Lanham, MD: Lexington Books, 2016), xi–xxi.

4. Janet Jacobs, "Descendants of Holocaust Survivors," in *The Holocaust across Generations: Trauma and Its Inheritance among Descendants of Survivors* (New York: NYU Press, 2017), 136, 147.

5. Litvak-Hirsch and Bar-On, "Livnot et hahaim m'hadash," 243–71.

6. Julia Chaitin, "Yeladim v'nechadim shel nitzolei hashoah" [Children and Grandchildren of Holocaust Survivors Coping with the Holocaust], in *Yaldut b'tzel hashoah: yeladim-nitsolim vedor sheni* [Childhood in the Shadow of the Holocaust: Child Survivors and Second Generation], ed. Zehava Solomon and Julia Chaitin (Tel Aviv: Kibbutz Hameuchad, 2007), 418–35; Yahav Telem, "Mifgashim m'hasug hashlishi" [Encounters with the Third Generation], *Yediot Acharonot*, July 4, 2013, 4–5.

7. Adi Goren, *The Meaning of Grandparenting for Grandchildren of Holocaust Survivors* (master's thesis, University of Haifa, 2004); Flora Hogman, "Memory of the Holocaust," Echoes of the Holocaust, June 4, 1995, http://www.holocaustechoes.com/4hogman.html; Eva Fogelman, "Psychological Dynamics in the Lives of Third-Generation Holocaust Survivors," *Hidden Child* 16 (2008), http://www.drevafogelman.com/_psychological_dynamics_in_the_lives_of_third_generation_holocaust_survivors_94110.htm.

8. Nora, "Bein zikaron l'historia," 4–19.

9. Tal Litvak Hirsch and Julia Chaitin, "The Shoah Runs through Our Veins: The Relevance of the Holocaust for Jewish-Israeli Young Adults," *Idea*, May 1, 2010, http://www.ideajournal.com/articles.php?id=49.

10. Friedman, "Witnessing for the Witness," 81–82, 86.

11. Noah Shenker, *Reframing Holocaust Testimony* (Bloomington: Indiana Univ. Press, 2015), 196.

Filmography

Third-Generation Holocaust Survivors Documentaries

A Documentary about the Holocaust [*Seret Doqomentary al hashoah*]. Directed by Itay Ziv, 2012.

Address: Germany [*Hactovet: Germania*]. Directed by Ruth Shiloni, 2017.

A Film Unfinished [*Shtikat haarchion*]. Directed by Yael Hersonski, 2010.

Aida's Secrets [*Hasodot shel Aida*]. Directed by Alon Schwarz, 2016.

Art Liberates [*Ha'omanut m'shachreret*]. Directed by Solo Avital and Adam Horowitz, 2004.

Café Nagler. Directed by Mor Kaplansky, 2015.

The Cahana Sisters [*Ha'ahayot Cahana*]. Directed by Gilad Melzer, 2006.

The Cemetery Club [*Moadon beit hakvarot*]. Directed by Tali Shemesh, 2006.

The Dark Side [*Hazad ha'afel*]. Directed by Natalie Assouline Travilio, 2015.

The Decent One [*Adam hagun*]. Directed by Vanessa Lapa, 2014.

Farewell Herr Schwarz [*Heye shalom, Peter Schwartz*]. Directed by Yael Reuveny, 2013.

The Flat [*Hadira*]. Directed by Arnon Goldfinger, 2011.

The Green Dumpster Mystery [*Hata'aluma bamechola hayeruka*]. Directed by Tal Haim Yoffe, 2008.

Hitler's Children [*Yaldei Hitler*]. Directed by Chanoch Ze'evi, 2011.

Kleiner Rudi. Directed by Michelle Stein Teer, 2006.

Lerner's Revenge [*Nikmat Lerner*]. Directed by Gila'ad Tokatly, 2006.

Martin. Directed by Ra'anan Alexandrowicz, 1999.

The Most Beautiful Woman [*Hayafa banashim*]. Directed by Maya Sarfaty, 2016.

My German Children [*Yeladim Germanim sheli*]. Directed by Tom Tamar Pauer, 2012.

Numbered [*S'furim*]. Directed by Dana Doron and Uriel Sinai, 2011.

Out of the Forest [*M'kivun hayaar*]. Directed by Yaron Kaftory Ben-Yosef and Limor Pinhasov Ben-Yosef, 2004.

Oy Mama. Directed by Noa Maiman, 2010.

Screaming Silence [*Shtika zoe'ket*]. Directed by Ronnie Sarnat and Gil Lesnik, 2015.

Shalom Italia [*Shloshah ahim v'me'ara*]. Directed by Tamar Tal-Anati, 2016.

Stalags [*Stalagim*]. Directed by Ari Liebsker, 2008.

There [*Shama*]. Directed by Yael Hersonski, 2001.

Watermarks [*Hachoach lishot*]. Directed by Yaron Zilberman, 2004.

Second-Generation Holocaust Documentaries

Because of That War [*Biglal ha'milhama ha'hi*]. Directed by Orna Ben-Dor, 1988.

Choice and Destiny [*Habhira v'hagoral*]. Directed by Tsipi Reibenbach, 1993.

Daddy, Come to the Fair [*Abbaleh, bo laluna park*]. Directed by Nitza Gonen, 1993.

Girlfriends [*Habanot m'libau*]. Directed by Yoel Kaminski, 1994.

Hanuszka. Directed by Nurit Kedar, 2006.

Healing by Killing [*Ripui b'hereg*]. Directed by Nitzan Aviram, 1989.

Hugo. Directed by Yair Lev, 1989.

Hugo 2. Directed by Yair Lev, 2008.

Kapo. Directed by Tor Ben-Mayor and Dan Setton, 1999.

The Kozalchik Affair [*Parashat kozalchik*]. Directed by Roni Ninio, 2015.

Love in Auschwitz [*Ahava b'Auschwitz*]. Directed by Tor Ben-Mayor, 2003.

My 100 Children [*100 hayeladim sheli*]. Directed by Amalia Margolin and Oshra Swartz, 2003.

One, Two, Three, Four, Adolf Hitler at My Door [*Ehad, shtaym, shalosh, arba m'germania, Hitler ba*]. Directed by Tammy Gross and Yuval Cohen, 2002.

Pizza in Auschwitz [*Pizza b'Auschwitz*]. Directed by Moshe Zimmerman, 2008.

Shores of Light [*Or b'ktzei hamagaf*]. Directed by Yael Katzir, 2015.

Tango of Slaves [*Tango shel avadim*]. Directed by Ilan Ziv, 1992.

Three Sisters [*Shalosh ahayot*]. Directed by Tsipi Reibenbach, 1998.

Bibliography

Aarons, Victoria, ed. *Third-Generation Holocaust Narratives: Memory in Memoir and Fiction*. Lanham, MD: Lexington Books, 2016.

Aarons, Victoria, and Alan L. Berger. *Third-Generation Holocaust Representation: Trauma, History, and Memory*. Evanston, IL: Northwestern Univ. Press, 2017.

Adams, Jenni. "Introduction." In *Representing Perpetrators in Holocaust Literature and Film*, edited by Jenni Adams and Jenni Vice, 1–12. Portland, OR: Vallentine Mitchell, 2013.

Adorno, Theodor W. *Negative Dialectics*. London: Routledge, 2000.

Aharoni, Matan. "Hatiud ha'ayzmi v'mishtar hamabat batelevizia" [Self-Representation and the Governing of the Gaze in Television]. *Panim* (2015): 68–69. http://www.ruvik.co.il/.

Alexander, Jeffrey C. "Toward a Theory of Cultural Trauma." In *Cultural Trauma and Collective Identity*, edited by Jeffrey C. Alexander et al., 1–30. Berkeley: Univ. of California Press, 2009.

Améry, Jean. *At the Mind's Limits: Contemplations by a Survivor on Auschwitz and Its Realities*. Bloomington: Indiana Univ. Press, 2009.

Anderman, Nirit. "Nashim sheyeholelu et hamahapecha bakolnoa hay-israeli" [Women Who Are Revolutionizing Israeli Cinema]. *Haaretz*, September 19, 2013.

———. "Ta'amula nazit ba'aron shel savta: hadira, sirto hatiudi shel arnon goldfinger" [Nazi Propaganda in Grandmother's Closet: The Flat, Arnon Goldfinger's Documentary Film]. *Haaretz*, May 9, 2011.

Arendt, Hannah. *Eichmann in Jerusalem: A Report on the Banality of Evil*. New York: Viking Press, 1963.

———. *The Origins of Totalitarianism*. London: Andre Deutsch, 1951.

"Arise America: Documentary Film 'The Decent One.'" YouTube, October 9, 2014. https://www.youtube.com/watch?v=UD_6z-2R80A.

Ash, Mimi, and Assaf Tal. "Total Horror Is Not Representable." Yad Vashem. http://www.yadvashem.org/yv/he/education/film_reviews/shoah.asp#04.

Ashkenazi, Ofer. "Homecoming as a Dead End: Place and Displacement in the New Israeli Documentary Film." *Jewish Culture and History* 15, no. 3 (2014): 212–33.

Aston, Judith, and Sandra Gaudenzi. "Interactive Documentary: Setting the Field." *Studies in Documentary Film* 6, no. 2 (2012): 125–39.

Ataria, Yohai. "Truyma: ne'emanut lashtika" [Trauma: Loyalty to Silence]. *History and Theory* 29 (n.d.). http://bezalel.secured.co.il/zope/home/he/1376936935/1388333556.

Avisar, Ilan. "The Holocaust in Israeli Cinema as a Conflict between Survival and Morality." In *Israeli Cinema: Identities in Motion*, edited by Miri Talmon and Yaron Peleg, 151–67. Austin: Univ. of Texas Press, 2013.

"Az'akat emet" [A True Alarm]. *Dyukan*, July 14, 2017, 36–40.

Bal, Mieke. "Intimacy, Modesty, Silence." In *The Philosophy of Documentary Film: Image, Sound, Fiction, Truth*, edited by David LaRocca, 261–86. Lanham, MD: Lexington Books, 2017.

Ballinger, Alexander, and Danny Graydon. *The Rough Guide to Film Noir.* London: Rough Guides, 2007.

Bar-Ilan, Limor. "The Representation of Holocaust Survivors in Israeli Documentaries." Yad Vashem, n.d. http://www.yadvashem.org/yv/he/education/newsletter/24/survivors_films.asp.

Barnett, Victoria. J. *Bystanders: Conscience and Complicity during the Holocaust.* Westport CT: Greenwood Press, 1999.

———. "The Changing View of the 'Bystander' in Holocaust Scholarship: Historical, Ethical, and Political Implications." *Utah Law Review* 4 (2017): 633–47.

Barnouw, Erik. *Documentary: A History of the Non-Fiction Film.* Oxford: Oxford Univ. Press, 1993.

Bar-On, Dan. *Bein pahad letikva: sipurei haim shel hamesh mishpahot nitsolei shoah shlosha dorot bamishpaha* [Fear and Hope: Three Generations of the Holocaust]. Tel Aviv: Beit Lochamei Haghetaot and Kibbutz Hameuchad Press, 1994.

———. "Descendants of Nazi Perpetrators: Seven Years after the First Interview." *Journal of Humanistic Psychology* 36, no. 1 (1996): 55–74.

———. *Hapsychologia shel hashoah* [The Psychology of the Holocaust]. Ra'anana, Israel: Open Univ. Press, 2006.

———. *Legacy of Silence: Encounters with Children of the Third Reich.* Cambridge MA: Harvard Univ. Press, 1989.

———. "The Use of a Limited Morality to Rationalize Horrendous Evil: Interviews with an Auschwitz Doctor and his Son." *Journal of Traumatic Stress* 3, no. 3 (1990): 415–27.

Bar-On, Dan, and Amalia Gaon. "We Suffered Too: Nazi Children's Inability to Relate to the Suffering of the Victims of the Holocaust." *Journal of Humanistic Psychology* 31, no. 4 (1991): 77–95.

Bar-On, Dan, and Israel Charny. "The Logic of Moral Argumentation of Children of the Nazi Era." *International Journal of Group Tensions* 22, no. 1 (1992): 3–20.

Bar-On, Dan, Tal Ostrovsky, and Dafna Fromer. "Who Am I in Relation to My Past, in Relation to the Other? German and Israeli Students Confront the Holocaust and Each Other." In *International Handbook of Multigenerational Legacies of Trauma*, edited by Yael Danieli, 97–118. New York: Plenum Press, 1998.

Baron, Lawrence. "Imagining the Shoah in American Third-Generation Cinema." In *The Impact of the Holocaust in America: An Annual Review*, vol. 6, edited by Bruce Zuckerman et al., 103–18. West Lafayette, IN: Purdue Univ. Press, 2008.

———. "Statuettes of Limitations: Oscar-Winning 'Holocaust' Films 1945–1948." Paper presented at the Conference on Film and History, Milwaukee, WI, November 4, 2017.

———. "The Wandering Review: 'Numbered.'" *San Diego Jewish World*, December 25, 2012. http://www.sdjewishworld.com/2012/12/25/the-wandering-review-numbered.

Baron, Zvi, and Dov Levin. "Be'ayat hashe'eilon l'heker hashoa" [The Problem of Questionnaires on the Holocaust]. *Yad Vashem Studies* 3 (1959): 87–108.

Barsam, Richard. *Non-Fiction Film: A Critical History.* Bloomington: Indiana Univ. Press, 1992.

Bar-Tal, Daniel. *Lichyot im hasichsuch* [Living with the Conflict]. Haifa: Carmel, 2007.

Bartov, Omer. *Anatomy of Genocide: The Life and Death of a Town Called Buczacz.* New York: Simon & Schuster, 2018.

———. *The Jew in Cinema*. Bloomington: Indiana Univ. Press, 2005.

———. "Kitsch vesadism baplaneta ha'aheret shel kazetnik" [Kitsch and Sadism in Ka-Tzetnik's Other Planet: Israeli Youth Imagine the Holocaust]. *Alpayim* 17 (1999): 148–75.

Barzel, Naima. *Al hab'hira batov: maasei hazala b'polin u'b'holand b'milhemet haolam hashniya* [Choosing the Good: Righteous among the Nations in Poland and the Netherlands during World War II]. Tel Aviv: Hakibbutz Hameuchad, 2007.

Bayer, Gerd. "After Post-Memory: Holocaust Cinema and the Third Generation." *Shofar: An Interdisciplinary Journal of Jewish Studies* 28, no. 4 (2010): 116–32.

Behrend, Fred, and Larry Hanove. *Rebuilt from Broken Glass: A German-Jewish Life Remade in America*. West Lafayette, IN: Purdue Univ. Press, 2017.

Beit Zvi, Shabtai. Hazionut hapost ugandit bemashber hashoah [Post-Ugandan Zionism on Trial]. Tel Aviv: Bronfman, 1977.

Bender, Arik. "Tzatza'ei nazim baknesset: ne'avek b'antishemiyut" [Nazi Descendants in the Knesset: We Will Fight Anti-Semitism]. NRG, November 22, 2011. http://www.nrg.co.il/online/1/ART2/309/033.html.

Bock, Gizla. "Challenging Dichotomies: Perspectives on Women's History." In *Writing Women's History*, edited by Karen Offen, Ruth Roach Pierson, and Jane Rendall, 1–24. Bloomington: Indiana Univ. Press, 1991.

Bogiinski, Yuval. "A Historical Overview of the Concept of a Holocaust Survivor." Knesset, January 24, 2014. http://www.knesset.gov.il/mmm/data/pdf/m03154.pdf.

Bridenthal, Renate, Atina Grossmann, and Marion Kaplan, eds. *When Biology Became Destiny: Women in Weimar and Nazi Germany*. New York: New Feminist Library, 1984.

Brown, Hannah. "Out of the Forest: Movie Review." *Jerusalem Post*, May 4, 2004.

Browning, Christopher R. *Ordinary Men: Reserve Police Battalion 101 and the Final Solution in Poland*. New York: HarperCollins, 1992.

———. *Remembering Survival: Inside a Nazi Slave-Labor Camp*. New York and London: W. W. Norton & Company, 2010.

Brutin, Batya. "Min hahulayim el hamerkaz: hashoah baomanut haisraelit" [From the Margins to the Mainstream: Israeli Art and the Holocaust]. *Massuah* 33 (2005): 110–38.

Bruzzi, Stella. *New Documentary: A Critical Introduction*. London: Routledge, 2000.

Butchart, Garnet. "Al etica v'kolnoa ti'udi: al emet mamashit vema'asit" [On Ethics and Documentary Cinema: Practical Truth]. *Takriv*, August 2015. http://takriv.net/wp-content/uploads/2015/09/PDF-translatedarticle-updt.pdf.

Burstein, Igal. *Ti'ud, seret ti'udi b'dia* [Documentation: A Documentary: A Fiction]. Tel Aviv: Sal Tarbut Artzi, 2004.

"Café Nagler." Go 2 Films. http://www.go2films.com/Family-Social-issues/Cafe-Nagler.

"Café Nagler." Israeli Film Center. http://www.israelfilmcenter.org/israeli-film-database/films/cafe-nagler.

Callon, Michel. "Some Elements of a Sociology of Translation: Domestication of the Scallops and the Fishermen of St. Brieuc Bay." In *Power, Action and Belief: A New Sociology of Knowledge*, edited by John Law, 196–233. London: Routledge and Kegan Paul, 1986.

Caruth, Cathy. "An Introduction: Recapturing the Past." In *Trauma: Explorations in Memory*, edited by Cathy Caruth, 151–57. Baltimore: John Hopkins Univ. Press, 1995.

———. *Unclaimed Experience: Trauma, Narrative, and History*. Baltimore: Johns Hopkins Univ. Press, 2016.

Chaitin, Julia. "Yeladim v'nechadim shel nitzolei hashoah" [Children and Grandchildren of Holocaust Survivors Coping with the Holocaust]. In *Yaldut b'tzel hashoah: yeladim-nitsolim vedor sheni* [Childhood in the Shadow of the Holocaust: Child Survivors and Second Generation], edited by Zehava Solomon and Julia Chaitin, 418–35. Tel Aviv: Kibbutz Hameuchad, 2007.

———. "Yeladim v'nechadim shel nitzolim mitmodedim im hashoah" [Children and Grandchildren of Holocaust Survivors Deal with the Holocaust]. In *Yaldut b'tzel hashoah: yeladim-nitsolim vedor sheni* [Childhood in the Shadow of the Holocaust: Child Survivors and Second Generation], edited by Zehava Solomon and Julia Chaitin, 304–36. Tel Aviv: Hakibbutz Hameuchad, 2007.

Cohen, Boaz. "Early Children's Holocaust Testimonies: Historical Sources or Anecdotes?" Paper presented at the Emerging Questions in Holocaust Testimonies Research Conference, University of Virginia, Charlottesville, VA, November 6, 2017.

Cole, Tim. "Please Mind the Gap: Integrated Histories and Geographies of the Holocaust and Holocaust Memory." Paper presented at the Beyond Camps and Forced Labor Conference, Birkbeck, University of London, January 10–12, 2018.

"Colloquium: 'shtikat ha'arkhiyon'" [Colloquium: 'A Film Unfinished']. *Theory and Criticism* 40 (Summer 2012): 269–87.

Confino, Alon. "From Psychohistory to Memory Studies: Or How Some Germans Became Jews and Some Jews Nazis." In *History Flows through Us: Germany, the Holocaust, and the Importance of Empathy*, edited by Roger Frie, 17–30. London: Routledge, 2018.

Cooper Marcus, Clare. *House as a Mirror of Self: Exploring the Deeper Meaning of Home*. San Francisco: Conari Press, 1995.

Corner, John. *The Art of Record: A Critical Introduction to Documentary*. Manchester: Manchester Univ. Press, 1996.

Cowie, Elizabeth. *Recording Reality, Desiring the Real*. Minneapolis: Univ. of Minnesota Press, 2011.

Dagan, Hagai, and Gidi Dishon. "Nostalgiat shoah: iyun mehudash betrauma ubenostalgia leor hamikre shel 'pizza beauschwitz'" [Holocaust Nostalgia: Rethinking Trauma and Nostalgia in Light of "Pizza in Auschwitz"]. *Teoria v'bikoret* 38/39 (Winter 2011): 185–209.

"'The Decent One': A Behind-the-Scenes Look." YouTube, September 26, 2014. https://www.youtube.com/watch?v=FAbhWUnRcII.

Deuel-Lusky, Haim, and Oded Wolkstein. "Al shtikat ha'archion" [On A Film Unfinished]. *Takriv* 2 (n.d.). http://takriv.gisight.net/index.php?option=com_contentandview=articleandid=27:2011-07-20-13-49-24andcatid=10:2011-08-14-09-14-03andItemid=15.

Duvdevani, Shmulik. *Guf rishon matzlema* [First-Person Camera]. Jerusalem: Keter, 2010.

———. "Nichnas latmuna" [Getting into the Frame]. YNet News, August 3, 2008. http://www.ynet.co.il/articles/0,7340,L-3576843,00.html.

Ebbrecht, Tobias. "Migrating Images: Iconic Images of the Holocaust and the Representation of War in Popular Film." *Shofar: An Interdisciplinary Journal of Jewish Studies* 28, no. 4 (Summer 2010): 86–103.

Edgren, Henrik, ed. *Looking at the Onlookers and Bystanders: Interdisciplinary Approaches to the Causes and Consequences of Passivity*. Stockholm: Living History Forum, 2012.

Ehrenreich, Robert, and Tim Cole. "The Perpetrator-Bystander-Victim Constellation: Rethinking Genocidal Relationships." *Human Organization* 64, no. 3 (Fall 2005): 213–24.

Epstein Elias, Bat-Chen. "Germany tov" [A Good German]. *Israel Today*, August 2, 2013. http://www.israelhayom.co.il/site/newsletter_article.php?id=26709andhp=1andnewsletter=08.02.2013.

Evans, Richard J. *In Hitler's Shadow: West German Historians and the Attempt to Escape from the Nazi Past*. London: I. B. Tauris, 1989.

Eyerman, Ron. *Cultural Trauma: Slavery and the Formation of African American Identity*. Cambridge: Cambridge Univ. Press, 2002.

Feldman, Jacky. *Above the Death Pits, Beneath the Flag: Youth Voyages to Poland and the Performance of Israeli National Identity*. New York: Berghahn Books, 2008.

Felman, Shoshana, and Dori Laub. *Testimony: Crises of Witnessing in Literature, Psychoanalysis, and History*. London: Routledge, 1992.

Figley, Charles, ed. *Compassion Fatigue: Secondary Traumatic Stress Disorders from Treating the Traumatized*. New York: Brunner/Mazel, 1995.

Flanzbaum, Hilene. "The Trace of Trauma: Third-Generation Holocaust Survivors." *Phi Kappa Phi Forum* 91, no. 1 (Spring 2012): 32–35.

Fogelman, Eva. "Psychological Dynamics in the Lives of Third-Generation Holocaust Survivors." *Hidden Child* 16 (2008). http://www.drevafogelman.com/_psychological_dynamics_in_the_lives_of_third_generation_holocaust_survivors__94110.htm.

———. "Third-Generation Descendants of Holocaust Survivors and the Future of Remembering." Jewcy, May 1, 2008. http://jewcy.com/jewish-religion-and-beliefs/third_generation_descendants_holocaust_survivors_and_future_remembering.

Forsyth, Hardey, ed. *Grierson on Documentary*. London: Faber and Faber, 1966.

Fox, Nicole. "Their History Is Part of Me: Third-Generation American Jews and Intergenerational Transmission of Memory." *Trauma and History: Yalkut Moreshet Journal for the Study of the Holocaust and Antisemitism* 4, no. 87 (2010): 9–35.

Frei, Norbert. "Y'kumim makbilim? madua yesh lahkor et nekudot hamaga shabein hahistoryografya lezichronot mishpahtiyim" [Parallel

Universes? Why Should We Examine the Touch Points between Historiography and Familial Memories?]. In *Zikaron v'shichecha: germania v'hashoah* [Memory and Amnesia: Germany and the Holocaust], edited by Gilad Margalit and Yifat Weiss, 216–20. Tel Aviv: Hakibbutz Hameuchad, 2005.

Frie, Roger. "Historical Trauma and Lived Experience: An Introduction." In *History Flows through Us: Germany, the Holocaust, and the Importance of Empathy*, edited by Roger Frie, 1–14. London: Routledge, 2018.

———. *Not in My Family: German Memory and Responsibility after the Holocaust.* Oxford: Oxford Univ. Press, 2017.

Friedländer, Saul. "Trauma, Memory, and Transference." In *Holocaust Remembrance: The Shapes of Memory*, edited by Geoffrey Hartman, 252–64. Oxford: Basil Blackwell, 1992.

———. "Trauma, Transference, and Working Through in Writing the History of the Shoah." *History and Memory* 4 (1992): 39–59.

Friedman, Michal. "The Double Legacy of Arbeit Macht Frei." *Prooftexts* 22, no. 1/2 (Winter/Spring 2002): 200–220.

———. "Witnessing for the Witness: Choice and Destiny by Zipi Reibenbach." *Shofar: An Interdisciplinary Journal of Jewish Studies* 24, no. 1 (Fall 2005): 81–93.

Frisch, Michael. *A Shared Authority: Essays on the Craft and Meaning of Oral and Public History.* Albany: State Univ. of New York Press, 1990.

Fulbrook, Mary. "Guilt and Shame among Communities of Experience, Connection and Identification." In *Reverberations of Nazi Violence in Germany and Beyond: Disturbing Pasts*, edited by Stephanie Bird et al., 15–32. London: Bloomsbury, 2016.

Gan, Alon. *Korbanutam omanutam: mesiach korbani lesiach riboni* [From Sovereignty to Victimhood: An Analysis of the Victimization Discourse in Israel]. Jerusalem: Israel Democracy Institute, 2014.

Gavison, Ruth, ed. *Coping with Global Migration: A Strategy for Immigration Policy in Israel.* Jerusalem: Metzilah Center for Zionist, Jewish, Liberal, and Humanist Thought, 2009.

Gertz, Nurith. *Makhela aheret: nitzoley shoah zarim v'aherim* [A Different Choir: Holocaust Survivors, Aliens and Others in Israeli Cinema and Literature]. Tel Aviv: Am Oved and Open Univ., 2004.

Geva, Sharon. *El ha'ahot halo yedu'a* [To the Unknown Sister]. Tel Aviv: Hakibbutz Hameuchad, 2010.

Ghert-Zand, Renee. "After 70 Years, Man Born in DP Camp Meets Unknown Brother(s)." *Times of Israel*, May 22, 2016. http://www.timesofisrael.com/after-70-years-man-born-in-dp-camp-meets-unknown-brothers.

Giesen, Bernhard. "From Denial to Confessions of Guilt: The German Case." In *Remembering the Holocaust: A Debate*, edited by Jeffrey C. Alexander, 114–34. Oxford: Oxford Univ. Press, 2009.

Gil, Idit. "The Shoah in Israeli Collective Memory: Changes in Meanings and Protagonists." *Modern Judaism: A Journal of Jewish Ideas and Experiences* 32, no. 1 (2012): 76–101.

Gladstone, Kay. "Separate Intentions: The Allied Screenings of Concentration Camp Documentaries in Defeated Germany in 1945–1946: Death Mills and Memory of the Camps." In *Holocaust and the Moving Image: Representations in Film and Television since 1933*, edited by Toby Haggith and Joanna Newman, 50–64. New York: Wallflower Press, 2005.

Gluzman, Michael. *Haguf hatzioni: leumiyut, migdar uminiyut basifrut haivrit hachadasha* [The Zionist Body: Nationality, Gender, and Sexuality in Modern Hebrew Literature]. Tel Aviv: Hakibbutz Hameuchad, 2007.

Godfrey, Mark. *Abstraction and the Holocaust*. New Haven, CT: Yale Univ. Press, 2007.

Golan, Yvonne Kozlovsky. "Cinematic Love and the Shoah: Abnormal Love during Abnormal Times." *Post Script* 30, no. 3 (Fall 2011): 40–57.

———. *Masach shel shichecha: al header chavayat hashoah shel yehudei hamizrach bimedia vebaomanut beisrael* [Forgotten from the Frame: The Absence of the Holocaust Experience of Mizrahim from the Visual Arts and Media in Israel]. Tel Aviv: Resling, 2017.

Goldberg, Amos. "Hashoah vehahistoria: netaqim beidan postmoderni" [The Holocaust and History: Disconnections in a Postmodern Age]. *Theory and Criticism* 40 (Summer 2012): 121–54.

———. "Introduction." In Dominick LaCapra, *Writing History, Writing Trauma*, 7–28. Baltimore: Johns Hopkins Univ. Press, 2000.

Goldenberg, Myrna. "Women Remembering the Holocaust." In *Thinking the Unthinkable: Meanings of the Holocaust*, edited by Roger S. Gottlieb, 150–66. New York: Paulist, 1990.

Goldenberg, Myrna, and Amy H. Shapiro, eds. *Different Horrors, Same Hell: Gender and the Holocaust*. Seattle: Univ. of Washington Press, 2013.

Goldhagen, Daniel Jonah. *Hitler's Willing Executioners: Ordinary Germans and the Holocaust*. New York: Vintage, 1996.

Goldman, Ron. "Emet v'ziuf al shulhan ha'aricha" [Truth and Deceit in the Editing Room]. *Panim* 32 (2005). http://www.itu.org.il/Index.asp?ArticleID=4926andCategoryID=762andPage=1.

Greenspan, Henry. "Lives as Text: Symptoms as Modes of Recounting in the Life Histories of Holocaust Survivors." In *Storied Lives: The Cultural Politics of Self-Understanding*, edited by George C. Rosenwald and Richard L. Ochberg, 145–65. New Haven, CT: Yale Univ. Press, 1992.

Grodzinsky, Yosef. *In the Shadow of the Holocaust: The Struggle between Jews and Zionists in the Aftermath of World War II*. Monroe, ME: Common Courage Press, 2004.

Gross, Larry, John Stuart Katz, and Jay Ruby, eds. *Image Ethics: The Moral Rights of Subjects in Photographs, Film, and Television*. New York: Oxford Univ. Press, 2000.

Guntag, Nir. "Tohar hashoah" [The Purity of the Holocaust]. *7th Eye*, April 15, 2015. http://www.the7eye.org.il/155119.

Gurevich, David, and Dan Arev. "Trauma, ashma, mehila: hameavel ce'ed basia'ah shel haconflict batelevizia vebakolnoa haisraelim" [Trauma, Guilt, Forgiveness: The Perpetrator as a Witness in the Discourse of Conflict in Israeli Television and Cinema]. *Takriv*, n.d., https://takriv.net/.

Gurevich, Zali, and Gideon Aran. "Al hamakom" [About the Place]. *Alpaim* 4 (1991): 9–44.

Gutwein, Daniel. "The Privatization of the Holocaust: Memory, Historiography, and Politics." *Israel Studies* 14, no. 1 (2009): 36–64.

Habia, Liron. "Yitzug nitzolot hashoah bakolnoa hadocomentary bashanim 1980–2010" [The Representation of Women Survivors of the Holocaust in Documentaries between 1980 and 2010]. Seminar paper for the course Holocaust Survivors in Israeli Cinema, Open University, Ra'anana, Israel, 2012.

"Hagermanim shehechlitu la'alot v'l'hitgayer: dor sheni lashoah" [Germans Who Decided to Immigrate to Israel and Convert to Judaism: Second Generation of the Holocaust]. *Channel 2 News*, April 25, 2012. https://www.youtube.com/watch?v=4nEv1_Iuk6Q.

Haggith, Toby. "Filming the Liberation of Bergen-Belsen." In *Holocaust and the Moving Image: Representations in Film and Television since 1933*, edited by Toby Haggith and Joanna Newman, 33–49. New York: Wallflower Press, 2005.

———. "How the German Concentration Camps Factual Survey (1945/2014) became the World's First Holocaust Documentary." *Archive Zone*, n.d. http://s2s.focalint.tv/Publications/AZ_articles/az2015winter_iss96_german_concentration_camps_factual_survey_part_2.pdf.

Halamish, Aviva. *B'merutz kaful neged hazman: mediniyut ha'aliya hazionit beshnot hashloshim* [The Double Race against Time: The Zionist Immigration Policy in the 1930s]. Jerusalem: Yad Ben Zvi, 2006.

Hartmann, Gertrud. "Children of Nazis: A Psychotomimetic Perspective." In *International Handbook of Multigenerational Legacies of Trauma*, edited by Yael Danieli, 85–96. New York: Plenum Press, 1998.

Harel, Nitza. "Yetzugam shel hanazism v'hashoah bakolnoa hama'aravi: diyun b'shlosha narrativim kolno'in: hanarrativ hakolno'i hagermani" [The Representation of the Holocaust and Nazism in Western Cinema: Three Cinematic Narratives: The German Narrative]. In *Kolnoa v'zikaron: yahasim mesukanim?* [Cinema and Memory: Dangerous Relationship?], edited by Haim Bresheeth, Moshe Zimmermann, and Shlomo Sand. Jerusalem: Zalman Shazar Center, 2004. http://lib.cet.ac.il/pages/item.asp?item=15911.

Haus, Jeffrey. "The Younger Generation: Jews and Diaspora in Frank Capra's America." Forthcoming.

Hazan, Yoram. "Dor sheni lashoah: musag besafek" [The Second Generation of the Holocaust: A Questionable Concept]. *Sihot: Israel Journal of Psychotherapy* 1 (1987): 104–8.

Hedgepeth, Sonja M., and Rochelle G. Saidel, eds. *Sexual Violence against Jewish Women during the Holocaust*. Hanover, NH: Univ. Press of New England, 2010.

Heilbronner, Oded, and Moshe Zimmermann. "Hakdama" [Introduction]. In *Hagermanim 1945–1990* [The Germans 1945–1990], edited by Oded Heilbronner and Moshe Zimmermann, 415–26. Jerusalem: Magnes Press, 1997.

Heineman, Elizabeth D. "Sexuality and Nazism: The Doubly Unspeakable?" *Journal of the History of Sexuality* 11, no. 1/2 (2002): 22–66.

Heinemann, Marlen E. *Gender and Destiny: Women Writers and the Holocaust.* New York: Greenwood Press, 1986.

Herman, Judith L. *Trauma v'hachlama* [Trauma and Healing]. Tel Aviv: Am Oved, 1994.

Hersonski, Yael. "Witnessing the Archive." In *Probing the Ethics of Holocaust Culture*, edited by Claudio Fogu, Wulf Kasteiner, and Todd Presner, 277–82. Cambridge MA: Harvard Univ. Press, 2016.

Herzog, Esther, ed. *Nashim bashoah* [Women and Family in the Holocaust]. Netanya, Israel: Otzar Hamishpat, 2006.

Hess, Aharon. *B'tzel hashoah: hador hasheni* [In the Shadow of the Holocaust: The Second Generation]. Or Yehuda, Israel: Hed Artzi, 1990.

Hilberg, Raul. *Perpetrators, Victims, Bystanders: The Jewish Catastrophe, 1933–1945.* New York: HarperCollins, 1992.

"Himmler: harotzeach hanazi ahshav shehu ish tov" [Himmler: The Nazi Murderer Who Thought He Was a Good Person]. YouTube, January 27, 2014. https://www.youtube.com/watch?v=q2NiWfvUQwk.

Himmler, Katrin. *The Himmler Brothers: A German Family History.* Basingstoke, UK: Palgrave Macmillan, 2007.

Hirsch, Marianne. "Past Lives, First Memories in Exile." *Poetics Today* 17, no. 4 (Winter 1996): 659–67.

———. "Surviving Images: Holocaust Memories and the Works of Postmemory." *Yale Journal of Criticism* 14, no. 1 (2001): 5–37.

Hoffman, Eva. *After Such Knowledge: A Mediation of the Aftermath of the Holocaust.* New York: Vintage, 2005.

Hogman, Flora. "Memory of the Holocaust." Echoes of the Holocaust, June 4, 1995. http://www.holocaustechoes.com/4hogman.html.

Hoppe, Reiter. "The Next Generation of Young Yekkes in Preserving the Yekke Heritage." Facebook group, http://www.facebook.com/groups/HoppeHoppeReiter.

Hopper, Elad. "Lo miflazot, bnei adam: Izogey hanazim veyaldehem bakolnoa hadocomentary haisraeli" [Not Monster, Human Beings:

Representations of Nazis and their Offspring in Israeli Documentary Cinema]. Seminar paper for the course Holocaust Survivors in Israeli Cinema, Open University, Ra'anana, Israel, 2016.

Ilani, Ofri. "Medinat ashkenaz" [The Ashkenazi Country]. *Haaretz*, October 13, 2017, 1–2.

Ilany, Itay. "K'she tzatza'ei hanazim sharim hatikva berap lifney nitzolim" [When Nazis' Descendants Sing a Rap-Style Hatikva in Front of Survivors]. YNet News, December 18, 2016. http://www.ynet.co.il/articles/0,7340,L-4894262,00.html.

Interview with Lawrence Langer at the Emerging Questions in Holocaust Testimonies Research Conference, University of Virginia, Charlottesville, VA, November 7, 2017.

Interview with Yehudith Inbar, Yad Vashem, n.d. http://www.yadvashem.org/he/articles/interviews/yeudit.html.

Irgun yotsei merkaz eropa (Association of Israelis of Central European Origin). http://www.irgun-jeckes.org/?CategoryID=200andArticleID=461.

Izikovich, Gili. "B'zroa hazaka" [With a Strong Arm]. *Haaretz*, April 4, 2013. https://www.haaretz.co.il/gallery/television/.premium-1.1985164.

———. "Tzatzaeihem shel b'chirei hamishtar hanazi nechsafim baseret 'Yaldei Hitler'" [Descendants of Prominent Nazi Officials Are Represented in the Film "Hitler's Children"]. *Haaretz*, May 1, 2011. https://www.haaretz.co.il/gallery/1.1172643.

Jacobs, Janet. "Gender and Collective Memory: Women and Representation at Auschwitz." *Memory Studies* 21, no. 1 (2008): 211–25.

———. *The Holocaust across Generations: Trauma and Its Inheritance among Descendants of Survivors*. New York: NYU Press, 2017.

Jarecka, Urzula. "Wounded Memory: Rhetorical Strategies Used on Public Discourse on the Katyn Massacre. In *The Long Aftermath: Cultural Legacies of Europe at War, 1936–2016*, edited by Manuel Braganca and Peter Tame, 302–15. New York: Berghahn Books, 2016.

Jilovsky, Esther. *Remembering the Holocaust: Generations, Witnessing and Place*. London: Bloomsbury, 2015.

Jilovsky, Esther, Jordana Silverstein, and David Slucki, eds. *In the Shadows of Memory: The Holocaust and the Third Generation*. Portland, OR: Vallentine Mitchell, 2016.

Jordans, Frank. "Germania: hasidra shesho'elet ma hahorim asu Bashoah" [Germany: The Series That Asks What the Parents Did during the Holocaust]. YNet News, March 28, 2013. http://www.ynet.co.il/articles/0,7340,L-4361823,00.html.

Jucovy, Milton E. "Telling the Holocaust Story: A Link between the Generations." *Psychoanalytic Inquiry* 5, no. 1 (1985): 31–50.

Kaes, Anton. "History and Film: Public Memory in the Age of Electronic Dissemination." *History and Memory* 2, no. 1 (Fall 1990): 111–29.

Kangisser Cohen, Sharon. "The Survivors and Their Stories." Paper presented at the Beyond Camps and Forced Labor Conference, Birkbeck, University of London, January 10–12, 2018.

Keinan, Irith. *Lo nirga hara'av: she'arit hapleita v'shlihei eretz yisrael b'germania 1945–1948* [Holocaust Survivors and Eretz Israeli Delegations in Germany 1945–1948]. Tel Aviv: Am Oved, 1996.

Keis, Anton. "Historia v'kolnoa: zikaron tziburi b'idan hatikshoret ha'elektronit" [History and Cinema: Collective Memory in the Age of Electronic Media]. *Zmanim* 39/40 (1991): 28–37.

Kellermann, Nathan. "Ha'avar shel traumat hashoah" [Transmission of the Holocaust Trauma]. In *Yaldut b'tzel hashoah: yeladim-nitsolim vedor sheni* [Childhood in the Shadow of the Holocaust: Child Survivors and Second Generation], edited by Zehava Solomon and Julia Chaitin, 286–303. Tel Aviv: Hakibbutz Hameuchad, 2007.

Kerner, Aaron. *Film and the Holocaust: New Perspectives on Dramas, Documentaries, and Experimental Films*. London: Bloomsbury, 2011.

Kidron, Carol. "Hahavnaya hahevratit shel dor sheni lashoah" [The Social Construction of Second-Generation Survivors: Support Group Narratives of Wounded Carriers of Memory]. In *Yaldut b'tzel hashoah: yeladim-nitsolim vedor sheni* [Childhood in the Shadow of the Holocaust: Child Survivors and Second Generation], edited by Zehava Solomon and Julia Chaitin, 261–85. Tel Aviv: Hakibbutz Hameuchad, 2007.

Kimhi, Carmel Gottlieb. *Hapoetica shel habayit: yezug habait vahabait haleumi bekolnoa otobiografy doqomentary israeli* [The Poetics of the Home: Representation of Home and National Home in Autobiographical Documentary Israeli Cinema]. Jerusalem: Carmel, 2009.

———. "Teivat pandora b'gordon shtrasse" [Pandora's Box on Gordonstrasse]. *Takriv* 16 (2016). https://takriv.net/.

Klein, Hillel. "Hipus nitzolei hashoah ahar mashmaut v'zehut" [The Survivors' Search for Meaning and Identity]. In *Nazi Concentration Camps, Lectures and Discussions at the 4th Yad Vashem International Historical Conference of Holocaust Researchers*, edited by Israel Gutman and Rachel Manber, 543–53. Jerusalem: Yad Vashem, 1980.

Klein, Uri. "M'kivun haya'ar" [Out of the Forest]. *Haaretz*, June 10, 2004.

Kobrynskyy, Oleksandr, and Gerd Bayer, eds. *Holocaust Cinema in the Twenty-First Century: Images, Memory, and the Ethics of Representation*. New York: Wallflower Press, 2015.

Kohen-Raz, Odeya. "Arnon Goldfinger's 'The Flat' (2011): Ethics and Aesthetics in Third-Generation Holocaust Cinema." *Studies in Documentary Film* 6, no. 3 (2012): 323–38.

Krill, Ariel. "Holocaust 2.0: On 'A Film Unfinished' by Yael Hersonski." Walla, November 16, 2010. http://e.walla.co.il/?w=/267/1756326.

———. "The Truth Is Not Two-Dimensional: An Interview with Noemi Schory and Itay Ken-Tor, Producers of 'A Film Unfinished.'" Walla, January 21, 2011. http://e.walla.co.il/?w=//1783133.

LaCapra, Dominick. *Writing History, Writing Trauma*. Baltimore: Johns Hopkins Univ. Press, 2000.

Lachowitz, Anat. "Megamot hadashot beyetsug hashoah bakolnoa hatiudi beshnot haalpaim" [New Trends in Holocaust Representation in Documentary Filmmaking of the 21st Century]. Seminar paper for the course Holocaust Survivors in Israeli Cinema, Open University, Ra'anana, Israel, 2012.

Landsberg, Alison. *Prosthetic Memory: The Transformation of American Remembrance in the Age of Mass Culture*. New York, Columbia Univ. Press, 2004.

Lane, Jim. *The Autobiographical Documentary in America*. Madison: Univ. of Wisconsin Press, 2002.

Lang, Berel. "Imagining the Past, Remembering the Future." Paper presented that the Emerging Questions in Holocaust Testimonies Research Conference, University of Virginia, Charlottesville, VA, November 6, 2017.

Langer, Lawrence. "Gender Suffering? Women in Holocaust Testimonies." In *Women in the Holocaust*, edited by Dalia Ofer and Lenore Weitzman, 351–63. New Haven, CT: Yale Univ. Press, 1998.

———. "Holocaust Testimonies." Paper presented at the Emerging Questions in Holocaust Testimonies Research Conference, University of Virginia, Charlottesville, VA, November 5, 2017.

LaRocca, David. "Introduction: Representative Qualities and Questions of Documentary Film." In *The Philosophy of Documentary Film: Image, Sound, Fiction, Truth*, edited by David LaRocca, 1–54. Lanham, MD: Lexington Books.

Latour, Bruno. *Reassembling the Social: An Introduction to Actor-Network-Theory*. Oxford: Oxford Univ. Press, 2005.

Lavsky, Hagit. *The Creation of the German-Jewish Diaspora: Interwar German-Jewish Immigration to Palestine, the USA, and England*. Berlin: DeGruyter, 2017.

———. *New Beginnings: Holocaust Survivors in Bergen-Belsen and the British Zone in Germany, 1945–1950*. Detroit: Wayne State Univ. Press, 2002.

———. "Then and Now: Immigration and Absorption of Jews in Germany, between History and Historical Consciousness." In *Culture, Memory and History, Volume 2: Israelis' Culture and Memory*, edited by Meir Hazan and Uri Cohen, 251–74. Jerusalem: Zalman Shazar Center and Tel Aviv Univ., 2010.

Laub, Dori. "Bearing Witness on the Vicissitudes of Listening." In *Testimony: Crises of Witnessing in Literature, Psychoanalysis, and History*, edited by Shoshana Felman and Dori Laub, 57–74. London: Routledge.

Law, John. "Notes on the Theory of the Actor-Network: Ordering, Strategy, and Heterogeneity." *Systems Practice* 5, no. 4 (1992): 379–93.

Lebert, Norbert, and Stefan Lebert. *Harei ata nosei et shmi: hamoreshet hamara shel yaldei hanazim hab'chirim* [You Bear My Name: The Bitter Legacy of High-Ranking Nazis' Offspring]. Tel Aviv: Am Oved, 2014.

Lebovic, Nitzan. "Freeze-Framing: Temporality and the Archives in Forgacs, Hersonski, and Friedländer." In *Probing the Ethics of Holocaust Culture*, edited by Claudio Fogu, Wulf Kasteiner, and Todd Presner, 257–76. Cambridge MA: Harvard Univ. Press, 2016.

Leibowitz, Nizan. "Beit haz'chuchit" [House of Glass]. *Takriv* 5 (n.d.). http://takriv.net/.

Lentin, Ronit. *Israel and the Daughters of the Shoah: Reoccupying the Territories of Silence.* New York: Berghahn Books, 2000.

———. "Lichbosh m'hadash et territoriot hashtika: sofrot vekolnaniyot yisraeliot k'banot l'nitzolei shoah" [To Recapture the Territory of Silence]. In *Zikaron Galu'i, Zikaron Samu'i* [Overt Memory, Covert Memory], edited by Yoel Rappel, 169–95. Tel Yitzhak, Israel: Massuah, 1998.

Lerner, Merav. "Me'at midai, me'uhar midai? Tzatzaei hanazim sharim hatikva" [Too Little, Too Late? Nazis' Descendants Sing Hatikva]. Channel 20, August 16, 2016. http://www.20il.co.il/.

Lev, Itai. "Hataboo ha'acharon" [The Last Taboo]. *Globes*, April 15, 2015. https://www.calcalist.co.il/consumer/articles/0,7340,L-3656861,00.html.

Levenkron, Nomi. "Ha'alamot v'hamavet: znut, oness v'avdut minit b'milhemet ha'olam hashniya" [Death and the Maidens: Prostitution, Rape, and Sexual Slavery during World War II]. *Theory and Criticism* 32 (2009): 15–44.

Levi, Hadas. "Pianuach hasod shel hatzofe: hashimush bamedium hakolno'i k'kli avoda im kvutzot" [Revealing the Viewers' Secret: Cinema as a Tool for Group Therapy]. *Mikbatz* (2003): 77–98.

Levi, Hagai. "Habuz: hagai levi neged Jean-Luc Godard" [The Contempt: Hagai Levi and Jean-Luc Godard]. Walla, November 12, 2010. http://news.walla.co.il/?w=/227/1754877.

Levi, Primo. *Hashokim vehanitzolim* [The Drowned and the Saved]. Tel Aviv: Am Oved, 1991.

———. *Survival in Auschwitz.* New York: Simon & Schuster, 1996.

Levin, Itamar. *Mi'ba'ad la'dmaot: humor Yehudi that hashilton hanatsi* [Through the Tears: Jewish Humor under the Nazi Regime]. Jerusalem: Yad Vashem, 2004.

Lidtka, Alf. "Hitmodedut im ha'avar: ashlayot shel zcira, drachim l'shchichat hanazism begermania hamiaaravit" [Ways of Dealing with the Past in Western Germany]. In *The Germans 1945–1990*, edited by Oded Heilbronner and Moshe Zimmermann, 417–39. Jerusalem: Magnes Press, 1997.

Liebman, Stuart, ed. *Claude Lanzmann's* Shoah*: Key Essays.* Oxford: Oxford Univ. Press, 2007.

———. "Documenting the Liberation of the Camps: The Case of Alexander Ford's *Vernichtungslager Majdanek: Cmentarzysko Europy* (1944)." In *Lesson and Legacies VII: The Holocaust in International Perspective*, edited by Dagmar Herzog, 333–51. Evanston, IL: Northwestern Univ. Press, 2006.

Litvak Hirsch, Tal, and Alon Lazar. "Bein avar l'atid: zikaron hashoah ketrauma qoleqtivit tarbutit vehantsahato be'einei bnei hador hashlishi beisrael" [Between the Past and the Future: Holocaust Memory as a Collective Trauma and Its Commemoration by Third-Generation Holocaust Survivors in Israel]. Moreshet, n.d. http://www.moreshet.org/?CategoryID=414andArticleID=1388.

Litvak Hirsch, Tal, and Dan Bar-On. "Livnot et hahaim m'hadash: mehqar ma'qav 'l ha'vara bein droit shel traumat hashaoh" [Rebuilding Your Life: A Follow-Up Study on Intergenerational Transference of Trauma of the Holocaust]. *Megamot: Journal of Behavioral Sciences* 45, no. 2 (December 2007): 243–71.

Litvak Hirsch, Tal, and Julia Chaitin. "Hakdama" [Introduction]. In *Drachim Miztalvot* [Intersecting Roads], edited by Tal Litvak Hirsch and Julia Chaitin, 2–13. Beer Sheva, Israel: Ben Gurion Univ. of the Negev, 2011.

———. "The Shoah Runs through Our Veins: The Relevance of the Holocaust for Jewish-Israeli Young Adults." *Idea*, May 1, 2010. http://www.ideajournal.com/articles.php?id=49.

"Lizkor: Ein matzav lishkoach." *Reiting*, May 26, 2004.

Lory, Aviva. "*Ho, kama savalnu*" [Oh, How Much We Suffered]. *Haaretz*, August 6, 2007. http://www.haaretz.co.il/misc/1.1431956.

Loshitzky, Yosefa. *Identity Politics on the Israeli Screen*. Austin: Univ. of Texas Press, 2002.

———, ed. *Spielberg's Holocaust: Critical Perspectives on* Schindler's List. Bloomington: Indiana Univ. Press, 1997.

McGlothlin, Erin. *Second-Generation Holocaust Literature: Legacies of Survival and Perpetration*. New York: Camden House, 2006.

Mandel, Naomi. *Against the Unspeakable: Complicity, the Holocaust, and Slavery in America*. Charlottesville: Univ. of Virginia Press, 2007.

Mann, Barbara E. *Space and Place in Jewish Studies*. New Brunswick, NJ: Rutgers Univ. Press, 2012.

Marangoly, Rosemary George. *The Politics of Home: Postcolonial Relocations and Twentieth-Century Fiction.* Cambridge: Cambridge Univ. Press, 1996.

Margalit, Gilad. *Ashma, sevel v'zikaron: Germania zocheret et meteiha b'milhemet ha'olam hashniya* [Guilt, Suffering, and Memory: Germany Remembers Its World War II Dead]. Haifa: Haifa Univ. Press, 2007.

———. "Toda'at ha'ashma hagermanit v'hashlachoteiha acharei 1945" [German Guilt and Its Implications after 1945]. In *Zikaron v'shichicha: germania v'hashoah* [Memory and Amnesia: Germany and the Holocaust], edited by Gilad Margalit and Yifat Weiss, 228–66. Tel Aviv: Hakibbutz Hameuchad, 2005.

Markowitz, Dalia, and Kziaa Alon. "Moadon beit hakvarot" [The Cemetery Club]. In *Documentally*, edited by Maayan Amir, 199–206. Tel Aviv: Am Oved, 2007.

McGlothlin, Erin. *Second-Generation Holocaust Literature: Legacies of Survival and Perpetration.* New York: Camden House, 2006.

Meidan, Kobi. "Reayon im Yael Hersonski" [An Interview with Yael Hersonski]. *Hotzei Yisrael*, April 23, 2012. http://www.youtube.com/watch?v=87uq16cV1lI.

Meyers, Oren, Motti Neiger, and Eyal Zandberg. *Communicating Awe: Media Memory and Holocaust Commemoration.* Basingstoke, UK: Palgrave Macmillan, 2014.

Michalczyk, John J. *Filming the End of the Holocaust: Allied Documentaries, Nuremberg and the Liberation of the Concentration Camps.* London: Bloomsbury, 2014.

Milner, Iris. *Kirey avar* [A Torn Past]. Tel Aviv: Am Oved, 2004.

Miron, Guy. "Lately, Almost Constantly, Everything Seems Small to Me: The Lived Space of German Jews under the Nazi Regime." *Jewish Social Studies* 20, no. 1 (Fall 2013): 121–49.

Miron, Guy, and Dorit Yosef. "Burganut v'tzionut b'hayei habayit shel yoyzot merkaz europa b'yisrael" [Bourgeoisie and Zionism in the Domestic Life of Immigrants from Central Europe in Israel]. *Iyunim B't'kumat Israel* 28 (2017): 197–224.

Mitscherlich, Margarete. "Hayecholet shel hagermanim l'hitabel: ashlaya o tikva?" [The Germans' Ability to Mourn: An Illusion or Hope?]. In

The Germans 1945–1990, edited by Oded Heilbronner and Moshe Zimmermann, 440–48. Jerusalem: Magnes Press, 1997.

Mitscherlich, Margareta, and Alexander Mitscherlich. *The Inability to Mourn: Principles of Collective Behavior.* New York: Grove Press, 1975.

Morrow, Paul. "In the Matter of Testimony." Paper presented at the Emerging Questions in Holocaust Testimonies Research Conference, University of Virginia, Charlottesville, VA, November 3, 2017.

Munk, Yael. "Arnon Goldfinger's 'The Flat': Holocaust Memory, Film Noir, and the Pain of Others." *Jewish Film and New Media: An International Journal* 4, no. 1 (Spring 2016): 25–42.

Nagler-Cohen, Liron. "Shovrim shtika: tzatzaei nazim sharim hatikva" [Breaking the Silence: Nazis' Descendants Sing Hatikva]. YNet News, August 16, 2016. http://www.ynet.co.il/articles/0,7340,L-4842043,00.html.

Namer, Esther. "Nashim nitsolot shoah bakolnoa haisraeli" [Women Holocaust Survivors in Israeli Cinema]. Seminar paper for the course Holocaust Survivors in Israeli Cinema, Open University, Ra'anana, Israel, 2018.

Nanus, Zion. "Hasodot m'ahorey hatmuna" [The Secrets behind the Photo]. *Mako*, May 5, 2016. http://www.mako.co.il/news-channel2/Channel-2-Newscast-q2_2016/Article-95c284fdcf18451004.htm.

Naremore, James. *More than Night: Film Noir in Its Contexts.* 2nd ed. Berkeley: Univ. of California Press, 2008.

Natan, Gilad. "Yaldei ovdim zarim um'vakshei miklat b'ma'arechet hahinuch" [Children of Foreign Workers and Asylum Seekers in the Education System]. Knesset, December 12, 2010. http://www.knesset.gov.il/mmm/data/pdf/m02716.pdf.

Ne'eman Arad, Gulie. "Israel and the Shoah: A Tale of Multifarious Taboos." *New German Critique* 90 (Autumn 2003): 5–26.

Netzer, Ruth. *Hakolno'a metapel banu: yihasei metapel-metupal bakolno'a* [Cinema Takes Care of Us: The Rapist-Patient Relationship in Cinema]. Tel Aviv: Resling, 2013.

Neumann, Boaz, Ronny Hirsh-Ratzkovsky, and Shahar Galili, eds. *Historia belo nahat: bein yehudim legermanim* [History and Discontent: Between Jews and Germans]. Tel Aviv: Am Oved, 2012.

"New Jewish Cinema: Vanessa Lapa, Director of 'The Decent One.'" YouTube, October 9, 2014. https://www.youtube.com/watch?v=aledk49EM1g.

Nichols, Bill. *Blurred Boundaries: Questions of Meaning in Contemporary Culture*. Bloomington: Indiana Univ. Press, 1994.

———. "Documentary Reenactment and the Fantasmatic Subject." *Critical Inquiry* 35, no. 1 (Autumn 2008): 72–89.

———. *Introduction to Documentary*. Bloomington: Indiana Univ. Press, 2001.

———. *Representing Reality: Issues and Concepts in Documentary*. Bloomington: Indiana Univ. Press, 1991.

"Nitzolei shoah l'netanyahu: al tigaresh yaldei ovdim zarim" [Holocaust Survivors to Netanyahu: Don't Deport the Children of Foreigners]. YNet News, August 8, 2010. http://www.ynet.co.il/articles/0,7340,L-3931953,00.html.

Nora, Pierre. "Bein zikaron l'historia" [Between Memory and History]. *Zmanim* 45 (1993): 4–19.

———. "Between Memory and History: Les Lieux de Mémoire." *Representations* 26 (Spring 1989): 7–24.

Novak, Yuli, and Yaniv Ron-El. "Colloquium: hakdama" [Colloquium: Introduction]. *Theory and Criticism* 40 (Summer 2012): 263–68.

Novick, Peter. *That Noble Dream: The "Objectivity Question" and the American Historical Profession*. Cambridge: Cambridge Univ. Press, 1988.

Ofer, Dalia. "Estrategiot shel nashim bama'avak l'haim b'tkufat hashoah" [Women's Strategies in the Struggle for Life during the Holocaust]. In *Women and Family in the Holocaust*, edited by Esther Herzog, 27–44. Netanya, Israel: Otzar Hamishpat, 2006.

———. "The Past That Does Not Pass: Israelis and Holocaust Memory." *Israel Studies* 14, no. 1 (Spring 2009): 1–35.

———. "Sheerit hapleta bahistoryografya haisraelit" [The Holocaust Survivors in Israeli Historiography]. *Iyunim B'tkumat Israel* 17 (2006): 465–511.

Ofer, Dalia, and Lenore J. Weitzman. "Tafkid hamigdar b'heker hashaoah" [Gender and the Study of the Holocaust]. Matah, n.d. http://lib.cet.ac.il/pages/item.asp?item=20458.

———, eds. *Women in the Holocaust.* New Haven, CT: Yale Univ. Press, 1998.

Ofer, Miriam. *Haluk lavan bageto* [White Coats inside the Ghetto]. Jerusalem: Yad Vashem, 2015.

Or, Anat. "Sinema balash" [Cinema Detective]. *Haaretz*, June 27, 2008. http://www.haaretz.co.il/misc/1.1333472.

Ornstein, Anna. "Foreword." In *Not in My Family: German Memory and Responsibility after the Holocaust*, edited by Roger Frie, ix–xiii. Oxford: Oxford Univ. Press, 2017.

Ostrower, Haya. *L'lo humor hayinu mitabdim* [Without Humor We Would Have Killed Ourselves]. Jerusalem: Yad Vashem, 2009.

Oz, Almog. *Hatzabar: dyukan* [The Sabra: A Portrait]. Tel Aviv: Am Oved, 1997.

Oz-Salzberger, Fania. *Yisraelim, Berlin* [Israelis, Berlin]. Tel Aviv: Keter, 2001.

Paz, Ayala. "In the Shadow of Dark Times: A Reading of Hannah Arendt's *Eichmann in Jerusalem* through the Lens of *The Origins of Totalitarianism*." Forthcoming.

Piotrowska, Agnieszka. *Psychoanalysis and Ethics in Documentary Film.* London: Routledge, 2014.

Polak, Dana Weiler. "Noa Maiman, bito shel Yossi Maiman, nilhemet begerush haovdim hazarim bshem savta" [Noa Maiman, Yossi Maiman's Daughter, Fights against the Deportation of Foreign Workers in the Name of Her Grandmother]. *Haaretz*, October 14, 2009. http://www.haaretz.co.il/news/education/1.1285079.

Pollin-Galay, Hannah. *Ecologies of Witnessing: Language, Place, and Holocaust Testimony.* New Haven, CT: Yale Univ. Press, 2018.

Pollock, Griselda, and Max Silverman, eds. *Concentrationary Cinema: Aesthetics as Political Resistance in Alan Renais's* Night and Fog. New York: Bergham Books, 2011.

Popescu, Diana. "Performance, Memory, and Identity: The Israeli Third Generation in Yael Ronen's Third Generation Play." In *In the Shadows of Memory: The Holocaust and the Third Generation*, edited by Esther Jilovsky, Jordana Silverstein, and David Slucki, 209–26. Portland, OR: Vallentine Mitchell, 2016.

Porat, Dina. *Café haboker b're'ach ha'ashan* [Smoke-Scented Morning Coffee]. Jerusalem and Tel Aviv: Yad Vashem and Am Oved, 2011.

Portelli, Alessandro. "What Makes Oral History Different?" In *The Oral History Reader*, edited by Robert Perks and Thomson Alistair, 63–74. London: Routledge, 1998.

Prager, Brad. *After the Fact: The Holocaust in Twenty-First Century Documentary Film*. London: Bloomsbury, 2015.

Pryluck, Calvin. "Ultimately We Are All Outsiders: The Ethics of Documentary Filming." In *New Challenges for Documentary*, edited by Alan Rosenthal, 255–68. Berkeley: Univ. of California Press, 1988.

"PTSD." *Diagnostic and Statistical Manual of Mental Disorders*, 5th ed., edited by the American Psychiatric Association, 271–80. Arlington, VA: American Psychiatric Publishing, 2013.

Ramon, Amnon. *Doctor mul doctor gar: shcunat rehavia beyerushalyim* [A Doctor in Every House: Jerusalem's Rehavia Neighborhood]. Jerusalem: Yad Ben Zvi, 1998.

Raskin, Richard. Nuit et Brouillard *by Alain Resnais: On the Making, Reception, and Functions of a Major Documentary Film*. Aarhus, Denmark: Aarhus Univ. Press, 1987.

Renov, Michael. *The Subject of Documentary*. Minneapolis: Univ. of Minnesota Press, 2004.

———, ed. *Theorizing Documentary*. London: Routledge, 1993.

Ringelheim, Joan M. "The Unethical and the Unspeakable: Women and the Holocaust." *Simon Wiesenthal Center Annual* 1 (1984): 69–87. http://motlc.wiesenthal.com/site/pp.asp?c=gvKVLcMVIuG&b=394977.

Rittne, Carol, and John Roth, eds. *Different Voices: Women and the Holocaust*. St. Paul, MN: Paragon House, 1993.

Rosenfeld, Alan. *The End of the Holocaust*. Bloomington: Indiana Univ. Press, 2013.

Rosenfeld, Gavriel. *Hi Hitler: How the Nazi Past Is Being Normalized in Contemporary Culture*. Cambridge: Cambridge Univ. Press, 2015.

Rosenstone, Robert. *Revisioning History: Film and the Construction of a New Past*. Princeton, NJ: Princeton Univ. Press, 1995.

———. *Visions of the Past: The Challenge of Film to Our Idea of History*. Cambridge MA: Harvard Univ. Press, 1995.

Rosenthal, Perihan Aral, and Stuart Rosenthal, "Holocaust Effect in the Third Generation: Child of Another Time." *American Journal of Psychotherapy* 34, no. 4 (October 1980): 572–80.

Rosh White, Naomi. "Holocaust Testimony and History." In *The Oral History Reader*, edited by Robert Perks and Alistair Thomson, 172–82. London: Routledge, 1998.

Rotha, Paul. "Some Principles of Documentary." In *A Paul Rotha Reader*, edited by Duncan Petrie and Robert Kruger, 148–60. Exeter: Univ. of Exeter Press, 1999.

Roth-Cohen, Osnat, and Yehiel Limor. "The German (Fifth) Aliyah and the Development of Israel's Advertising Industry." *Israel Studies Review* 33 (2018): 126–45.

Rozenbaum, Ron. *Hitler: masa el shorshei haro'a* [Hitler: A Journey to the Roots of Evil]. Tel Aviv: Matar, 1999.

Rosenzweig, Orit Merlin. "Shlosha ahim v'me'ara: hazru l'hapess et hamakom bo histatru bashoah" [Shalom Italia: Went Back to Search for Their Hiding Place in the Holocaust]. Xnet, August 9, 2016. http://xnet.ynet.co.il/articles/0,7340,L-4839222,00.html.

Ruby, Jay. *Picturing Culture: Explorations of Film and Anthropology.* Durham, NC: Duke Univ. Press, 2000.

Sagi-Schwartz, Abraham, Marinus van IJzendoorn, and Marian J. Bakermans-Kranenburg. "Does Intergenerational Transference of Trauma Skip a Generation? No Meta-Analytic Evidence for Tertiary Traumatization with Third Generation Holocaust Survivors." *Attachment and Human Development* 10, no. 2 (June 2008): 105–21.

Salzborn, Samuel. "Hamitus hagermani, l'hargish k'uma shel korbanot: hatzaga v'yetzug shel hagermanim k'korban bapulmus hahadash al briha v'girush" [The German Myth: To Feel like a Nation of Victims]. *Dapim l'heker hashoa* 21 (2007): 239–60.

Sand, Shlomo. *Hakolnoa kehistoria: ledamyen velevayem et hameah haesrim* [Film as History: Imagining and Screening the Twentieth Century]. Tel Aviv: Am Oved and Open Univ. Press, 2002.

Saxton, Libby. "Shneihem sonim et Spielberg" [They Both Hate Spielberg]. *Mita'am*, December 2007, 106–24.

Scharf, Miri. "The Trace of Trauma: Third-Generation Holocaust Survivors." *Development and Psychopathology* 19, no. 2 (April 2007): 603–22.

Scharf, Miri, and Ofra Mayseless. "Adolescents' Attachment Representations and Their Capacity for Intimacy in Close Relationships." *Journal of Research on Adolescence* 17, no. 1 (2007): 23–50.

———. "Disorganizing Experiences in Second- and Third-Generation Holocaust Survivors." *Qualitative Health Research* 21, no. 11 (November 2011): 1539–53.

Schlor, Joachim. "Ha'aretz 'kan' ha'aretz 'sham': hirhurim al shiva" [The Land 'Here,' the Land 'There': Reflections on Returning]. Association of Israelis of Central European Origin, December 25, 2012. http://irgun-jeckes.org/%D7%94%D7%90%D7%A8%D7%A5-%D7%9B%D7%90%D7%9F-%D7%94%D7%90%D7%A8%D7%A5-%D7%A9%D7%9D-%D7%94%D7%A8%D7%94%D7%95%D7%A8%D7%99%D7%9D-%D7%A2%D7%9C-%D7%A9%D7%99%D7%91%D7%94-%D7%9E%D7%90%D7%AA-%D7%A4/.

Schneider, Ella. "Sho'ot mishelahen" [Their Own Holocausts]. *Ma'ariv*, November 1, 2006, 14.

Schneidman, Ronen. "A Holocaust Survivor's Confounding Choices." Forward, January 7, 2015. http://forward.com/schmooze/212162/a-holocaust-survivors-confounding-choices/.

Schwab, Gabriele. *Haunting Legacies: Violent Histories and Transgenerational Trauma*. New York: Columbia Univ. Press, 2010.

Schwartz, Alon. "A Talk at the Lev Cinema." Shoham, Israel, December 20, 2016.

Schweitzer, Ariel. "Archiv, bidyon, ta'amule: America bemilhama" [Archive, Fiction, Propaganda: America in War]. *Takriv*, n.d. https://takriv.net/.

———. "The 'Jew' of Cinema." *Haaretz* (English edition), December 17, 2010. http://www.haaretz.com/israel-news/the-jew-of-cinema-1.331109.

Segev, Tom. *Hamillion hashvi'i: haisraelim vehashoah* [The Seventh Million: The Israelis and the Holocaust]. Jerusalem: Keter, 1991.

Sela, Maya Galina. "Hashoa: niputz mitosim bakolnoa haisraeli vebaomanut bishnot hashmonim" [The Holocaust: Shattering Myths in Israeli Film and Art as of the 1980s]. Seminar paper in the course Holocaust Survivors in Israeli Cinema, Ra'anana, Israel, Open University, 2014.

Shandler, Jeffrey. *Holocaust Memory in the Digital Age: Survivors' Stories and New Media Practices*. Stanford, CA: Stanford Univ. Press, 2017.

Shapira, Anita. "Hashoah: zikaron prati v'zikaron tziburi" [The Holocaust: Private Memory and Public Memory]. In *Yehudim Yeshanim, Yehudim Hadashim* [New Jews, Old Jews], 103–86. Tel Aviv: Am Oved, 1997.

———. "Le'an halcha shlilat hagalut: sugiyot bazehut haisraelit" [Where Did the Exile Go: Issues in Israeli Identity]. *Shvut* (2004): 13–61.

———. *Yehudim Yeshanim, Yehudim Hadashim* [New Jews, Old Jews]. Tel Aviv: Am Oved, 1997.

Shapira, Avner. "Ma oseh Dudu Topaz b'kenes al kolnoa nazi?" [What Is Dudu Topaz Doing at a Conference about Nazi Cinema?]. *Haaretz*, November 3, 2016. http://www.haaretz.co.il/gallery/cinema/.premium-1.2153857.

Sharett, Yaakov, ed. *Pulmis hashilumim* [The Reparations Controversy]. Tel Aviv: Moshe Sharett Heritage Society, 2007.

Shavit, Avner. "Bamai 'hadira' metzig: ma saba shelachem asa bashoah?" ["The Flat's" Director Presents: What Did Your Grandfather Do during the Holocaust?]. Walla, September 5, 2011. https://e.walla.co.il/item/1856747.

———. "Hadira: re'ayon im Arnon Goldfinger al hatzlahato hamadhima b'germania" [The Flat: An Interview with Arnon Goldfinger on His Tremendous Success in Germany]. Walla, April 7, 2013. https://e.walla.co.il/item/2630758.

———. "Hadira: shalosh perspectivot al haseret" [The Flat: Three Different Perspectives on the Film], Walla, April 19, 2012. http://e.walla.co.il/?w=/267/2524988.

Sheffi, Na'ama. "Review of Guy Miron's 'German Jews in Israel: Memories and Past Images.'" *Journal of Israeli History* 25, no. 2 (2006): 377–81.

Shenker, Noah. *Reframing Holocaust Testimony*. Bloomington: Indiana Univ. Press, 2015.

Shik, Na'ama. "Haguf hamisken haze: hitnasut nashit al pi autobiografiot shel nitzolot Auschwitz-Birkenau 1946–2000" [That Poor Body: Women's Experiences in the Autobiographies of Survivors of Auschwitz-Birkenau 1946–2000]. Master's thesis, Tel Aviv University, 2004.

———. "Kavim merkazim bahistoriografia shel heker nashim bashoah" [Central Themes in the Historiography of Research on Women in the Holocaust]. *Zika* 12 (Autumn 2007). https://www.yadvashem.org/he/articles/general/women-holocaust-historiography.html.

Schnitzer, Meir. "Bata'ar baya'ar" [In the Forest, in the Forest]. *Ma'ariv*, April 30, 2004.

Schwab, Gabriele. *Haunting Legacies: Violent Histories and Transgenerational Trauma*. New York: Columbia Univ. Press, 2010.

Shohat, Ella. *Mizrah v'ma'arav bakolnoa hayisraeli* [East and West in Israeli Cinema]. Ra'anana, Israel: Open Univ. Press, 2007.

Shemesh, Tali, dir. *The Cemetery Club*. Jerusalem: Israeli Films, 2016. http://www.israelifilms.co.il/The-Cemetery-Club.html.

Shtauber, Shuki. *Yisraelim b'berlin* [Israelis in Berlin]. Tel Aviv: Yediot Aharonot, 2017.

Sternschuss, Michal. "Nitsolei shoah bakolnoa haisraeli" [Holocaust Survivors in Israeli Cinema.] Seminar paper from the course Holocaust Survivors in Israeli Cinema, Open University, Ra'anana, Israel, 2013.

Sipe, Dan. "The Future of Oral History and Moving Images." In *The Oral History Reader*, 2nd ed., edited by Robert Perks and Thomson Alistair, 379–88. London: Routledge, 2006.

Slavin, Marit. "Bnei adam zochrim gam havayot shelo havu" [People Also Remember Events They Did Not Experience]. Walla, June 12, 2005. https://news.walla.co.il/item/730398.

Stav, Yehuda. "Ya'ar hazvaot" [Forest of Horrors]. *Yediot Aharonot*, May 13, 2004.

Stier, Oren Baruch. *Committed to Memory: Cultural Mediations of the Holocaust*. Amherst: Univ. of Massachusetts Press, 2013.

Steir-Livny, Liat. "Dvarim shero'im mikan lo ro'im misham: shoah, nitsolei shoah, shikum veqlita bereyi hakolnoa vehaitonut shel irgunim tsionim beertz Israel vebeartsot habrit 1945–1948" [A World of Difference: The Representation of Holocaust, Holocaust Survivors, and Their Rehabilitation in the Films and Journalism of Zionist Organizations in Eretz Israel and the United States, 1945–1948]. PhD diss., Tel Aviv University, 2006.

———. "Hagalut hameshuleshet: dimuya shel nitsolat hashoah bakolnoa' haisraeli haalilaty" [The Threefold Exile: The Female Holocaust Survivor in Israeli Cinema]. In *Gender in Israel: New Studies on Gender in the Yishuv and the State*, edited by Margalit Shilo and Gideon Katz, 497–520. Beersheba, Israel: Ben-Gurion Univ. of the Negev, 2011.

———. "Hakambeck shel hagalut: meyehudi galuti leyahudi hadash ubehazara" [The Comeback of Jewish Diaspora in Israeli Culture]. In *Identity in Transition in Israeli Culture: A Book in Honor of Prof.*

Nurit Gertz, edited by Yael Munk, Adia Mendelson Maoz, Sandra Meiri, and Liat Steir-Livny, 461–81. Ra'anana, Israel: Open Univ. Press, 2013.

———. *Har hazikaron yizkor bimkomi* [Let the Memorial Hill Remember]. Tel Aviv: Resling, 2014.

———. *Is It OK to Laugh about It? Holocaust Humour, Satire and Parody*. Portland, OR: Vallentine Mitchell, 2017.

———. *One Trauma, Two Perspectives, Three Years*. Haifa: Herzl Institute for the Study of Zionism, Univ. of Haifa, forthcoming.

———. *Shtei panim bamara'a: yetsug nitsolei hashoah bakolnoa haisraeli* [Two Faces in the Mirror: The Representation of Holocaust Survivors in Israeli Cinema]. Jerusalem: Eshkolot Magnes, 2009.

Stern, Itay. "Haseret hayisraeli 'hayafa banashim' zacha b'taharut hastudentim shel haoscar ha'amerikani" [The Israeli Film "The Most Beautiful Woman" Won the Students' Competition at the American Oscars]. *Haaretz*, June 29, 2016. https://www.haaretz.co.il/gallery/cinema/1.3052773.

Stone, Dan. *The Liberation of the Camps: The End of the Holocaust and Its Aftermath*. New Haven, CT: Yale Univ. Press.

Teege, Jennifer, and Nikola Sellmair. *Amon: saba sheli haya yore bi* [Amon: My Grandfather Would Have Shot Me]. Tel Aviv: Hakibbutz Hameuchad, 2014.

Tal, Alon. "Hamechkar shehosef ma be'emet hoshvim hagermanim al hayisraelim" [The Research that Shows what Germans Really Think about Israelis] *Spitz*, January 15, 2015. http://spitzmag.de/issues/spitz_15/5759.

Tal, Ran, and Even, Anat. "Ra'ayon im Ra'anan Alexandrowicz" [An Interview with Ra'anan Alexandrowicz]. *Takriv*, n.d. https://takriv.net/article/%D7%A8%D7%90%D7%99%D7%95%D7%9F-%D7%A2%D7%9D-%D7%A8%D7%A2%D7%A0%D7%9F-%D7%90%D7%9C%D7%9B%D7%A1%D7%A0%D7%93%D7%A8%D7%95%D7%91%D7%99%D7%A5/.

Telem, Yahav. "Mifgashim m'hasoog hashlishi" [Encounters of the Third Generation]. *Yediot Aharonot*, July 4, 2013, 4–5.

Tanner, Anat. "Hayot b'seret shelahen" [Living in Their Own Movie]. YNet News, March 17, 2017. http://www.ynet.co.il/articles/0,7340,L-4936703,00.html.

Toby, Yaacov. *Hahurban v'haheshbon: medinat yisrael v'hashilumim mi-germanua 1949–1953* [The Reparations Agreement between Germany and Israel 1949–1953]. Ramat Gan and Tel Aviv: Bar Ilan Univ. and Tel Aviv Univ., 2015.

Trachtenberg, Barry. *The United States and the Nazi Holocaust: Race, Refuge, and Remembrance*. London: Bloomsbury Academic, 2018.

Tydor-Baumel Schwartz, Judith. *Double Jeopardy: Gender and the Holocaust*. London: Valentine Mitchell, 1998.

———. "Heker ha'isha, hamigdar v'hamishpaha b'tkufat hashoah: hitpatchuta shel disciplina historit" [The Study of Women, Gender, and Family during the Holocaust: The Development of a Historical Discipline]. In *Nashim Bashoah* [Women and Family in the Holocaust], edited by Esther Herzog, 1–26. Netanya, Israel: Otzar Hamishpat, 2006.

"Tzatza'ei hanazim hahaim b'yisrael" [Nazis' Descendants Who Live in Israel]. *Orly and Guy: The Morning Show*, June 20, 2013. https://www.youtube.com/watch?v=4nEv1_Iuk6Q.

"Tzatza'ei hanazim: moreshet stanit" [Nazis' Descendants: A Diabolical Heritage]. *Erev Hadash*, June 12, 2013. https://www.youtube.com/watch?v=juVyDqx7Mws.

"Vanessa Lapa: Charney Report." YouTube, January 15, 2015. https://www.youtube.com/watch?v=94VhOq1TekQ.

von Plato, Alexander. "Eifo hayeladim shelo m'aminim l'horeihem? Bikoret 'l kama tezot min haproyeqt 'hanhala shel mudut historit'" [Where Are the Children Who Don't Believe Their Parents? Critique on a Few Theses from the Endowment of Historical Awareness Project]. In *Zikaron v'shichecha: germania v'hashoah* [Memory and Amnesia: Germany and the Holocaust], edited by Gilad Margalit and Yifat Weiss, 221–27. Tel Aviv: Hakibbutz Hameuchad, 2005.

Walker, Janet. *Trauma Cinema: Documenting Incest and the Holocaust*. Berkeley: Univ. of California Press, 2005.

Waller, James. *Becoming Evil: How Ordinary People Commit Genocide and Mass Killing*. Oxford: Oxford Univ. Press, 2002.

Walzer, Harald. "Heroizatzia mitztaberet: hafihat 'haomdim menegd' veposhim legiborei hahitnagdut lanatsism basiach habein dori" [Cumulative Heroization: Turning Bystanders and Criminals into Heroes of Nazi Resistance]. In *Zikaron v'shichecha: germania v'hashoah* [Memory and Amnesia: Germany and the Holocaust], edited by Gilad

Margalit and Yifat Weiss, 198–215. Tel Aviv: Hakibbutz Hameuchad, 2005.

Wardi, Dina. *Nosei hahotam: dialog im bnei hador hasheni lashoah* [Memorial Candles: Children of the Holocaust]. Jerusalem: Keter, 1990.

Warren, Charles, ed. *Beyond Document: Essays on Nonfiction Film*. Lebanon, NH: Univ. Press of New England, 1996.

Warth, Danny. "Hamusika shelanu" [Our Music]. Danny Warth's blog, January 24, 2010. http://www.dannywarth.co.il/tag/%D7%94%D7%99%D7%A1%D7%98%D7%95%D7%A8%D7%99%D7%95%D7%AA-%D7%A9%D7%9C-%D7%A7%D7%95%D7%9C%D7%A0%D7%95%D7%A.

Weckel, Ulrike. "Shamed by Nazi Crimes: The First Step Towards Germans' Re-Education or a Catalyst for Their Wish to Forget?" In *Reverberations of Nazi Violence in Germany and Beyond: Disturbing Pasts*, edited by Stephanie Bird et al., 33–46. London: Bloomsbury, 2016.

Weitz, Yechiam. "Haderech l'vasenar: keitsad ushra hahahlata al masa umatan yashir bein Israel legermania" [The Way to Wassenaar: How the Decision for Direct Negotiations between Israel and Germany Was Approved]. *Yad Vashem Studies* 28 (2000): 275–47.

———. *Ha'ish shenirtzah pa'ama'im: hayav mishpato umoto shel dr. Israel kastner* [The Man Who Was Murdered Twice: The Life, Trial, and Death of Dr. Israel Kastner]. Jerusalem: Keter, 1995.

White, Hayden. "The Historical Text as Literary Artifact." In *Topics of Discourse: Essays in Cultural Criticism*, edited by Hayden White, 221–36. Baltimore: Johns Hopkins Univ. Press, 1978. Republished in Geoffrey Roberts, ed., *The History and Narrative Reader*. London: Routledge, 2001.

Wiesel, Elie. "Art and the Holocaust: Trivializing Memory." *New York Times*, June 11, 1989. http://www.nytimes.com/1989/06/11/movies/art-and-the-holocaust-trivializingmemory.html?pagewanted=all.

Winston, Brian. *The Documentary Film Book*. London: British Film Institute, 2013.

———. *Lies, Damn Lies, and Documentaries*. London: British Film Institute, 2000.

———. "The Tradition of the Victim in Griersonian Documentary." In *New Challenges for Documentary*, edited by Alan Rosenthal, 269–87. Berkeley: Univ. of California Press, 1988.

Winston, Brian, Gail Vanstone, and Wang Chi. *The Act of Documenting: Documentary Film in the 21st Century*. London: Bloomsbury Academic, 2017.

Yablonka, Hanna. *Ahim zarim: nitsolei hashoah bemdinat Israel 1948–1952* [Alien Brethren: Survivors of the Holocaust in Israel 1948–1952]. Jerusalem: Yad Yitzhak Ben-Zvi, 1994.

———. "Hahok l'asiyat din banazim u'b'ozreihem" [Nazis and Nazi Collaborators Punishment Law]. *Katedra* 82 (1997): 135–52.

———. *Harhek m'hamesila: mizrahim v'hashoah* [Off the Beaten Track: The Mizrahim and the Holocaust]. Tel Aviv: Yediot Aharonot, 2008.

———. *Medinat Israel neged Adolf Eichmann* [The State of Israel vs. Adolf Eichmann]. Tel Aviv: Yediot Aharonot, 2001.

———. "Nitzolei hashoah b'yisrael: sikumim rishonim" [Holocaust Survivors in Israel: First Summary]. *B'shvil hazikaron* 27 (1998). http://lib.cet.ac.il/Pages/item.asp?item=16227.

———. "Nitzoleu hashoah v'hayeshuv hayisraeli: mitos v'metziut" [Holocaust Survivors and the Jewish Yishuv: Myth and Reality]. YouTube, February 10, 2015. https://www.youtube.com/watch?v=QpxKv8nVnj0.

———. "Z'huyot sotrot, z'huyot mashlimot: nitsolim, zichron hashoah vehazehut hayehudit" [Conflicting Identities, Complementary Identities: Holocaust Survivors, the Memory of the Holocaust, and Israeli Identity]. *Massuah* 28 (2000): 301–17.

Yablonka, Hannah, Bella Guterman, and Avner Shalev, eds. *Anahnu po: nitzolei hashoah b'medinat Yisrael* [We Are Here: Holocaust Survivors in Israel]. Jerusalem: Yad Vashem, 2008.

Yahav, Galia. "Parodia meshubahat hosefet et habanalya shel teud hashoah" [A Great Parody Exposes the Banality of Holocaust Documentation.] *Haaretz*, January 23, 2012. http://www.haaretz.co.il/gallery/art/1.1623550.

Yair, Gad. *Ahava ze lo praktish* [Love Is Not Practical]. Tel Aviv: Hakibbutz Hameuchad, 2015.

"Yekke." The Yekke, December 20, 2012. http://lib.yeke.cet.ac.il/pages/item.asp?item=19602.

Young, James E. "Toward a Received History of the Holocaust." *History and Theory* 36, no. 4 (1997): 21–43.

———. *Writing and Rewriting the Holocaust: Narrative and the Consequence of Interpretation*. Bloomington: Indiana Univ. Press, 1988.

Ze'evi, Chanoch. "Yaldei Hitler" [Hitler's Children]. Yaldut avuda: yeladim sordei shoah (Lost Childhood Association), n.d., http://www.ylas.org/117983/%D7%99%D7%9C%D7%93%D7%99-%D7%94%D7%99%D7%98%D7%9C%D7%A8.

Zertal, Idith. *Ha'uma v'hamavet: historia, zikaron, politiqa* [Death and the Nation: History, Memory, Politics]. Or Yehuda, Israel: Kinneret Zmora-Bitan Dvir, 2002.

Zerubavel, Yael. "The 'Mythological Sabra' and Jewish Past: Trauma, Memory, and Contested Identities." *Israel Studies*, 7, no. 2 (2002): 115–44.

Zimmerman, Moshe. *Al tigu li bashoah* [Don't Touch My Holocaust]. Haifa: Haifa Univ. Press, 2002.

Zimmermann, Moshe. "Georgrafia shel asiyat din" [Geography of Justice]. Weiner Lectures 2015–2016, January 14, 2016. https://www.youtube.com/watch?v=__kESqNUgxIandt=3440s.

Zimmermann, Moshe, and Yotam Hotam, eds. *Bein hamoladot: hayekim bemehozoteihem* [Between Homelands: The Yekkes in Their Districts]. Jerusalem: Zalman Shazar Center, 2005.

Ziv, Avner. *Humor veishiyut* [Personality and Sense of Humor]. Tel Aviv: Papyrus, 1996.

Index

Liat Steir-Livny is a senior lecturer in the Department of Culture at Sapir Academic College, and a tutor and course coordinator for the Cultural Studies MA program and in the Department of Literature, Language, and the Arts at the Open University of Israel. She has authored numerous articles that analyze Holocaust commemoration in Israel from the 1940s until the present and has published four books: *Shtei panim bamara'a* (Two Faces in the Mirror, 2009), *Har hazikaron yizkor bimkomi* (Let the Memorial Hill Remember, 2014), *Is It O.K. to Laugh about It?* (2017), and *Trauma ahat, shtei perspectivot, shalosh shanim* (One Trauma, Two Perspectives, Three Years, 2018).